Scott, Foresman

SPRINGBOARD for PASSING THE GED

Writing Skills Test

Scott, Foresman and Company
Lifelong Learning Division

1900 East Lake Avenue
Glenview, Illinois 60025
1-800-628-4480
1-708-729-3000

Authors

Carole Thompson
Mary T. Brown
Linda Barnes

Library of Congress Cataloging-in-Publication Data
Barnes, Linda, 1938–
Scott, Foresman springboard for passing the GED writing skills test.

Includes index.
1. General educational development tests—Study guides. 2. English language—Composition and exercises—Examinations, questions, etc. I. Brown, Mary T. II. Thompson, Carole, 1948– . III. Title.
LB3060.33.G45B375 1987 373.12'6 87-4580
ISBN 0-673-24319-2

5678910-WEB-9897969594939291

Acknowledgments

Posttest directions on pp. **231** and **251** adapted from p. 3 of the Official GED Practice Test, Form A, 2nd Edition, © 1981. Used by permission from the OFFICIAL GED PRACTICE TEST, prepared by the GED Testing Service of the American Council on Education and distributed by Cambridge, the Adult Education Company, 888 Seventh Avenue, New York, NY, 10106. Directions for Part I of the GED Writing Skills Test on pp. **14, 36, 108, 224, 232,** and **252** excerpted from p. 9 of the 1988 TESTS OF GENERAL EDUCATIONAL DEVELOPMENT: A PREVIEW. Copyright © 1985, the GED Testing Service of the American Council on Education. All rights reserved. Reprinted by permission. Directions for Part II of the GED Writing Skills Test on pp. **20, 128, 160, 225, 244,** and **264** excerpted from p. 16 of the 1988 GED TESTS OF GENERAL EDUCATIONAL DEVELOPMENT: A PREVIEW. Copyright © 1985, the GED Testing Service of the American Council on Education. All rights reserved. Reprinted by permission. GED Spelling List on pp. **278–282** from the "Master List of Frequently Misspelled Words" from the GED TEST ITEM WRITER'S MANUAL, version 2.3 Copyright © 1985 by the GED Testing Service of the American Council on Education. All rights reserved. Reprinted by permission.

16 "Mail Order Rights Consumer Card." Copyright © 1982 by American Express Company. Reprinted by permission. **84** Country music passage adapted from Violet M. Malone, ed., "People," SCOTT, FORESMAN ADULT READING: COMPREHENSION, Level F. Scott, Foresman and Company, 1981, p. 14. **87** Animal tranquilizer passage adapted from Olive Stafford Niles et al., READING TACTICS A. Scott, Foresman and Company, 1981, p. 108. **88** Roller coaster passage adapted from Olive Stafford Niles et al., SKILLS FOR READING E. Scott, Foresman and Company, 1984, p. 190. **91** Number 13 passage adapted from Violet M. Malone, ed., "Cultures," SCOTT, FORESMAN ADULT READING: COMPREHENSION, Level E. Scott, Foresman and Company, 1982, p. 16.

Cartoon on page **29** by Cary Cochrane.
All other cartoon art by Anne Swiderski.

Contents

What You Should Know About Preparing for the GED Test

What Is the GED Test?

The initials GED stand for General Educational Development. You may have heard the GED Test called the High School Equivalency Test. That is because the test measures your ability against that of graduating high-school students. If you pass, you will earn a certificate that is the *equivalent* of a high-school diploma. You do not have go back to school to get it. That's quite an opportunity if you think about it!

Why Take the Test?

Every state in the Union, the District of Columbia, six United States territories or possessions, and many Canadian provinces use GED Test results as the basis for giving high-school equivalency credentials. A credential is something that credits a person with an achievement. GED credentials give credit for achieving the same amount of learning as high-school graduates. Those credentials are accepted for employment, promotion, and licensing just as high-school diplomas are.

There's another good reason for taking the test. Many colleges and universities now accept satisfactory GED Test scores in place of completed high-school grades to admit students.

Who Takes the Test?

In this country about 44 million people over eighteen do not have high-school diplomas. This means that about 26 percent of the adult population of the United States has not graduated from high school.

In recent years more than one-half million people each year have taken the GED Test. A lot of people must think it makes good sense to have a high-school equivalency credential.

Getting Ready for the GED Test

If you are not already enrolled in a GED preparation program and would like help preparing for the test, you should make some phone calls. The office of the superintendent of schools or your local vocational school, community college, or adult education center is a good place to contact. Ask if there are GED preparation courses available nearby. A call or two should be enough to get the information.

Many people prefer to study on their own rather than in a class. If you are one of those independent spirits, you can still benefit by calling one of the places suggested above. You may ask for information on the GED Test and about fees, application forms, and test times. If, however, you can't get the information you need, write to the following address:

General Educational Development
GED Testing Service of the American
Council on Education
One Dupont Circle
Washington, DC 20036

What's the GED Test Like?

Most questions on the GED Test are multiple-choice, and there are five answer choices for each. You need only to mark one of the five answer spaces for each question. You also have to write a short essay for the Writing Skills Test.

The GED Test measures if you have mastered the skills and general knowledge that are usually acquired in a four-year high-school education. However, you are not expected to remember many details, definitions, and facts. Therefore, being out of school for some time should not be a handicap at all.

The five subtests on the GED Test have been created to test whether an adult has the knowledge and skills that the average high-school graduate has in these areas:

Test 1: Writing Skills
Test 2: Social Studies
Test 3: Science
Test 4: Interpreting Literature and the Arts
Test 5: Mathematics

The GED Test does not base your score on your ability to race against the clock, as some tests do. You will have plenty of time to finish each subtest. Even so, you will want to work steadily and not waste any time. It is important that you answer every question, *even if you just guess,* because your score depends on the number of answers you get right.

Now read on to find out more about the GED Writing Skills Test.

The GED Writing Skills Test

What's on the Test?

The GED Writing Skills Test consists of 55 multiple-choice questions and an essay assignment. The test takes 2 hours to complete.

The multiple-choice section of the GED Writing Skills Test is sometimes called the conventions of English test. That is because this section tests the standard rules, or conventions, of formal English. The multiple-choice questions have five options each and are based on written passages from about 10 to 12 sentences long. The questions ask you to spot errors and choose how to rewrite sentences. They cover these areas of the conventions of English:

Sentence Structure	35%	19 questions
Usage	35%	19 questions
Mechanics (spelling, capitalization, and punctuation)	30%	17 questions

Sentence structure deals with the way words and punctuation are put together to form complete sentences. Usage involves the correct matching of subjects with verbs, verbs with verbs, and pronouns with the words they refer to. Capitalization tests the use of capital letters with the names of people, places, and things. Punctuation on the GED Test deals only with specific uses of the comma. Spelling, of course, involves the correct way to spell words. The words are in the passages, not in isolated lists; all the words that can be tested are taken from a list of frequently misspelled words.

Actually, many of the multiple-choice questions test more than one of these areas at the same time, since the correct answer to a question may involve sentence structure, but the four wrong options bring up points of usage and mechanics. You will be given 1 hour and 15 minutes to finish the multiple-choice questions.

For the essay, you will be given a specific topic and asked to write about 200 words on it. You will not have a choice in the matter, so you won't have to waste time deciding which topic to pick. The topic will be a general subject that adults know about. Special knowledge or research will not be needed—just good thinking and writing skills. You will be given scratch paper to plan your essay and a total of 45 minutes to produce a completed one.

Your essay will then be holistically scored. That means that two scorers will take turns reading your essay among many other GED candidates' essays. They won't look for errors but will instead judge your essay on the overall impression they get from it. They will compare it in their heads to model papers that have been assigned scores from 1 to 6. The worst paper is scored 1, the best 6. (Note that the highest score is *not* a *perfect* paper; it is merely the best of the lot.) Each scorer will then rate your paper on that same scale. Scores of 1 to 3 mean that the paper is in the lower half; scores of 4 to 6 put it in the upper half. A score of 0 will be given to an essay that is written on a topic that was not assigned, to an essay that cannot be read because of bad handwriting, and, of course, to a blank sheet of paper.

Each scorer will not know how the other scorer rated your essay. Their two scores will be added. Your total essay score will then be weighted in relation to your score on the conventions test, and the two will be added and reported to you as *one* score.

Life Experience: A "Plus" for GED Test-Takers

If you've been out of school for a while, you may be anxious about preparing for the GED Writing Skills Test. You may think that you've forgotten how to study, or you may feel that you're just not good at writing. If that sounds like the kind of thinking you've been doing, you're forgetting one very important thing you've got on your side: the *experience* you have.

For example, if you take down phone messages or write letters or postcards, you've got a head start with writing paragraphs and essays. Perhaps you've had to prepare your résumé or write business memos, letters, or reports. Sending letters to the editor, complaints about poor service, or questions about bills you've received may also have given you experience with writing. And if you've ever had to check someone else's writing—your child's, a friend's, your boss's—that "editing" experience will help you with the GED multiple-choice questions.

You don't have to remember all the special grammar terms that are taught in school. Instead, much of the test lets you put your experience to work for you. Working through this book will help you learn to apply your experience to your preparation for the GED Writing Skills Test.

How to Use This Book

What Is a Springboard?

You probably already know what a real springboard can do for athletes like divers and tumblers. A springboard is used to increase the height of their leaps. In the same way, this *Springboard* is your take-off point for making the big leap—passing the GED Writing Skills Test. This book starts each lesson at a very basic level. Then it brings you right up to the point where you can answer questions like those on the actual GED Test.

Taking the Skills Survey

The Skills Survey can be used as a pretest to show you how much you know already. It has about half the number of multiple-choice questions as the GED Writing Skills Test. The passages and questions are very much like those on the actual GED Test, and the skills they measure are the same. It also has an essay assignment like the one on the GED Test. Taking the Skills Survey and then carefully reading the answer explanations and scoring your essay will show you which skills you need to work on. When you come to a lesson in the book that teaches one of those skills, you can give more of your time and attention to it. In that way you can plan your studies to meet your own special needs.

When you work through the Skills Survey, you may do well on certain skills, such as sentence structure. If that happens, it would still be a good idea to read quickly through the lessons dealing with that skill and then answer all the GED-level questions in them. That will strengthen the skills you already have and give you practice in answering questions like those on the GED Test.

Working the Lessons

The lessons in this book carefully guide you through all the steps you need to understand the material. Each lesson is easy to read and understand.

First it presents important ideas about a skill. Next, in *Here's an Example,* you'll find one or more specific examples of how to use the skill that has just been explained. A section called *Try It Yourself* lets you see if you have understood what you've just read by giving you an opportunity to use the skill yourself and then explaining how you should have gone about doing so. Then comes a *Warm-up,* in which you can get plenty of practice with the skill by completing different kinds of exercises and writing sentences and paragraphs of your own. The Warm-up will end with a "prewriting" session in which you'll prepare notes for a longer writing exercise.

Another section, called *Coming to Terms,* defines important words related to writing skills. Although you do not have to memorize these terms, you may find it helpful to learn their meanings. You can do this by reading each definition twice, thinking about it, and then reading it again. You'll also find many *Test-Taking Tips* throughout the lessons. These are practical suggestions about how to answer certain types of questions that often appear on the GED Writing Skills Test.

Each lesson then introduces a very important step, one that helps you leap from a lower level to a higher, GED, one. This step is a special section called *On the Springboard.* This section contains a passage with one or two multiple-choice questions that are similar to those on the GED Test (but not quite as difficult), a writing exercise, or both. On the Springboard is not only a jumping-off point but also a step that helps you gain confidence in your ability to answer questions like those on the actual test. If you have any problems answering the Springboard questions correctly, this book will tell you exactly what to review before going on. After all, you need to be in top shape before taking the final leap.

That leap is the section called *"The Real Thing."* There you will find a passage and questions like those on the GED Test, a GED-level essay topic, or both. Because you've just completed On the Springboard, your chances of success with "The Real Thing" will be greatly increased.

Checking Your Answers

You can check some of your answers to the Warm-up exercises quickly and easily in the *Warm-up Answers* section nearby. One thing you will soon learn, however, is that in writing there is usually no one, "correct" way to do things. Writing is creative and personal; your thoughts are your own, and your way of expressing them is your own. So answers to many of the exercises in this book cannot really be given. Instead, you'll sometimes find "answers" in a *Sample Warm-up Answers* section nearby that you can use as guides.

In addition, it is a good idea to have someone work with you to help check your writing. If you're taking a GED class, your teacher, of course, will be a great help. But if you're studying on your own, try to think of someone who can read all your writing: your spouse, a close friend, a co-worker, your boss, a teacher in your neighborhood, or perhaps a librarian. The person should be someone who is a good writer, not just someone who knows you and likes you.

Answers for On the Springboard and "The Real Thing" multiple-choice questions in each section are near the end of the section, after all the lessons. Solid color strips run along the edges of these pages to help you locate them quickly. On these pages you'll find not only each correct answer but also an explanation of why that answer makes sense. Reading the explanation, even if you got the answer right, will help you check your thinking and strengthen what you have already learned. It will also add confidence in your ability to make good judgments. In addition, "sample" answers to writing topics are often provided for you to use as models of good writing. As with the Warm-up exercises, you'll also want your teacher or checker to read your writing for On the Springboard and "The Real Thing."

Keeping Track

After the answer explanations for "The Real Thing" multiple-choice questions in each lesson in the first and last sections of the book, you'll find a *Keeping Track* box that will help you do just that—keep track of how well you are doing. There you can record how many "Real Thing" answers you got right. Once you've finished all "The Real Thing" questions in a section, you can transfer your scores to the Keeping Track chart that follows the explanations. You'll be able to see which skills you've learned and which ones you need to review before you go on.

Taking Advantage of the Extra Practice

Following each section is some extra practice for the particular writing skills covered in that section. These Extra Practice sections measure the same skills that the GED Test measures. Doing the extra practice for a section lets you know whether you've learned the skills needed to do well in that area on the GED Test.

Charting Your Progress

The Progress Chart on the inside back cover is for you to keep a record of how many multiple-choice questions you got correct on the Extra Practice. Notice how many correct answers you need to get a passing score, a good score, and a very good score on each test. A good or very good score means you are ready to go on to the next section. If you just barely get a passing score or less, take the time to go back over those lessons that gave you trouble.

Taking the Posttests

After you've finished studying all three writing sections, done the extra practice, and reviewed any material you need to, make an appointment with yourself to take the first of the two Posttests. When you finish, check your answers and have your essay rated. Then find your score and the explanation of your results.

If you pass, you are ready to take the GED Writing Skills Test. If you don't, you can review those sections of the book for which you still need practice and then take the second Posttest.

Referring to the Style Guide

The Style Guide near the back of this book is a good source of information about capitalization, punctuation, word usage, and spelling. You can refer to it whenever a question comes up in your own writing about one of these matters.

Using the Index

When you need to review certain skills, the Index at the back of this book can help you. It lists all the important topics in the book and the numbers of the pages on which the topics are discussed. In addition, all the terms whose definitions appear in Coming to Terms throughout the book appear in the Index in **bold** type. That helps you locate and review their meanings.

In preparing you for the GED Test, this *Springboard* takes nothing for granted, leaves nothing to chance. That's how the training of a championship athlete works, and the training of a successful GED candidate is no different.

Getting Ready to Write

How Do *You* Feel About Writing?

If you're like many people, the thought of writing can leave you cold. Writing takes time, energy, thought—in other words, work. Many people usually find it easier to pick up the phone, say it in person, or just forget the whole thing. And any writing that is to be evaluated—such as the GED essay—can really make an otherwise able person nervous and insecure. That anxiety, in turn, can make it even more difficult for the person to put his or her thoughts down in writing.

Yet you don't have to be a gifted writer to produce a successful GED essay. You just have to be able to think about a topic and get across your ideas on it clearly and logically using the working parts of standard written English—words, sentences, and paragraphs. If you can do that, you'll possess a valuable skill that you can use for much more than merely a one-time essay test. Why is that?

The Thinking-Writing Connection

Often people don't really know what they think about an issue until they take the time to write about it. Trying to find the words to express their thoughts requires them to determine what those thoughts *are*. Then their writing makes them think some more. They make their thinking clearer, sometimes question it, and perhaps even change it. So writing and thinking go hand in hand. Clear thinking helps clear writing, and vice versa. Together they are a process. So if you can improve your thinking-writing process to the point where you can write a successful GED essay, you'll also be able to help yourself at home and on the job. You'll be able to discover your thoughts on problems and issues in your life and express those thoughts in letters, memos, reports, even your own personal journal.

To improve your thinking-writing process, you need to write, write, and write some more. You can't improve your writing skills by just reading about writing; you have to do it for yourself. So complete as many of the exercises in this book as you can, and write on your own as well. Write letters to businesses, utility companies, newspapers, friends. Get a large folder or notebook and keep copies of *all* your writing in it.

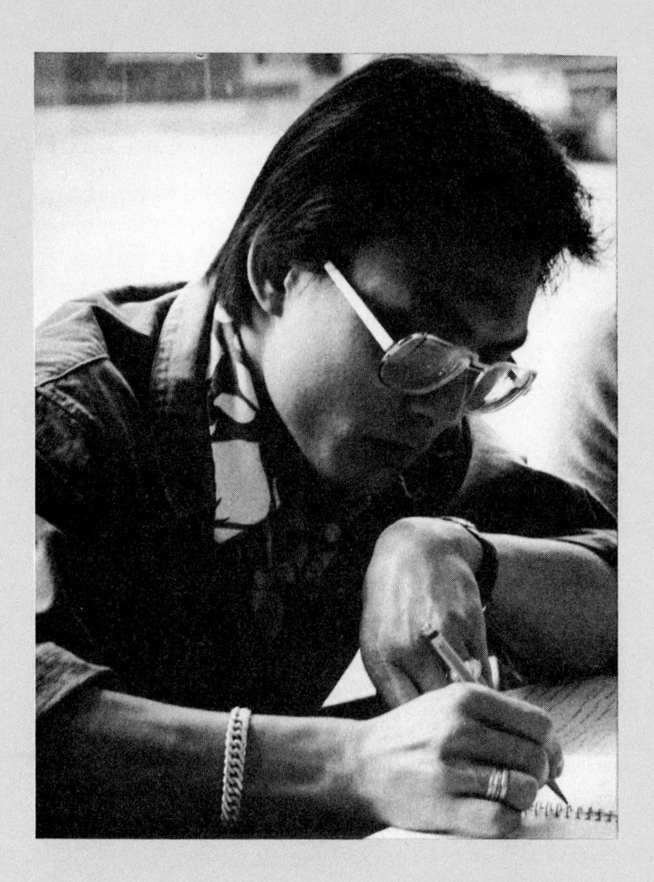

(Even if this is your own book, it would be a good idea if you wrote your answers to the exercises on separate sheets of paper. That way you can keep all your writing in one place.) Once you've finished studying for the GED Writing Skills Test, it will be satisfying for you to look back on all your work and see how far you've come.

Tools of the Trade

Before you begin to write, you need to find the writing situation that works best for you. Writing is a personal, creative act. Professional writers can be very picky about where they write and what they write with. So treat yourself with the same respect.

Even if you are enrolled in a GED class, you will need to find a spot at home where you will be comfortable and undisturbed. You can't think and write with the television blaring in the background or your family constantly demanding things. Experiment with different ways of writing—different types of paper, pens, and pencils, a typewriter or possibly even a word processor. These are the tools of the trade just the way a hammer, saw, and plane are the tools of a carpenter, so it's fine to be as particular about your own tools as a carpenter would be about his or hers.

Finding the Words to Express Your Thoughts

Another tool that can help you prepare for the GED Writing Skills Test is a dictionary. Writing deals with words. And if you don't know the meanings of many words, you won't be able to get your ideas across clearly and precisely. So if you don't already have a dictionary that's handy to use, you might want to consider buying one. Then you can note any unfamiliar words you see in your reading or hear someone speak, look those words up in your dictionary, and add them to your "writing vocabulary" by trying to use them when you write.

Before you can use a dictionary to find the meaning of a word, of course, you must be able to find the word. In a dictionary, words are arranged in alphabetical order. A word's place in a dictionary can be determined by its second letter, its third letter, and so on.

For example, note the order in which these words are arranged:

goggle
golden
greasy
great
guide

If the first letters of two words are the same, the words are placed according to the second letters. If the first and second letters are the same, they are placed according to the third letters. Can you explain, then, why you find *official* after *officer* in a dictionary?

The two words in heavy black type at the top of every dictionary page are called guide words. Every word on the page falls alphabetically between the two guide words at the top.

Suppose, for example, that you are trying to find the word *monotonous.* Would it be on the page with the guide words *monologue* and *monopoly* or on the page with the guide words *monorail* and *monsoon?* The second choice is correct because the *t* in *monotonous* comes after the *r* in *monorail,* but the second *o* comes before the *s* in *monsoon.*

For a little bit of practice with this system, put a check before any words below that you would find on a page with the guide words *spring* and *spur.*

___ sprinkle	___ sprig
___ sputter	___ spruce
___ spry	___ sprocket
___ spurt	___ spread

If you checked the words *sprinkle, spry, spruce,* and *sprocket,* you understand how to use guide words.

Once you have found a word in your dictionary, you can check its complete spelling to make sure you know it. Then you can learn the word's meaning. Most words have more than one meaning. Some dictionaries list the original or the oldest meaning of a word first. Others give the meaning that is used most often first. More limited and more technical definitions come later.

Often a dictionary will also use the word in a phrase or sentence to help you understand a particular meaning. These examples are especially helpful, since it is sometimes difficult to get the true, precise meaning of a word "out of context," that is, from its definition alone. And you want to be sure you are using a word correctly when you use it in your writing.

Still another way a dictionary can be a big help is by listing synonyms, which are words that mean almost the same thing as the word you've looked up. Perhaps you've already used a word in your writing a number of times. You want to use that particular word again, but you want to avoid repeating it. If you look the word up in a good dictionary, you may find one or more synonyms for it listed after the word's definitions. These synonyms will have slightly different shades of meaning; you can choose the most appropriate one.

For example, look again at the third sentence in the paragraph above: "You want to use that particular word again, but you want to avoid repeating it." The sentence sounds repetitive because the word *want* is used twice. The dictionary lists these synonyms after the definitioms for *want: desire, wish, crave, demand.* The word *wish* comes closest to meaning what *want* does in that particular sentence, so it would be a good replacement for it the second time around: "You want to use that particular word again, but you wish to avoid repeating it."

A thesaurus is a book that gives nothing but synonyms for words. You may want to buy a paperbook thesaurus to help in your search for new and precise words, especially if your dictionary doesn't have this feature.

Armed with these tools—pen and paper, a dictionary and possibly a thesaurus, this book, and *you*—you can begin to improve your own thinking-writing connection and end with the ability to write a successful GED essay.

Test Anxiety: How to Cope with It

When you think about actually taking the GED Test, you may feel anxious. This is perfectly normal. Plenty of people—no matter how prepared, intelligent, or self-confident they may be—feel test anxiety. Recent studies show that men are just as apt to have test anxiety as women and that younger people are as prone to it as older ones.

Test anxiety can make you so afraid of failing that you put off studying. It can make you panic so that you do not think clearly. You may begin to jump from one area to the next in an impossible attempt to learn everything at once without any plan.

Test anxiety can work against you during the test too. You may feel so anxious that you can't concentrate on the questions. That is the most dangerous result of test anxiety. Just when you need every bit of energy, you waste that energy thinking, "I didn't answer the last question fast enough," or "I'm probably behind everyone else now," or "I never did understand this."

Making Anxiety Work for You

Most people do get nervous about taking a test. The successful ones are those who make that nervousness work *for* them. Test anxiety can actually help you if you learn to channel it correctly. For example, anxiety can cause many people to put their noses to the grindstone and spend plenty of time preparing for a test. They try harder to answer the test questions—even difficult ones. Their anxiety makes them alert and careful.

If you use this book properly, you can avoid the buildup of harmful test anxiety. You can make your anxiety work for you by using your energy to prepare thoroughly for the exam.

As you work through this book, be honest in grading yourself on the sections called On the Springboard and "The Real Thing." You can fool yourself by saying, "Oh, I marked answer 5, but I thought it might be 3, so I'll give myself credit for that answer." But if you do this, you will begin to feel uneasy. You may doubt that you really have covered the material. Then you have created your own test anxiety. So don't rush your study. The extra time it takes you to review sections is well worth it.

Positive Thinking Can Raise Your Scores

While you've been away from school, you've done many things that show your basic strengths. You may have held down a job; received raises or promotions; had children; supported a family; bought, built, or rented a home; saved some money; traveled; acquired interesting hobbies; or made good friends. However, when facing a new challenge like a test, you may forget that you've done such things. You may feel unsure of yourself because now you're entering unknown territory—and the ground begins to feel shaky!

Look at the Accomplishments Chart below. Take time now to write down five things you've done since you left school that you feel good about. Don't think, "I'm proud of that, but it's too silly to write down." Be honest and put down whatever you want. After all, no one but you has to see your list.

Once you've written your list, ask yourself if any of those things took hard work, courage, patience, or the ability to put your experience to work for you. Then put checks in the boxes where you deserve them.

If you start feeling bad about your abilities later, come back to this chart and take another good look at those checks. Then tell yourself that you have no reason to feel bad.

Accomplishment	Hard work	Courage	Patience	Experience
1.				
2.				
3.				
4.				
5.				

Feeling depressed or anxious takes a surprising amount of energy. By thinking positively, you will find it easier to prepare for this new challenge in a steady, organized way.

Relax!

Following that order is not always as easy as it might seem. If you are one of the many people who feel anxious about taking a test, you can *learn* to relax.

Exercise can be one of the best ways to relax your mind. You might try jogging or doing simple stretching exercises for fifteen minutes after each study session. Don't think about what you have just studied. For this short period of time, think only of how you will soon pass the GED Test.

Another way to relax is to find a quiet spot where you can be alone for fifteen minutes after every study session. Close your eyes. Think about how you are working steadily to pass the GED Test and that you will soon achieve your goal.

Still another way to relax is to tense and then relax your muscles. For example, you might try tensing your muscles while saying to yourself, "I am working hard to pass the GED Test." Then relax your muscles and say, "And I am going to pass it soon." Each time, appreciate the relaxation for a little while and think about how good it feels to be working toward something you want.

Research shows that people forget less of what they have studied if they relax immediately after studying. That's another good reason to do one of the relaxation activities right after studying for the GED Test.

The Endurance Factor

Some people confuse two things: studying in a steady way and studying until they are tired or bored or both. You will be wasting a lot of your time if you study too long or if you study when you are too tired to concentrate.

Decide before you begin to study what hours you will set aside each day to prepare for the GED Test. Probably you should spend between forty-five minutes and two hours per session. You can choose to study once or, if you have the time, two or even three times a day.

Set up your schedule so that you can use your periods of greatest energy for study. Some people study best in the early morning hours. You will have to decide which times are best for you.

If you have a job, try to make use of your lunch hour and coffee breaks. If you take a bus or train to work, you can use your travel time for study. If you do this regularly, chances are you'll be able to squeeze in a surprising amount of extra study time.

Remember, whenever you feel yourself concentrating poorly or when you feel tired, close your book and do something else. You might do some of the relaxation exercises mentioned earlier.

Tips for Passing the GED Writing Skills Test

Long-Range Planning

1. As you prepare for the GED Writing Skills Test, keep in mind that what you are learning will benefit you for the rest of your life, not just until you pass the test. Certainly, passing the test is foremost in your mind right now, and it should be. But don't assume that once the test is over, you will no longer use what you are learning. Consider the skills you are now mastering to be a permanent part of your life. This attitude will help you value what you learn. It will also give you a greater sense of purpose as you prepare for the GED Test.

2. Give yourself plenty of time to prepare for the GED Writing Skills Test. Don't think you can do all your studying in one weekend. Your brain can't continue to work at its peak if you cram too much into it at once.

3. If you think you might have a vision problem, have your eyes checked before you begin to study for the test. All your knowledge and ability may not help if you have trouble seeing and end up misreading some of the questions.

4. Be sure that your study conditions help you, not hold you back. Check to see that you have good lighting. Use a desk or table that is large enough for all your study materials. Make certain that you are not too warm or too cold. If you are, you may not be able to concentrate as well as you could. Use a comfortable chair that supports your back well.

5. Keep all your study materials in one place and have them ready before you sit down to study. You will probably want to have plenty of pencils, pens, and paper, a notebook or folder, and, of course, a dictionary.

6. Begin slowly and build your endurance. Don't spend more than an hour each time you study until you are sure that covering this amount of material doesn't wear you out. Preparing for the GED Writing Skills Test is, in this sense, like preparing for running a marathon race.

7. As you study, take notes. If you jot down main ideas and important facts, you reinforce what you are learning. Then later you can use these notes to review. But be careful not to write down too much. Too many notes are just as bad as no notes at all. If you are in a GED class, your notes can also help you keep track of questions to ask your teacher. Take time to think carefully about his or her answers. Make sure that you really do understand what has been explained. Don't be afraid to ask for further explanations. The first big step in understanding something is being able to ask questions about it.

8. People study best at different speeds. This book will help you decide how long to spend on each section. The answer explanations, Keeping Track charts, and Progress Chart can help you judge your progress and decide if you are moving at the right pace. Make the most of these self-checks as you work through the lessons.

9. Be sure to review what you have studied each day. It is easy to forget what you have read if you do not go over it once more before closing your book. You can review by going through your notes, by looking at the headings in your book, and by asking yourself to explain what was covered in each section. Try explaining aloud to your self, as if you were a teacher talking to a class, the important ideas that you just read. This builds your confidence. You won't just *think* you know it—you can actually *hear* that you know it. This is probably the best way to see whether you really understood what was being taught.

10. Put your newly acquired writing skills to use in your daily life. Practice with other writing that you do on the job or at home.

Short-Range Planning—The Last 24 Hours

1. If you have prepared for a long time in advance, do something relaxing the night before the GED Test. You might want to go to a movie or to a sports event.

2. Getting a good night's sleep before the exam is one of the best things you can do for yourself. Cramming is not wise for any exam. It doesn't make sense at all for the GED Test. To pass the GED Test, you must read and think carefully and use common sense. A good night's sleep will help you do just that.

3. It's not smart to drink too much coffee or soft drinks with caffeine or take any other kind of stimulant. After an initial "high," you may begin to feel nervous or tired. This jittery sensation won't help you concentrate.

4. Steer clear of tranquilizers as well. Even though they help you feel less nervous, they will also affect your ability to think quickly and read carefully. The trade-off is just not worth it when you're taking an important test.

5. Don't dress too warmly when you go to take the test. Psychologists have found that if people feel slightly cool, they tend to do better on a test. You may become drowsy if you are too warm.

6. If you are left-handed, get a desk with a left-handed writing board. Ask the examiner about this before the exam, if possible.

During the Test

1. No matter how much or how little people study for a test, they often go into it with the attitude they developed toward test-taking long ago. Some students get too rattled to make good use of what they have learned with all their study. Others pride themselves on not getting nervous and take the test without being serious about it. They trust that their good luck will see them through and don't really give the test their complete attention. What is the best attitude to take during the GED Test? The best attitude is to be very serious about doing your best, but never panic.

2. The people who give the GED Test know that many people are anxious about taking the test. They will make every effort to make you feel at ease. Before you begin the test, they will let you know where the restrooms and smoking areas are located. They will also try to make sure that the testing room is quiet and at a comfortable temperature and that the lighting is good. A wall clock will probably be in the room. If not, about every fifteen minutes the examiner will announce the time remaining during the test. Even so, you may want to wear a watch so you will know exactly how much time you have to finish.

3. Some GED questions are missed only because test-takers don't mark answer sheets correctly. In some places the answers are corrected by a machine that can recognize only a completely filled-in space as a correct answer. If the machine sees an answer that is marked in some other way—like this, or like this, or like this—it cannot count that mark as a correct answer.

Remember that the machine is fair. However, if you confuse it with markings that it does not understand, it will mark your answer wrong even if it is correct. To avoid this, fill in the space so that the answer is definitely clear, but not so hard that you can't erase later if you want to change an answer. Check to make sure you have not made any extra marks near that answer or filled in any other space in that row of choices.

When you write your GED essay, make sure your handwriting is neat enough to be read. It doesn't have to be perfect, and you can cross out words and phrases, but if the scorers can't read your essay, they will have to give you a score of 0.

4. Put both the answer sheet and the test booklet on your desk so that they are easy to see and reach. Keep your place by putting one hand near the multiple-choice question you are working on and the other hand next to the number of that question on the answer sheet. Otherwise, one of your hands must move back and forth from the answer sheet to the test booklet. This wastes time and increases your chances of making an error.

5. Try to answer every multiple-choice question on the test. Your score will be based on the number of answers you get right. You do not get any points taken off for marking wrong answers. *So don't be afraid to guess.* Try to answer every question on the exam.

6. Each multiple-choice question counts exactly the same when the final score is being determined. Don't spend too much time on a difficult question and then leave others blank. Try to ration your time.

7. Try to answer each multiple-choice question for yourself *before* you read the five possible choices. After you decide what you think the answer should be, match your idea to the five choices and pick the one that is most similar.

8. You may first want to go through and answer the questions that are easy for you. Then you can go back and answer those that take more time. *Warning:* If you follow this suggestion, be very careful to mark the answer space whose number is the same as that of the question you are answering. Test-takers often skip one question, say number 19, but they forget to skip an answer on the answer sheet. Then, when they mark the answer for question number 20, they put that answer by mistake in the space for number 19. You can probably guess what happens next—their answers to all the following problems are also in the wrong spaces. If they don't catch the problem, they can actually fail the test just because of this mix-up. *Make sure that you have the right answer in the right answer space.* When you do skip a question, make a very light *X* beside the number for it on your answer sheet so that you can find it easily when you come back. Remember to erase the *X* when you've answered the question.

9. From time to time breathe deeply and stretch. Did you know that stretching is the most natural exercise to help you feel refreshed and relaxed?

10. On multiple-choice tests that have five answer choices, like the first part of the GED Writing Skills Test, you can sometimes see quite easily that three of the choices are wrong. Then it becomes a problem of deciding between two very logical-looking options. If you really can't make up your mind about which of two good options is best, follow your intuition. By answering this way, you have a better than 50 percent chance of getting the right answer. Hunches, after all, are one way of arriving at perfectly good conclusions.

11. Don't choose any answer on the basis of its number. In other words, don't choose answer (3) just because it's been a while since you chose the third answer. On the other hand, if you think choice (1) is the correct answer, choose it even if the answer right before it was also (1).

12. Try to stick to your first impressions. Don't change your answer once you've marked it unless you are certain it is wrong.

13. Some people work faster, though not necessarily more accurately, than others. If you finish early, don't turn in your test. Use every minute you have to go back and check your answers. Go over each mark to see that you have filled in the correct space. Some students get poor scores just because they are careless. They know that the correct answer is, say, (2), but they accidentally mark the space for (1) or (3). Be sure to check before turning in your exam to see that the answer you have marked is really the number of the answer you have chosen.

14. You will be given scratch paper on which to write notes and plan your essay. Be sure to use it. Otherwise your essay will show a lack of thought and organization and will not get a good score. The notes you make will not be scored, only your essay.

Make a date with yourself to reread this section the day before you take the GED Writing Skills Test. With these tips and all the study aids this book provides fresh in your mind, you should pass the test with flying colors.

Skills Survey

Directions

On the following pages is a skills survey. Here is where you get the chance to show yourself how much you already know.

Don't look at this skills survey as a test. That may only make you nervous, and you won't do as well as you otherwise would. Instead, look at this skills survey as a personal guide. First, it is a guide to what is on the GED Writing Skills Test. It has passages like the kind found on the GED Test. It has the same kinds of multiple-choice questions that the GED Test has. It gives you an essay assignment similar to a GED essay topic. And it asks you to use the same skills that the GED Test does.

This is the second way in which you can use this survey as a guide. The survey shows you which skills you are already good at, which skills you need to practice, and which skills you need to learn.

To use this guide correctly, you will need to be good to yourself. Get yourself a comfortable chair next to a desk or table in a well-lighted area. Most important, demand some peace and quiet. You will want to be able to concentrate so you can work to the best of your ability.

There is no time limit on this survey. Doing things like reading passages, answering multiple-choice questions, and writing an essay *quickly* is a skill in itself. That is a skill you will get to practice as you work through the lessons, the extra practice sections, and the Posttests in this book. For now, forget about the clock.

Read each passage on the Skills Survey carefully. Next read the questions for the passage and answer as many as you can. Try to answer every question. Then go on to write your essay.

If this is your own book, you can mark your answers in the answer circles after the questions. Completely fill in the circle of the number you have chosen as the correct answer. For example, if you think the fourth choice is the correct answer to a question, fill in circle 4 like this:

Filling in the circle completely will give you practice in marking an answer sheet correctly. That will help you when you go to take the actual GED Writing Skills Test. Use the blank sheets for preparing and writing your essay.

If this is not your book, number a separate sheet of paper from 1 to 28. You can write the number of each answer you have chosen after the number of the question. Plan and write your essay on separate paper, but be sure to keep it as you work through this book.

Are you ready to find out how much you already know? Then turn the page and start the Skills Survey.

Part I

Directions: The following items are based on paragraphs that contain numbered sentences. Some of the sentences contain errors in sentence structure, usage, or mechanics. A few sentences, however, are correct as written. Read each paragraph and then answer the items based on it. For each item, choose the answer that would result in the most effective writing of the sentence or sentences. The best answer must be consistent with the meaning and tone of the rest of the paragraph.

Items 1–9 refer to the following passage.

(1) How does the U.S. government decide that paper money is wore out, and how does it dispose of this "wealth"? (2) There are thirty-seven Federal Reserve Banks, and they all have at least one sorting and shredding machine. (3) Each machine sorts thorough 50,000 bills an hour. (4) The sorting machine in Washington, D.C., works eight hours a day five days a week. (5) The machine can "look" at the bills to see which ones are too ragged, or dirty to stay in circulation. (6) After the machine sorts out the bad bills, it automatically counts the good ones into stacks of 100 these good bills are banded together and put into a vault. (7) The old bills continue in the machine, which then shreds them. (8) They are cut into such tiny bits that they could never be glued back together. (9) Up to this point, no Human hands or eyes have been involved in the operation. (10) The sorting machines have been in use since 1980. (11) Before that time however, all the sorting was done by specially trained people. (12) Once the bills are shredded, all the pieces onto dump trucks. (13) Then trash that used to be worth millions of dollars is buried in local dumps.

1. Sentence 1: **How does the U.S. government decide that paper money is wore out, and how does it dispose of this "wealth"?**

   What correction should be made to this sentence?

   (1) change How does to How do
   (2) change the spelling of government to goverment
   (3) change decide to deciding
   (4) change wore to worn
   (5) remove the word and

   (1) (2) (3) (4) (5)

2. Sentence 2: **There are thirty-seven Federal Reserve Banks, and they all have at least one sorting and shredding machine.**

   If you rewrote sentence 2 beginning with

   Each of the thirty-seven Federal Reserve Banks

   the next word(s) should be

   (1) has (2) have (3) having
   (4) is having (5) has had

   (1) (2) (3) (4) (5)

3. Sentence 3: **Each machine sorts thorough 50,000 bills an hour.**

   What correction should be made to this sentence?

   (1) change sorts to sorting
   (2) change sorts to sorted
   (3) replace thorough with through
   (4) replace thorough with threw
   (5) no correction is necessary

   (1) (2) (3) (4) (5)

4. Sentence 5: **The machine can "look" at the bills to see which ones are too ragged, or dirty to stay in circulation.**

   Which of the following is the best way to write the underlined portion of this sentence? If you think the original is the best way, choose option (1).

   (1) ragged, or
   (2) ragged or
   (3) ragged; or
   (4) ragged. Or
   (5) ragged or,

   (1) (2) (3) (4) (5)

5. Sentence 6: **After the machine sorts out the bad bills, it automatically counts the good ones into stacks of 100 these good bills are banded together and put into a vault.**

   Which of the following is the best way to write the underlined portion of this sentence? If you think the original is the best way, choose option (1).

   (1) of 100 these
   (2) of 100. these
   (3) of 100, but these
   (4) of 100; and these
   (5) of 100. These

   (1) (2) (3) (4) (5)

6. Sentence 7: **The old bills continue in the machine, which then shreds them.**

   Which of the following is the best way to write the underlined portion of this sentence? If you think the original is the best way, choose option (1).

   (1) which
   (2) who
   (3) that
   (4) it
   (5) whom

   (1) (2) (3) (4) (5)

7. Sentence 9: **Up to this point, no Human hands or eyes have been involved in the operation.**

   What correction should be made to this sentence?

   (1) remove the comma after point
   (2) change Human to human
   (3) insert a comma after hands.
   (4) change are to is
   (5) no correction is necessary

   (1) (2) (3) (4) (5)

8. Sentence 11: **Before that time however, all the sorting was done by specially trained people.**

   What correction should be made to this sentence?

   (1) change the spelling of Before to Befour
   (2) insert a comma after time
   (3) remove the word was
   (4) change the word was to been
   (5) change the spelling of specially to specialy

   (1) (2) (3) (4) (5)

9. Sentence 12: **Once the bills are shredded, all the pieces onto dump trucks.**

   What correction should be made to this sentence?

   (1) replace Once with Whenever
   (2) remove the comma after shredded
   (3) change the spelling of pieces to peaces
   (4) insert is loaded after pieces
   (5) insert are loaded after pieces

   (1) (2) (3) (4) (5)

GO ON TO THE NEXT PAGE.

Items 10–18 refer to the following passage.

(1) When you shop at home from mail order companies you get convenience, better service, a wider selection, and more complete product information, but there are several tips to remember to keep your mail order shopping trouble-free. (2) It is always a good idea to check several places to find out if a firm is reliable; for example, you can contact the Better Business Bureau, the consumer protection agency where the company is located, or the Direct Marketing Association. (3) Read advertisements carefully, and contact the company about its exchange policy missing facts, or questionable claims. (4) Always pay by money order, check, or credit or charge card so that you have a record, never send cash. (5) Since it helps to know one's legal rights as a consumer, find out what laws covering purchases by mail are enforced by the U.S. Postal Service and the Federal Trade Commission. (6) If a package is late, first check your local post office because it may be holding the item for you. (7) A mail order company must ship your order within the time promised or, if no time is stated, within thirty days of receipt of your properly completed order and payment.
(8) The seller must notify you in case of delay.
(9) After a product you didn't order comes by U.S. mail, it is illegal for the sender to pressure you to return it or to pay for it. (10) A product may be unsatisfactory. (11) Then you should check the warranty and ask the seller about replacement, repair, or refund. (12) Remember that most firms are reliable and depend upon repeat orders and your valueable goodwill to stay in business.

10. Sentence 1: **When you shop at home from mail order companies you get convenience, better service, a wider selection, and more complete product information, but there are several tips to remember to keep your mail order shopping trouble-free.**

Which of the following is the best way to write the underlined portion of this sentence? If you think the original is the best way, choose option (1).

(1) companies you
(2) compaines. You
(3) companies; you
(4) companies, you
(5) companies and you

① ② ③ ④ ⑤

11. Sentence 2: **It is always a good idea to check several places to find out if a firm is reliable; for example, you can contact the Better Business Bureau, the consumer protection agency where the company is located, or the Direct Marketing Association.**

If you rewrote sentence 2 beginning with

You can find out if a firm is reliable

the next word should be

(1) by (2) to (3) so
(4) and (5) for

① ② ③ ④ ⑤

12. Sentence 3: **Read advertisements carefully, and contact the company about its exchange policy missing facts, or questionable claims.**

What correction should be made to this sentence?

(1) change the spelling of advertisements to advertizements
(2) change the spelling of carefully to carefuly
(3) change contact to contacting
(4) replace its with it's
(5) insert a comma after policy

① ② ③ ④ ⑤

13. Sentence 4: **Always pay by money order, check, or credit or charge card so that you have a record, never send cash.**

Which of the following is the best way to write the underlined portion of this sentence? If you think the original is the best way, choose option (1).

(1) record, never
(2) record never
(3) record, and never
(4) record; nevertheless, never
(5) record; never

① ② ③ ④ ⑤

14. Sentence 5: **Since it helps to know one's legal rights as a consumer, find out what laws covering purchases by mail are enforced by the U.S. Postal Service and the Federal Trade Commission.**

What correction should be made to this sentence?

(1) replace Since with While
(2) replace one's with your
(3) change the spelling of rights to wrights
(4) change right to Rights
(5) change are to is

① ② ③ ④ ⑤

15. Sentence 6: **If a package is late, first check your local post office because it may be holding the item for you.**

Which of the following is the best way to write the underlined portion of this sentence? If you think the original is the best way, choose option (1).

(1) is
(2) was
(3) had been
(4) will be
(5) be

① ② ③ ④ ⑤

16. Sentence 9: **After a product you didn't order comes by U.S. mail, it is illegal for the sender to pressure you to return it or to pay for it.**

What correction should be made to this sentence?

(1) replace After with If
(2) change didn't to doesn't
(3) remove the comma after mail
(4) change mail to Mail
(5) no correction is necessary

① ② ③ ④ ⑤

17. Sentences 10 and 11: **A product may be unsatisfactory. Then you should check the warranty and ask the seller about replacement, repair, or refund.**

The most effective combination of sentences 10 and 11 would include which of the following groups of words?

(1) A product should be checked
(2) to be unsatisfactory and then
(3) If a product is unsatisfactory, check
(4) Because an unsatisfactory product
(5) A product may be replaced, repaired,

① ② ③ ④ ⑤

18. Sentence 12: **Remember that most firms are reliable and depend upon repeat orders and your valueable goodwill to stay in business.**

What correction should be made to this sentence?

(1) change are to will be
(2) insert a comma after reliable
(3) change depend to will depend
(4) change the spelling of valueable to valuable
(5) no correction is necessary

① ② ③ ④ ⑤

GO ON TO THE NEXT PAGE.

Items 19–28 refer to the following passage.

(1) Have you ever wondered how skiing became a popular sport in the Sierra Nevada? (2) It all started in 1853, when a young Norwegian immigrant named Jon Torsteinson arrived in the gold country of the west to make his fortune. (3) Not long after his arrival, Jon changed his name to John Thompson, gave up prosspecting for gold, and tried ranching instead. (4) After an unsuccessful attempt at ranching, he saw an ad that said, "People Lost to the World: Uncle Sam Needs a Mail Carrier." (5) John made himself some heavy oak skis that were modeled after skis he had used as a boy in Norway. (6) They were 10 feet (300 centimeters) long, 2 inches thick, and weighed 25 pounds each, in comparison, modern skis average 200 centimeters in length and weigh about 7 pounds each. (7) Because few people on his route ever seen skis, he laughingly called them "Norwegian snowshoes." (8) He was promptly nicknamed "Snowshoe" Thompson. (9) The Sierra region's only communication link in winter, he travels alone with no compass or gun, braving wolf packs, blizzards, forty-foot snowdrifts, and endless mountain peaks. (10) He carried the mail on his back. (11) Often it weighed at least 100 pounds. (12) Sometimes he also carried medicine to isolated townspeople and miners one time he carried a printing press in parts over many trips. (13) Young people along his route became fascinated and then asked for lessons on building and using skis, and then skiing became a sport. (14) Soon races were held, and ski clubs were formed throughout the Sierras.

19. Sentence 2: **It all started in 1853, when a young Norwegian immigrant named Jon Torsteinson arrived in the gold country of the west to make his fortune.**

What correction should be made to this sentence?

(1) insert the word be after all
(2) remove the word when
(3) change Norwegian to norwegian
(4) change arrived to arrives
(5) change west to West

(1) (2) (3) (4) (5)

20. Sentence 3: **Not long after his arrival, Jon changed his name to John Thompson, gave up prosspecting for gold, and tried ranching instead.**

What correction should be made to this sentence?

(1) remove the comma after arrival
(2) change changed to will change
(3) remove the comma after Thompson
(4) change the spelling of prosspecting to prospecting
(5) change the spelling of instead to insted

(1) (2) (3) (4) (5)

21. Sentence 5: **John made himself some heavy oak skis that were modeled after skis he had used as a boy in Norway.**

Which of the following is the best way to write the underlined portion of this sentence? If you think the original is the best way, choose option (1).

(1) were
(2) was
(3) be
(4) is
(5) are

(1) (2) (3) (4) (5)

22. Sentence 6: **They were 10 feet (300 centimeters) long, 2 inches thick, and weighed 25 pounds each, in comparison, modern skis average 200 centimeters in length and weigh about 7 pounds each.**

Which of the following is the best way to write the underlined portion of this sentence? If you think the original is the best way, choose option (1).

(1) each, in comparison,
(2) each in comparison,
(3) each. In comparison,
(4) each, in comparison
(5) each in comparison

(1) (2) (3) (4) (5)

23. Sentence 7: **Because few people on his route ever seen skis, he laughingly called them "Norwegian snowshoes."**

What correction should be made to this sentence?

(1) insert the word had after route
(2) change seen to see
(3) remove the comma after skis
(4) change called to calls
(5) replace them with it

(1) (2) (3) (4) (5)

24. Sentence 9: **The Sierra region's only communication link in winter, he travels alone with no compass or gun, braving wolf packs, blizzards, forty-foot snowdrifts, and endless mountain peaks.**

What correction should be made to this sentence?

(1) change winter to Winter
(2) remove the comma after winter
(3) change travels to is traveling
(4) change travels to traveled
(5) remove the comma after blizzards

(1) (2) (3) (4) (5)

25. Sentences 10 and 11: **He carried the mail on his back. Often it weighed at least 100 pounds.**

The most effective combination of sentences 10 and 11 would include which of the following groups of words?

(1) Carrying the mail on his back, it often
(2) He carried and weighed 100 pounds of
(3) his back, whereas it often weighed
(4) Weighing at least 100 pounds, he carried
(5) He often carried at least 100 pounds of

(1) (2) (3) (4) (5)

26. Sentence 12: **Sometimes he also carried medicine to isolated townspeople and miners one time he carried a printing press in parts over many trips.**

Which of the following is the best way to write the underlined portion of this sentence? If you think the original is the best way, choose option (1).

(1) miners one
(2) miners, one
(3) miners, and one
(4) miners; therefore, one
(5) miners because one

(1) (2) (3) (4) (5)

27. Sentence 13: **Young people along his route became fascinated and then asked for lessons on building and using skis, and then skiing became a sport.**

If you rewrote sentence 13 beginning with

Skiing became a sport when

the next word(s) should be

(1) fascination
(2) young people
(3) his route
(4) skiing lessons
(5) building and using

(1) (2) (3) (4) (5)

28. Sentence 14: **Soon races were held, and ski clubs were formed throughout the Sierras.**

Which of the following is the best way to write the underlined portion of this sentence? If you think the original is the best way, choose option (1).

(1) held, and
(2) held and
(3) held. And
(4) held; and
(5) held,

(1) (2) (3) (4) (5)

GO ON TO THE NEXT PAGE.

Part II

Directions: This part will help you find out how well you write. It has one question that asks you to present an opinion on an issue or to explain something. In preparing your answer for this question, you should take the following steps:

1. Read all of the information accompanying the question.
2. Plan your answer carefully before you write.
3. Use scratch paper to make any notes.
4. Write your answer.
5. Read carefully what you have written and make any changes that will improve your writing.
6. Check your paragraphing, sentence structure, spelling, punctuation, capitalization, and usage, and make any necessary corrections.

You will have 45 minutes to write on the question below. Write legibly and use a ballpoint pen.

> Friendship is something that most people seek throughout their lifetimes.
>
> Does the kind of friendship a person looks for change over the course of his or her lifetime? Write your answer to this question in a composition of about 200 words. Be specific, and give examples.

Answers: Skills Survey

1. (4) The right verb form to use with the word *is* is *worn,* not *wore.*

2. (1) *Each of the thirty-seven Federal Reserve Banks has at least one sorting and shredding machine.* The subject of the rewritten sentence is *Each,* which is singular. You have to choose a verb to go with it that is also singular and that shows the correct time—the present. *Has* is the only option that does that.

3. (3) The correct spelling for the word that's needed in the sentence is *through.*

4. (2) You don't need a comma or any other mark of punctuation to separate just two elements in a sentence—*ragged* and *dirty*—that are connected by *or.*

5. (5) The original sentence is called a run-on. A run-on is two complete thoughts mistakenly written as one sentence. The period and the capital letter separate those two thoughts and make them two sentences.

6. (1) *Which* is the correct pronoun to use in this sentence. It refers to the word before it, *machine.*

7. (2) There's no need to capitalize *human* in this sentence. You use capital letters only for the names of particular people.

8. (2) You could have gotten this answer correct for two reasons: (a) if you knew that *however* was an interrupting word and needed a comma both before and after it or (b) if you sounded the sentence out in your head and heard a pause after *time.* Commas are used to signal such pauses.

9. (5) The sentence is not complete as it is. You need a verb to go with the subject *pieces. Are loaded* is a plural verb, and *is loaded* is singular. Since the subject *pieces* is plural, option (5) is correct.

How does the U.S. government decide that paper money is worn out, and how does it dispose of this "wealth"? Each of the thirty-seven Federal Reserve Banks has at least one sorting and shredding machine. Each machine sorts through 50,000 bills an hour. The sorting machine in Washington, D.C., works eight hours a day five days a week. The machine can "look" at the bills to see which ones are too ragged or dirty to stay in circulation. After the machine sorts out the bad bills, it automatically counts the good ones into stacks of 100. These good bills are banded together and put into a vault. The old bills continue in the machine, which then shreds them. They are cut into such tiny bits that they could never be glued back together. Up to this point, no human hands or eyes have been involved in the operation. The sorting machines have been in use since 1980. Before that time, however, all the sorting was done by specially trained people. Once the bills are shredded, all the pieces are loaded onto dump trucks. Then trash that used to be worth millions of dollars is buried in local dumps.

10. (4) A dependent thought that comes at the beginning of a sentence needs a comma after it. *When you shop at home from mail order companies* is an example of that kind of sentence part.

11. (1) *You can find out if a firm is reliable by contacting the Better Business Bureau, the consumer protection agency where the company is located, or the Direct Marketing Association.* The only option that logically and smoothly connects the ideas in the sentence is *by contacting.*

12. (5) You need a comma to separate three or more items in a list. *Exchange policy* is the first of three items mentioned.

13. (5) A comma is not strong enough to separate two complete thoughts; a semicolon is. Option (5) is the best way to join the two closely related ideas.

14. (2) The pronouns *you* and *your* are used throughout the passage. *One's* does not follow through with this usage.

15. (1) *Is* is correct because it shows an action that takes place in present time. *Was, had been,* and *will be* do not show present time. *Be* must always be used with a helper *(will be, would be).*

16. (1) *If* correctly expresses the relationship between the idea in the first part of the sentence and the idea in the last part.

17. (3) *If a product is unsatisfactory, check the warranty and ask the seller about replacement, repair, or refund.* The two verbs (*check* and *ask*) match. The verbs in the other options do not match *check.*

18. (4) *Valuable* is the correct spelling.

When you shop at home from mail order companies, you get convenience, better service, a wider selection, and more complete product information, but there are several tips to remember to keep your mail order shopping trouble-free. You can find out if a firm is reliable by contacting the Better Business Bureau, the consumer protection agency where the company is located, or the Direct Marketing Association. Read advertisements carefully, and contact the company about its exchange policy, missing facts, or questionable claims. Always pay by money order, check, or credit or charge card so that you have a record; never send cash. Since it helps to know your legal rights as a consumer, find out what laws covering purchases by mail are enforced by the U.S. Postal Service and the Federal Trade Commission. If a package is late, first check your local post office because it may be holding the item for you. A mail order company must ship your order within the time promised or, if no time is stated, within thirty days of receipt of your properly completed order and payment. The seller must notify you in case of delay. If a product you didn't order comes by U.S. mail, it is illegal for the sender to pressure you to return it or to pay for it. If a product is unsatisfactory, check the warranty and ask the seller about replacement, repair, or refund. Remember that most firms are reliable and depend upon repeat orders and your valuable goodwill to stay in business.

19. (5) The word *west* should be capitalized in this sentence because it refers to a particular section of the country; it is a geographical place name.

20. (4) *Prospecting* is the correct spelling.

21. (1) The original verb *(were)* is correct. *That* refers to *skis,* so the verb must be plural, and it must also show past time.

22. (3) There are two complete thoughts in the original and a comma is not strong enough to separate them. A comma *is* needed after *In comparison* because it is an interrupting phrase.

23. (1) *Seen* must always be used with a helper. *People seen* and *people see* are incorrect.

24. (4) The action in this passage took place in the past. Therefore, *traveled* (not *travels* or *is traveling*) is correct. The seasons of the year are not capitalized.

25. (5) *He often carried at least 100 pounds of mail on his back.* That is the clearest, shortest way to combine the two ideas.

26. (3) The original wording is a run-on; it is two complete thoughts incorrectly run together as one sentence. One way to separate the thoughts is with a connecting word *(and)* and a comma.

27. (2) *Skiing became a sport when young people along his route became fascinated and asked for lessons on building and using skis.* The original wording is awkward and repetitious. "And then" is used twice. That skiing became a sport is the most important idea in this sentence, so it is placed first. The rest of the sentence then explains how skiing became a sport.

28. (1) The original wording is correct because when *and* joins two complete thoughts, a comma must be used before it. Option (3) is incorrect because *And ski clubs were formed throughout the Sierras* would not be a complete sentence.

Have you ever wondered how skiing became a popular sport in the Sierra Nevada? It all started in 1853, when a young Norwegian immigrant named Jon Torsteinson arrived in the gold country of the West to make his fortune. Not long after his arrival, Jon changed his name to John Thompson, gave up prospecting for gold, and tried ranching instead. After an unsuccessful attempt at ranching, he saw an ad that said, "People Lost to the World: Uncle Sam Needs a Mail Carrier." John made himself some heavy oak skis that were modeled after skis he had used as a boy in Norway. They were 10 feet (300 centimeters) long, 2 inches thick, and weighed 25 pounds each. In comparison, modern skis average 200 centimeters in length and weigh about 7 pounds each. Because few people on his route had ever seen skis, he laughingly called them "Norwegian snowshoes." He was promptly nicknamed "Snowshoe" Thompson. The Sierra region's only communication link in winter, he traveled alone with no compass or gun, braving wolf packs, blizzards, forty-foot snowdrifts, and endless mountain peaks. He often carried at least 100 pounds of mail on his back. Sometimes he also carried medicine to isolated townspeople and miners, and one time he carried a printing press in parts over many trips. Skiing became a sport when young people along his route became fascinated and asked for lessons on building and using skis. Soon races were held, and ski clubs were formed throughout the Sierras.

Now circle the number of each item you got wrong on the answer key below.

1. (4)	**11.** (1)	**21.** (1)
2. (1)	**12.** (5)	**22.** (3)
3. (3)	**13.** (5)	**23.** (1)
4. (2)	**14.** (2)	**24.** (4)
5. (5)	**15.** (1)	**25.** (5)
6. (1)	**16.** (1)	**26.** (3)
7. (2)	**17.** (3)	**27.** (2)
8. (2)	**18.** (4)	**28.** (1)
9. (5)	**19.** (5)	
10. (4)	**20.** (4)	

Scoring Your Essay The essay is the one part of the Skills Survey that you cannot correct yourself. A sample essay appears below that you can use as a model, but you will also need someone to help you score your own essay.

Sample essay:

Friends fill many different needs as we make our way through life. Little children, for example, pick friends to have fun with—to play ball, dolls, or videogames. Some even create imaginary friends. Older children often look for a "best friend" to share their ideas and secrets with.

Teenagers need friends to help them become independent of their parents. With their friends, teenagers often create a life away from home, with its own fashions, music, and language. Teen friends often share special interests—sports, computers, drama, or even, unfortunately, drugs.

As adults, we look for friends who will provide comfort and assistance in times of trouble as well as help us celebrate our good times. They are true friends. Such friends can also help us learn what we need to know at various steps of adult life—marriage, parenthood, work, midlife, old age.

Some self-employed people seek friendships as a way to help their businesses. People who are divorced or widowed seek out other single people for companionship. Today support groups of all kinds provide adults with special kinds of help through friendship. Such groups serve alcoholics, dieters, heart patients, gamblers, and widows.

The most interesting people seem to have the widest variety of friends. They realize that satisfying others' different needs for support, interest, and help is as rewarding as having their own needs satisfied.

If you're in a GED class, your teacher will be able to read your own essay and help you plan a course of study. If you're studying alone, however, you'll need to find someone to read and score your paper. Choose someone who you know is a good writer—a teacher, your boss, a friend—someone you trust to be honest with you about your abilities.

First give the person you have chosen the checklist on the next page to preview, so that he or she can understand better what is needed. (In fact, the scorer might want to read this whole section, "Scoring Your Essay," before beginning in order to fully understand what is going on.) Once the scorer has previewed the checklist, give him or her the topic assignment and then your essay to read.

Essay Scoring Checklist

To the scorer: Preview this entire checklist before you read and score the essay.

Read the essay topic on page 20. Next, read the essay written on that topic *quickly.* Take no more than two minutes. Try to achieve an overall impression of the writing. Then put the essay aside and, without referring back to it, rate it using the following criteria.

	Satisfactory	Needs Work
Message— the presence of a clear, controlling idea	☐	☐
Details— the use of examples and specific details to support the message	☐	☐
Organization— a logical presentation of ideas	☐	☐
Expression— the clear, precise use of language to convey the message	☐	☐
Sentence Structure— the use of complete sentences that avoid a repetitive, singsong rhythm	☐	☐
Mechanics and Usage— knowledge of the conventions of standard English (grammar, punctuation, and so on)	☐	☐

Using the Survey Results

How did you do on the Skills Survey? Here's a chart to show you the skills that were tested by the questions. By comparing the answers you got wrong with the chart, you can see which skills you need to concentrate on when you study the lessons in this book. The chart also shows the areas covered by the essay checklist and which lessons give you instruction and practice in those areas.

You will still probably want to work through every lesson, of course. That will help you develop skills that weren't tested directly on the Skills Survey as well as strengthen the skills you already have. Those new and strengthened skills will help guarantee your chances of passing the GED Writing Skills Test.

Question Number	**Skill**	**Lesson**
5, 9, 11, 13, 16, 17, 22, 25, 26, 27	Sentence structure	1, 2, 5, 6, 7, 8, 9
	Usage	
2, 21	Subject-verb agreement	3, 20
1, 15, 23, 24	Verb forms and tenses	4, 18, 19
6, 14	Pronouns	21
	Mechanics	
4, 8, 10, 12, 28	Punctuation	5, 6, 7, 23
7, 19	Capitalization	22
3, 18, 20	Spelling	Spelling breaks
	If your essay rating shows you need work in	*Pay special attention to lesson*
	Message	10, 17
	Details	15, 17
	Organization	11, 12, 13, 14, 17
	Expression	16
	Sentence structure	1–2, 5–9
	Mechanics and usage	3–4, 18–23, Spelling breaks

Writing Sentences

Did you ever listen to yourself speak to a friend? When you speak, you seldom start at the beginning of your thoughts and go clearly, directly, and in an orderly way to the end. Your words don't show a clear finish to one idea and the beginning of another. Instead, your words and ideas run together. Sometimes they bunch up; at other times they string themselves out. You may use expressions such as "um" or "you know" to help connect your thoughts or give you time to think of others. You may even interrupt yourself to say a new idea that suddenly popped into your head or to explain a thought from a minute ago.

The ideas you speak can become the ideas you write about. When you write, however, your thoughts must be presented in a more organized, formal way. It's as if you're boxing and presenting your thoughts to your reader. The boxes you use are sentences.

You have to know the best way to pack those boxes. In other words, you have to know how to move the information around in each sentence so that you come up with the best "fit." There are also ways of slowing down the ideas you are presenting and of speeding them up. There are even ways of interrupting your written ideas, but you have to know the right ways to do it. That is what writing good, effective sentences is all about. You'll need to produce such sentences when you write your GED essay.

In addition to writing your own sentences, you'll need to act as an "editor" of someone else's sentences on the GED Writing Skills Test. On the first part of the test you'll be reading passages from ten to twelve sentences long and answering multiple-choice questions about them. One kind of question will ask you to analyze a part of a sentence and, if needed, choose the best way to rewrite it. For example, look at the sample GED item in the next column.

Some people insist that they never dream scientists state that normally everyone dreams several times during a night's sleep.

Which of the following is the best way to write the underlined portion of this sentence? If you think the original is the best way, choose option (1).

(1) dream scientists
(2) dream, scientists
(3) dream, yet scientists
(4) dream. And scientists
(5) dream, and scientists

To answer that question, you have to look at the entire sentence and see how the parts are related. The original is actually two complete thoughts with nothing separating them; they are mistakenly run together. One way to fix this problem is to use a comma and a connecting word. Options (3) and (5) both do that, but the word *yet* makes more sense as a connecting word in this situation than *and* does, so option (3) is the best way to fix the problem: "Some people insist that they never dream, yet scientists state that normally everyone dreams several times during a night's sleep."

Another kind of GED multiple-choice item about sentences will ask you to spot an error in a sentence by choosing the necessary correction. Here's an example.

Contrary to popular belief, people generally dream in color all the time.

What correction should be made to this sentence?

(1) remove the comma after belief
(2) insert they after people
(3) change dream to dreaming
(4) insert a comma after color
(5) no correction is necessary

In this kind of question, half the time the fifth option will be "no correction is necessary." Sometimes that will be the correct answer, as it is in this case. A comma is helpful after an introductory phrase, so option (1) is not correct. The word *they* is not needed because *people* is already the subject of the sentence. Changing *dream* to *dreaming* would make the sentence incomplete because *dreaming* is the wrong kind of verb form to use as the main verb of a sentence. And finally, no comma is needed before the ending phrase *all the time.* So option (5) is the right answer.

There's a third kind of GED multiple-choice item. With this kind of question, the original sentence doesn't have an actual mistake. It is, however, written in a wordy or unclear way, and you have to pick the best way to rewrite ("repack") it. Here's an example of this kind of item.

> Your brain usually follows a certain logic, but that logic does not apply when dreaming.
>
> If you rewrote that sentence beginning with <u>When you dream, the logic</u> the next words should be
>
> (1) does not apply
> (2) that your brain
> (3) is usually followed
> (4) of dreaming is not
> (5) follows but does not
>
> (1) (2) (3) (4) (5)

How would you answer that question? Say the beginning of the new sentence in your head. Then ask yourself what information from the old sentence would follow that beginning to keep the meaning of the original sentence. The actual *words* from the original are not as important as their *meaning.* Two ideas from the original still have to be expressed in the new sentence: (1) your brain usually follows logic and (2) logic does not apply.

Add the first option to the new beginning: "When you dream, the logic does not apply." That picks up the second idea but leaves no way to express the first idea. Try the beginning with option (2): "When you dream, the logic that your brain . . ." That begins to express the first idea and leaves room in the sentence for the second as well: "When you dream, the logic that your brain usually follows does not apply." Option (2) is the best choice.

One tip: Always read all five answer choices before you make your final choice. You may think the first or second option is correct, but then you'll find a later option that brings up an important point you had forgotten about.

The fourth and final kind of GED multiple-choice item involves *two* sentences. Again, there is no obvious error in them, but you must pick out the best way to combine the two into one. Here's an example.

> In a dream, you can be in your living room one moment. Then in the next moment, you have been transported to the middle of the ocean.
>
> The most effective combination of these sentences would include which of the following groups of words?
>
> (1) one moment, and then in the next
> (2) In a dream, you can be transported to
> (3) Having been transported to the middle
> (4) and in the middle of the ocean the next
> (5) Your living room and the middle of
>
> (1) (2) (3) (4) (5)

To combine the sentences effectively, you have to choose the important information from both, combine it in an easy-to-understand way, and drop the words you don't need. Remember: Actual words aren't important; information is. The important ideas from the second sentence are "in the next moment" and "the middle of the ocean." If you picked up those ideas, you could attach them to the first sentence and drop all the other, unnecessary words from the second sentence. And that's precisely what the fourth option lets you do: "In a dream you can be in your living room one moment and in the middle of the ocean the next." Doesn't that *sound* like a good, effective sentence?

The following section of this book will help you develop the skills you need to answer multiple-choice questions about sentences like those. It will also give you plenty of opportunities to write your own good, effective sentences as a first step to writing a successful GED essay.

LESSON 1

Sentence Sense

From Body Language to Talking

You've probably heard the old saying "A picture is worth a thousand words." Seeing people talk can be just like seeing a picture. They use gestures, facial expressions, and other types of body language to do some of their communicating for them. When you are face-to-face with someone, you don't have to find words for all the information you want to get across.

Here's an Example

Look at the picture below. This man is using the look on his face and a gesture to show that he has no money. The hotel clerk is certainly getting the message.

Obviously, the man in the picture, Fred, needs money. Suppose he calls his wife on the telephone. Then he would have to communicate everything with words. This might be Fred's end of a phone conversation with his wife:

"Fred here. Need money, honey."
"Because my wallet was stolen."
"No, no credit cards, nothing."
"Wire me $250. Okay? Good-bye."

Fred's wife needs more words than the hotel clerk does because she isn't there to see him. Yet Fred isn't careful to fill her in on every last detail. And when you think about it, he doesn't have to. Fred's wife at least knows where he is and why he is there. And she can *ask* Fred for any information she needs. Fred also doesn't have to impress her with the way he explains himself.

From Talking to Writing

Without body language or speech to aid them, writers have to use more words to convey their messages. When you write, always be aware that your reader may need more information than you are used to giving when you speak.

A piece of writing is actually a series of **sentences.** Sentences are like word boxes that you pack and unpack with information. If your readers don't understand a sentence, it's as if you've just handed them an empty box.

Many writing situations require that you use only well-formed and complete sentences to get your message across. The GED Test is one of those situations. A complete sentence must have two basic kinds of information: a **verb** and a **subject.**

The verb supplies the most important information in a sentence. It sets the time of the sentence. Some verbs tell you what action is going on. Action verbs are words like *see, shove, giggle, think,* and *write.*

Other verbs describe a condition, or a "state of being." State-of-being verbs are words like *are, seem, was, feel,* and *taste.*

Sometimes several verbs have to work together to be complete. For example, you might say, "We *will give* her a going-away present." In that sentence *give* is the main verb, and *will* is a helping verb. In "He *may have left* for the day," *left* is the main verb and *may have* are helping verbs. Main verbs and helping verbs working together are called **verb phrases.**

The subject is the naming part of a sentence. It names who or what is producing the action or displaying the condition the verb describes. Subjects are words like *bulldozer, Fred,* and *she.*

Do a subject and a verb always make a group of words a complete sentence? No, not quite—the group of words must also form an independent, complete thought. Your reader should need no further information to understand what your sentence means. "When *I saw* you last" has a subject *(I)* and a verb *(saw).* Yet it is not a complete thought and therefore not a complete sentence. You still don't know what happened "when I saw you last."

Coming to Terms

sentence a complete thought containing a subject and a verb

verb the part of a sentence that shows action or state of being

verb phrase a main verb and one or more helping verbs working together

subject the part of a sentence that names who or what is acting or being the way the verb describes

A Test-Taking Tip

On the GED Test you will have to tell whether sentences are complete. You probably remember that a complete sentence begins with a capital letter and ends with a mark of punctuation. A period (.) puts a "stop" after a sentence that gives facts or directions. A question mark (?) shows that something is being asked. An exclamation point (!) shows the end of a sentence that expresses strong feeling. On the GED Test, however, even incomplete sentences will begin with capital letters and end with punctuation. So telling whether a sentence is complete may be hard.

Don't just see if a sentence *sounds* like a complete thought because people don't always speak in complete thoughts. To tell whether a sentence is complete, check what information the sentence has and what information it doesn't have. Check to see that it is actually a complete thought.

Here's an Example

Look back at Fred's phone conversation with his wife. Each group of words is a statement his wife will understand. Yet look again at how each group appears when it is written down.

"Fred here. Need money, honey."

"Because my wallet was stolen."

"No, no credit cards, nothing."

"Wire me $250. Okay? Good-bye."

While all the word groups begin with capital letters and end with periods, most of Fred's statements are not complete thoughts.

"Fred here" is a type of expression many people use on the telephone. The verb *(is)* is missing. Verbs are often left out. The result is an incomplete but perfectly understandable *spoken* sentence.

The group of words "Need money, honey" is an incomplete thought because it doesn't name *who* needs the money. Fred didn't include that information because his wife would know whom he meant. People sometimes leave the subjects out of statements when they are talking. The complete thought (and therefore the complete sentence) would be "*I* need money, honey."

"No, no credit cards, nothing" is an incomplete thought because it has no verb or subject. Fred uses these five words instead of the complete sentences "*I have* no credit cards" and "*I have* nothing."

Even when speaking, people sometimes must communicate in complete thoughts. If Fred walked up to you in a hotel lobby and said, "Because my wallet was stolen," you wouldn't know how to react. You are a stranger and wouldn't know his situation. Yet that group of words has a subject *(wallet)* and a verb phrase *(was stolen).* Even so, Fred would have conveyed an incomplete thought. You might reply, "Because your wallet was stolen, what?" Fred's complete sentence would have to be "*I need to borrow money* because my wallet was stolen."

Be on guard for sentences that command or request someone to do something. These sentences often have no stated subjects. In "Wire me $250" the word *you* is understood. Fred is talking directly to his wife: "*You* wire me $250." "Wire me $250" is the only complete sentence that Fred used in his conversation.

Try It Yourself

Fred's wife Ruth sent him a money order to pay his hotel bill. She included the following telegram. Do you think she wrote the way she talks? Did she use any complete sentences in her message?

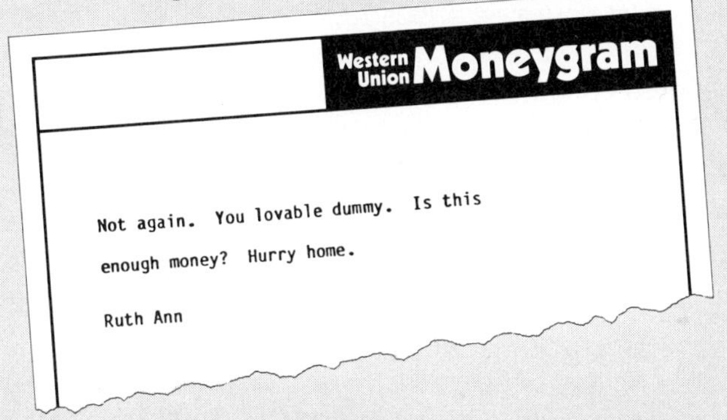

Look at the first group of words: "Not again." Why isn't this a complete sentence? For one thing, it has no subject or verb. For another, it is an incomplete thought. Only Fred knows what "Not again" means. Anyone else who read the telegram would say, "Not again what?"

Why isn't "You lovable dummy" a complete sentence? What information is missing? The verb is missing, as in "You *are* a lovable dummy."

Look at "Is this enough money?" Is the end punctuation correct? Yes it is, because a question is being asked. Is the question a complete sentence? To answer that, find the subject and the verb. One good way to find the subject and the verb in a question is to turn the words around into an answer: "This is enough money." The subject is *this* and the verb is *is.*

Now what about "Hurry home"? What kind of sentence is this? Is there a subject and a verb? "Hurry home" is a command sentence. *You* is the understood subject. *Hurry* is the verb. Remember that commands often don't need to show subjects to be complete sentences.

Ruth's message was perfectly acceptable for her writing situation. But in other situations, she would have to write all complete sentences. How would she have written her message if she had sent it to the hotel clerk to forward to Fred?

Warm-up

Supply a punctuation mark at the end of each of these sentences. Use a period, a question mark, or an exclamation point.

1. Linda and Seva asked how you were doing
2. Kill the umpire
3. How are you feeling now that you've lost ten pounds
4. I wonder whether he knows what I think about him

Here are some incomplete sentences. Make each a complete sentence by supplying one of these:

- **a.** a subject
- **b.** a verb or verb part
- **c.** both a subject and a verb

5. Forgiven me yet?

____

____

6. Miss you and wish you were here.

____

____

7. Two left.

____

____

8. Frank sitting at home doing nothing.

____

____

9. Repair the leaky faucet by myself.

____

____

10. Maria frustrated by Carlos's stubbornness.

____

____

Compare your answers with the Sample Warm-up Answers below. While your sentences may vary, all should express complete thoughts.

Sample Warm-up Answers

1. . **2.** ! **3.** ? **4.** . **5.** *Have you* forgiven me yet? **6.** *I* miss you and wish you were here. **7.** Two *are* left. (It would also be all right to write, "*There are* two left." Just remember that *there* can never be the subject of a sentence because it doesn't name anyone or anything. In the sentence "There are two left," *two* is the subject.) **8.** Frank *is* sitting at home doing nothing. **9.** *I can* repair the leaky faucet by myself. **10.** Maria *was* frustrated by Carlos's stubbornness.

Parts of the following passage are more like spoken English than written English. See if you can find any incomplete sentences. Add your own subjects or verbs to these, and then rewrite the passage on the lines below.

Always want to be in the know. The United States Census Bureau is an example of Americans' mania for information. The Census Bureau publishes a book nearly 1,000 pages long. Has the boring title of *Statistical Abstracts of the United States.* Yet this set of numbers, charts, and graphs is a best-seller. It contains facts about everything from the federal budget to sales of electric popcorn poppers. More than enough information to satisfy any curious American.

____

____

____

____

____

____

____

____

____

____

____

____

Compare your rewrite to the one in the Sample Warm-up Answer below. Don't worry if your subjects and verbs are different. Do check to see whether you have any incomplete sentences left in your passage.

Sample Warm-up Answer

Americans always want to be in the know. The United States Census Bureau is an example of Americans' mania for information. The Census Bureau publishes a book nearly 1,000 pages long. *This book* has the boring title of *Statistical Abstracts of the United States.* Yet this set of numbers, charts, and graphs is a best-seller. It contains facts about everything from the federal budget to sales of electric popcorn poppers. *It has* more than enough information to satisfy any curious American.

Writing Complete Sentences

You know now that you must write in complete sentences, especially when your reader does not know you personally. Your reader will also expect your sentences to follow rules of punctuation and grammar. These rules are sometimes called the conventions of English. The more formal the writing situation, the more important it is for you to use the conventions of English. And the GED Writing Skills Test is a very formal situation.

Your GED essay will give you the chance to show that you can write and correct your own sentences following the English conventions. On the multiple-choice test, you'll find and fix incorrect grammar and punctuation in sentences that other people wrote. You will, for example, have to find and fix **fragments,** which are incomplete sentences.

You have already seen some fragments and fixed them by adding subjects and verbs. When you are revising fragments in passages on the GED conventions test or in your own essay, you can also combine the fragments with other fragments or with sentences in the passage.

Coming to Terms

fragment an incomplete sentence

Here's an Example

Below are the first four sentences from an essay by a GED student. Three of the sentences are fragments. In two, the writer did not provide enough information to give the essay reader a clear picture of what he was trying to say. The third fragment should be attached to another sentence from the passage to form one complete sentence.

■ *Wow, the automobile! Been so many changes.* In my own neighborhood, I can see changes. *Like more noise, dirtier air, and less safe streets.*

In this case, writing the way he talks hurt this GED student. Look at the three sentences that are *italicized.* "Wow, the automobile!" is more like an expression of emotion than a sentence. Besides, this fragment has no subject or verb. The essay reader would have no way of knowing why this writer put *wow* and *the automobile* in the same sentence.

The statement "Been so many changes" is missing a subject and part of the verb phrase. But when you add the subject from the first fragment, the rest of the verb, and a little more information, you create the following complete sentence:

■ The automobile has been responsible for so many changes.

The third fragment is "Like more noise, dirtier air, and less safe streets." This fragment gives examples of the changes mentioned in the sentence before it. The fragment can be attached to the end of that sentence.

■ In my own neighborhood, I can see changes like more noise, dirtier air, and less safe streets.

Notice that no comma was used when the fragment was attached to the end of the sentence. That is usually the case unless you "hear a pause" between the parts of the sentence. That means that if you spoke the sentence aloud, you would pause at that spot. In that case, you need a comma. When you attach a fragment to the *beginning* of a sentence, you almost always need to use a comma.

On the GED Test, try one of these techniques when you need to fix a fragment in your essay or in one of the written passages:

1. Add a missing subject or verb and any other information, if necessary.

2. Move and attach the fragment to the beginning or end of another fragment or sentence. You may have to add or drop a word or two. Be sure to change the fragment's punctuation, if necessary. Drop the final period. If you are attaching the fragment to the beginning of a sentence, you will probably need to use a comma after it. If you are attaching it to the end, you *usually* don't need a comma before it. Say the sentence to yourself, and listen for a pause.

Try It Yourself

Here is more of the essay on automobiles. Look the passage over carefully. Can you find two fragments among these sentences? How would you fix them?

■ Other big changes are positive. By owning automobiles. People can save a great deal of time. This invention has also created jobs. For many people I know.

The two fragments are "By owning automobiles" and "For many people I know." You can fix both fragments by attaching them to other sentences. The first fragment belongs with the sentence about saving time: "By owning automobiles, people can save a great deal of time." (*Or:* "People can save a great deal of time by owning automobiles.")

The second fragment belongs with the sentence about jobs: "This invention has also created jobs for many people I know." (*Or:* "For many people I know, this invention has also created jobs.")

Warm-up

There is one fragment and one complete sentence in each of the pairs below. Underline the fragment in each pair. Then attach it to the beginning or end of the complete sentence.

1. With his wife's money. Fred was able to pay his hotel bill.

____

____

2. The store delivered my new washer and dryer. Just in time for laundry day.

____

____

3. With each and every day. I try to do more and more push-ups.

____

____

4. We budgeted in more money for salaries. To hire more workers.

____

____

Now reverse the order of the statements in each sentence. Write your new sentences on the lines below.

5. ______________________________

____

6. ______________________________

____

7. ______________________________

____

8. ______________________________

____

Compare your rewritten sentences with the Sample Warm-up Answers in the next column. Remember that your answers do not have to match the samples exactly. In each set you could have fixed the fragment by placing it at the beginning *or* the end.

Parts of the following passage were written as if they were spoken English. On the lines below, rewrite the passage. Use the kind of English you will use on the GED Test.

There are five fragments. Fix them by attaching them to nearby sentences or adding subjects or verbs.

A Soviet nuclear reactor accident in 1986. It was a dangerous problem. A problem for the Soviets and for others as well. It was even more dangerous than Three Mile Island. People were contaminated by the radiation. Escaping from the reactor. Spread into northern and eastern Europe and even drifted into the United States. To find whether the radiation levels were safe. Scientists tested the air in America.

____

____

____

____

____

____

____

____

____

____

____

Now compare your rewrite with the one in the Sample Warm-up Answers below. Are there any fragments left in your passage? Does your passage contain enough information for the reader to get your message?

Use this "stretching" exercise to prepare for the writing assignment in On the Springboard. It will get you ready for the mental exercise of writing in the same way that stretching gets you ready for physical exercise.

Think about your goals and why you are preparing to take the GED Test. Do you want a better job? Are you interested in going on to college? Would you like to gain the sense of personal satisfaction and accomplishment that comes from learning?

Whatever your reasons, imagine you are going to write an explanation of your decision to earn a GED credential. You're going to write it for someone who knows you personally, like your spouse or a good friend. List any information that you would include in your explanation. You can just jot down notes; you don't have to worry about writing complete sentences at this point.

Now go back and consider what information you would need to include if you were going to write your explanation for someone who does *not* know you well. List that information as well.

Keep your list of reasons. You'll be using it soon.

Sample Warm-up Answers

1. With his wife's money, Fred was able to pay his hotel bill. **2.** The store delivered my new washer and dryer just in time for laundry day. **3.** With each and every day, I try to do more and more push-ups. **4.** We budgeted in more money for salaries to hire more workers. **5.** Fred was able to pay his hotel bill with his wife's money. **6.** Just in time for laundry day, the store delivered my new washer and dryer. **7.** I try to do more and more push-ups with each and every day. **8.** To hire more workers, we budgeted in more money for salaries.

A Soviet nuclear reactor accident happened in 1986. It was a dangerous problem for the Soviets and for others as well. It was even more dangerous than Three Mile Island. People were contaminated by the radiation escaping from the reactor. Some radiation spread into northern and eastern Europe and even drifted into the United States. To find whether radiation levels were safe, scientists tested the air in America.

On the Springboard

Directions: Read this paragraph carefully and then answer the questions that follow it. For each question, choose the answer that would correct an error or show the best way to write the sentence.

(1) People who write history believe. (2) That the earliest telegraphs were drums and smoke signals from fires. (3) The ancient Greeks are thought to have invented the modern telegraph. (4) They were the first to link alphabet letters to signals. (5) The word "telegraph" itself can be traced back to a signaling system that Claude Chappe established in France in the 1790s. (6) Since then, inventors given the world today's telegraph, telephone, teletype, television, and many other communication breakthroughs.

1. Sentences 1 and 2: **People who write history believe. That the earliest telegraphs were drums and smoke signals from fires.**

   Which of the following is the best way to write the underlined portion of these sentences? If you think the original is the best way, choose option (1).

   (1) believe. That
   (2) believe, that
   (3) believe that

   (1) (2) (3)

2. Sentences 3 and 4: **The ancient Greeks are thought to have invented the modern telegraph. They were the first to link alphabet letters to signals.**

   Which of the following is the best way to write the underlined portion of these sentences? If you think the original is the best way, choose option (1).

   (1) telegraph. They
   (2) telegraph, they
   (3) telegraph they

   (1) (2) (3)

3. Sentence 6: **Since then, inventors given the world today's telegraph, telephone, teletype, television, and many other communication breakthroughs.**

   What correction should be made to this sentence?

   (1) remove the comma after then
   (2) change inventors to invent
   (3) insert have after inventors

   (1) (2) (3)

Each year many adults decide to complete their high-school education. Often these adults study and take the GED Test instead of enrolling in high school.

Write a short composition about why you are studying for the GED Test. Write for someone who does not know you at all. Use complete sentences and the information you listed in the Warm-up exercise. Try to write at least five or six sentences.

Check your answers for On the Springboard questions 1–3 on page 98. If you avoided fragments by answering the questions correctly, congratulations. Try your skill on "The Real Thing" that follows. If you had trouble with the passage or questions, review this lesson on writing in complete sentences and your responses in the Warm-up before you go on.

“The Real Thing”

Directions: The following items are based on a paragraph that contains numbered sentences. Some of the sentences contain errors in sentence structure, usage, or mechanics. A few sentences, however, are correct as written. Read the paragraph and then answer the items based on it. For each item, choose the answer that would result in the most effective writing of the sentence or sentences. The best answer must be consistent with the meaning and tone of the rest of the paragraph.

(1) Sending telegrams used to be serious business. (2) Telegrams were often used in an emergency to convey bad news, so people opened them. (3) With a sense of fear and anticipation. (4) Novelty companies eventually took over. (5) They came up with downright silly telegrams. (6) The phone book lists these gimmicks. (7) It is filling up with telegram gimmicks. (8) You can barely find Western Union's number among singing-telegram and balloon-o-gram ads. (9) There are tap-o-grams featuring tap dancers and revenge telegrams featuring a pie in the face. (10) Giant telegrams five feet high and seven feet wide available. (11) There is even a complete Arabian-nights-feast telegram!

1. Sentences 2 and 3: **Telegrams were often used in an emergency to convey bad news, so people opened them. With a sense of fear and anticipation.**

   Which of the following is the best way to write the underlined portion of these sentences? If you think the original is the best way, choose option (1).

   (1) them. With
   (2) them, with
   (3) them with
   (4) them? With
   (5) them! With

   (1) (2) (3) (4) (5)

2. Sentences 6 and 7: **The phone book lists these gimmicks. It is filling up with telegram gimmicks.**

   The most effective combination of sentences 6 and 7 would include which of the following groups of words?

   (1) and it is filling up
   (2) lists and fills up
   (3) It lists
   (4) The phone book is
   (5) filling the phone book up with

   (1) (2) (3) (4) (5)

3. Sentence 9: **There are tap-o-grams featuring tap dancers and revenge telegrams featuring a pie in the face.**

   Which of the following is the best way to write the underlined portion of this sentence? If you think the original is the best way, choose option (1).

   (1) dancers and
   (2) dancers. And
   (3) dancers, and
   (4) dancers! And
   (5) dancers. Revenge

   (1) (2) (3) (4) (5)

4. Sentence 10: **Giant telegrams five feet high and seven feet wide available.**

   What correction should be made to this sentence?

   (1) replace Giant with There
   (2) insert a comma after telegrams
   (3) insert as much as after telegrams
   (4) insert are after wide
   (5) no correction is necessary

   (1) (2) (3) (4) (5)

Check your answers and record your score on page 101.

LESSON 2

Adding Details

If sentences are boxes you fill with information, then some sentences can have smaller boxes within them. These smaller boxes have detailed information. When you write a sentence, you may need to add many descriptive words to explain exactly what you mean. These details make your sentences much more interesting and informative.

Using Descriptive Words with Nouns

You may remember from school that **nouns** are words that name persons, places, things, or ideas. The subject of a sentence is a noun, but you use nouns elsewhere in sentences too. In addition, you can add details to those nouns. You can use descriptive words to answer some of these questions about nouns: What kind? How many? Which one? Whose? How does it look, feel, smell, sound, or taste?

Coming to Terms

noun a word that names a person, place, thing, or idea

Here's an Example

A magazine reporter began an article this way. The details that describe the nouns are in **bold.**

■ A **dark, stormy** afternoon set the stage for the **ugly** incident that followed. The strikers, **cold and wet,** marched through the **hard** rain with their **hand-lettered** signs. **United,** they were protesting that the **company's proposed** paycut was **unjust.**

Now look at some of those sentences without their details.

■ An afternoon set the stage for the incident that followed. The strikers marched through the rain with their signs.

You probably noticed that in some cases, the sense of the sentence depends on descriptive words. "An afternoon set the stage" doesn't make much sense, but "a dark, stormy afternoon set the stage" certainly does. "The paycut was" makes no sense at all without the detail "unjust." Other details strengthen the picture you get of the strikers.

When you add details to your own complete sentences, you need to know a few rules about commas. Place a comma after a detail that comes at the beginning of a sentence.

■ **Exhausted,** the search party returned from the mountain.

Place commas around a detail immediately following the noun it describes.

■ The search party**, exhausted,** returned from the mountain.

Sometimes you'll want to use two details to help describe a noun. For example, take the sentence about the search party. If you wanted to add that the members of the party were also successful, you could write it this way.

■ The exhausted search party returned from the mountain. They were successful.

But if you wanted your writing to sound smoother and more natural, you could combine the details in one sentence. You could combine them with a connecting word such as *but* and leave out any unnecessary words from the second sentence.

■ The **exhausted but successful** search party returned from the mountain.

What if the exhausted search party were wet? You'd probably want to combine the details with the connecting word *and.*

■ The **exhausted and wet** search party returned from the mountain.

In a sentence like that, you could also drop the *and.* If you choose this way, you need to separate the details with a comma.

■ The **exhausted, wet** search party returned from the mountain.

You need this comma *only* if the details could be separated by *and* and still make sense. If they cannot be separated by *and,* don't use a comma.

■ The search party returned with the **missing ten-year-old** boy.

Try It Yourself

The sentences below express some opinions about people's attitudes. Look for details that could be combined. Think of details that could be added in the blanks.

■ Many people are becoming less trusting. They are also less neighborly. Some city dwellers are insecure. These cautious people would rather be left alone. This ______ situation exists partly because of television. Studies show that people who watch a lot of television overestimate the amount of crime that actually occurs. Their ______ feelings would change if they only turned off the TV.

Did you see that *people* and *They* in the first two sentences referred to the same group? That means the details describing them could be combined: "Many people are becoming less trusting and neighborly." The unnecessary words "They are also less" should be dropped.

What about the details describing city dwellers? There are a number of ways you could have combined them. Here are four: (1) "Some insecure, cautious city dwellers would rather be left alone." (2) "Insecure and cautious, some city dwellers would rather be left alone." (3) "Some city dwellers, insecure and cautious, would rather be left alone." (4) "Some city dwellers are insecure and cautious and would rather be left alone."

What about the blank before the word *situation?* Any number of details could have gone there: *sad, disturbing, alarming,* or *interesting.* The same is true of the blank before *feelings.* You could have used *suspicious, fearful, unrealistic, distrustful,* or any other word that helps describe the feelings those people have.

Warm-up

Combine the following sentences from horoscope predictions by pairing the details. Remember to use commas and connecting words appropriately.

1. You will receive an invitation soon.
The invitation will be exciting.
It will be mysterious.

____

____

2. A Virgo will come into your life.
She will be strong-willed.
She will be capable.

____

____

3. A relationship with a family member may become strained for a time.
This relationship may become unhappy.

____

____

4. On the other hand, your chances of passing a test in the near future are good.
The test will be difficult.
The test is worthwhile.

____

____

Now compare your answers with the Sample Warm-up Answers. Remember that there is sometimes more than one way to combine details.

Add details to these sentences.

5. The beggar asked the businessman for money.

____

____

6. That music is giving me a headache.

____

____

7. Who was that man I saw you with at the theater?

____

____

You can find sample sentences with details under the Sample Warm-up Answers below.

Think of two people you know who are very different from one another. List as many ways that they are different as you can. Then write sentences describing the people.

Sample Warm-up Answers
1. You will receive an exciting, mysterious invitation soon. **2.** A strong-willed and capable Virgo will come into your life. **3.** A relationship with a family member may become strained and unhappy for a time. **4.** On the other hand, your chances of passing a difficult yet worthwhile test in the near future are good. **5.** Hungry, the ragged beggar asked the young, well-dressed businessman for a little money. **6.** That loud rock music is giving me a tremendous headache. **7.** Who was that short, silly-looking man I saw you with at the new downtown theater?

Using Descriptive Words with Verbs

Just as you use descriptive words with the nouns in your sentences, you can also use them to add information to verbs and other words. You can add details to tell when something happened, where it happened, and how it happened.

Here's an Example

A sportswriter used details to describe the action she saw during a baseball game.

■ This team **always** keeps the fans **keenly** alert. **Yesterday** they played **somewhat inconsistently.** As usual with this year's team, though, they performed **well** enough to win. Once again the superb pitching **strongly** motivated the rest of the team to play **better** than they are. **Confidently,** manager Jim Fouts predicts a pennant.

See how much life is brought to that article by the writer's selection of descriptive words. You may have noticed that, without the details, the second sentence says only, "They played."

You can combine these kinds of details into one sentence, as you did with details about nouns. You can also pair them with a connecting word. Look at this example.

■ The frustrated player threw the ball into the stands. He was **obviously** frustrated. He threw the ball **angrily.** He threw the ball **disgustedly.** He threw it **high.**

The last four details can be combined into one sentence like this.

■ The **obviously frustrated** player **angrily and disgustedly** threw the ball **high** into the stands.

You usually don't need a comma with this kind of detail unless you put it right at the beginning of the sentence.

■ **Disgustedly,** the frustrated player threw the ball into the stands.

Try It Yourself

A GED student wanted to add more life and detail to his writing. Below is an example of the sentences he wrote. Can any of the details be combined into another sentence?

■ Some people rush past accidents. It happens often. They do it thoughtlessly. They ignore people in trouble. They do this deliberately even when the trouble is serious.

Did you find all the descriptive words used to explain verbs? Look at the first three sentences. They tell you that when people rush, they do so often and thoughtlessly. You can move those two details into the first sentence: "Some people often rush thoughtlessly past accidents." The detail *deliberately* helps describe *how* people ignore others, so it can be moved next to *ignore:* "They deliberately ignore people in trouble, even when the trouble is serious."

Have you noticed that sometimes you can change the way you use a detail by changing the form of the word slightly? For instance, people who rush *thoughtlessly* can be called *thoughtless* people. Watch for chances to change the form of descriptive words when you combine.

Warm-up

Here are some more predictions using details. Combine them whenever possible.

1. You will courageously defend a friend.
   You will do it unselfishly.
   This will happen tomorrow.

   ____

   ____

2. Your love life will improve.
   It will do so soon.
   It will do so drastically.

   ____

   ____

3. You will keep a promise made long ago.
   You will do it honorably.
   You will do it even though you made the promise carelessly.

   ____

   ____

4. You will solve a problem at work.
You will do it quickly.
You will not do it thoughtlessly.

Compare your answers with the Sample Warm-up Answers below. Remember that your answers don't have to match exactly.

Now add details that show how, when, or where to these sentences.

5. My boss yelled at him.

6. Her children don't know how to behave.

7. The spy turned and vanished into the trees.

You can find three sample sentences under the Sample Warm-up Answers below. Did you add details similar to the way they were added in the samples?

Sample Warm-up Answers
1. Tomorrow you will courageously and unselfishly defend a friend. **2.** Soon your love life will improve drastically. **3.** You will honorably keep a promise made carelessly long ago. **4.** You will solve a problem at work quickly but not thoughtlessly. **5.** My boss angrily yelled at him today. **6.** Unfortunately, her children don't know how to behave responsibly. **7.** The spy turned swiftly and silently and vanished into the trees.

Writing Descriptive Phrases

When you write, you can often use whole phrases to add details. In fact, you probably use phrases in your writing all the time without even thinking about them. Some of these phrases begin with words such as *over, into, at,* and *in.* These words show relationships.

You can also use some verb forms to add more information to a sentence. They aren't the main verbs of sentences. They are verbs in the *-ing* form (for example, *walking*) and the *to* form (for example, *to walk*). These verb forms are called **verbals.** When there are other words working with them, the words and the verbal make up a verbal phrase.

Coming to Terms

verbal a form of a verb that is not the main verb of a sentence but is used to add information to the sentence. Verbs ending in *-ing* when they are *not* part of the main verb phrase and verbs with *to* are verbals.

Here's an Example

These sentences have descriptive phrases marked in bold.

- She changed her clothes **after her exercise class.**
- Ahmad looked bored **sitting at his mother-in-law's house.**

In the first sentence, the descriptive phrase *after her exercise class* tells *when* the woman changed her clothes. In the second sentence, *sitting* is a verbal. The descriptive verbal phrase is *sitting at his mother-in-law's house.* It tells *where* Ahmad looked bored.

Like single words, phrases can be combined to add more information to your sentences and make them smoother to read.

- Roberto Jerez just moved here. Roberto moved **from Denver.** He came here **to find a new job.**

Those sentences can be combined into one good sentence by moving the descriptive phrases.

■ Roberto Jerez just moved here **from Denver to find a new job.**

You can place phrases at various spots in your sentences as long as it is clear which word each phrase is describing. For example, you could put the verbal phrase in the last example at the beginning of the sentence.

■ **To find a new job,** Roberto Jerez just moved here from Denver.

Notice that when a descriptive phrase comes at the beginning of a sentence, you usually use a comma after it. When you place the phrase in the middle or at the end of the sentence, you need a comma to separate it *only* if you hear a pause when you say the sentence to yourself.

■ The thief was trying to escape. He was trying to escape from the police. He was limping away.

Combined: The thief**, limping away,** was trying to escape **from the police.**

You can also pair phrases as you did with descriptive words, using a connecting word.

■ Dinah is a workaholic. She works **at night.** She works **on weekends.**

Combined: Dinah is a workaholic. She works **at night and on weekends.**

Whenever you add a detail, you need to place it as near to the word it is describing as possible. That usually isn't too difficult with single words. When you're adding phrases, however, you have to be especially careful. Misplaced phrases can be very funny, as in this ad.

■ For sale—grand piano by a retired music teacher with two broken legs

As you write more detailed sentences, you may accidentally write a phrase with no word to describe. This happens especially with verbals ending in *-ing* at the beginning of a sentence.

■ Being very small, soccer was a better choice than football.

That verbal phrase sounds as if it belongs with *soccer.* You have to add a different subject to give it something to describe.

■ Being very small, I chose soccer over football.

Try It Yourself

Read the paragraph below. Look for ways to combine details to make the sentences sound smoother. Be careful to keep each phrase near the word it describes.

■ Cigarette smoking is being restricted these days. It is being restricted in private homes. It is also being restricted in public places. Standing up for their rights, nonsmokers are working hard. Specifically, they're standing up for their right to breathe clean air. They're working hard to change laws.

The first three sentences all speak of restrictions and where they occur. You could have combined them along these lines: "Cigarette smoking is being restricted these days in people's homes and in public places."

What about the next two sentences? Rights are discussed in both, so you can move the phrase "to breathe clean air." The next sentence adds information about why nonsmokers are working hard, so you can move "to change laws" too: "Standing up for their right to breathe clean air, nonsmokers are working hard to change laws."

Your sentences do not have to match those to be good combinations, but they should make sense and be clear by having the details near the words they describe.

Warm-up

Combine these sentences by moving descriptive phrases. Make sure you place the phrases logically and use commas only when necessary.

1. Many voters believe that their votes don't matter.
These voters are unregistered.
These voters are living in this city.

____

____

2. A few votes have made a difference in many crucial situations.
They have made a difference in many situations throughout United States history.
They have made a difference in world politics.

____

____

3. John Kennedy could have been defeated in 1960.
   He could have lost by a few votes.
   Those votes were in certain precincts.
   Those precincts were in Illinois.

   ___

   ___

4. President Andrew Johnson just missed being impeached.
   He was being tried for incompetence.
   He missed by one vote.

   ___

   ___

Compare your combined sentences with those in the Sample Warm-up Answers below before you go on.

Rewrite the following paragraph. Move misplaced descriptive words and phrases to more logical places. Add new subjects if needed. Use commas only when necessary.

There is nothing so relaxing as ice cream. Leaning back on the porch swing, your spoon dips into a mass of cold, creamy deliciousness. You sit there quietly eating and remembering the past on your swing. Without even trying, the sights and sounds of childhood are thought of. No one can eat ice cream without smiling.

___

___

___

___

___

___

___

Compare your paragraph with the one below under Sample Warm-up Answers.

Sample Warm-up Answers
1. Many unregistered voters living in this city believe that their vote doesn't matter. **2.** A few votes have made a difference in many crucial situations throughout United States history and in world politics. **3.** John Kennedy could have been defeated in 1960 by a few votes in certain precincts in Illinois.
5. President Andrew Johnson, being tried for incompetence, just missed being impeached by one vote.

There is nothing so relaxing as ice cream. Leaning back on the porch swing, you dip your spoon into a mass of cold, creamy deliciousness. You sit there on your swing quietly eating and remembering the past. Without even trying, you think of the sights and sounds of childhood. No one can eat ice cream without smiling.

You know that adding details to your sentences is important. But before you can add details, you have to *notice* details to write about. You notice details by carefully observing.

Look at the picture below. Notice as much about it as you can—how the people look, what they are wearing, what they are doing, where they seem to be, and so on. Write as many complete, detailed sentences about the picture as you can. Combine details if that leads to more effective sentences.

Write five simple sentences about yourself. Use only nouns and verbs. For example,

I am a man.
I drive a cab.
I fish.
My dog is a collie.
I own my house.

Now think about yourself. List the details that you could add to your sentences. Be sure to include more than just how you look. Here are two examples:

I am a man.
  tall, slightly overweight, a cheerful smile
I fish.
  in the park in the spring, up north in autumn

Save the details about yourself for the Springboard exercise.

A Test-Taking Tip

Don't forget to include details in your GED essay. Use your imagination to picture the sights and hear the sounds of what you are writing about. Notice the details in your mind and include them in your writing.

On the Springboard

Directions: Read this paragraph carefully and then answer the questions that follow it.

(1) Who are the most satisfied employees? (2) Researchers conducted a survey and found that salespeople were the happiest workers. (3) Proud of their work, salespeople believe in helping people. (4) They also take pride in their role in the economy. (5) In addition, they get instant feedback on successful efforts. (6) A confident, determined salesperson can make good money and enjoy doing it.

1. Sentence 2: **Researchers conducted a survey and found that salespeople were the happiest workers.**

   If you rewrote sentence 2 beginning with

   After conducting a survey,

   the next word should be

   (1) salespeople (2) and
   (3) researchers

   (1) (2) (3)

2. Sentences 3 and 4: **Proud of their work, salespeople believe in helping people. They also take pride in their role in the economy.**

   The most effective combination of sentences 3 and 4 would include which of the following groups of words?

   (1) helping people and they also take
   (2) Proud of their work and of their role in the economy,
   (3) Proud of their work and they also take pride

   (1) (2) (3)

3. Sentence 6: **A confident, determined salesperson can make good money and enjoy doing it.**

   What correction should be made to this sentence?

   (1) remove the comma after confident
   (2) insert a comma after determined
   (3) no correction is necessary

   (1) (2) (3)

Imagine that you have just discovered a long-lost relative. Write a letter describing yourself to him or her. Use your notes from the last Warm-up. Make sure your details are placed logically.

Check your answers for On the Springboard on page 98.

Did you get all the Springboard questions correct? If so, and if you have used details in your Springboard writing, try "The Real Thing." If not, take time to practice adding details correctly, and then go on.

A Test-Taking Tip

When you choose an answer for a multiple-choice question on the GED Writing Skills Test, *always* go back and reread the sentence with the correction you've chosen. Sometimes an answer will look correct by itself, but if you put it back into the sentence, you can see that it is wrong.

“The Real Thing”

Directions: Read the paragraph and then answer the items based on it.

(1) Do you know why records spin at peculiar speeds? (2) Who decided on the speeds of 33⅓, 45, and 78 revolutions per minute? (3) Trying to produce a disc to play on his newly invented Gramophone, Emile Berliner decided to use 78 rpm. (4) The motor Berliner found for his Gramophone ran at 78 rpm. (5) Attempting to match the speed of the motor, grooves were cut into the discs. (6) However, more music would fit on a record if a slower speed was used. (7) RCA Victor trying to market a 33⅓-rpm record, failed during the Great Depression. (8) Finally, in the late 1940s, CBS succeeded in doing so. (9) RCA Victor developed the 45-rpm record. (10) By doing this, it competed for the small-disc market. (11) Avid collectors now have to rummage at garage sales to find the old 78s. (12) They also rummage for them in second-hand stores.

1. Sentence 3: **Trying to produce a disc to play on his newly invented Gramophone, Emile Berliner decided to use 78 rpm.**

   Which of the following is the best way to write the underlined portion of this sentence? If you think the original is the best way, choose option (1).

   (1) Gramophone, Emile Berliner decided
   (2) Gramophone. Emile Berliner decided
   (3) Gramophone Emile Berliner decided
   (4) Gramophone, it was decided
   (5) Gramophone, his decision was

   (1) (2) (3) (4) (5)

2. Sentence 5: **Attempting to match the speed of the motor, grooves were cut into the discs.**

   Which of the following is the best way to write the underlined portion of this sentence? If you think the original is the best way, choose option (1).

   (1) motor, grooves were cut
   (2) motor. He cut grooves
   (3) motor and cutting grooves
   (4) motor, he cut grooves
   (5) motor to cut grooves

   (1) (2) (3) (4) (5)

3. Sentence 7: **RCA Victor trying to market a 33⅓-rpm record, failed during the Great Depression.**

   What correction should be made to this sentence?

   (1) insert was after RCA Victor
   (2) insert a comma after RCA Victor
   (3) change trying to tried
   (4) remove the word failed
   (5) insert a comma after failed

   (1) (2) (3) (4) (5)

4. Sentences 9 and 10: **RCA Victor developed the 45-rpm record. By doing this, it competed for the small-disc market.**

   The most effective combination of sentences 9 and 10 would include which of the following groups of words?

   (1) the 45-rpm record and by doing this
   (2) RCA Victor developed and competed
   (3) By developing the 45-rpm record, RCA Victor
   (4) By doing this, RCA Victor
   (5) RCA Victor developed for the small-disc market

   (1) (2) (3) (4) (5)

5. Sentences 11 and 12: **Avid collectors now have to rummage at garage sales to find the old 78s. They also rummage for them in second-hand stores.**

   The most effective combination of sentences 11 and 12 would include which of the following groups of words?

   (1) In second-hand stores, avid collectors
   (2) to find the old 78s in second-hand stores
   (3) the old 78s and they also rummage
   (4) rummage at garage sales and in second-hand stores
   (5) Rummaging for old 78s, they

   (1) (2) (3) (4) (5)

Check your answers and record your score on page 101.

LESSON 3

Pairing Subjects

Connecting Subjects with *And*

People sometimes write the way they talk. But writing has an advantage over talking. As you've seen with adding details, you can rewrite sentences and combine your thoughts to create less repetitious, more interesting sentences.

Making pairs of subjects by using *and* is one way of combining sentences, but be careful. You may have to change the verb and some other words from **singular** to **plural.**

Coming to Terms

singular showing one

plural showing more than one

Here's an Example

Look at these sentences from a conversation between a talk show host and his guest. Their thoughts are not quite organized, so they often repeat ideas.

Host: "Did you ever want to direct? Woody Allen directs his own movies. Clint Eastwood does too. Do you see any challenge there?"

Guest: "I've thought about it. I've been attracted to producing too. But film directors take on an impossible job. For that matter, film producers take on impossible jobs too."

Notice the host's second and third sentences. The subjects are different, but the verbs mean basically the same thing. If the host had written those ideas, he might have combined them.

■ **Woody Allen and Clint Eastwood direct** their own movies.

You can see that when two singular subjects are paired, the singular verb *directs* is replaced with the plural verb *direct.* The singular words *his* and *movie* have to be changed to the plural words *their* and *movies* also.

As you can see, the guest repeated herself too. This time you can pair plural subjects with *and* without changing other words.

■ Film **directors and** film **producers take** on impossible jobs.

Later, the guest went on to say this:

"Only one American western has been made by Hollywood in the last few years. And only two good romantic love stories have been filmed."

When you pair a singular and a plural subject with *and,* always use a plural verb. Be sure you move the details that describe the subject *(two good romantic)* when you move the subject.

■ Only one American **western and** two good romantic **love stories have been made** by Hollywood in the last few years.

Try It Yourself

Read the next passage. Watch for subjects that you might pair.

■ Television has changed greatly since I was young. Movies are quite different too. Most films made today seem louder and rougher. Even TV soap operas have an abundance of violence. Cartoons have their share of violence too. All this is having an effect on people. My daughter wants to be a tough private eye when she grows up. My son wants to be one too.

Did you find some sentences to combine? Since the first two sentences say the same basic thing about their subjects, you might have combined them this way: "Television and the movies have changed greatly since I was young." Did you remember to change the verb from the singular *has* to the plural *have?*

You probably also noticed the repetition in the fourth and fifth sentences. The subjects and verbs are already plural and don't need to be changed: "Even TV soap operas and cartoons have an abundance of violence."

If you combined the sixth and seventh sentences, you should have changed two words, *eye* and *wants,* to plurals: "My daughter and son want to grow up to be tough private eyes."

Did you notice how the passage became shorter and more interesting by pairing subjects?

A Test-Taking Tip

When some people pair two subjects with *and,* they sometimes put a comma between the two. That is a mistake. You need commas only when you have three or more subjects connected by *and,* not just two. The GED Test often includes this kind of error in a multiple-choice question, so watch out for it there. And be sure you don't overuse commas this way in your essay.

Warm-up

Combine the following sentences. Use *and* to pair the subjects. Remember to change words from singular to plural when necessary.

1. My father often talks about walking four miles to school every morning. Uncle Stan tells us about it too.

____

____

2. In a farming region, schools can be miles away from many homes. Libraries might also be that far away.

____

____

3. My son complains if we don't drive him eight blocks to school. So do his sisters.

____

____

Compare your answers with the Sample Warm-up Answers below. You don't need to match the examples *exactly,* but do check to make sure that you changed verbs and other words to plural as necessary.

Often when people are asked to write on a topic, they say, "I can't think of anything to write." If this happens to you, try **free writing.**

Free writing is one way to prepare to write when you can't readily think of ideas to write about, as you did in Lessons 1 and 2. When you free write, write down whatever comes to your mind. You never let your pen stop. If you can't think of anything to write, you write *that* until an idea comes to you. Keep these suggestions in mind while free writing:

1. Set a time limit for yourself.
2. Start writing and *keep* writing.
3. Put down *all* your ideas, even ones that don't seem particularly useful at the time. Don't try to evaluate or organize them.
4. Don't worry about spelling or punctuation at this point. Don't even write in complete sentences.

Now try free writing. Your topic is this: How do I feel about having children? Allow yourself three minutes.

Below is one result of a free-writing session on this topic by a twenty-two-year-old man. He doesn't have any children.

Sometimes I envy my friends
with kids even though
they can be bratty and
noisy be fun to watch
them grow. They wake
you up in the mornings
even on weekends when
you really want to sleep.
You also have to earn
a lot of money to support
kids send them to school
buy clothes food and all
that I'm trying to think
of more you should have
kids only when you're ready
there's no partying with
kids babysitters The doctor
bills are another expense
to worry about insurance
too. You also need a nice
home so they can play.
My mother would love it
if I ever have kids, she'd
be a good grandmother

Sample Warm-up Answers
1. My father and Uncle Stan often talk about walking four miles to school every morning. **2.** In a farming region, schools and libraries can be miles away from many homes. **3.** My son and his sisters complain if we don't drive them eight blocks to school.

Did you think of some of these ideas? You may have had many other ideas too, especially if you have children. Different people think of different things. And in three minutes, you will not think of every idea on a topic.

Keep your free-writing list. You will use it in the next exercise.

Coming to Terms

free writing writing about a topic continuously to get ideas about it

On the Springboard

Directions: Read this paragraph carefully and then answer the questions that follow it.

(1) Countless movies, plays, books, and songs throb with stories of passionate lovers. (2) Some of these "star-crossed" lovers, and colorful characters have gone down in history. (3) Rhett Butler and Scarlett O'Hara was two such romantic characters. (4) For many, Romeo has become the symbol of a young lover defeated by an old feud. (5) Juliet is seen by many people this way too. (6) Modern Cleopatras still lose everything for the men they love. (7) And, like Samson, men blinded by love are double-crossed by their Delilahs.

1. Sentence 2: **Some of these "star-crossed" lovers, and colorful characters have gone down in history.**

   Which of the following is the best way to write the underlined portion of this sentence? If you think the original is the best way, choose option (1).

   (1) lovers, and
   (2) lovers. And
   (3) lovers and

   (1) (2) (3)

2. Sentence 3: **Rhett Butler and Scarlett O'Hara was two such romantic characters.**

   What correction should be made to this sentence?

   (1) insert a comma after Butler
   (2) replace was with were
   (3) change characters to character

   (1) (2) (3)

3. Sentences 4 and 5: **For many, Romeo has become the symbol of a young lover defeated by an old feud. Juliet is seen by many people this way too.**

   The most effective combination of sentences 4 and 5 would include which of the following groups of words?

   (1) feud and so has
   (2) feud, and Juliet
   (3) Romeo and Juliet have

   (1) (2) (3)

Now return to your free-writing list on the topic of having children. Pick a few of your best ideas, and write at least four or five sentences about them. If necessary, pair subjects by using *and* to reduce repetition.

Check your answers for the On the Springboard questions on page 98.

Did you get the answers correct? If so, and if you are satisfied with your writing, move on. If not, you might want to review the section before going on.

A Test-Taking Tip

On the GED Writing Skills Test, you will find questions that ask you about rewriting or combining sentences. When you read this kind of question, rewrite the sentence in your head before looking at any of the answers. This is the best way to prevent confusion.

The Real Thing

Directions: Read the paragraph and then answer the items based on it.

(1) Who really invented the game of baseball? (2) The typical baseball fan believes that Abner Doubleday invented the game. (3) The average player has the same idea. (4) Doubleday, as the story goes, laid out the first baseball diamond at Cooperstown, New York, in 1839. (5) That story, and others are based on the opinion of one small commission of people appointed by A. G. Spaulding. (6) The commission said that baseball was purely American and owed nothing to foreign games. (7) However, it is claimed by most Britishers that baseball developed from an English game called rounders, and many historians claim that as well. (8) The truth may never be known. (9) The name of the real inventor and his story remaining a mystery for all time.

1. Sentences 2 and 3: **The typical baseball fan believes that Abner Doubleday invented the game. The average player has the same idea.**

   The most effective combination of sentences 2 and 3 would include which of the following groups of words?

   (1) fan and the average player believes
   (2) invented the game and the average
   (3) typical baseball fan and player believes
   (4) Abner Doubleday and the average player
   (5) fan and the average player believe

   (1) (2) (3) (4) (5)

2. Sentence 4: **Doubleday, as the story goes, laid out the first baseball diamond at Cooperstown, New York, in 1839.**

   Which of the following is the best way to write the underlined portion of this sentence? If you think the original is the best way, choose option (1).

   (1) diamond at Cooperstown
   (2) diamond. At Cooperstown
   (3) diamond, at Cooperstown
   (4) diamond. And at Cooperstown
   (5) diamond. Doubleday was at Cooperstown

   (1) (2) (3) (4) (5)

3. Sentence 5: **That story, and others are based on the opinion of one small commission of people appointed by A. G. Spaulding.**

   What correction should be made to this sentence?

   (1) remove the comma after story
   (2) remove the word and
   (3) change are to is
   (4) remove the word are
   (5) insert a comma after based

   (1) (2) (3) (4) (5)

4. Sentence 7: **However, it is claimed by most Britishers that baseball developed from an English game called rounders, and many historians claim that as well.**

   If you rewrote sentence 7 beginning with

   However, most Britishers

   the next words should be

   (1) it is claimed
   (2) and many historians
   (3) called a game rounders
   (4) claim that rounders
   (5) developed baseball

   (1) (2) (3) (4) (5)

5. Sentence 9: **The name of the real inventor and his story remaining a mystery for all time.**

   What correction should be made to this sentence?

   (1) insert a comma after inventor
   (2) change remaining to remains
   (3) change remaining to may remain
   (4) insert a comma after mystery
   (5) no correction is necessary

   (1) (2) (3) (4) (5)

Check your answers on pages 101–102.

Connecting Subjects with *Or* and *Nor*

Sometimes you write sentences with two subjects in which you don't mean both one *and* the other. Sometimes you want to say one *or* the other; you want to show a choice is being made or a possibility exists. You use *or* and *either . . . or* to pair subjects in such cases.

■ Either Kim or Jamie will win the ten-kilometer run this Sunday.

When you want to show that both of two choices or two possibilities are being rejected, you can use *neither . . . nor.*

■ Neither Ted nor Allen likes to run as much as their wives.

When you use these words to pair, remember this rule about singular and plural: Always match the verb to the subject closest to it.

Here's an Example

Rita Pierri is taking a citizenship class at a community college. She was recently asked to give a speech about her decision to become a U.S. citizen. Below is part of the rough draft of her speech. The revisions that Rita decided to make are also shown.

■ I am not the first member of my family to become an American citizen. My long-lost uncle may have been the first to apply for citizenship. Possibly my parents were the first.

Rita decided to combine the second and third sentences.

■ I am not the first member of my family to become an American citizen. My long-lost **uncle or** possibly my **parents were** the first to apply for citizenship.

Notice how Rita avoided repetition by pairing the subjects with *or.* She also used a plural verb to match *parents,* which is the closest subject. She went on:

■ I am so excited about becoming a citizen. My husband is going with me to my citizenship test. If he can't, my two closest friends are going with me.

She revised this way:

■ Either my **husband or** my two closest **friends are going** with me to the citizenship test.

Then she wrote the following:

■ The hardest decision I ever made was to let go of my native land. My friends don't have any idea of the emotions I felt. My husband doesn't either.

In combining the second and third sentences below, Rita showed that both choices were rejected by using *neither . . . nor.*

■ *Neither my* **friends nor** my **husband has** any idea of the emotions I felt.

Notice that negative words such as *no* and *not (n't)* are dropped when *neither . . . nor* is used.

A Test-Taking Tip

Just as you don't use a comma between two subjects connected by *and,* you also don't use one when you pair subjects with *or* or *nor.* Watch out for that mistaken use of commas on the GED Test.

Try It Yourself

Here is part of a paper written by an adult student. Read it and watch for subjects to pair.

■ You can't imagine what a job interview is like until you have had one. Shaking hands are a sure sign of your nervousness. A dry, stuttering mouth is a good clue too.

Did you combine the second and third sentences? If so, you could have done it this way: "Shaking hands or a dry, stuttering mouth is a sure sign of your nervousness."

The paper continues:

■ A good résumé is not a guarantee of getting a job. Good references aren't either. During your interview, be confident, be courteous, and be ready to list your strengths.

Combine the first two sentences. Did you make the necessary words plural? Your sentence might say the following: "Neither a good résumé nor good references are guarantees of getting a job."

A Test-Taking Tip

Either and *neither* are important words to know how to use when you combine sentences on the GED Writing Skills Test. They are also on the GED Spelling List. That means you may be tested on whether these words are spelled correctly in a passage. When you see these words on the test, make sure they are used correctly and spelled correctly.

Warm-up

In the sentences below, a woman is writing about her family. Use *or* or *nor* to pair the subjects of her sentences when possible.

1. The television set is usually on in our house. When the TV isn't on, the radio is.

____

____

2. Sometimes my husband will turn off everything just for a little peace and quiet. Sometimes I will.

____

____

3. Unlike me, my daughters don't like the nighttime soap operas. My husband doesn't like them either.

____

____

Check your sentences with those in the Sample Warm-up answers. Were you able to find the subjects to pair in all the sentences?

Now think about television and what it does for you. What kinds of shows do you watch? Why do you watch them? Make a list of your thoughts about television. If you have trouble coming up with ideas, try free writing for three minutes.

Sample Warm-up Answers
1. Either the television set or the radio is usually on in our house. **2.** Sometimes my husband or I will turn off everything just for a little peace and quiet. **3.** Unlike me, neither my daughters nor my husband likes the nighttime soap operas.

On the Springboard

Directions: Read this paragraph carefully and then answer the questions that follow it.

(1) Blind dates have become big business recently. (2) Neither family nor friends has to find dates for single people anymore. (3) There must be fifty ways to meet someone new. (4) In many cases, personal ads help arrange the first meeting. (5) A dating service often helps arrange first dates too. (6) There are also singles bars, dial-a-date businesses, marriage brokers, and singles clubs. (7) Finding a date these days takes either money or nerve but not help from relatives.

4. Sentence 2: **Neither family nor friends has to find dates for single people anymore.**

   Which of the following is the best way to write the underlined portion of this sentence? If you think the original is the best way, choose option (1).

   (1) nor friends has
   (2) nor friends have
   (3) or friends have

   (1) (2) (3)

5. Sentences 4 and 5: **In many cases, personal ads help arrange the first meeting. A dating service often helps arrange first dates too.**

   The most effective combination of sentences 4 and 5 would include which of the following groups of words?

   (1) either personal ads or a dating service help
   (2) personal ads or a dating service helps
   (3) personal ads and a dating service helps

   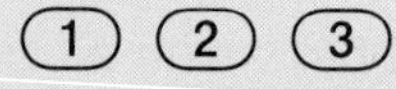

Write a short passage entitled "What Television Does for Me." Use the list you prepared in the Warm-up for ideas to include. Write interesting sentences using as many of the combining methods as you can.

Compare your answers for On the Springboard with those on page 98.

If you had some difficulty with the two questions, reviewing this section on choice words would be a good idea. If you did well and feel comfortably in control of combining, move on to "The Real Thing."

The Real Thing

Directions: Read the paragraph and then answer the items based on it.

(1) Every day, people seem to look for new ways to improve themselves. (2) Because of this interest in self-improvement, recreational sports and personal growth classes becoming available everywhere. (3) Depending on one's preference, either a group exercise class or a private teacher are available for improving the body. (4) In addition, there are classes in aerobic dancing, weight training, and yoga. (5) People are attacking bad habits with self-help too. (6) Meditation is not a surefire way to make one quit smoking, and neither is hypnosis, but either one can help. (7) Even industry is offering its employees self-improvement opportunities. (8) Employees of one company could take either an exercise class or a long run outside as a lunch-hour activity. (9) It is a sign of the times that only three people out of ninety chose neither option.

6. Sentence 2: **Because of this interest in self-improvement, recreational sports and personal growth classes becoming available everywhere.**

   What correction should be made to this sentence?

   (1) remove the comma after self-improvement
   (2) insert a comma after sports
   (3) insert the word is after classes
   (4) insert the word are after classes
   (5) no correction is necessary

   (1) (2) (3) (4) (5)

7. Sentence 3: **Depending on one's preference, either a group exercise class or a private teacher are available for improving the body.**

   What correction should be made to this sentence?

   (1) remove the comma after preference
   (2) change the spelling of either to eether
   (3) change are to is
   (4) insert a comma after available
   (5) no correction is necessary

   (1) (2) (3) (4) (5)

8. Sentence 5: **People are attacking bad habits with self-help too.**

   Which of the following is the best way to write the underlined portion of this sentence? If you think the original is the best way, choose option (1).

   (1) habits with
   (2) habits, with
   (3) habits. With
   (4) habits and with
   (5) habits or with

   (1) (2) (3) (4) (5)

9. Sentence 6: **Meditation is not a surefire way to make one quit smoking, and neither is hypnosis, but either one can help.**

   If you rewrote sentence 6 beginning with

   Neither meditation nor hypnosis

   the next word should be

   (1) makes
   (2) can
   (3) help
   (4) is
   (5) are

Check your answers and record your score for the entire lesson on page 102.

LESSON 4

Pairing Verb Forms

Connecting Main Verbs

You have already learned to pair subjects. You can also pair closely related verbs that work with the same subject. To do this, you state the subject once and then pair the verbs by using *and, or, either . . . or,* or *neither . . . nor.*

When you pair verbs, you have to remember that sometimes the verb is actually a verb phrase made up of a main verb and helping verbs. In addition, the main verb, its helpers, and all the details that work with them make up the **complete verb.**

All the details usually have to be moved with the main verb. Sometimes the helping verbs do too.

Coming to Terms

complete verb the main verb, its helpers (if any), and all the details that work with it

Here's an Example

Look at the complete verbs in these sentences.

■ Tim **pulled over to the curb.** He **jumped out of the car.**

Notice that the verbs in these sentences are related in time order. For that reason, you can pair them by using *and* to make one sentence.

■ Tim **pulled over to the curb** and **jumped out of the car.**

In combining these sentences, some words were moved, and unnecessary ones were dropped. Notice that, as with paired subjects, no comma was used before *and.* Now look at the complete verbs in the last two sentences below.

■ The car started rolling down the hill. Tim **should have used the emergency brake.** He **could also have parked in gear.**

You can combine two of these sentences with *or* because the verbs are related by being choices. Tim should have done one thing or the other.

■ Tim **should have used the emergency brake** or **parked in gear.**

Did you notice that part of the verb phrase from the second sentence (*could have* from *could have parked*) was dropped when it was paired with the verb from the first? The meaning of those helping verbs is contained in *should have* from the first sentence, so in this case it wasn't necessary to repeat them.

Don't pair verbs that are unrelated, even when they have the same subject.

■ Tim liked his car. Tim went to see about a new-car loan today.

Combined: Tim liked his car and went to see about a new-car loan today.

That sentence is illogical. Tim's liking his car has nothing to do with his going for a loan.

Try It Yourself

Here are some sentences from a letter to the editor in a newspaper. See if you can spot verbs to pair.

■ Public services in this town have been going downhill for years. For instance, my neighbors and I have a complaint about trash removal. We would like to see something done about the problem. At six in the morning, the garbage crews show up. They bang cans deliberately. They don't care about sleeping people. Nor do they worry about damaging the cans.

In the second and third sentences, the subjects refer to the same people (*neighbors and I* and *We*). Their verbs are closely related too. You should have located all the words that are part of the complete verb in the second sentence and moved them with the verb, like this: "For instance, my neighbors and I have a complaint about trash removal and would like to see something done about the problem."

The fourth and fifth sentences also have subjects referring to the same people (*crews* and *They*) as well as related verbs. You should have come up with a sentence similar to this: "At six in the morning, the crews show up and bang cans deliberately."

Finally, the last two sentences share a common subject and related verbs. Because the sentences have a negative meaning, you could have paired the verbs with *neither . . . nor:* "They neither care about sleeping people nor worry about damaging the cans." Or you could have kept the *not* and paired the verbs with *or:* "They don't care about sleeping people or worry about damaging the cans."

Warm-up

Below are five pairs of sentences that describe the writer's dream. First, determine whether you can combine each pair of sentences. If so, write a new sentence on the lines provided.

1. I went to sleep last night stuffed with pizza. I had a terrifying dream.

____

____

2. Six or seven people were chasing me, laughing loudly. They all wore tuxedoes.

____

____

3. Finally the people all caught up with me. They fell on top of me with a shout.

____

____

4. They landed right on my stomach. They all were the result of my eating too much before bedtime.

____

____

Compare your answers with the Sample Warm-up Answers below. While your sentences may vary, all should have appropriately paired verbs.

Select a short event that you saw or that happened to you (for example, a fire or an exciting football play). Make notes describing what happened or what you saw. Write down as many details as you can recall.

On the Springboard

Directions: Read this paragraph carefully and then answer the questions that follow it.

(1) Before World War II, most Americans did not know of the martial arts. (2) They were not impressed by the fighting ability of anyone who was not American. (3) Soldiers coming home from the Pacific brought information about karate and other martial arts with them. (4) In recent years, people of all ages and sizes practice martial arts and study the philosophy of Asian disciplines. (5) One such woman over eighty years old was in the news recently and had earned a black belt in karate.

1. Sentences 1 and 2: **Before World War II, most Americans did not know of the martial arts. They were not impressed with the fighting ability of anyone who was not American.**

   The most effective combination of sentences 1 and 2 would include which of the following groups of words?

   (1) did not know or were not impressed
   (2) not know of the martial arts, and
   (3) neither knew of the martial arts nor

   (1) (2) (3)

2. Sentence 5: **One such woman over eighty years old was in the news <u>recently and had earned</u> a black belt in karate.**

   Which of the following is the best way to write the underlined portion of this sentence? If you think the original is the best way, choose option (1).

   (1) recently and had earned
   (2) recently or had earned
   (3) recently. She had earned

Write a description of an event as if you were reporting it step by step. Use your notes from the Warm-up. Use verbs and their helpers so your reader can picture the activity well. Combine verbs or other words for better sentences whenever you can.

Sample Warm-up Answers
1. I went to sleep last night stuffed with pizza and had a terrifying dream. **2.** shouldn't be combined **3.** Finally the people all caught up with me and fell on top of me with a shout. **4.** shouldn't be combined

Now compare your answers for On the Springboard with those on page 98.

Are you spotting incorrect comma use quickly now? Do you understand how to move and pair verbs? If so, try your skill on "The Real Thing." If you had problems with the Springboard questions, you might want to review this section before moving on.

The Real Thing

Directions: Read the paragraph and then answer the items based on it.

(1) Many people think of their country as the center of the world. (2) They see all the other countries revolving around them. (3) The British, for example, don't consider the American Revolution to be a major historical event. (4) They don't give it much space in their schoolbooks. (5) To them, it was an event that interfered with the much more important relationship they had with France. (6) Brazil has developed a huge amount of industry in recent years. (7) It has joined the world market. (8) Most Americans neither know of this economic development nor care. (9) Both France and the United States ignored the history of Vietnam and so became involved in a difficult conflict there. (10) The world getting smaller. (11) Every country could benefit from teaching its people history from a world view.

1. Sentences 1 and 2: **Many people think of their country as the center of the world. They see all the other countries revolving around them.**

   The most effective combination of sentences 1 and 2 would include which of the following groups of words?

   (1) Many people think and see
   (2) of the world and see
   (3) They think they see
   (4) of the world around them
   (5) of the world and they

   (1) (2) (3) (4) (5)

2. Sentences 3 and 4: **The British, for example, don't consider the American Revolution to be a major historical event. They don't give it much space in their schoolbooks.**

   The most effective combination of sentences 3 and 4 would include which of the following groups of words?

   (1) historical event and don't
   (2) They don't, for example,
   (3) either consider or give
   (4) Consider the British
   (5) The British don't give it

   (1) (2) (3) (4) (5)

3. Sentences 6 and 7: **Brazil has developed a huge amount of industry in recent years. It has joined the world market.**

   Which of the following is the best way to write the underlined portion of these sentences? If you think the original is the best way, choose option (1).

   (1) years. It has (2) years has
   (3) years and has (4) years and it
   (5) years have

   (1) (2) (3) (4) (5)

4. Sentence 8: **Most Americans neither know of this economic development nor care.**

   What correction should be made to this sentence?

   (1) change the spelling of neither to niether
   (2) insert a comma after know
   (3) insert a comma after development
   (4) replace nor with or
   (5) no correction is necessary

   (1) (2) (3) (4) (5)

5. Sentence 10: **The world getting smaller.**

   Which of the following is the best way to write the underlined portion of this sentence? If you think the original is the best way, choose option (1).

   (1) getting (2) is getting
   (3) and getting (4) and gets
   (5) or getting

   (1) (2) (3) (4) (5)

Check your answers on page 102.

Connecting Other Verb Forms

You already know that you can use verb forms called verbals to add more information to a sentence. You can pair verbals in the same way you pair main verbs.

Here's an Example

Notice the verbals in these examples.

■ Sam Eli had just enough time **to see** the Badlands. He had just enough time **to take** a whitewater raft trip.

In both those sentences *had* is the main verb. The verbals are *to see* and *to take.* The verbal phrases are *to see the Badlands* and *to take a whitewater raft trip.*

Because those verbals are related, you can pair them with *and.* When you pair verbals that begin with *to,* you do not necessarily have to repeat the *to.*

■ Sam Eli had just enough time **to see** the Badlands **and take** a whitewater raft trip.

Look at these next examples of verbals ending with *-ing.*

■ Bronski didn't leave the session **believing** its outcome. He didn't leave **accepting** the vote as final.

In both those sentences *did leave* is the main verb. (*Did* comes from *didn't,* or *did not.*) The verbals are *believing* and *accepting.* The verbal phrases are *believing its outcome* and *accepting the vote as final.*

If you wanted to combine those sentences by pairing the verbals, you could replace the negative word *not* (from *didn't*) with *neither . . . nor.*

■ Bronski left the session **neither believing** its outcome **nor accepting** the vote as final.

Notice how the verb changes from *did leave* to *left* when you pair with *neither . . . nor.* If you wanted to, you could pair the two with *or* and keep *did leave* as the verb and *not* as the negative.

■ Bronski did**n't** leave the session **believing** its outcome **or accepting** the vote as final.

There is one very important thing to remember when you are pairing verb forms. The words you are pairing should be **parallel,** or in the same form. That is true of verbals as well as main verbs. For example, don't pair a verbal beginning with *to* and a verbal ending in *-ing.* Your sentence will not flow well then. Hear how the flow of this sentence shifts, or becomes rough.

■ Carlo enjoys flying to Italy and then to sail to the Greek islands.

The verbal phrases were paired, but each verb is in a different form. One verb has an *-ing* ending. The other verb begins with *to.* The shift in verb form makes the sentence awkward.

■ *Combined correctly:* Carlo enjoys **flying** to Italy and then **sailing** to the Greek islands.

Now that the verbals are parallel, the sentence flows. You don't hear a shift in form. Now look at the sentence below.

■ Most evenings Brian is either watching television or talks on the phone with his girl friend.

You may already see two ways to match the two main verbs in that sentence.

■ Most evenings Brian is either **watching** television or **talking** on the phone with his girl friend.

OR

Most evenings Brian either **watches** television or **talks** on the phone with his girl friend.

Coming to Terms

parallel matching in form

Try It Yourself

The movie review below has two sentences with paired verbs that are not parallel. Try to hear when the flow shifts.

■ Here's a weird but familiar science fiction plot. The hero becomes the victim of a freak accident and is landing in a world parallel to his. He finds a town just like his own and walks down the street. The people all seem to resemble his neighbors and acting as if nothing is wrong. But the hero senses danger. Something about this town is very wrong.

Which two sentences did you find? Did you decide the verbs *becomes* and *is landing* in the second sentence were not parallel? What about the verbals *to resemble* and *acting* in the fourth sentence?

Look at each pair of words now. What are your choices for making them match? Should you change *is landing* to *lands* or *becomes* to *is becoming?* The first way sounds more natural. How would you change the second sentence? Here's a good way to write these sentences: "The hero becomes the victim of a freak accident and lands in a world parallel to his. . . . The people all seem to resemble his neighbors and act as if nothing is wrong."

Warm-up

Combine the following pairs of sentences by pairing the verb forms using *and, or, either . . . or,* or *neither . . . nor.* Make the verbs parallel if necessary. If a sentence already has paired verbs or verbals, make them parallel.

1. Allergies give many people problems. They can even prevent them from working.

____

____

2. An allergic reaction is produced by breathing a substance that the body cannot tolerate. To touch such a substance also produces one.

____

____

3. Certain foods, such as cheese and yeast, also produce allergic reactions in many people, causing headaches and can make them black out.

____

____

4. Adults as well as children have been known to develop allergies suddenly. They have also recovered from them just as suddenly.

____

____

5. Some people I know seem to be allergic to work and avoiding it at all costs.

____

____

Compare your answers with the Sample Warm-up Answers below.

Now write this head on a sheet of paper: "Things I Enjoy **Doing** in My Spare Time." Then list your ideas under that head. Next write the head "Things I Want **to Do** in My Lifetime." Take three or four minutes to list the things you would do if you could.

Sample Warm-up Answers
1. Allergies give many people problems and can even prevent them from working. **2.** An allergic reaction is produced by breathing or touching a substance that the body cannot tolerate. *OR* An allergic reaction is produced by breathing a substance that the body cannot tolerate or by touching such a substance. **3.** Certain foods, such as cheese and yeast, also produce allergic reactions in many people, causing headaches and making them black out. **4.** Adults as well as children have been known to develop allergies suddenly and to recover from them just as suddenly. **5.** Some people I know seem to be allergic to work and avoid it at all costs.

On the Springboard

Directions: Read this paragraph carefully and then answer the questions that follow it.

(1) Macramé, or decorative knotwork, has a long history, starting in the Middle East in the 1200s. (2) It spread from there into Europe during the 1600s. (3) Sailors' and fishermen's knots formed the basic patterns for macramé. (4) In addition to producing handcrafts, tying knots was found to soothe nerves as well as helping people think more clearly. (5) Famous heads of state such as Winston Churchill and Charles de Gaulle relaxed by knotting and knitting.

3. Sentences 1 and 2: **Macramé, or decorative knotwork, has a long history, starting in the Middle East in the 1200s. It spread from there into Europe during the 1600s.**

   The most effective combination of sentences 1 and 2 would include which of the following groups of words?

   (1) in the 1200s and spread
   (2) in the 1200s and spreading
   (3) starting and spreading

   (1) (2) (3)

4. Sentence 4: **In addition to producing handcrafts, tying knots was found to soothe nerves as well as helping people think more clearly.**

   Which of the following is the best way to write the underlined portion of this sentence? If you think the original is the best way, choose option (1).

   (1) to soothe nerves as well as helping
   (2) soothing nerves and helping
   (3) to soothe nerves and help

   (1) (2) (3)

5. Sentence 5: **Famous heads of state such as Winston Churchill and Charles de Gaulle relaxed by knotting and knitting.**

   What correction should be made to this sentence?

   (1) replace relaxed with relaxing
   (2) insert a comma after knotting
   (3) no correction is necessary

   (1) (2) (3)

Go back to your notes from the last Warm-up about things you enjoy doing and things you want to do. Pick one of those topics and write about it, using your notes. When possible, pair verb forms. Also make sure you write in complete sentences, and pair subjects and other words when that is the most effective way to write.

You can check your answers to the Springboard multiple-choice questions on page 99.

Did you understand how to pair the verb forms? If so, you should be ready to move on to "The Real Thing." If you didn't get all the Springboard answers correct, review this section first.

The Real Thing

Directions: Read the paragraph and then answer the items based on it.

(1) Health care has taken an interesting turn. (2) In the beginning humans believed sickness was caused by angry gods or evil spirits. (3) Their way of curing sickness was to try to satisfy the gods or drive the spirits away. (4) Eventually humans began to rely on natural remedies such as herbs and plant extracts to relieve illness. (5) Then people began to study the human body. (6) They started experimenting with new medicines and surgery. (7) Bacteria were discovered in the 1600s. (8) Leading to the germ theory of disease. (9) First vaccinations were developed. (10) Then antibiotics were. (11) Technology such as X rays, EEGs, EKGs, and artificial organs followed. (12) Some people, however, have begun to believe that modern medicine can neither cure every ill nor answer every need. (13) They have returned to more traditional solutions such as herbal remedies, acupuncture, and even simple faith.

6. Sentence 3: **Their way of curing sickness was to try to satisfy the gods or drive the spirits away.**

   If you rewrote sentence 3 beginning with

   They tried to cure sickness by

   the next words would be

   (1) satisfying the gods or driving
   (2) to satisfy the gods or to drive
   (3) satisfying the gods or to drive
   (4) the satisfaction of the gods or driving
   (5) to satisfy the gods and driving

   (1) (2) (3) (4) (5)

7. Sentences 5 and 6: **Then people began to study the human body. They started experimenting with new medicines and surgery.**

   Which of the following is the best way to write the underlined portion of these sentences? If you think the original is the best way, choose option (1).

   (1) began to study the human body. They started experimenting
   (2) began to study the human body and experiment
   (3) began to study the human body and experimenting
   (4) beginning to study the human body and starting to experiment
   (5) beginning to study the human body and experimenting

   (1) (2) (3) (4) (5)

8. Sentences 7 and 8: **Bacteria were discovered in the 1600s. Leading to the germ theory of disease.**

   Which of the following is the best way to write the underlined portion of these sentences? If you think the original is the best way, choose option (1).

   (1) the 1600s. Leading
   (2) the 1600s to lead
   (3) the 1600s and lead
   (4) the 1600s and leading
   (5) 1600s, leading

   (1) (2) (3) (4) (5)

9. Sentences 9 and 10: **First vaccinations were developed. Then antibiotics were.**

   The most effective combination of sentences 9 and 10 would include which of the following groups of words?

   (1) developed and antibiotics were
   (2) developed or antibiotics were
   (3) and antibiotics were developed then
   (4) First vaccinations then were
   (5) vaccinations and then antibiotics

Check your answers and record your score for the entire lesson on pages 102–103.

LESSON 5

Making Lists

Writing About Three or More

You already know that you can pair subjects, verbs, and even some details in your sentences. Pairing can make sentences smoother and more interesting. You also know that sometimes you have to be careful about the form of the words you are pairing; they have to be in the same form, or parallel.

The same holds true when you're writing about three or more things in one sentence. Whether you're listing subjects or other nouns, verbs or verbals, or descriptive words or phrases, they must be parallel. In addition, you need to use commas when you make such lists.

Here's an Example

See how this example has a list of three nouns (one is part of a noun phrase) as its subjects.

- **Quickness, smartness, and** the **ability** to throw well are needed by a quarterback.

The sentence is smooth. The items in the list are parallel and separated by commas. Also, because there are three subjects connected with *and,* the verb is plural.

Now read the following sentence out loud.

- A quarterback must be quick, smart, and throw well.

In that sentence, the last item in the list is in a different form from the first two. The first two are descriptive words: *quick* and *smart.* The last is a verb. The sentence does not flow well. To make the list parallel, you could make the last item begin with a descriptive word.

- A quarterback must be **quick, smart, and able** to throw well.

Or you could make each item begin with a verb.

- A quarterback must **be** quick**, be** smart**, and throw** well.

Here's another example of a nonparallel list.

- People look to their leaders for encouragement, to be strong, and lead wisely.

In that sentence, you can see a noun, a verbal with *to,* and a verbal without *to.* (Remember that it's all right to drop the second *to* when you combine verbals.) Any one of the following would make that list parallel.

- People look to their leaders for **encouragement, strength, and leadership.**
- People look to their leaders **to encourage** them**, to be** strong**, and to lead** wisely.
- People look to their leaders to **encourage** them**, be** strong**, and lead** wisely.

Keeping words parallel is important whether you're pairing two items or listing three or more. The main difference between pairing and listing is the use of commas. Use a comma in pairing words *only* when you drop the *and* between two descriptive words before a noun (for example, *a tall, mysterious woman*). *Always* use commas to separate the items in a list.

Try It Yourself

In this paragraph from a GED student, look for lists that have nonparallel items. Decide how you would make them parallel.

- Calculators are an invention that has changed our lives. We can buy calculators cheaply, carry them in our wallets, and be running them on solar batteries. A calculator is fast, dependable, and a good way to compute your bill when you go shopping.

Look at the list of verb phrases in the second sentence: *can buy calculators cheaply, carry them in our wallets,* and *be running them on solar batteries.* Why are these phrases not parallel? Notice that the third verb phrase, *be running,* is in a different form from the first two. Now look at how the student revised her sentence: "We can buy calculators cheaply, carry them in our wallets, and run them on solar batteries." Is that how you chose to make the list parallel?

What about the last sentence? What is the list in that sentence made up of? *Fast* and *dependable* are descriptive words, but *a good way* is a noun phrase. The student revised the sentence this way: "Calculators are fast, dependable, and helpful in computing your bill when you go shopping." Is that similar to the way you would have rewritten it?

Warm-up

In their inaugural addresses, three presidents made the points listed below. Combine these sentences by making lists of the points. Be careful to use connecting words and commas correctly.

1. John F. Kennedy, calling upon all people to work together:
Together let us explore the stars.
Together let us conquer the deserts.
Let us eradicate disease.
Let us tap the ocean depths.
Let us encourage the arts and commerce.

2. Harry Truman, talking about events after World War II:
They will test our courage.
They will test our devotion to duty.
They will test our concept of liberty.

3. Jimmy Carter, speaking about his inauguration:
This inauguration ceremony marks a new beginning.
This ceremony marks a new dedication within our government.
This ceremony marks a new spirit among us all.

The Warm-up answers below show the sentences as the presidents actually wrote them.

Below is part of a manual entitled "How to Buy a Used Car." How can you improve it by combining sentences and making lists? Rewrite the paragraph on the lines following.

There's more to buying a used car than kicking the tires. There's more to it than checking the paint job. There's even more to it than shaking hands with the dealer. A knowledge of cars helps guarantee a good buy. A test drive does too. So does the choice of a dealer with a good reputation.

Compare your rewrite with the Sample Warm-up Answer below. Be sure that the forms you chose for the items are parallel and that you used commas to separate the items.

Now think of three or four things you hate to do. On a separate sheet of paper, write a sentence listing them.

Think of three or four qualities a good boss or supervisor should have. Write a sentence listing them.

Think of three or four ways to describe a good friend of yours. Write a sentence listing them.

Now think of yourself and the things you do best. Are you good at talking to people? Can you paint or cook well? Is your home a model of neatness and organization? Make a list of all the things you are good at doing. Don't worry about writing in complete sentences or even in parallel forms now; just list as many of your skills as you can. You'll use your list in the Springboard writing exercise.

Warm-up Answers
1. Together let us explore the stars, conquer the deserts, eradicate disease, tap the ocean depths, and encourage the arts and commerce. **2.** They will test our courage, our devotion to duty, and our concept of liberty. **3.** This inauguration ceremony marks a new beginning, a new dedication within our government, and a new spirit among us all.

Sample Warm-up Answer
There's more to buying a used car than kicking the tires, checking the paint job, or shaking hands with the dealer. A knowledge of cars, a test drive, and the choice of a dealer with a good reputation all help guarantee a good buy.

On the Springboard

Directions: Read this paragraph carefully and then answer the questions that follow it.

(1) Humans tend to be superstitious. (2) Some old-fashioned superstitions involve black cats, Friday the thirteenth, broken mirrors, and, spilled salt. (3) A horseshoe is considered good luck. (4) So are four-leaf clovers and rabbits' feet. (5) Athletes are often particularly superstitious. (6) Wearing "lucky" socks, eating a certain meal before a game, and running onto the field a certain way are all ways some players have of showing they are superstitious.

1. Sentence 2: **Some old-fashioned superstitions involve black cats, Friday the thirteenth, broken mirrors, and, spilled salt.**

   What correction should be made to this sentence?

   (1) remove the comma after thirteenth
   (2) change and to or
   (3) remove the comma after and

   (1) (2) (3)

2. Sentences 3 and 4: **A horseshoe is considered good luck. So are four-leaf clovers and rabbits' feet.**

   The most effective combination of sentences 3 and 4 would include which of the following groups of words?

   (1) Horseshoes, four-leaf clovers, and rabbits' feet are
   (2) Horseshoes, and four-leaf clovers, and rabbits' feet
   (3) Considered good luck is a horseshoe

   (1) (2) (3)

3. Sentence 6: **Wearing "lucky" socks, eating a certain meal before a game, and running onto the field a certain way are all ways some players have of showing they are superstitious.**

   If you rewrote sentence 6 beginning with

   Some players may wear "lucky" socks,

   the next words would be

   (1) eating a certain meal
   (2) or they may eat a certain meal
   (3) eat a certain meal

   (1) (2) (3)

Pretend you are filling out a job application form, and you are asked to write about the general job skills you have. Look back at your list of things you are good at. Pick four abilities that could become valuable job skills. For example, if you cook well, you're probably good at following written directions without a supervisor. If you're a neat and organized person at home, you'd probably be one on the job too. If you are good at talking to people, your interpersonal skills could help you deal with the different kinds of people in the business world.

In one sentence list the four general job skills you have chosen. Then write a few sentences explaining each skill further.

You can check the answers for On the Springboard on page 99.

If you are having trouble with parallel forms, try reading aloud all the nonparallel examples in this and the previous lesson. See if you can begin to hear the change in rhythm when the nonparallel form appears. If you have no problem identifying or writing parallel forms in pairs or lists, try your skill on "The Real Thing."

The Real Thing

Directions: Read the paragraph and then answer the items based on it.

(1) Excess stress is taking a toll on human health today. (2) A job, raising a family, and just getting through each day can cause a certain amount of stress. (3) Stress can also come from frustration, anger grief, and a loss of control. (4) After learning more about the harmful effects of stress, more and more adults are beginning to take measures to reduce the stress in their lives. (5) There are many ways to take a daily vacation from stress. (6) Either an exciting movie or a good book help you get your mind off the stressful aspects of your life. (7) Exercising or taking a nap can provide welcome relief too. (8) Such mini-vacations let you step back. (9) They enable you to take a fresh look at your life.

1. Sentence 2: **A job, raising a family, and just getting through each day can cause a certain amount of stress.**

   Which of the following is the best way to write the underlined portion of this sentence? If you think the original is the best way, choose option (1).

   (1) A job, raising a family, and
   (2) A job and raising a family and
   (3) A job, a family, and
   (4) Having a job, raising a family, and
   (5) To have a job, to raise a family, and

   (1) (2) (3) (4) (5)

2. Sentence 3: **Stress can also come from frustration, anger grief, and a loss of control.**

   What correction should be made to this sentence?

   (1) insert a comma after come
   (2) insert a comma after anger
   (3) insert and after anger
   (4) replace a loss of with losing
   (5) no correction is necessary

   (1) (2) (3) (4) (5)

3. Sentence 4: **After learning more about the harmful effects of stress, more and more adults are beginning to take measures to reduce the stress in their lives.**

   Which of the following is the best way to write the underlined portion of this sentence? If you think the original is the best way, choose option (1).

   (1) stress, more
   (2) stress and more
   (3) stress more
   (4) stress. More
   (5) stress. And more

   (1) (2) (3) (4) (5)

4. Sentence 6: **Either an exciting movie or a good book help you get your mind off the stressful aspects of your life.**

   What correction should be made to this sentence?

   (1) insert a comma after movie
   (2) change help to helping
   (3) change help to helps
   (4) change get to getting
   (5) insert a comma after mind

   (1) (2) (3) (4) (5)

5. Sentences 8 and 9: **Such mini-vacations let you step back. They enable you to take a fresh look at your life.**

   The most effective combination of sentences 8 and 9 would include which of the following groups of words?

   (1) step back and they
   (2) step back to enable
   (3) They let you take
   (4) letting you step back and enabling
   (5) step back and take

   (1) (2) (3) (4) (5)

Check your answers and record your score on page 103.

LESSON 6

Combining Complete Thoughts

Using Commas and Connecting Words

You've been writing complete sentences. You've also been combining parts of sentences—subjects, verbs, details—when those parts are related. Sometimes there are relationships between entire sentences. When you are writing, you can make these relationships clearer by combining the sentences.

One way to combine sentences is to insert a comma between them along with one of these connecting words: *and, but, or, for, so,* and *yet.* These words show the relationship between your ideas.

Here's an Example

Each of the following descriptions of weekly TV shows can be rewritten as one sentence. Notice how the sentences are connected to show the relationship between ideas.

If one idea is in addition to the other, you can use a comma and *and*.

■ A war drama: An army patrol is trapped behind enemy lines. Paratroopers must risk their lives in a rescue attempt.

Combined: An army patrol is trapped behind enemy lines**, and** paratroopers must risk their lives in a rescue attempt.

If one idea contrasts with the other, you can use a comma and *but* or *yet*.

■ A legal drama: Defense Attorney Boswick wins her case. She is not completely sure of her client's innocence.

Combined: Defense Attorney Boswick wins her case**, but** she is not completely sure of her client's innocence.

■ A comedy: Alice has planned a surprise party for Ralph. Ralph has made other plans for that night.

Combined: Alice has planned a surprise party for Ralph**, yet** Ralph has made other plans for that night.

If a choice or possibility exists between the two ideas, you can use a comma and *or*.

■ A medical show: A young mother must undergo a new, unproved operation. Otherwise she will die.

Combined: A young mother must undergo a new, unproved operation**, or** she will die.

If the first idea causes the second, you can use a comma and *so*.

■ Late-night movie: The crew of a jet airliner becomes deathly ill. An inexperienced passenger must try to land the plane.

Combined: The crew of a jet airliner becomes deathly ill**, so** an inexperienced passenger must try to land the plane.

If the second idea causes the first, you can use a comma and *for*.

■ A detective show: A popular actress hires Rock and R. J. to protect her. She feels someone is following her.

Combined: A popular actress hires Rock and R. J. to protect her**, for** she feels someone is following her.

Look at the difference between two complete ideas being connected and a sentence with a paired verb.

■ An army **patrol is trapped** behind enemy lines, and **paratroopers must risk** their lives in a rescue attempt.

An army **patrol is trapped** behind enemy lines and **must fight** its way out alone.

The first sentence has two subjects (*patrol* and *paratroopers*), each with its own verb. The second sentence has only one subject with two verbs. Use a comma with a connecting word only to connect two complete thoughts, not just two verbs.

Finally, remember what you learned about listing three or more items. Look at this example.

■ On the sports network tonight, two rugby teams meet in Liverpool, the Spartans battle the Wolverines in basketball, and ice dancers Torvill and Dean are interviewed.

You can "list" complete thoughts in the same way that you list other items—with commas in between and a connecting word between the last two. In the example, three complete thoughts are listed: (1) two rugby teams meet in Liverpool, (2) the Spartans battle the Wolverines in basketball, and (3) ice dancers Torvill and Dean are interviewed.

Try It Yourself

Read these opinions of a college student. Then reread the sentences and ask yourself these questions: Which of these sentences would I combine? What words would I use? How would I punctuate these sentences?

■ Some people wonder if we really do have things better than our grandparents did. The cost of living has risen considerably. The quality of goods and services is down. Violent crime increases each year. It doesn't just happen in the big cities anymore. Robots are appearing in our factories. More and more workers will become unemployed and unemployable. No period of history, however, is without its difficulties. Our grandparents faced and solved many problems themselves.

Did you notice that the second and third sentences are contrasting statements? For that reason, you can combine them with either *yet* or *but.* Did you find the next two sentences to be related? The second one gives additional information about crime, so it can be connected to the first with *and.* Finally, the sentence about robots gives a cause for unemployment, so it can be connected to the next sentence with *so.*

Now read the paragraph with the complete thoughts combined: "Some people wonder if we really do have things better than our grandparents did. The cost of living has risen considerably, yet the quality of goods and services is down. Violent crime increases each year, and it doesn't just happen in the big cities anymore. Robots are appearing in our factories, so more and more workers will become unemployed and unemployable. No period of history, however, is without its difficulties. Our grandparents faced and solved many problems themselves." Did you notice how smoothly the sentences flowed? The ideas were easier to understand.

Warm-up

Look at each pair of sentences carefully. Decide whether you can combine a pair using a comma and one of these connecting words: *and, but, or, for, so,* or *yet.* If so, combine the sentences on the lines. If the ideas aren't related enough to combine, write *can't combine*.

1. For many people, jogging is a healthy sport.
   There are risks involved.

   ____

   ____

2. The robber darted out of the liquor store.
   A police officer dashed down the street after him.

   ____

   ____

3. The Zacks' kitchen plumbing started to leak all over the floor.
   They called their landlord.

   ____

   ____

4. The basket didn't count.
   The buzzer had already sounded the end of the game.

   ____

   ____

5. My job is usually interesting.
   Today was a bore.

   ____

   ____

6. You can hire a photographer to take pictures at your wedding.
   You can rent a video camera to film the wedding yourself.

   ____

   ____

7. My friend Al is having trouble with the printer on his home computer.
   He bought the computer on sale last year.

   ____

   ____

8. This district is largely Democratic.
   A small core of Republican precincts is in the northern section of the city.

   ____

   ____

9. On that TV soap opera, Jessica finally filed for a divorce from Lance.
   She could no longer accept his affairs.

   ____

   ____

10. You are going to be late for your dentist appointment.
    You should call his office to inform the receptionist.

    ____

    ____

Now compare your combined sentences with those under Sample Warm-up Answers below. Pay attention to the connecting word that was used in each sentence and to the placement of the comma.

Complete each of the following sentence stems using your own words. Use a comma and a connecting word; then add a complete thought. Remember to put a period at the end.

11. Some people believe in marriage ______

    ____

12. The love of money is the root of all evil ____

    ____

13. Children should be protected, encouraged, and loved ______________________

14. Voting is often a chore ______________

    ____

Sample answers are given below. Just make sure you used a comma and the right connecting word to introduce the idea you were putting into the sentence.

Sample Warm-up Answers
1. For many people, jogging is a healthy sport, yet there are risks involved. **2.** The robber darted out of the liquor store, and a police officer dashed down the street after him. **3.** The Zacks' kitchen plumbing started to leak all over the floor, so they called their landlord. **4.** The basket didn't count, for the buzzer had already sounded the end of the game. **5.** My job is usually interesting, but today was a bore. **6.** You can hire a photographer to take pictures at your wedding, or you can rent a video camera to film the wedding yourself. **7.** can't combine **8.** This district is largely Democratic, but a small core of Republican precincts is in the northern section of the city. **9.** On that TV soap opera, Jessica finally filed for a divorce from Lance, for she could no longer accept his affairs. **10.** You are going to be late for your dentist appointment, so you should call his office to inform the receptionist. Sample completions: **11.** Some people believe in marriage, and they cannot understand the high divorce rate in this country. **12.** The love of money is the root of all evil, yet you need some money to survive. **13.** Children should be protected, encouraged, and loved, for the future rests with them. **14.** Voting is often a chore, so many people just don't bother to vote.

Do you vote in every election? Do you vote only in certain elections? Do you vote at all? Take the time now to think about why you vote or don't vote. List your ideas; they don't have to be in complete sentences. If you have trouble thinking of ideas, free write for three minutes, jotting down all your thoughts on the subject.

A Test-Taking Tip

When you take the GED Writing Skills Test, look carefully at each sentence to see if a correction needs to be made. Try to rewrite the sentence in your head, if that's what the question asks for. However, if you've tried these things and still can't determine the right answer, don't be afraid to guess. Remember that even a wrong guess won't hurt your score, but a blank answer circle can't help it.

On the Springboard

Directions: Read this paragraph carefully and then answer the questions that follow it.

(1) There is a brand-new house on the market called a "smart house." (2) It is expected to take over the construction industry in the near future. (3) A smart house has an air conditioner and a security system that can be turned on by telephone. (4) Anything plugged into the house's wiring system can be programmed to go on and off automatically. (5) The new wiring system virtually eliminates electrical fires, so it makes a smart house a safer house.

1. Sentence 1 and 2: **There is a brand-new house on the market called a "smart house." It is expected to take over the construction industry in the near future.**

   Which of the following is the best way to write the underlined portion of these sentences? If you think the original is the best way, choose option (1).

   (1) "smart house." It
   (2) "smart house," for it
   (3) "smart house," and it

   (1) (2) (3)

2. Sentence 5: **The new wiring system virtually eliminates electrical fires, so it makes a smart house a safer house.**

   If you rewrote sentence 5 beginning with

   A smart house is a safer house,

   the next word should be

   (1) so
   (2) yet
   (3) for

   (1) (2) (3)

Take the time now to write an explanation of why you vote or don't vote. Use your notes from the Warm-up exercise. If you write any related sentences, try to combine them with commas and connecting words.

You can check your Springboard answers on page 99. If you have a good grasp on commas and connecting words, go on to "The Real Thing." If you got even one of the Springboard answers wrong, review this section first.

The Real Thing

Directions: Read the paragraph and then answer the items based on it.

(1) A phobia is a strong fear that has no basis in reality. (2) There are many types of such unreasonable fears. (3) For example, claustrophobia is the extreme fear of enclosed places, and a person suffering from claustrophobia could not stand being in an elevator. (4) Inside the elevator, the person would feel tightness in the chest, have a rapid pulse, or even fainting. (5) People with agoraphobia are afraid to be in open places. (6) They often cannot even leave their own homes. (7) Acrophobia is the fear of heights. (8) Acrophobic people often experience vertigo, or dizziness, when they are up off the ground. (9) These phobias, though not involving a loss of contact with reality, may severely limit a person's life. (10) Some therapists treat phobias by gradually exposing the individual to the thing that he or she fears. (11) This treatment is fairly painless and often effective.

1. Sentence 3: **For example, claustrophobia is the extreme fear of enclosed places, and a person suffering from claustrophobia could not stand being in an elevator.**

   Which of the following is the best way to write the underlined portion of this sentence? If you think the original is the best way, choose option (1).

   (1) places, and a
   (2) places and a
   (3) places. And a
   (4) places. A
   (5) places and, a

2. Sentence 4: **Inside the elevator, the person would feel tightness in the chest, have a rapid pulse, or even fainting.**

   What correction should be made to this sentence?

   (1) remove the comma after elevator
   (2) change feel to feeling
   (3) remove the comma after chest
   (4) insert or before have
   (5) change fainting to faint

3. Sentences 5 and 6: **People with agoraphobia are afraid to be in open places. They often cannot even leave their own homes.**

   The most effective combination of sentences 5 and 6 would include which of the following groups of words?

   (1) in open places, so they
   (2) They are afraid to be
   (3) People often cannot
   (4) are afraid and often cannot
   (5) to be in open places and to leave

4. Sentence 9: **These phobias, though not involving a loss of contact with reality, may severely limit a person's life.**

   If you rewrote sentence 9 beginning with

   These phobias do not involve a loss of contact with reality,

   the next word should be

   (1) and (2) for (3) so
   (4) yet (5) or

   1 2 3 4 5

5. Sentence 11: **This treatment is fairly painless and often effective.**

   What correction should be made to this sentence?

   (1) change is to being
   (2) insert a comma after is
   (3) insert a comma after painless
   (4) remove the word and
   (5) no correction is necessary

Check your answers on pages 103–104.

Using Semicolons

You've combined sentences with commas and connecting words. Another way is to use a semicolon (;). Using a semicolon is a more formal way to connect two related and complete thoughts. Since the GED Writing Skills Test is a formal situation, you might find learning how to use semicolons helpful.

Here's an Example

These two complete sentences could be connected with just a semicolon because their ideas are related.

- Emotional factors are not the only triggers of headaches. Certain physical postures can lead to head and neck pain.

  Combined: Emotional factors are not the only triggers of headaches**;** certain physical postures can lead to head and neck pain.

Often a semicolon is used to connect two sentences when the second idea begins with one of these special connecting words: *moreover, furthermore, however, nevertheless, therefore,* and *consequently.* Perhaps you already use these words at the beginnings of some of your sentences. They are related in meaning to the short connecting words *and, but,* and *so.* But when you combine sentences with the long words, you need to handle them differently. Notice below that a semicolon comes *before* a long connecting word and a comma *after* it.

Instead of using *and,* you can sometimes use *moreover* or *furthermore.*

- Last year Americans spent over $1 billion on arthritis cures. Many of them were worthless.

  Combined: Last year Americans spent over $1 billion on arthritis cures**; moreover,** many of them were worthless.

- Second-degree burns should be placed under cold water, cleaned, and dressed. The victim should be taken to a doctor as soon as possible.

  Combined: Second-degree burns should be placed under cold water, cleaned, and dressed**; furthermore,** the victim should be taken to a doctor as soon as possible.

Can you see how *moreover* and *furthermore* can express the idea of "in addition to" a little more forcefully than *and* does?

Instead of using *but,* you can sometimes use *however* or *nevertheless*.

- Ear infections are so common among children that parents often ignore them. Such infections can have serious effects.

  Combined: Ear infections are so common among children that parents often ignore them**; however,** such infections can have serious effects.

- The outlook has brightened for potential heart attack victims. Heart disease is still a major threat.

  Combined: The outlook has brightened for potential heart attack victims**; nevertheless,** heart disease is still a major threat.

Instead of using *so,* you can sometimes use *therefore* or *consequently*.

- Cold germs are transmitted more often by hands than by sneezing. Wash your hands frequently if you are with someone with a cold.

  Combined: Cold germs are transmitted more often by hands than by sneezing**; therefore,** wash your hands frequently if you are with someone with a cold.

- An anorexic person refuses to eat. He or she may die without treatment.

  Combined: An anorexic person refuses to eat**; consequently,** he or she may die without treatment.

Using long connecting words with semicolons as well as short ones with commas can add variety to your sentences. Variety makes your writing sound more interesting to your reader.

A Test-Taking Tip

You'll find that practicing with the words *therefore* and *consequently* can help you in *two* ways on the GED Writing Skills Test. First, you can use them in your essay if you need to combine two ideas that show cause. Second, they are on the GED Spelling List, so you may need to identify whether they are spelled correctly in one of the passages on the test.

Try It Yourself

How would you combine these sentences? What long connecting word would you use?

- For many years, environmental groups have worked to protect the earth and its resources. Many of our environmental problems still exist.

The writer is showing both sides of an issue. Both bad and good things have happened. A contrasting word is needed to show this. What contrasting word did you think of using to combine the first two sentences? You could have used *however:* "For many years, environmental groups have worked to protect the earth and its resources; however, many of our environmental problems still exist."

Now read that sentence three more times; each time substitute one of these words for *however: but, yet,* and *nevertheless.* What kind of punctuation would you use with each?

Often the choice of connecting words is a matter of opinion. Sometimes, however, you'll find that one is better than the others.

Warm-up

Combine each of the following sentences using a semicolon, a long connecting word, and a comma. Keep the meaning of each word in mind to help yourself choose the best one.

1. Some people say that houseplants are like people. They are more like kittens or puppies.

____

____

2. A houseplant cannot get the water, light, and temperature it needs by itself. You are responsible for supplying these requirements.

____

____

3. You can keep the air around your plants humid by spraying with a mister. Pebbles on the surface of the soil help keep moisture in.

____

____

4. Different kinds of plants require differing amounts of light. Make sure you know the needs of each of your plants.

____

____

Compare your combined sentences with those in the Sample Warm-up Answers below. Make sure you used the right punctuation and an appropriate connecting word.

Now rewrite the paragraph below, combining sentences wherever you think that will improve the writing. Since it is never a good idea to use *only* long connecting words, include some short connecting ones as well.

Most people today believe that banks are safe and reliable places to put their money in. Some people still prefer to keep their money in other places. There are those who insist on hiding their money in a mattress at home. Perhaps they place it in a bank's safe deposit box but not in an account. Often these are older people who lived through the bank failures of the 1930s. They do not trust banks. However, the government now insures deposits in most banks. It will pay back up to a certain amount money that is lost when a bank collapses.

____

____

____

____

____

____

____

____

____

____

____

____

In the Sample Warm-up Answers below, you'll find a sample paragraph that you can use to compare your own with. Remember that in certain situations there may be more than one connecting word that can be used. Be sure that you placed semicolons before your long connecting words and commas before the short ones.

If you're like most people, you need to make a budget. Budgets help you figure out how much money you have coming in and how much is going out.

Think now about your own budget. List the sources of income you have. Next list your necessary expenses each month, such as food and doctor bills. Finally, list the expenses you have when there's money left over, such as going to the movies or buying more clothes. You'll use your lists in the Springboard writing exercise.

Sample Warm-up Answers

1. Some people say that houseplants are like people; however, they are more like kittens or puppies. **2.** A houseplant cannot get the water, light, and temperature it needs by itself; consequently, you are responsible for supplying these requirements. **3.** You can keep the air around your plants humid by spraying with a mister; moreover, pebbles on the surface of the soil help keep moisture in. **4.** Different kinds of plants require differing amounts of light; therefore, make sure you know the needs of each of your plants.

Most people today believe that banks are safe and reliable places to put their money in; however, some people still prefer to keep their money in other places. There are those who insist on hiding their money in a mattress at home, or perhaps they place it in a bank's safe deposit box but not in an account. Often these are older people who lived through the bank failures of the 1930s; consequently, they do not trust banks. However, the government now insures deposits in most banks, and it will pay back up to a certain amount money that is lost when a bank collapses.

On the Springboard

Directions: Read this paragraph carefully and then answer the questions that follow it.

(1) Do you know anyone who hates chocolate? (2) Children enjoy it in milk and candy bars. (3) The taste of chocolate doesn't appeal just to the young. (4) Adults crave chocolate too. (5) On cold days we drink hot chocolate to keep warm and on hot days we cool off with chocolate sundaes. (6) Chocolate is disastrous for diets; nevertheless, it sneaks its way into many of them.

3. Sentences 2 and 3: **Children enjoy it in milk and candy bars. The taste of chocolate doesn't appeal just to the young.**

   The most effective combination of sentences 2 and 3 would include which of the following groups of words?

   (1) bars, and
   (2) bars; therefore,
   (3) bars; however,

   (1) (2) (3)

4. Sentence 5: **On cold days we drink hot chocolate to keep warm and on hot days we cool off with chocolate sundaes.**

   What correction should be made to this sentence?

   (1) insert a semicolon after warm
   (2) insert a comma after warm
   (3) replace and with so

   (1) (2) (3)

Write an explanation of your budget. Contrast the money you have coming in with the money you need for living expenses such as food. Show how the amount of money you need for living expenses affects the amount of money you have left over for other things, such as leisure activities or more clothes. Combine sentences when that will improve your writing. Use both short and long connecting words.

Now check your answers to the Springboard questions on page 99. If you understand how to use connecting words to combine sentences, go on to "The Real Thing." If you had problems, review this lesson and practice writing your own combined sentences.

"The Real Thing"

Directions: Read the paragraph and then answer the items based on it.

(1) Fast-food restaurants are popular and handy. (2) Some people feel that fast food is not the most healthful you can buy. (3) Think about a meal you have had at a fast-food restaurant. (4) It may have been tasty but chances are at least some of the items were deep-fried. (5) Potatoes, chicken, and even fruit pies, take a dunk in sizzling oil. (6) Ketchup, relish, and dressings are also loaded. (7) With salt, yet salt is already overused by many. (8) With all that salt and oil, you need something to drink. (9) Looking cool and refreshing, soda pop and creamy shakes are sure to contain either sugar or artificial sweeteners. (10) Oil, salt, and sugar don't appear on the fast-food menu, but they are most likely in the fast food.

6. Sentences 1 and 2: **Fast-food restaurants are popular and handy. Some people feel that fast food is not the most healthful you can buy.**

   The most effective combination of sentences 1 and 2 would include which of the following groups of words?

   (1) handy, and some people
   (2) popular and handy and not the most healthful
   (3) Some people feel that fast-food restaurants
   (4) handy; however, some
   (5) handy, yet nevertheless some

   (1) (2) (3) (4) (5)

7. Sentence 4: **It may have been tasty but chances are at least some of the items were deep-fried.**

   What correction should be made to this sentence?

   (1) insert a comma after tasty
   (2) replace but with so
   (3) replace but with and
   (4) insert a comma after but
   (5) change are to being

   (1) (2) (3) (4) (5)

8. Sentence 5: **Potatoes, chicken, and even fruit <u>pies, take</u> a dunk in sizzling oil.**

   Which of the following is the best way to write the underlined portion of this sentence? If you think the original is the best way, choose option (1).

   (1) pies, take
   (2) pies, and take
   (3) pies; take
   (4) pies take
   (5) pies; nevertheless, take

     3  5

9. Sentences 6 and 7: **Ketchup, relish, and dressings are also <u>loaded. With</u> salt, yet salt is already overused by many.**

   Which of the following is the best way to write the underlined portion of these sentences? If you think the original is the best way, choose option (1).

   (1) loaded. With
   (2) loaded with
   (3) loaded, with
   (4) loaded; moreover, with
   (5) loaded, and with

10. Sentence 9: **Looking cool and refreshing, soda pop and creamy shakes are sure to contain either sugar or artificial sweeteners.**

    If you rewrote sentence 9 beginning with

    <u>Soda pop and creamy shakes may look cool and refreshing,</u>

    the next words should be

    (1) moreover, they
    (2) and containing
    (3) yet they
    (4) are sure to
    (5) consequently, they

Check your answers and record your score for the entire lesson on page 104.

LESSON 7

Combining Unequal Ideas

Sometimes you'll write two complete thoughts that are closely related, but they are not of equal importance. One is the main idea; the other is a secondary idea. This secondary idea is almost like a detail, yet it has its own subject and verb. You can combine such unequal ideas by using one of these connecting words to show their exact relationship.

To show time or place
after, until
as long as, when
as soon as, whenever
before, where
once, wherever
since, while

To set up a condition
if
unless
whether

To give a reason or an effect
because
since
so that

To show one idea is in spite of another
although
even though
though

Sometimes these secondary connecting words require commas, and sometimes they don't. It all depends on how you use them.

Placing a Secondary Idea at the Beginning

Often you'll want to put a secondary idea at the beginning of one of your sentences. It will lead your reader into the main idea. When you do so, you need to put the right connecting word at the beginning of the secondary idea and a comma at the end of it.

Here's an Example

Here are two sentences that could have a number of different relationships between their ideas.

■ I made the gravy.
My husband carved the turkey.

If the actions happened at the same time, they can be combined by using the word *while* to introduce one of the complete ideas and make it secondary to the other.

■ **While** I made the gravy, my husband carved the turkey.

Note what the word *while* does to the idea it is attached to. If you read only *while I made the gravy,* you wonder what happened while this person was making the gravy. The idea is no longer a complete thought that can stand independently. Instead, it now depends on the main part of the sentence for you to understand its meaning. For that reason, this kind of secondary idea is sometimes called a **dependent thought.** The main idea of the sentence is then called the **independent thought.**

In the example above, you could also make the other idea the dependent thought by introducing it with *while.*

■ **While** my husband carved the turkey, I made the gravy.

Sometimes you have a choice about which idea to make secondary, or dependent. Other times you don't. It depends on the relationship between the ideas. For example, look at these sentences. They mean two different things.

■ After my husband carved the turkey, I made the gravy.

■ After I made the gravy, my husband carved the turkey.

Sometimes you have to change a few words in one or both sentences when you combine ideas by making one dependent on the other. Look at this example.

■ Artificial turf is used in some places. In those places athletes suffer more injuries.

Combined: **Wherever** artificial turf is used, athletes suffer more injuries.

Since the meaning of *wherever* takes in the meaning of *in some places* and *in those places,* you don't need to repeat those words.

Now look at a few more examples of dependent thoughts at the beginnings of sentences. Notice the subject and verb of each, study the connecting word at the beginning, and note the comma separating the dependent and independent thoughts.

■ **Because** *Julian proposed* to Mary Beth at the Dragon Inn, *it became* their favorite restaurant.

■ **Unless** *I am mistaken*, the *punishment* for drunk driving in this state *is* one year.

■ **Even though** small *businesses are* risky, *thousands* of new ones *open* up each year.

You might have noticed that introductory dependent thoughts are a little like the introductory descriptive phrases you learned about in Lesson 2. They may even begin with some of the same words (for example, *after* and *before*). The comparison is useful because both are followed by commas and neither can stand alone as a complete sentence.

A Test-Taking Tip

The spelling of many words has become shortened or simplified in casual English. You may have seen these spellings in advertisements and other informal writing: *tho* and *altho.* Remember that the GED Writing Skills Test is a formal situation. You should spell these words *though* and *although* if you use them on the test.

Coming to Terms

independent thought a group of words with a subject and verb that expresses a complete idea and can stand alone as a complete sentence.

dependent thought a group of words with a subject and a verb that is introduced by a connecting word. It cannot stand alone.

Try It Yourself

Below are parts of an office memo. How could you combine each pair of sentences by placing a connecting word before the first sentence so that it becomes dependent on the second sentence to complete its meaning?

■ I stopped to change a woman's flat tire. I was late coming in to work today.

How is the first sentence related to the second? It is giving a cause for the writer's lateness. Therefore, you could use the word *Because* or *Since* in front of the first idea and make it dependent on the second: "Because I stopped to change a woman's flat tire, I was late coming in to work today." Did you remember that the dependent idea needed to be followed by a comma?

You may have noticed that some connecting words have more than one meaning. The word *since* can name a time (for example, *since you've been gone*) or state a reason (for example, *since you are so stubborn*).

Now try this one.

■ The Simpson report requires a lot more work. I can still finish it by tonight.

Did you see that the idea in the second idea is *in spite of* the first? For that reason, you could use *Even though* at the beginning of one long sentence: "Even though the Simpson report requires a lot more work, I can still finish it by tonight."

Warm-up

Combine each pair of sentences below. Choose an appropriate connecting word to place at the beginning of the first idea to make it dependent on the second. You may have to change another word or two.

1. Cats and dogs are quite different from each other.
   People tend to like one or the other but not both.

   ____

   ____

2. Cats may seem cold and uncaring.
   That is not necessarily the case.

   ____

   ____

3. Cats want to cuddle with you at times.
   Then they can be quite affectionate.

   ____

   ____

4. Dogs need long walks and companionship.
   Busy people may not be good dog owners.

   ____

   ____

Check your combined sentences with those given below under Sample Warm-up Answers. You may have used different connecting words, but all your introductory dependent ideas should have commas after them.

Now read through this accident report. Then decide which connecting word to use in each blank to make the next sentence dependent on the sentence following it. Rewrite the paragraph. Don't forget about commas.

______ The first snowfall is always dangerous. I was driving especially carefully. ______ Mr. Watt's car ran the stop sign on my right. I began to pump my brakes. ______ I was traveling slowly. I skidded quite a distance and hit Mrs. Cortesi's car. ______ Mr. Watt was breaking the law. He is responsible for the accident. ______ He could have stopped. Then nothing would have happened.

Compare your rewritten paragraph with the one below under Sample Warm-up Answers.

Consider this situation. Suppose a credit-card company sends you a bill for $132.40. You have no record of that purchase. In fact, you never even heard of the store where the purchase was made. Prepare to write a letter to the credit-card company explaining the situation. Make a list of the ideas you would want to include in such a letter. This list will help you write your Springboard exercise.

Sample Warm-up Answers
1. Because cats and dogs are quite different from each other, people tend to like one or the other but not both. **2.** Although cats may seem cold and uncaring, that is not necessarily the case. **3.** When cats want to cuddle with you, they can be quite affectionate. **4.** Since dogs need long walks and companionship, busy people may not be good dog owners.

Because the first snowfall is always dangerous, I was driving especially carefully. When Mr. Watt's car ran the stop sign on my right, I began to pump my brakes. Even though I was traveling slowly, I skidded quite a distance and hit Mrs. Cortesi's car. Since Mr. Watt was breaking the law, he is responsible for the accident. If he had stopped, nothing would have happened.

On the Springboard

Directions: Read this paragraph carefully and then answer the questions that follow it.

(1) Many Americans do not realize it, but the federal income tax did not exist until 1913. (2) In that year, the Sixteenth Amendment was added to the Constitution; it gave Congress the right to tax private incomes. (3) However, it wasn't until 1942 that the income tax first began to reach into the pocket of the average citizen. (4) Because the government needed funds to build weapons for World War II. (5) Congress raised the tax and allowed it to be withheld from employees' paychecks. (6) A whole generation of workers has never known what it is like to bring home all the money they have earned.

1. Sentence 1: **Many Americans do not realize it, but the federal income tax did not exist until 1913.**

   If you rewrote sentence 1 beginning with

   Although many Americans do not realize it,

   the next word should be

   (1) until
   (2) the
   (3) but

   (1) (2) (3)

2. Sentence 2: **In that year, the Sixteenth Amendment was added to the Constitution; it gave Congress the right to tax private incomes.**

   What correction should be made to this sentence?

   (1) replace In with Because in
   (2) insert and after Constitutuion;
   (3) no correction is necessary

   (1) (2) (3)

3. Sentences 4 and 5: **Because the government needed funds to build weapons for World War II. Congress raised the tax and allowed it to be withheld from employees' paychecks.**

   Which of the following is the best way to write the underlined portion of this sentence? If you think the original is the best way, choose option (1).

   (1) World War II. Congress
   (2) World War II; Congress
   (3) World War II, Congress

   (1) (2) (3)

Remember the credit-card situation from the Warm-up? You've been billed $132.40 for a purchase that you did not make. Review the notes you made during the Warm-up. Write the body of a letter to the company explaining the situation. If appropriate, use your knowledge of sentence structure to make some ideas dependent on others.

Now take the time to check your Springboard multiple-choice answers on page 99.

If you got all three correct, read the tip that follows and then try "The Real Thing." If you got one or more questions wrong, review this section. Also, practice writing sentences of your own with dependent ideas at the beginning.

A Test-Taking Tip

Very often on the GED Writing Skills Test, a passage will contain a sentence fragment that is actually a dependent thought. The fragment may look like a complete sentence because it has a subject and a verb. However, the secondary connecting word at the beginning will be a clue to you that it is not a complete sentence.

"The Real Thing"

Directions: Read the paragraph and then answer the items based on it.

(1) Today's astronomers have charted 88 star patterns, or constellations. (2) Because of its ladle-like appearance, one such constellation is called the Big Dipper. (3) However, the Big Dipper has also been known as the Greater Bear and as the Great Bear and Hunters. (4) There is a legend of the Iroquois Indians. (5) It states that the three stars that make up the tail of the bear are remnants of a mighty hunting party. (6) After the party was attacked by stone giants, the great bear and the three surviving Indians was carried to the sky by invisible hands. (7) There the Indians still chase the bear today. (8) The first Indian carries a bow; and the second carries a kettle. (9) The third carries sticks to make a fire for cooking the bear when he is slain. (10) The blood that drips from the bear tints the leaves and gives us our fall colors every year.

1. Sentence 2: **Because of its ladle-like appearance, one such constellation is called the Big Dipper.**

   Which of the following is the best way to write the underlined portion of this sentence? If you think the original is the best way, choose option (1).

   (1) appearance, one
   (2) appearance one
   (3) appearance, and one
   (4) appearance, so one
   (5) apppearance. One

   (1) (2) (3) (4) (5)

2. Sentences 4 and 5: **There is a legend of the Iroquois Indians. It states that the three stars that make up the tail of the bear are remnants of a mighty hunting party.**

   The most effective combination of sentences 4 and 5 would include which of the following groups of words?

   (1) Indians, stating that the three stars
   (2) According to a legend of the Iroquois Indians,
   (3) Because there is a legend of the Iroquois Indians,
   (4) Indians; consequently, it states that
   (5) There is a legend that states

   (1) (2) (3) (4) (5)

3. Sentence 6: **After the party was attacked by stone giants, the great bear and the three surviving Indians was carried to the sky by invisible hands.**

   What correction should be made to this sentence?

   (1) replace After with Even though
   (2) insert a comma after party
   (3) remove the comma after giants
   (4) insert and after the comma
   (5) change was to were

   (1) (2) (3) (4) (5)

4. Sentence 8: **The first Indian carries a bow; and the second carries a kettle.**

   Which of the following is the best way to write the underlined portion of this sentence? If you think the original is the best way, choose option (1).

   (1) bow; and
   (2) bow, and
   (3) bow and
   (4) bow. And
   (5) bow; and,

   (1) (2) (3) (4) (5)

5. Sentence 10: **The blood that drips from the bear tints the leaves and gives us our fall colors every year.**

   If you rewrote sentence 10 beginning with

   Blood then drips from the bear, tinting the leaves and

   the next word should be

   (1) gives
   (2) give
   (3) giving
   (4) to give
   (5) gave

   (1) (2) (3) (4) (5)

Check your answers on page 104.

Placing a Secondary Idea at the End

You may have already discovered for yourself that you can also place secondary ideas at the ends of sentences. Such an idea is still dependent on the main part of the sentence. The one big difference is that you usually don't need to use a comma to separate the dependent and independent thoughts. You have to listen to the sound of the sentence. Only if you hear a pause between the two thoughts do you use a comma.

Here's an Example

Look at some of the same sentences you studied in the last section. This time, the dependent thoughts come at the end.

- I made the gravy **while** my husband carved the turkey.
- Athletes suffer more injuries **wherever** artificial turf is used.
- The Dragon Inn became Julian and Mary Beth's favorite restaurant **because** he proposed to her there.
- Thousands of small businesses open up each year **even though** they are risky.

Now look at these examples. Say the sentences aloud or sound them out in your head. Can you "hear" that each one needs a comma to signal the pause between the independent and the dependent thought?

- The punishment for drunk driving in this state is one year**, unless** I am mistaken.
- A landmark year for the space program was 1969**, when** U.S. astronauts walked on the moon.

Usually you don't need to use a comma before a dependent thought at the end of a sentence. Just remember that this "rule" does not always apply. Always listen to the sound of your sentences. Punctuate the way your ear tells you to.

Finally, take a look at these two sentences.

- Please be at the union hall by seven **so that** we can start the meeting on time.
- Please be at the union hall by seven **so** we can start the meeting on time.

Sometimes writers drop the word *that* from the secondary connecting term *so that.* If you do so, just be careful not to confuse the secondary *so* of *so that* with the main connecting word *so,* which is used in this sentence.

- Five members were not at the hall by seven, **so** we could not start the meeting on time.

A Test-Taking Tip

If you read or write a sentence on the GED Writing Skills Test in which *so* is connecting two thoughts, try this little test: In your mind replace the word *so* with the words "with the result that." If the sentence makes sense, *so* is being used as a main connecting word, and it needs a comma before it. If you can replace the word *so* with "in order that" and still have the sentence make sense, you're dealing with the secondary connecting word *so* from the phrase *so that.* You probably won't need to use a comma.

Try It Yourself

The short passage below is taken from a letter written by a soldier. Watch for two opportunities to combine sentences by making one idea dependent on another. This time, place the secondary idea at the end of the new sentence.

- We arrived in Dallas late. The plane had several problems before leaving Chicago. We drove into boot camp at 5:15 in the morning. Hundreds of guys were outside exercising and running. I am really looking forward to the next eight weeks. I am a bit nervous. Am I crazy?!

Did you see the relationship between the first two sentences? The second sentence gave a cause, or reason, for the first. You could combine these two sentences to show how these two events fit together: "We arrived in Dallas late because the plane had several problems before leaving Chicago." There is no need to use a comma to separate the two ideas.

Look at the fifth and sixth sentences. The writer was feeling both anticipation and nervousness. You could express that by writing this sentence: "I am really looking forward to the next eight weeks, though I am a bit nervous." You could also have used *although* or *even though* in that sentence. Did you hear the pause between the independent and dependent thoughts and use a comma?

The soldier went on to say the following. Remember what you know about parallel writing. Can you figure out a better way to write the dependent thought in this sentence?

■ I enlisted in the army to serve my country and because I wanted an education.

The recruit made the common mistake of combining a verbal ("to serve my country") with an entire dependent thought ("because I wanted an education"). They are not parallel. To make them parallel, you could make both ideas verbals: "I enlisted in the army to serve my country and to get an education." You could also make both ideas part of one dependent thought: "I enlisted in the army because I wanted to serve my country and to get an education."

Warm-up

Here are the same sentence pairs you worked with in the last Warm-up. This time, make one idea dependent on the other and place it at the *end* of the sentence. Listen for any spot in which you may need to use a comma. You'll also need to change some words around.

1. Cats and dogs are quite different from each other.
People tend to like one or the other but not both.

____

____

2. Cats may seem cold and uncaring.
That is not necessarily the case.

____

____

3. Cats want to cuddle with you at times.
Then they can be quite affectionate.

____

____

4. Dogs need long walks and companionship.
Busy people may not be good dog owners.

____

____

Compare your combined sentences with those in the Sample Warm-up Answers.

Complete each statement below by writing a dependent thought before or after the independent thought. Use commas if you need to.

5. I was determined to run in the marathon

____

6. ______________________________

______________ hundreds of runners were at the starting line ahead of me.

7. ______________________________

______________ I was exhausted by the fifteenth mile.

8. I made up my mind to finish ______________

____

9. You never really know what you can do ______

____

Check your answers with the Sample Warm-up Answers given below. You will have written different ideas, but make sure your sentences are logical.

Now list ten events and decisions in your life on a separate sheet of paper. Write a sentence about each event. Complete the sentence by using a connecting word to relate it to another idea. Use as many different connecting words as you can. Put dependent thoughts at the beginnings and ends of your sentences.

Example: I was born shortly before President Nixon was elected the first time.

Pick one of the following topics. Make a list of your ideas on the subject. Remember that you don't need to worry about sentence structure or punctuation at this point. Just write phrases that you can later expand into sentences.

the death penalty
women's rights
sex on television and in movies

Sample Warm-up Answers
1. People tend to like cats or dogs but not both because they are quite different from each other. **2.** Cats may seem cold and uncaring, though that is not necessarily the case. **3.** Cats can be quite affectionate when they want to cuddle with you. **4.** Busy people may not be good dog owners since dogs need long walks and companionship. **5.** I was determined to run in the marathon because I wanted to test my strength and endurance. **6.** When I arrived at the beginning of the race, hundreds of runners were at the starting line ahead of me. **7.** Even though I had trained long hours, I was exhausted by the fifteenth mile. **8.** I made up my mind to finish whether or not I had a chance to win. **9.** You never really know what you can do until you try.

On the Springboard

Directions: Read this paragraph carefully and then answer the questions that follow it.

(1) The ability to read is vital in a democracy. (2) Voters must be informed in order to vote intelligently. (3) Many American adults, however, are illiterate. (4) Illiteracy will remain a serious problem as long as we continue to ignore it. (5) We must begin to solve this problem if we hope to have informed citizens voting.

4. Sentences 1 and 2: **The ability to read is vital in a democracy. Voters must be informed in order to vote intelligently.**

   The most effective combination of sentences 1 and 2 would include which of the following groups of words?

   (1) democracy so that
   (2) Although the ability
   (3) democracy because voters

   (1) (2) (3)

5. Sentence 4: **Illiteracy will remain a serious problem as long as we continue to ignore it.**

   Which of the following is the best way to write the underlined portion of this sentence? If you think the original is the best way, choose option (1).

   (1) problem as long as we
   (2) problem; as long as we
   (3) problem. As long as we

   (1) (2) (3)

Look back at the list of ideas you prepared in the Warm-up exercise. Jot down the topic you picked at the top of a fresh sheet of paper. Write a composition explaining your ideas on the subject. Write for someone who doesn't know you well, such as your congressional representative or a GED scorer. Experiment with different ways of relating ideas and making them dependent on each other.

You can check your Springboard multiple-choice answers on page 100.

How did you do? Two correct answers mean you're ready to try "The Real Thing." If you got any wrong, you might want to take the time to review dependent ideas.

"The Real Thing"

Directions: Read the paragraph and then answer the items based on it.

(1) Humans are capable of remarkable feats of strength and courage. (2) Our physical abilities are not entirely known. (3) We don't really know what their limits are either. (4) Sometimes people are able to do seemingly impossible things in spite of their limitations. (5) One man saw a child trapped under a heavy pipe. (6) The man had to lift the pipe, or else the child would be crushed. (7) He ran forward and lifted it off the child; the pipe weighed 400 pounds. (8) Another man crossed a field, crawled through a hedge, and climbed stairs to save a drowning baby. (9) Though he had lost his legs in Vietnam. (10) People like these are almost superhuman in the moment when they act.

6. Sentences 2 and 3: **Our physical abilities are not entirely known. We don't really know what their limits are either.**

   The most effective combination of sentences 2 and 3 would include which of the following groups of words?

   (1) entirely known, and we don't
   (2) abilities and their limits are not
   (3) Although our physical abilities
   (4) entirely known, yet we don't
   (5) Either our physical abilities or limits

   (1) (2) (3) (4) (5)

7. Sentence 4: **Sometimes people are able to do seemingly impossible things in spite of their limitations.**

   What correction should be made to this sentence?

   (1) replace Sometimes with Although
   (2) remove the word are
   (3) insert a comma after impossible
   (4) replace in spite of with although
   (5) no correction is necessary

   (1) (2) (3) (4) (5)

8. Sentence 6: **The man had to lift the pipe, or else the child would be crushed.**

   If you rewrote sentence 6 beginning with

   The child would be crushed

   the next word should be

   (1) or
   (2) and
   (3) although
   (4) unless
   (5) since

9. Sentence 7: **He ran forward and lifted it off the child; the pipe weighed 400 pounds.**

   Which of the following is the best way to write the underlined portion of this sentence? If you think the original is the best way, choose option (1).

   (1) child; the pipe
   (2) child, even though the pipe
   (3) child, weighing
   (4) child and the pipe weighed
   (5) child. The pipe weighed

10. Sentences 8 and 9: **Another man crossed a field, crawled through a hedge, and climbed stairs to save a drowning baby. Though he had lost his legs in Vietnam.**

    Which of the following is the best way to write the underlined portion of these sentences? If you think the original is the best way, choose option (1).

    (1) baby. Though
    (2) baby; though,
    (3) baby, even though
    (4) baby, but though
    (5) baby, and though

    (1) (2) (3) (4) (5)

Check your answers and record your score for the entire lesson on pages 104–105.

LESSON 8

Placing Information Within Sentences

Using Dependent Thoughts to Identify Nouns

You've learned how to add details to give more information about the nouns in your sentences. And you've just learned a great deal about changing complete sentences into dependent thoughts. You can also change independent thoughts to dependent thoughts and then use them as details to identify your nouns. It's like placing a smaller box of information within the larger box of your sentence. In fact, you may already write sentences this way without even realizing that you're doing so.

Here's an Example

Below is part of a GED student's composition. Notice the thoughts that begin with *who* and *that.*

■ The idea **that** *people are more good than bad* appeals to me. We all know people **who** *concentrate on the negative all the time.* They notice only the bad things **that** *happen to them.* It is those people **who** *say,* "The cashier always leaves the register just as I get there." According to them, a line forms quickly at the bank teller's window **that** *they are walking up to.* They always notice people **who** *do discourteous or dishonest things.* However, I see things differently. When I get up in the morning, I tell myself to have a nice day and to help others **that** *I meet* have a nice one too. When you expect good things to happen, you don't notice the bad as much.

In that paragraph, whole dependent thoughts were placed inside sentences. In the first sentence, for example, *idea* and *appeals* are the subject and verb of the independent thought. The word *that* introduces a different thought in which *people* and *are* are the subject and verb. In the second sentence, *We* and *know* are the subject and verb. The word *who* begins a new, dependent thought and is actually the subject of that thought; *concentrate* is its verb.

The words *who* and *that* are special connecting words in these cases. *Who* always refers to people; *that* can refer to people or things. Remember that nouns name people or things. The words *who* and *that* help identify the noun that comes before them by beginning a thought that helps pinpoint the noun. For example, "that they are walking up to" helps pinpoint *which* bank teller's window. Sometimes *who* and *they* are even the subjects of these dependent thoughts.

You use these kinds of dependent thoughts very often when you speak. So you may already be using them when you write. Sometimes, however, you may write two or three sentences that sound short and choppy because such thoughts weren't placed within sentences. In such cases, you can rewrite your sentences to make them sound smoother. For example, the GED student had initially written these sentences.

■ Sometimes bad things happen to them. They notice only those bad things.

When he reread his paragraph, he didn't like the sound of those sentences. He combined them into the one, smooth sentence that you read in the paragraph by using *that* to refer to *things*.

■ They notice only the bad things that happen to them.

Try It Yourself

A judge took the following notes on contestants in a talent show. Watch for ways to combine each set of notes into one sentence by using *who* or *that*.

■ the first woman
sang a sweet love song
she wrote it herself

Were you able to combine those three notes? The last note helps identify the song that was sung, so you could have used *that* to combine the ideas into one sentence like this: "The first woman sang a sweet love song that she wrote herself."

Now try these notes.

■ dance group
performed to music from *Fame*
had terrific technique

The second note helps identify which dance group. Because the group is made up of people, you could use either *who* or *that* to start the dependent thought: "The dance group who performed to music from *Fame* had terrific technique" or "The dance group that performed to music from *Fame* had terrific technique."

Warm-up

Expand the complete sentences below. Identify the person or thing by adding a dependent thought beginning with *who* or *that.*

1. I love movies ______________________________

____

2. I have a friend ______________________________

____

3. Please don't get the idea ______________________

____

4. Pizza is one kind of food ______________________

____

5. The movie star ______________________________

______________________________ was Cary Grant.

6. People ______________________________

______________________________ bother me.

Compare your sentences with those under Sample Warm-up Answers below. Check to make sure you used *who* and *that* correctly and that your added thoughts help identify the nouns that come before them. What verbs did you use in your additions? Did you also use subjects?

Sample Warm-up Answers
1. I love movies that have a lot of action. **2.** I have a friend who always makes me laugh. **3.** Please don't get the idea that you can get away with that. **4.** Pizza is one kind of food that gives me heartburn. **5.** The movie star who always made me smile was Cary Grant. **6.** People who don't use their turn signals when driving bother me. **7.** We all know people who are never content. **8.** The part of the city that was destroyed by a tornado will take several years to rebuild. **9.** She wore a dress that was too tight for her to her job interview. **10.** A man who was talking to himself sat next to me on the bus this morning.

Now combine these sentences by using *who* and *that* to make one thought identify the person or thing being discussed.

7. Some people are never content.
We all know people like that.

____

____

8. Part of the city was destroyed by a tornado.
It will take several years to rebuild.

____

____

9. She wore a dress to her job interview.
It was too tight for her.

____

____

10. A man sat next to me on the bus this morning.
He was talking to himself.

____

____

You can compare your combined sentences with the sample answers given in the previous column. Again, be sure that you used *who* and *that* correctly.

Do you think people are basically good, bad, or somewhere in between? Think about that question for about five minutes. List your thoughts on the matter. You can make notes like the judge's notes in Try It Yourself. You'll use your notes to finish the Springboard writing exercise.

On the Springboard

Directions: Read this paragraph carefully and then answer the questions that follow it.

(1) As he is walking his dog, your neighbor may be helping himself as much as his pet. (2) In addition, the habit of stroking your cat under its chin might actually add a few years to your own life. (3) According to researchers, pets can have a positive effect on their owners' health, both mental and physical. (4) Pets offer companionship that can ease a person's loneliness. (5) Petting an animal reduces anxiety and depression, lowers blood pressure, and consequentally increases the chances for a longer, happier life.

1. Sentence 1: **As he is walking his dog, your neighbor may be helping himself as much as his pet.**

   If you rewrote sentence 1 beginning with

   The neighbor who

   the next words should be

   (1) may be helping
   (2) is walking
   (3) may be walking

   (1) (2) (3)

2. Sentence 4: **Pets offer companionship that can ease a person's loneliness.**

   Which of the following is the best way to write the underlined portion of this sentence? If you think the original is the best way, choose option (1).

   (1) companionship that can
   (2) companionship who can
   (3) companionship can

   (1) (2) (3)

3. Sentence 5: **Petting an animal reduces anxiety and depression, lowers blood pressure, and consequentally increases the chances for a longer, happier life.**

   What correction should be made to this sentence?

   (1) insert that after animal
   (2) remove the comma after depression
   (3) change the spelling of consequentally to consequently

   (1) (2) (3)

Write the title "Are People Basically Good or Bad?" at the top of a sheet of paper and then write your thoughts on that matter. Use your notes from the Warm-up exercise. Be sure to keep in mind ways to combine thoughts with *who* and *that* as well as other ways you've studied.

Take the time now to check the answers to On the Springboard on page 100. Did you get all three questions correct? If so, see what you can do with the GED-level "Real Thing." If you had trouble with one or more of the Springboard items, review this first section and practice writing your own sentences with *who* and *that* before you go on.

The Real Thing

Directions: Read the paragraph and then answer the items based on it.

(1) Americans are becoming more and more fond of drinking tea; especially a hot mug of tea on a cold winter's day. (2) Whether you drink black tea or herbal tea the goal of every tea drinker is to brew the perfect pot of tea. (3) To perform this feat, first fill a teakettle with cold tap water. (4) Such water is full of oxygen. (5) It will bring out the full flavor of the tea. (6) Bring the water to a full rolling boil. (7) Next, fill the china cup or teapot who will be used to brew the tea with some of the water to warm it. (8) Let the water sit for a few minutes, pour it out, and then add your favorite teabags or loose tea. (9) Pour the boiling water over the top of your tea, and let it brew for the recommended time. (10) It is important to brew the tea only for that time, or it will be too bitter to enjoy.

1. Sentence 1: **Americans are becoming more and more fond of drinking tea; especially a hot mug of tea on a cold winter's day.**

   What correction should be made to this sentence?

   (1) insert who after Americans
   (2) remove the word are
   (3) change the semicolon to a comma
   (4) insert a comma after especially
   (5) no correction is necessary

   (1) (2) (3) (4) (5)

2. Sentence 2: **Whether you drink black tea or herbal tea the goal of every tea drinker is to brew the perfect pot of tea.**

   Which of the following is the best way to write the underlined portion of this sentence? If you think the original is the best way, choose option (1).

   (1) tea the goal (2) tea that the goal
   (3) tea, the goal (4) tea, and the goal
   (5) tea. The goal

   (1) (2) (3) (4) (5)

3. Sentences 4 and 5: **Such water is full of oxygen. It will bring out the full flavor of the tea.**

   The most effective combination of sentences 4 and 5 would include which of the following groups of words?

   (1) It is full of oxygen
   (2) oxygen and it will bring
   (3) is full of oxygen and will bring
   (4) Such water is full of oxygen and flavor
   (5) oxygen for it will bring

   (1) (2) (3) (4) (5)

4. Sentence 7: **Next, fill the china cup or teapot who will be used to brew the tea with some of the water to warm it.**

   Which of the following is the best way to write the underlined portion of this sentence? If you think the original is the best way, choose option (1).

   (1) teapot who will be used
   (2) teapot. Who will be used
   (3) teapot it will be used
   (4) teapot will be used
   (5) teapot that will be used

   (1) (2) (3) (4) (5)

5. Sentence 10: **It is important to brew the tea only for that time, or it will be too bitter to enjoy.**

   If you rewrote sentence 10 beginning with

   If you brew the tea longer than that,

   the next word should be

   (1) or (2) and (3) time
   (4) it (5) but

   (1) (2) (3) (4) (5)

Check your answers to "The Real Thing" on page 105.

Using Dependent Thoughts to Give More Information

Have you ever been talking about something and then found the need to "interrupt" yourself by giving some side information about the person or thing you're discussing? Then you go on with your main point. Such an interrupting thought is not really necessary to identify the person or thing you're talking about; instead, it just gives your listener some added information.

You can do the same for your reader when you write. You can use the words *who* and *which* to introduce dependent thoughts that give additional information about people or things.

Here's an Example

Look again at the conversation about the record album. If the man were writing that sentence, he would probably write it something like this.

- My new album**, which** *was recorded live in L.A.***,** is really great. Luther Jackson**, who** *plays drums on the album***,** is a friend of mine.

Notice that *who* is used to give more information about a person; *which* (not *that*) is used to refer to a thing. Also, unlike the dependent thought that is necessary to help identify a person or thing, the dependent thought that merely gives extra information requires commas. That's because this kind of dependent thought is more like a descriptive detail. You learned in Lesson 2 that a descriptive detail immediately following the noun is separated by commas, like this.

- His drumming**, inspired and driving,** always makes me stop and listen.

That detail is just a shortened form of a dependent thought with its own subject and verb.

- His drumming**, which is inspired and driving,** always makes me stop and listen.

Try It Yourself

Below is part of a job performance review. See if you can find how to combine the four sentences into two by turning some of the information into dependent thoughts beginning with *who* or *which*.

- During this performance period, this employee has successfully met the responsibilities of her job. These responsibilities were agreed upon twelve months ago. This employee has performed well under difficult conditions. It is recommended that this employee be given a merit increase in pay.

What did you decide to do with the first two sentences? The second sentence gives added information about the responsibilities that were mentioned in the first sentence. Because responsibilities are things, you could use *which* to make the information in the second sentence dependent on the first: "During this performance period, this employee has successfully met the responsibilities of her job, which were agreed upon twelve months ago."

What about the next two sentences? Both talk about the employee. Since the merit increase is especially important, the information in that sentence should probably remain the main idea, and the information in the sentence before it can be made into a dependent thought, like this: "It is recommended that this employee, who has performed well under difficult conditions, be given a merit increase in pay." Did you remember to use *who* because you were writing about a person?

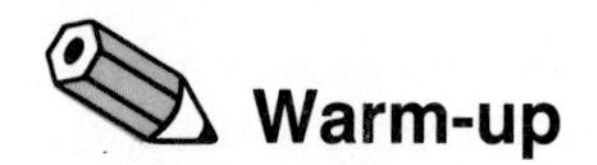

Warm-up

Complete each sentence by choosing *who* or *which* and then adding information. Don't forget to use commas.

1. My best friend ______________________ ______________________ called me last night.
2. The most exciting place I've ever been to is ______________, ______________________.
3. The family member I feel closest to is my ______________________, ______________.

Compare your answers with those below. Be sure you included a verb, a subject if *who* or *which* was not the subject of the dependent thought, and commas.

Now combine these sentences. For each pair, choose the thought that you want to make the main idea of the sentence. Make the other thought dependent by using *who* or *which* and placing the thought within the main sentence.

4. Alcoholism is a disease.
   It affects the physical, mental, and financial well-being of its victims.
   ____
   ____
5. Rock 'n' roll became popular in the 1950s.
   It has its roots in blues and country music.
   ____
   ____
6. Muhammad Ali changed his name from Cassius Clay when he changed religions.
   He was the most famous athlete of his day.
   ____
   ____

Now rewrite each sentence on your own paper. Make the main idea in each sentence the dependent thought, and change the dependent thought to be the main idea. Then compare your answers with the samples below.

Think about the kind of music you like best and why you like it. For three or four minutes, make a list of the reasons you like that kind of music best. You'll expand your notes into sentences in the Springboard writing exercise.

Sample Warm-up Answers
1. My best friend, who I've known for more than ten years, called me last night. **2.** The most exciting place I've ever been to is Alaska, which is beautiful and wild at the same time. **3.** The family member that I feel closest to is my wife, who is always there when I need her. **4.** Alcoholism, which is a disease, affects the physical, mental, and financial well-being of its victims. Alcoholism, which affects the physical, mental, and financial well-being of its victims, is a disease. **5.** Rock 'n' roll, which became popular in the 1950s, has its roots in blues and country music. Rock 'n' roll, which has its roots in blues and country music, became popular in the 1950s. **6.** Muhammad Ali, who changed his name from Cassius Clay when he changed religions, was the most famous athlete of his day. Muhammad Ali, who was the most famous athlete of his day, changed his name from Cassius Clay when he changed religions.

On the Springboard

Directions: Read this paragraph carefully and then answer the questions that follow it.

(1) Country music is about feelings, but it is also about real life. (2) These feelings and experiences come mainly from the lives of poor, rural southern people, which gave us country music. (3) People who don't like country music put it down by calling it hillbilly music. (4) They don't realize the deep roots that this music has in many other kinds of music, such as gospel, blues, and American folk music.

4. Sentence 2: **These feelings and experiences come mainly from the lives of poor, rural southern people, which gave us country music.**

   Which of the following is the best way to write the underlined portion of this sentence? If you think the original is the best way, choose option (1).

   (1) people, which
   (2) people, who
   (3) people, that

   (1) (2) (3)

5. Sentence 3: **People who don't like country music put it down by calling it hillbilly music.**

   What correction should be made to this sentence?

   (1) insert a comma after who
   (2) replace who with which
   (3) no correction is necessary

   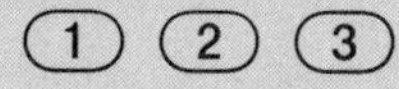

On a fresh sheet of paper, write a composition telling what kind of music you like best and *why* you like it. Use your notes from the Warm-up exercise, but expand them into sentences. Experiment with different ways of making some thoughts dependent on others. If you think of new ideas as you are writing, include them too.

You can check your Springboard multiple-choice answers on page 100. Are you becoming more comfortable and skillful with using dependent thoughts? If you got both answers correct, work with the dependent thoughts in "The Real Thing" that follows. If not, review this section and practice writing more sentences with added information in the form of dependent thoughts.

"The Real Thing"

Directions: Read the paragraph and then answer the items based on it.

(1) Living abroad is totally different from reading about or even visiting a foreign country. (2) Former exchange students number in the hundreds of thousands, and they look back on their experiences fondly. (3) However, most are also quick to say that living in another country was demanding and challenging. (4) Differences between cultures at times overwhelmed students. (5) So did homesickness. (6) They began to succeed when they began to make new friends, which helped them find their way in new surroundings and a new language. (7) It seems that being an exchange student and living with a host family mean much more than just stepping into a scene from a travel poster. (8) Those people who take part in overseas study programs not only master other languages and make new friends. (9) They also learn about themselves and their ability to cope.

6. Sentence 2: **Former exchange students number in the hundreds of thousands, and they look back on their experiences fondly.**

   If you rewrote sentence 2 beginning with

   Former exchange students, who number in the hundreds of thousands,

   the next word should be

   (1) and (2) look (3) they
   (4) which (5) for

   ① ② ③ ④ ⑤

7. Sentences 4 and 5: **Differences between cultures at times overwhelmed students. So did homesickness.**

   The most effective combination of sentences 4 and 5 would include which of the following groups of words?

   (1) students, and so did
   (2) students, yet so did
   (3) cultures, which at times
   (4) cultures and homesickness at times
   (5) So did differences between

   ① ② ③ ④ ⑤

8. Sentence 6: **They began to succeed when they began to make new friends, which helped them find their way in new surroundings and a new language.**

   What correction should be made to this sentence?

   (1) insert a comma after succeed
   (2) remove the comma after friends
   (3) replace which with that
   (4) replace which with who
   (5) insert a comma after surroundings

   ① ② ③ ④ ⑤

9. Sentence 8: **Those people who take part in overseas study programs not only master other languages and make new friends.**

   Which of the following is the best way to write the underlined portion of this sentence? If you think the original is the best way, choose option (1).

   (1) people who
   (2) people, who
   (3) people which
   (4) people, which
   (5) people

   ① ② ③ ④ ⑤

Check your answers on page 105.

Using Noun Phrases to Give More Information

There's a certain kind of noun phrase that you can use to give more information about the person or thing you are writing about. In fact, this noun phrase is really just a shortened form of a dependent thought.

Here's an Example

This is one of the sentences that you worked with in the last Warm-up exercise, with just one difference. Can you spot it?

■ Muhammad Ali**, the most famous athlete of his day,** changed his name from Cassius Clay when he changed religions.

In that sentence, the information after Muhammad Ali's name is just a noun phrase. The subject *who* and the verb *was* are missing.

■ Muhammad Ali, ~~who was~~ the most famous athlete of his day, changed his name from Cassius Clay when he changed religions.

Whenever a dependent thought tells who or what a person or thing is, you have the choice of dropping the subject of the thought (*who* or *which*) and the verb *(is, are, was,* or *were).* That is one way of adding variety to your sentences.

Try It Yourself

Here is a letter from the teacher in a preschool to the parents of one of her students. Two sentences can be combined by making one a noun phrase and placing it within the other sentence. In another sentence, the dependent thought can be shortened to a noun phrase. Can you find where to make these two changes?

■ Raul continues to progress. He recognizes the letters of the alphabet as well as colors and shapes. His ability to count, which was his weakest skill, has improved markedly. Shannon and Peter are two of Raul's friends. They are one year older and love to help him.

The first two sentences are fine. Did you notice the dependent thought in the third sentence? It begins with *which* and a form of the verb *be (was),* followed by a noun phrase. Therefore, you could drop the subject and verb *(which was)* and rewrite the sentence this way: "His ability to count, his weakest skill, has improved markedly."

The next two sentences both give information about Shannon and Peter. They can be combined by picking up the information from the first sentence about who Shannon and Peter are (two of Raul's friends) and making that a noun phrase within a sentence: "Shannon and Peter, two of Raul's friends, are one year older and love to help him."

✓ A Test-Taking Tip

Knowing about noun phrases that add information will help you not only on the GED Writing Skills Test but also on the GED Science Test, the GED Social Studies Test, and the GED Test of Interpreting Literature and the Arts. Very often such a phrase is used to define or explain a difficult or unknown term. Now that you can recognize noun phrases, you can use them as clues to the meanings of unfamiliar words in reading passages on the other GED Tests.

Warm-up

Here are some more of the sentences you worked with in the last Warm-up. Then you added dependent thoughts beginning with *who* or *which.* This time, add a noun phrase. For some of the sentences, you may even be able to use the same information and just omit the subject and verb. Don't forget to use commas to separate the noun phrases.

1. My best friend ______________________ ______________________ called me last night.
2. The movie ______________________ ______________ will be on TV this Friday night.
3. The most exciting place that I've ever been to is ______________, ______________.
4. The family member I feel closest to is my ______________, ______________.

Compare your sentences with those under Sample Warm-up Answers. Were you able to use some of the same information that you did last time? Did you use commas to separate the noun phrases?

Now write five sentences about five persons you know. In each sentence, include a noun phrase that tells who that person is.

Next, write five sentences about things you own, events you've seen, or places you've gone. In each sentence, include a noun phrase that gives added information about the thing, event, or place.

Some people believe that seriously ill people who have little hope of ever recovering should have the right to die. In other words, such people should be able to refuse medicines and artificial means of supporting life. Another belief some people have is that abortion is wrong under any circumstances; these people say that they believe in the "right to life."

Pick one of these beliefs—the right to die or the right to life—and list your thoughts about the issue. Allow yourself at least three minutes for this preparation.

Sample Warm-up Answers
1. My best friend, David Juleen, called me last night. **2.** The movie, the last one made by Steve McQueen, will be on TV this Friday night. **3.** The most exciting place that I've ever been to is Alaska, a beautiful and wild land. **4.** The family member that I feel closest to is my wife, a warm and supportive woman.

On the Springboard

Directions: Read this paragraph carefully and then answer the questions that follow it.

(1) In the past, many animals died or suffered needlessly because a veterinarian was unable to give them medicine. (2) For example, Gargantua was a famous circus gorilla. (3) He died of pneumonia complicated by aching wisdom teeth. (4) He might have lived longer, but no animal doctor could get near him. (5) Now a special device, it is a gun with a needle instead of a bullet, is used to quiet a sick animal. (6) The needle is fired into the animal's hide. (7) When the drug has taken effect, the doctor can treat the animal.

6. Sentence 2 and 3: **For example, Gargantua was a famous circus gorilla. He died of pneumonia complicated by aching wisdom teeth.**

   The most effective combination of sentences 2 and 3 would include which of the following groups of words?

   (1) was a famous circus gorilla and died
   (2) Gargantua, a famous circus gorilla, died
   (3) Gargantua died of pneumonia

   ① ② ③

7. Sentence 5: **Now a special device, it is a gun with a needle instead of a bullet, is used to quiet a sick animal.**

   Which of the following is the best way to write the underlined portion of this sentence? If you think the original is the best way, choose option (1).

   (1) device, it is a gun
   (2) device is a gun
   (3) device, a gun

   ① ② ③

Pick one of these topics and write down your thoughts on the issue: the right to die or the right to life. Expand the ideas you listed in the Warm-up into complete sentences. Relate your ideas using some of the ways you've practiced so far. If noun phrases come in handy, be sure to use them.

You can check your Springboard answers on page 100. You are learning some fairly complex sentence structures now, so you want to be sure you understand them fully before you go on. If you need to, review this section before you attempt "The Real Thing" that follows. You also might want to go back to the Springboard writing topic that you didn't choose the first time. Practice writing sentences with noun phrases and dependent thoughts about it. Be sure to take the time to think about the topic and list ideas before you begin to write.

The Real Thing

Directions: Read the paragraph and then answer the items based on it.

(1) Roller coasters, the most frightening rides at amusement parks also have the longest lines of riders. (2) Several parks have five or more roller coasters, and each one wilder than the next. (3) The excitement of the rides is suggested by the names of the more popular coasters, such as the Beast the Demon, and the Screaming Eagle. (4) The Bat, at Kings Island near Cincinnati, was the first roller coaster with the cars suspended under the tracks. (5) When the cars turn a corner, they swing from side to side. (6) A very exciting ride, the Jetscream at Six Flags over Mid-America, carries you twenty turns in eleven seconds. (7) At Great America near Chicago, you can ride the American Eagle and reach a top speed of sixty miles an hour. (8) The Mighty Canadian Mine Buster is a roller coaster in Toronto. (9) It is as thrilling as any ride in the United States.

10. Sentence 1: **Roller coasters, the most frightening rides at amusement parks also have the longest lines of riders.**

What correction should be made to this sentence?

(1) remove the comma after coasters
(2) replace the comma with the word are
(3) insert a comma after rides
(4) insert the word they after parks
(5) insert a comma after parks

(1) (2) (3) (4) (5)

11. Sentence 2: **Several parks have five or more roller coasters, and each one wilder than the next.**

Which of the following is the best way to write the underlined portion of this sentence? If you think the original is the best way, choose option (1).

(1) each one wilder
(2) each one who is wilder
(3) each one which is wilder
(4) each one that is wilder
(5) each one is wilder

(1) (2) (3) (4) (5)

12. Sentence 3: **The excitement of the rides is suggested by the names of the more popular coasters, such as the Beast the Demon, and the Screaming Eagle.**

What correction should be made to this sentence?

(1) replace The with Because the
(2) insert the word that after rides
(3) remove the word is
(4) insert a comma after Beast
(5) no correction is necessary

(1) (2) (3) (4) (5)

13. Sentence 6: **A very exciting ride, the Jetscream at Six Flags over Mid-America, carries you twenty turns in eleven seconds.**

If you rewrote sentence 6 beginning with

Carrying you twenty turns in eleven seconds, the Jetscream at Six Flags over

the next words should be

(1) Mid-America is a
(2) Mid-America, a
(3) Mid-America, carries
(4) Mid-America, and it is
(5) Mid-America because it is

(1) (2) (3) (4) (5)

14. Sentences 8 and 9: **The Mighty Canadian Mine Buster is a roller coaster in Toronto. It is as thrilling as any ride in the United States.**

The most effective combination of sentences 8 and 9 would include which of the following groups of words?

(1) Buster, a roller coaster in Toronto, is
(2) Buster, who is a roller coaster
(3) in Toronto yet it is as thrilling
(4) It is a roller coaster in Toronto
(5) Being a roller coaster in Toronto

(1) (2) (3) (4) (5)

Check your answers and record your score for the entire lesson on page 106.

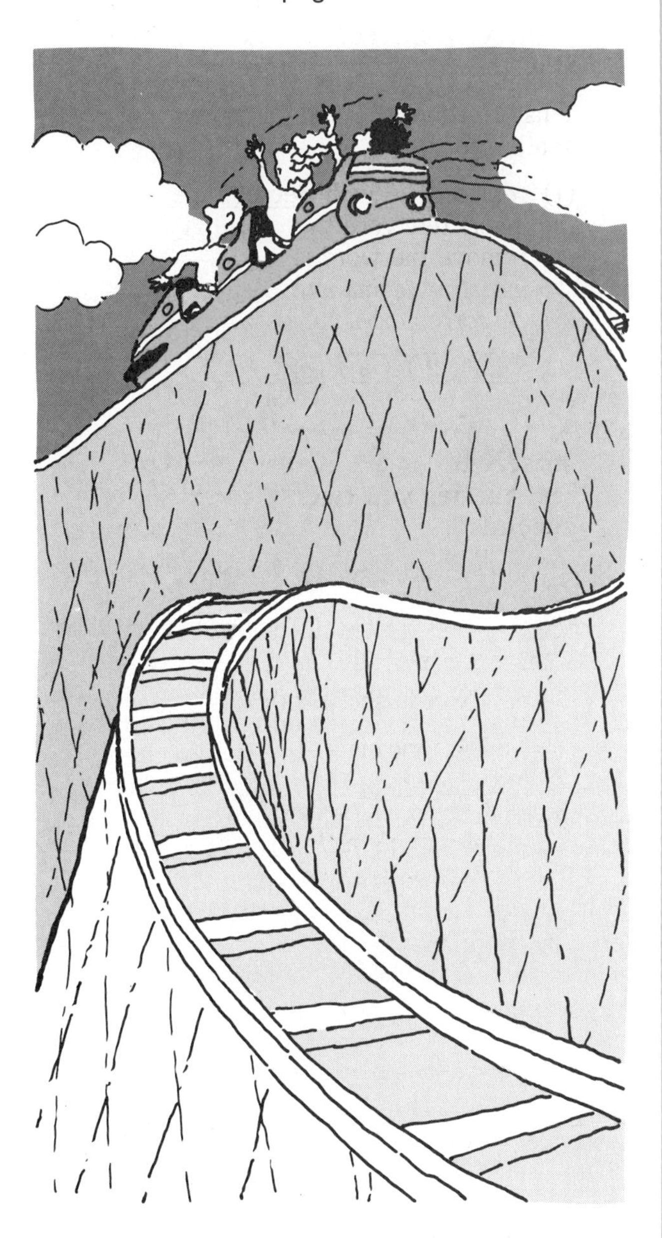

LESSON 9

Going Too Far

Run-on Sentences

By now you are writing sentences that have many parts. They may be quite long. This can lead to two common problems that many writers face. The first is called a run-on sentence because the writer "runs on" beyond the point where the sentence should end. The result is two or more complete thoughts written as one sentence.

The problem with detecting run-on sentences is that they may sound fine when you read them. You need to learn how to spot and fix run-on sentences in your own writing and in paragraphs on the GED Test.

Coming to Terms

run-on a mistake in which two or more complete thoughts are written as one sentence

Here's an Example

The writing sample below is from a GED student's paragraph on her family before she had a chance to revise it. The places where two thoughts are running together are in **bold.**

■ The most interesting members of my family are my twins, Karen and **Kevin they** are five years old and always into something. My mother and uncle were **twins therefore** I wasn't too surprised when the doctor heard two heartbeats. Raising twins can be **difficult it's** also a lot of fun.

This passage appears to have three sentences, but actually has six complete thoughts. Look at the first "sentence." The words *members* and *are* are the subject and verb of the first complete thought. The words *Karen and Kevin* are a noun phrase that gives more information about *twins.* The word *they* begins an entirely new and complete thought; in fact, it is the subject of that thought. The student chose to split the ideas with a period and a capital letter.

■ The most interesting members of my family are my twins, Karen and **Kevin. They** are five years old and always into something.

The next run-on sentence has two independent thoughts connected only by the word *therefore.* You've already had practice in combining and introducing by using a long connecting word such as *therefore.* You can see that there are two ways to correct this run-on.

■ My mother and uncle were twins**; therefore,** I wasn't too surprised when the doctor heard two heartbeats.

My mother and uncle were twins**. Therefore,** I wasn't too surprised when the doctor heard two heartbeats.

Did you also recognize that the second independent thought ("I wasn't too surprised") had a dependent thought that went with it ("when the doctor heard two heartbeats")?

Although it is easy to run on long sentences, it is not the length of a sentence that makes it a run-on. Some very long sentences are well written and correct. Some very short sentences are run on. Look at the last "sentence" of the paragraph. It contains two fairly short yet independent thoughts. The student decided to fix this run-on by inserting a comma and a short connecting word between the two thoughts.

■ Raising twins can be difficult**, yet** it is also a lot of fun.

Of course, you could use any of the ways you've studied about combining ideas to fix any of these sentences. For example, look at a few other ways that the first run-on could be fixed.

■ The most interesting members of my family are my twins, Karen and Kevin, who are five years old and always into something.

The most interesting members of my family are my twins, Karen and Kevin, because they are five years old and always into something.

Because my twins, Karen and Kevin, are five years old and always into something, they are the most interesting members of my family.

My twins, Karen and Kevin, the most interesting members of my family, are five years old and always into something.

My five-year-old twins, Karen and Kevin, are always into something, so they are the most interesting members of my family.

✓ A Test-Taking Tip

You've learned that there are usually a number of ways to write a particular thought as a complete sentence. Some ways may be better than others, but sometimes two or three ways are equally good. On the multiple-choice questions on the GED Writing Skills Test, you will not be asked to choose between two perfectly acceptable answers. One answer will always be clearly better than the other four. Apply what you know about sentence structure, and you should be able to pick the right one.

Try It Yourself

A town council member took notes during a meeting. Her secretary had to correct them for a written report. Be the secretary. Watch for run-ons. Decide how you would fix them.

■ Ben Goldberg of 2399 Third Street requested a stop sign at the corner of Third and Main it has been the scene of several minor accidents. Councilman Ferrara promised to look into it. A man on Maple Street is building a garage he says it is for private use. However, it looks like a business to the neighbors they are angry and upset. The mayor asked me to take a look at it by next week.

As secretary, how did you straighten out these hastily written notes? Did you see the spot in the first "sentence" where one independent thought ended and another one began? "At the corner of Third and Main" is a descriptive phrase that ends one complete thought. The word *it* begins a new and independent thought. You could fix the run-on this way: "Ben Goldberg of 2399 Third Street requested a stop sign at the corner of Third and Main. It has been the scene of several minor accidents."

The next sentence is correct. Could you tell?

In the third "sentence," you may have noticed that a second complete thought starts with *he.* Did you simply capitalize and punctuate, like this: "A man on Maple Street is building a garage. He says it is for private use." Or perhaps you thought a semicolon would be better: "A man on Maple Street is building a garage; he says it is for private use."

The next "sentence" is also a run-on. It can be corrected by using a short connecting word and a comma to show the relationship between the thoughts: "However, it looks like a business to the neighbors, and they are angry and upset." Did you choose that way or some other way?

Warm-up

There are three run-on sentences in the following paragraph. Rewrite the paragraph and fix them.

In some European countries, you can't live in a house with a number 13 address the address does not exist. Instead, the address 12 is followed by 12½ and then by 14. Many office buildings in the United States skip the thirteenth floor some airlines and sports arenas omit thirteen as a seat number. Athletes may refuse to wear the number thirteen on their sports uniforms. Some people will not start a trip on the thirteenth day of any month others will not buy or use thirteen of anything.

____

Compare your rewritten paragraph with the Sample Warm-up Answer. Remember that there is often more than one way to fix a run-on. On the lines that follow, rewrite the three run-ons again. This time, fix them in a way that is different from the way you chose the first time and from the way they are shown in the Sample Warm-up Answer.

1. ______________________________________

2. ______________________________________

3. ______________________________________

Because we live in a democracy, a long and often complex process is needed for an idea to become law. If you had the power to snap your fingers and make one of your ideas the law of the land, what would it be? Why would you choose to make it a law? List your thoughts on the matter for about five minutes. If you are having trouble thinking of ideas, try free writing. Write down anything you think of when you hear the word *law.* That may help you think of your own idea for a law. You will use your notes in the Springboard exercise.

A Test-Taking Tip

You learned that the word *that* in the secondary connecting term *so that* is sometimes omitted. In speech and informal writing, the word *that* may also be omitted when it is being used as a connecting word to identify a person or thing (for example, "He told me to take the one *(that)* he had left on his desk") or when it is introducing another kind of dependent thought (for example, "He told me *(that)* they were leaving at five").

You may find such a sentence in a paragraph on the GED Writing Skills Test. If a sentence has two thoughts and looks as if it might be a run-on, first try inserting *that* between the thoughts to check the meaning of the sentence. If the sentence makes sense with *that,* it is all right. If not, you may be dealing with a run-on.

In your GED essay, you might find it helpful to include *that* to connect thoughts even when it would be okay to omit it. That way, you will be keeping the relationship between your thoughts clear in your mind as well as in your writing.

Sample Warm-up Answer
In some European countries, you can't live in a house with a number 13 address; the address does not exist. Instead, the address 12 is followed by 12½ and then by 14. Many office buildings in the United States skip the thirteenth floor, and some airlines and sports arenas omit thirteen as a seat number. Athletes may refuse to wear the number thirteen on their sports uniforms. Some people will not start a trip on the thirteenth day of any month, while others will not buy or use thirteen of anything.

On the Springboard

Directions: Read this paragraph carefully and then answer the questions that follow it.

(1) Even though there are more Americans needing health care every year hospitals have been closing all over the United States. (2) Hospital care has become very expensive. (3) Many insurance plans limit the number of days that they will pay for one person's stay in the hospital. (4) As a result, hospitals are releasing patients earlier. (5) According to many experts, people wait longer to enter hospitals they leave sooner. (6) Home nursing care and halfway houses are being developed to fill the needs of people who are discharged while still needing help and care.

1. Sentence 1: **Even though there are more Americans needing health care every year hospitals have been closing all over the United States.**

   Which of the following is the best way to write the underlined portion of this sentence? If you think the original is the best way, choose option (1).

   (1) year hospitals
   (2) year. Hospitals
   (3) year, hospitals

   (1) (2) (3)

2. Sentence 5: **According to many experts, people wait longer to enter hospitals they leave sooner.**

   Which of the following is the best way to write the underlined portion of this sentence? If you think the original is the best way, choose option (1).

   (1) hospitals they
   (2) hospitals, and they
   (3) hospitals; therefore, they

   (1) (2) (3)

3. Sentence 6: **Home nursing care and halfway houses are being developed to fill the needs of people who are discharged while still needing help and care.**

   What correction should be made to this sentence?

   (1) insert a semicolon after people
   (2) insert a semicolon after discharged
   (3) no correction is necessary

   (1) (2) (3)

If you had the power to make one law, what would it be? Why would you make it? Take out your notes from the Warm-up exercise and use them to answer those two questions. Expand your notes into complete sentences, and, of course, make sure you fix any run-on sentences that you may write.

See if you correctly spotted and fixed all the errors in the Springboard paragraph by checking your answers on page 100. If you don't have a problem with run-ons, go on to "The Real Thing" that follows. If you do have a problem spotting run-ons in your own or in someone else's writing, take the time to review this section before you go on. Practice noting the subjects and verbs in the independent and dependent thoughts you read in this book and write in the exercises.

“The Real Thing”

Directions: Read the paragraph and then answer the items based on it.

(1) In the Northern Hemisphere, there have long been celebrations in late December. (2) As the sun moves farther north in the sky. (3) People have celebrated its return and the lengthening of the days. (4) Yarol was the god of light and warmth of early European people, and they used to light the largest log they could find for him. (5) They were trying to get the sun to rise high in the sky so that it would catch fire from the log and warm the earth again. (6) It seemed to work every year. (7) This ritual became the Christmas celebration of burning the Yule (Yarol) log. (8) Jewish people celebrate the Feast of Lights at this time they are celebrating a miracle in their temple long ago. (9) These celebrations have deep religious meaning, yet they serve another purpose as well. (10) Remembering that the days are growing longer helps people stay cheerful in the frigid days of January.

1. Sentences 2 and 3: **As the sun moves farther north in the sky. People have celebrated its return and the lengthening of the days.**

   Which of the following is the best way to write the underlined portion of these sentences? If you think the original is the best way, choose option (1).

   (1) sky. People
   (2) sky; people
   (3) sky, people
   (4) sky people
   (5) sky, so people

   (1) (2) (3) (4) (5)

2. Sentence 4: **Yarol was the god of light and warmth of early European people, and they used to light the largest log they could find for him.**

   If you rewrote sentence 4 beginning with

   Early European people used to light the largest log they could find for Yarol,

   the next word should be

   (1) their (2) was (3) he
   (4) which (5) because

   (1) (2) (3) (4) (5)

3. Sentences 6 and 7: **It seemed to work every year. This ritual became the Christmas celebration of burning the Yule (Yarol) log.**

   Which of the following is the best way to write the underlined portion of these sentences? If you think the original is the best way, choose option (1).

   (1) year. This
   (2) year this
   (3) year, but this
   (4) year; nevertheless, this
   (5) year even when this

   (1) (2) (3) (4) (5)

4. Sentence 8: **Jewish people celebrate the Feast of Lights at this time they are celebrating a miracle in their temple long ago.**

   What correction should be made to this sentence?

   (1) insert who after people
   (2) insert which after Lights
   (3) insert a semicolon after time
   (4) insert a comma after miracle
   (5) no correction is necessary

   (1) (2) (3) (4) (5)

5. Sentence 9: **These celebrations have deep religious meaning, yet they serve another purpose as well.**

   If you rewrote sentence 9 beginning with

   Having deep religious meaning,

   the next words should be

   (1) serving another purpose
   (2) yet they serve
   (3) as well as serving
   (4) these celebrations serve
   (5) and another purpose

   (1) (2) (3) (4) (5)

Check your answers on page 106.

Comma Splices

The second way to "go too far" in writing a sentence is to combine two independent thoughts by putting a comma between them without a main connecting word to go with it. A comma just isn't strong enough for that job. Such a "sentence" is sometimes called a **comma splice.** You can fix comma splices in the same ways you used to fix run-on sentences.

Coming to Terms

comma splice two independent thoughts joined only by a comma

Here's an Example

Below is a description of a dog found in a dog owner's manual. The commas that are causing comma splices are in **bold.**

■ Newfoundlands are marvelous, giant dogs**,** they were first bred by the early Canadians. Because its coat is oily, a Newfoundland's fur keeps water away from its body. The dog is therefore a good hunting dog**,** it can retrieve ducks from the coldest water. It is also famous for saving people from drowning. However, Newfoundlands are gentle giants**,** they do not make good watch dogs. In fact, they are wonderful with children**,** they make good guardians and good friends.

There are two independent thoughts separated only by a comma in the first "sentence." The subject and verb of the first thought are *Newfoundlands are;* the subject and verb of the second thought are *they* and *were bred.* The writer should have used different punctuation between the two (a semicolon or a period and capital letter). Or he could have used the connecting word *that* to combine the two thoughts by making one help identify the other.

■ Newfoundlands are marvelous, giant dogs **that** were first bred by the early Canadians.

In the second sentence the comma is *not* causing a comma splice; it is needed to separate the introductory dependent thought *(Because its coat is oily)* from the dependent one.

The third sentence is a comma splice that can probably best be fixed by using a semicolon or a period and a capital letter.

■ The dog is therefore a good hunting dog**;** it can retrieve ducks from the coldest water.

The dog is therefore a good hunting dog**. I**t can retrieve ducks from the coldest water.

The fifth sentence is a comma splice. Since the two independent thoughts have a cause-and-effect relationship, a connecting word that shows that relationship would be a good idea. The writer could have used *consequently,* along with a semicolon and comma, of course.

■ However, Newfoundlands are gentle giants**; consequently,** they do not make good watch dogs.

The last comma splice also has a cause-and-effect relationship. The second thought is a reason for the first, so a connecting word like *because* would be appropriate. It can be used in between the thoughts, as here.

■ In fact, they are wonderful with children **because** they make good guardians and good friends.

Or it could be used at the beginning, like this.

■ In fact, **because** they make good guardians and good friends, they are wonderful with children.

Try It Yourself

Here is another selection from the dog owner's manual. This one gives a few helpful guidelines on training a dog. See if you can find the four comma splices. Decide how *you* would fix them.

■ Once your dog is used to wearing a collar and leash, you can start to teach it such commands as "sit" and "heel." Dogs respond especially well to short, clipped sounds, you should pronounce your command clearly and distinctly. Don't try to teach more than one command at a time, that will only confuse the dog. A dog is like a person, it learns best when it gets immediate feedback. Therefore, praise your dog immediately after a desired action, correct it immediately after a wrong one. Dogs naturally want to please their owners, so praise usually works better than punishment.

Is the first sentence a comma splice? There are two thoughts in the sentence, but the first is dependent on the second. It begins with the connecting word *once.* Therefore, the first sentence is all right.

What about the second sentence? The comma separating the descriptive words *short* and *clipped* is correct (if you don't remember why, you might want to review Lesson 2). However, the second comma is not. Before it, there is an independent thought whose subject and verb are *Dogs respond.* After it, there is an independent thought whose subject and verb are *you should pronounce.* Since the sentence needs a connecting word to show the cause-and-effect relationship between the two ideas, you could have corrected it, among other ways, like this: "Dogs respond especially well to short, clipped sounds; therefore, you should pronounce your command clearly and distinctly."

What about the next sentence? Did you spot the two independent thoughts with only a comma between them? (The subject of the first thought is the understood *you.*) Did you decide to use another cause-and-effect connecting word such as this: "Don't try to teach more than one command at a time because that will only confuse the dog."

Now look at the fourth sentence. Again there are two independent thoughts. The subject and verb of the first are *dog is;* the subject and verb of the second are *it learns.* (Did you notice that *when it gets immediate feedback* is a secondary thought that is dependent on *it learns best,* so it is written correctly?) You could have decided to fix the comma splice with a different mark of punctuation, such as a semicolon: "A dog is like a person; it learns best when it gets immediate feedback."

Did you spot the fourth and final comma splice in the fifth sentence? The understood *you* is the subject of both independent thoughts; *praise* and *correct* are the verbs. Probably the best way you could choose to correct the sentence would be to leave the comma and insert the main connecting word *and:* "Therefore, praise your dog immediately after a desired action, and correct it immediately after a wrong one."

If you thought that the last sentence was a comma splice, you probably forgot that *so* is a main connecting word that can be used with a comma to connect two independent thoughts. The last sentence is fine.

Warm-up

The following account of a baseball game has four comma splices in it. Rewrite the paragraph on the lines below. Fix each comma splice you find. Try to use different ways to correct the splices.

The catcher signaled for a fastball, the pitcher went into his windup. Chewing nervously on his cigar, the manager glanced skyward. A dark gray cloud began blocking the sun. The batter hit a low line drive, the runner at second took off. An argument erupted at home plate over the umpire's call. The angry baserunner kicked dust at the umpire, he was tossed out of the game. Just then the rain came down in torrents, the game had to be called.

____

____

____

____

____

____

____

____

____

____

You can compare your rewritten paragraph with the Sample Warm-up Answer below. Did you find all four comma splices?

Now rewrite each of the corrected sentences on your own paper. This time, choose a way to fix each that is different from the way you chose the first time.

Think again about why you are studying to take the GED Test. If possible, go back to the notes you used to write on that topic in the first lesson. Add to them if you think of any new ideas. Don't look at your actual writing from that lesson, however. You'll use your new set of notes to complete the next Springboard writing exercise.

Sample Warm-up Answer
The catcher signaled for a fastball, and the pitcher went into his windup. Chewing nervously on his cigar, the manager glanced skyward. A dark gray cloud began blocking the sun. As soon as the batter hit a low line drive, the runner at second took off. An argument erupted at home plate over the umpire's call. The angry baserunner kicked dust at the umpire; consequently, he was tossed out of the game. Just then the rain came down in torrents; the game had to be called.

On the Springboard

Directions: Read this paragraph carefully and then answer the questions that follow it.

(1) Circuses are not as common as they once were. (2) Before the days of television and Disneyland, people waited eagerly for circuses to come. (3) Now people are used to spectacular things. (4) We can watch rockets take off for space, we can see deep into the ocean with sonar, and we can travel inside the human body with cameras. (5) Circuses seem quaint and old-fashioned to some, many people still turn out when the circus comes to town.

4. Sentence 2: **Before the days of television and Disneyland, people waited eagerly for circuses to come.**

   Which of the following is the best way to write the underlined portion of this sentence? If you think the original is the best way, choose option (1).

   (1) Disneyland, people
   (2) Disneyland people
   (3) Disneyland. People

   1 2 3

5. Sentence 4: **We can watch rockets take off for space, we can see deep into the ocean with sonar, and we can travel inside the human body with cameras.**

   Which of the following is the best way to write the underlined portion of this sentence? If you think the original is the best way, choose option (1).

   (1) space, we
   (2) space, and we
   (3) space and we

   1 2 3

6. Sentence 5: **Circuses seem quaint and old-fashioned to some, many people still turn out when the circus comes to town.**

   What correction should be made to this sentence?

   (1) remove the comma
   (2) insert yet after the comma
   (3) insert a comma after out

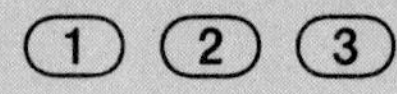

Write again about why you are studying to take the GED Test. Use your notes from the last Warm-up and, if you like, from the Warm-up in the first lesson. Don't look back, however, at the composition you wrote for Lesson 1. Instead, write a new composition. Try to use some of the things you've studied about combining and inserting information in sentences. After you've finished, compare the two pieces of writing. Can you see an improvement in your writing? Can you spot some areas where you still need more practice?

Check your Springboard multiple-choice answers with those on page 100. Did you understand why one sentence was a comma splice and the others were not? If so, good; try noting and fixing the comma splices and other errors that occur in "The Real Thing" that follows. If you had difficulty with the Springboard questions, review this section on comma splices before you go on. Try analyzing some of the sentences in this book to see when commas and connecting words are used.

“The Real Thing”

Directions: Read the paragraph and then answer the items based on it.

(1) Bombarded daily by food ads many consumers often find it difficult to make sensible, nutritious choices. (2) The wise shopper knows about nutrition, and uses that knowledge to plan healthful menus. (3) One of the most reliable sources of information on food can be the product label itself it often lists the food's ingredients. (4) The label may also tell the consumer how long the food has been on the shelf and the date by which it must be sold. (5) In some instances, such information is put there voluntarily by the manufacturers, federal law requires it in other cases. (6) The amount of information varies, but all food labels must contain at least the name of the product, the net weight, and the name and location of the manufacturer, packer, or distributor. (7) On canned food, the net weight includes the liquid in which the product is packed. (8) In addition, some manufacturers include nutritional information on the label. (9) They list such things as the vitamin, mineral, fat, and fiber content of the food.

6. Sentence 1: **Bombarded daily by food ads many consumers often find it difficult to make sensible, nutritious choices.**

   Which of the following is the best way to write the underlined portion of this sentence? If you think the original is the best way, choose option (1).

   (1) ads many (2) ads, many
   (3) ads. Many (4) ads; therefore, many
   (5) ads, and many

   (1) (2) (3) (4) (5)

7. Sentence 2: **The wise shopper knows about nutrition, and uses that knowledge to plan healthful menus.**

   What correction should be made to this sentence?

   (1) insert who after shopper
   (2) remove the comma after nutrition
   (3) change uses to using
   (4) insert a comma after knowledge
   (5) change to plan to plans

   (1) (2) (3) (4) (5)

8. Sentence 3: **One of the most reliable sources of information on food can be the product label itself it often lists the food's ingredients.**

   Which of the following is the best way to write the underlined portion of this sentence? If you think the original is the best way, choose option (1).

   (1) itself it
   (2) itself, it
   (3) itself and it
   (4) itself because it
   (5) itself; consequently, it

   (1) (2) (3) (4) (5)

9. Sentence 5: **In some instances, such information is put there voluntarily by the manufacturers, federal law requires it in other cases.**

   What correction should be made to this sentence?

   (1) remove the word is
   (2) insert a comma after voluntarily
   (3) insert the word but before federal
   (4) change requires to requiring
   (5) insert a comma after it

   (1) (2) (3) (4) (5)

10. Sentences 8 and 9: **In addition, some manufacturers include nutritional information on the label. They list such things as the vitamin, mineral, fat, and fiber content of the food.**

    The most effective combination of sentences 8 and 9 would include which of the following groups of words?

    (1) on the label, and they list
    (2) In addition, they include nutritional
    (3) on the label; consequently, they
    (4) some manufacturers include and list
    (5) information on the label, such as the

    (1) (2) (3) (4) (5)

Check your answers and record your score for the entire lesson on pages 106–107.

Answers: On the Springboard

1 Sentence Sense

Writing Complete Sentences
(page 35)

1. (3) *That the earliest telegraphs were drums and smoke signals from fires* is a fragment.

2. (1) The original is the correct way.

3. (3) The verb *given* is always used with an extra verb, like *have.* Without *have,* sentence 6 is a fragment.

People who write history believe that the earliest telegraphs were drums and smoke signals from fires. The ancient Greeks are thought to have invented the modern telegraph. They were the first to link alphabet letters to signals. The word "telegraph" itself can be traced back to a signaling system that Claude Chappe established in France in the 1790s. Since then, inventors have given the world today's telegraph, telephone, teletype, television, and many other communication breakthroughs.

2 Adding Details

Writing Descriptive Phrases
(page 43)

1. (3) *After conducting a survey, researchers found that salespeople were the happiest workers.* The verbal phrase *After conducting a survey* describes something the researchers (not the salespeople) did.

2. (2) *Proud of their work and of their role in the economy, salespeople believe in helping people.* Salespeople are proud of two things: *their work* and *their role in the economy.* Option (2) smoothly combines these two things.

3. (3) No error.

Who are the most satisfied employees? After conducting a survey, researchers found that salespeople were the happiest workers. Proud of their work and of their role in the economy, salespeople believe in helping people. In addition, they get instant feedback on successful efforts. A confident, determined salesperson can make good money and enjoy doing it.

3 Pairing Subjects

Connecting Subjects with *And*
(page 47)

1. (3) Don't put a comma between two subjects *("star-crossed" lovers and colorful characters).* Option (2) creates a fragment.

2. (2) Subjects joined by *and* are considered plural and must match with a plural verb *(were).*

3. (3) *For many, Romeo and Juliet have become the symbols of young lovers defeated by an old feud.* To avoid repetition, the two subjects *(Romeo and Juliet)* were combined. Notice that three words in the sentence were changed to their plural form to match *Romeo and Juliet: have, symbols, lovers.*

Countless movies, plays, books, and songs throb with stories of passionate lovers. Some of these "star-crossed" lovers and colorful characters have gone down in history. Rhett Butler and Scarlett O'Hara were two such romantic characters. For many, Romeo and Juliet have become the symbols of young lovers defeated by an old feud. Modern Cleopatras still lose everything for the men they love. And, like Samson, men blinded by love are double-crossed by their Delilahs.

Connecting Subjects with *Or* and *Nor*
(page 50)

4. (2) *Friends* is the subject closer to the verb. Therefore, *have* is the correct verb.

5. (2) *In many cases, personal ads or a dating service helps arrange the first meeting.* For a smooth sentence, you should combine the two subjects *(ads, service).* Remember, though, that the verb always matches the subject closer to it, which is *service.*

Blind dates have become big business recently. Neither family nor friends have to find dates for single people anymore. There must be fifty ways to meet someone new. In many cases, personal ads or a dating service helps arrange the first meeting. There are also singles bars, dial-a-date businesses, marriage brokers, and singles clubs. Finding a date these days takes either money or nerve but not help from relatives.

4 Pairing Verb Forms

Connecting Main Verbs
(page 53)

1. (3) *Before World War II, most Americans neither knew of the martial arts nor were impressed with the fighting ability of anyone who was not American.* Option (3) pairs closely related verbs *(knew, were impressed)* with the same subject *(Americans).*

2. (3) Neither *and* nor *or* shows the correct relationship between the verbs *was* and *had earned.*

Before World War II, most Americans neither knew of the martial arts nor were impressed with the fighting ability of anyone who was not American. Soldiers coming home from the Pacific brought information about karate and other martial arts with them. In recent years, people of all ages and sizes practice martial arts and study the philosophy of Asian disciplines. One such woman over eighty years old was in the news recently. She had earned a black belt in karate.

Connecting Other Verb Forms
(page 57)

3. (2) *Macramé, or decorative knotwork, has a long history, starting in the Middle East in the 1200s and spreading from there into Europe during the 1600s.* Option (2) is the best choice because the two verbals (*starting* and *spreading*) have the same ending.

4. (3) Option (3) is correct because *soothe* and *help* are parallel. It is not necessary to put another *to* in front of *help.*

5. (3) No error.

Macramé, or decorative knotwork, has a long history, starting in the Middle East in the 1200s and spreading from there into Europe during the 1600s. Sailors' and fishermen's knots formed the basic patterns for macramé. In addition to producing handcrafts, tying knots was found to soothe nerves and help people think more clearly. Famous heads of state such as Winston Churchill and Charles de Gaulle relaxed by knotting and knitting.

5 Making Lists

Writing About Three or More
(page 61)

1. (3) In lists, commas are used only after each item on the list and not after *and.*

2. (1) *Horseshoes, four-leaf clovers, and rabbits' feet are considered good luck.* Option (1) correctly combines the three items that are considered good luck.

3. (3) *Some players may wear "lucky" socks, eat a certain meal, or run onto the field a certain way to show they are superstitious.* Notice that option (3) creates a smoothly flowing sentence with three parallel verbs in the list: *wear, eat, run.* It is not necessary to repeat *may* in front of *eat* and *run.*

Humans tend to be superstitious. Some old-fashioned superstitions involve black cats, Friday the thirteenth, broken mirrors, and spilled salt. Horseshoes, four-leaf clovers, and rabbits' feet are considered good luck. Athletes are often particularly superstitious. Some players may wear "lucky" socks, eat a certain meal, or run onto the field a certain way to show they are superstitious.

6 Combining Complete Thoughts

Using Commas and Connecting Words
(page 66)

1. (3) The ideas in the two sentences are so closely related that they should be joined with *and* rather than remain two separate sentences.

2. (3) *A smart house is a safer house, for the new wiring system virtually eliminates electrical fires. For* is the correct connecting word because the second idea causes the first. In other words, the new wiring system causes the house to be safer.

There is a brand-new house on the market called a "smart house," and it is expected to take over the construction industry in the near future. A smart house has an air conditioner and a security system that can be turned on by telephone. Anything plugged into the house's wiring system can be programmed to go on and off automatically. A smart house is a safer house, for the new wiring system virtually eliminates electrical fires.

Using Semicolons
(page 70)

3. (3) *Children enjoy it in milk and candy bars; however, the taste of chocolate doesn't appeal just to the young. However* expresses the contrasting relationship between children liking chocolate and adults liking chocolate.

4. (2) Remember to use a comma between two complete sentences joined by *and.*

Do you know anyone who hates chocolate? Children enjoy it in milk and candy bars; however, the taste of chocolate doesn't appeal just to the young. Adults crave chocolate too. On cold days we drink hot chocolate to keep warm, and on hot days we cool off with chocolate sundaes. Chocolate is disastrous for diets; nevertheless, it sneaks its way into many of them.

7 Combining Unequal Ideas

Placing a Secondary Idea at the Beginning
(page 74)

1. (2) *Although many Americans do not realize it, the federal income tax did not exist until 1913.* The only connecting word you need in this sentence is *Although.*

2. (3) No error.

3. (3) *Because the government needed funds to build weapons for World War II* cannot stand alone as a sentence. Since it is an introductory dependent thought, option (3) is correct.

Although many Americans do not realize it, the federal income tax did not exist until 1913. In that year, the Sixteenth Amendment was added to the Constitution; it gave Congress the right to tax private incomes. However, it wasn't until 1942 that the income tax first began to reach into the pocket of the average citizen. Because the government needed funds to build weapons for World War II, Congress raised the tax and allowed it to be withheld from employees' paychecks. A whole generation of workers has never known what it is like to bring home all the money they have earned.

Placing a Secondary Idea at the End
(page 78)

4. (3) *The ability to read is vital in a democracy because voters must be informed in order to vote intelligently. Because* is a logical connecting word to use since it shows why reading is vital.

5. (1) Nothing is wrong with the original sentence.

The ability to read is vital in a democracy because voters must be informed in order to vote intelligently. Many American adults, however, are illiterate. Illiteracy will remain a serious problem as long as we continue to ignore it. We must begin to solve this problem if we hope to have informed citizens voting.

8 Placing Information Within Sentences

Using Dependent Thoughts to Identify Nouns
(page 81)

1. (2) *The neighbor who is walking his dog may be helping himself as much as his pet.* The verb *is walking* correctly describes the neighbor's action.

2. (1) Nothing is wrong with the original sentence.

3. (3) *Consequently* is the correct spelling.

The neighbor who is walking his dog may be helping himself as much as his pet. In addition, the habit of stroking your cat under its chin might actually add a few years to your own life. According to researchers, pets can have a positive effect on their owners' health, both mental and physical. Pets offer companionship that can ease a person's loneliness. Petting an animal reduces anxiety and depression, lowers blood pressure, and consequently increases the chances for a longer, happier life.

Using Dependent Thoughts to Give More Information
(page 84)

4. (2) *Who* is the correct connecting word because it refers to people.

5. (3) No error. A comma is not used after a connecting word like *who.*

Country music is about feelings, but it is also about real life. These feelings and experiences come mainly from the lives of poor, rural southern people, who gave us country music. People who don't like country music put it down by calling it hillbilly music. They don't realize the deep roots that this music has in many other kinds of music, such as gospel, blues, and American folk music.

Using Noun Phrases to Give More Information
(page 87)

6. (2) *For example, Gargantua, a famous circus gorilla, died of pneumonia complicated by aching wisdom teeth.* Option (2) is the best revision because the information in the first sentence was reduced to the descriptive phrase, *a famous circus gorilla.* Option (3) omits the necessary information about Gargantua's being a famous circus gorilla.

7. (3) It is unnecessary to use *it* and *is* because they are repeated information.

In the past, many animals died or suffered needlessly because a veterinarian was unable to give them medicine. For example, Gargantua, a famous circus gorilla, died of pneumonia complicated by aching wisdom teeth. He might have lived longer, but no animal doctor could get near him. Now a special device, a gun with a needle instead of a bullet, is used to quiet a sick animal. The needle is fired into the animal's hide. When the drug has taken effect, the doctor can treat the animal.

9 Going Too Far

Run-on Sentences
(page 92)

1. (3) A comma is needed after the introductory dependent thought.

2. (2) The comma and the connecting word *and* correctly join the two independent thoughts.

3. (3) No error.

Even though there are more Americans needing health care every year, hospitals have been closing all over the United States. Hospital care has become very expensive. Many insurance plans limit the number of days that they will pay for one person's stay in the hospital. As a result, hospitals are releasing patients earlier. According to many experts, people wait longer to enter hospitals, and they leave sooner. Home nursing care and halfway houses are being developed to fill the needs of people who are discharged while still needing help and care.

Comma Splices
(page 96)

4. (1) No error.

5. (1) This sentence is really a list of three independent thoughts. *We can watch rockets take off for space* is the first independent thought in the list.

6. (2) The original wording is a comma splice. Option (2) is the only choice that uses a connecting word with the comma.

Circuses are not as common as they once were. Before the days of television and Disneyland, people waited eagerly for circuses to come. Now people are used to spectacular things. We can watch rockets take off for space, we can see deep into the ocean with sonar, and we can travel inside the human body with cameras. Circuses seem quaint and old-fashioned to some, yet many people still turn out when the circus comes to town.

Answers: "The Real Thing"

1 Sentence Sense

Writing Complete Sentences
(page 36)

1. (3) Sentence 3 is a fragment because it lacks a subject and a verb. Therefore, options (1), (4), and (5) are incorrect. Option (2) is incorrect because the comma is unnecessary; there is no pause between *them* and *with.*

2. (4) *The phone book is filling up with these telegram gimmicks.* In this option, the subject from sentence 6 is combined with the last part of sentence 7. It is not necessary to repeat words like *gimmicks.*

3. (1) Options (2), (4), and (5) create fragments. Option (3) is incorrect because there is no pause between *tap dancers* and *revenge telegrams.*

4. (4) The original wording is a fragment that lacks a verb. Option (4) is the only option with a verb.

Sending telegrams used to be serious business. Telegrams were often used in an emergency to convey bad news, so people opened them with a sense of fear and anticipation. Novelty companies eventually took over. They came up with downright silly telegrams. The phone book is filling up with these telegram gimmicks. You can barely find Western Union's number among singing-telegram and balloon-o-gram ads. There are tap-o-grams featuring tap dancers and revenge telegrams featuring a pie in the face. Giant telegrams five feet high and seven feet wide are available. There is even a complete Arabian-nights-feast telegram!

KEEPING TRACK
Top Score = 4
Your Score = ☐

2 Adding Details

Writing Descriptive Phrases
(page 44)

1. (1) Option (1) is the best choice because the verbal phrase *Trying to produce a disc to play on his newly invented Gramophone* is followed by a comma. Also, this verbal phrase describes *Emile Berliner,* not *it* or *his decision.* Option (2) creates a sentence fragment.

2. (4) Option (4) is correct because *Attempting to match the speed of the motor* clearly describes *he.* The original wording is incorrect because the verbal phrase does not describe *grooves.*

3. (2) When a descriptive phrase is in the middle of a sentence, use commas to separate it from the rest of the sentence. If you chose option (1), you probably didn't take the time to read the entire sentence. Does *RCA Victor was trying to market a 33⅓-rpm record, failed during the Great Depression* make sense?

4. (3) *By developing the 45-rpm record, RCA Victor competed for the small-disc market.* Option (3) logically combines the sentences by changing sentence 9 into a verbal phrase that describes *RCA Victor.* Option (4) is not the best choice because it is not clear to the reader what *this* refers to.

5. (4) *Avid collectors now have to rummage at garage sales and in second-hand stores to find the old 78s.* By combining similar information about where collectors rummage, you can smoothly combine the two sentences. If you chose option (5), be sure you make introductory verbal phrases describe something definite. *They* is too vague.

Do you know why records spin at peculiar speeds? Who decided on the speeds of 33⅓, 45, and 78 revolutions per minute? Trying to produce a disc to play on his newly invented Gramophone, Emile Berliner decided to use 78 rpm. The motor Berliner found for his Gramophone ran at 78 rpm. Attempting to match the speed of the motor, he cut grooves into the discs. However, more music would fit on a record if a slower speed was used. RCA Victor, trying to market a 33⅓-rpm record, failed during the Great Depression. Finally, in the late 1940s, CBS succeeded in doing so. By developing the 45-rpm record, RCA Victor competed for the small-disc market. Avid collectors now have to rummage at garage sales and in second-hand stores to find the old 78s.

KEEPING TRACK
Top Score = 5
Your Score = ☐

3 Pairing Subjects

Connecting Subjects with *And*
(page 48)

1. (5) *The typical baseball fan and the average player believe that Abner Doubleday invented the game.* Options (1) and (5) combine the two subjects (*basefall fan* and *average player*), but only option (5) uses a plural verb *(believe)* to match the subject.

2. (1) Options (2) and (4) create fragments. Option (3) is incorrect because there is no reason to insert a comma after *diamond.* Try reading sentence 4 to yourself, and you won't hear a pause after *diamond.*

3. (1) No comma is needed between two subjects. Removing the word *are* creates a fragment.

4. (2) *However, most Britishers and many historians claim that baseball developed from an English game called rounders.* Option (2) is the best choice because it gets rid of extra words by combining the subjects with *and.*

5. (3) When two subjects (*name* and *story*) are joined by *and,* they must be matched with a plural verb. Therefore, option (2) is incorrect. The original wording of the sentence is a fragment because it lacks a verb.

Who really invented the game of baseball? The typical baseball fan and the average player believe that Abner Doubleday invented the game. Doubleday, as the story goes, laid out the first baseball diamond at Cooperstown, New York, in 1839. That story and others are based on the opinion of one small commission of people appointed by A. G. Spaulding. The commission said that baseball was purely American and owed nothing to foreign games. However, most Britishers and many historians claim that baseball developed from an English game called rounders. The truth may never be known. The name of the real inventor and his story may remain a mystery for all time.

Connecting Subjects with *Or* and *Nor*
(page 51)

6. (4) The original wording is a fragment because it lacks a verb. *Are* is the correct choice because it is a plural verb, to match the two subjects joined by *and (sports and classes).* Remember that two subjects joined by *and* are considered plural.

7. (3) The verb must match the subject closer to it, which is *teacher.* Option (1) is incorrect because a comma *is* needed after a verbal phrase that comes at the beginning of a sentence.

8. (1) Option (3) creates a fragment because *with self-help too* is a phrase and contains neither a subject nor a verb. Options (4) and (5) are not logical. Option (2) is incorrect because a comma is not needed in this sentence.

9. (4) *Neither meditation nor hypnosis is a surefire way to make one quit smoking, but either one can help.* When you combine two subjects with *neither . . . nor,* make sure the verb matches the subject closer to it. *Hypnosis* matches *is.*

Every day, people seem to look for new ways to improve themselves. Because of this interest in self-improvement, recreational sports and personal growth classes are becoming available everywhere. Depending on one's preference, either a group exercise class or a private teacher is available for improving the body. In addition, there are classes in aerobic dancing, weight training, and yoga. People are attacking bad habits with self-help too. Neither meditation nor hypnosis is a surefire way to make one quit smoking, but either one can help. Even industry is offering its employees self-improvement opportunities. Employees of one company could take either an exercise class or a long run outside as a lunch-hour activity. It is a sign of the times that only three people out of ninety chose neither option.

KEEPING TRACK

Top Score = 9

Your Score = ☐

4 Pairing Verb Forms

Connecting Main Verbs
(page 54)

1. (2) *Many people think of their country as the center of the world and see all the other countries revolving around them.* Option (2) logically pairs two related verbs (*think* and *see*) with a common subject *(people).* Option (5) adds the unnecessary *they.*

2. (1) *The British, for example, don't consider the American Revolution to be a major historical event and don't give it much space in their schoolbooks.* Again, two related verbs (*consider* and *give*) are paired with a common subject *(British).*

3. (3) Option (3) creates a smooth-sounding sentence by not repeating the subject *(It).* Options (2) and (5) are not logical. For option (4) to be correct, it should contain a comma after *years.*

4. (5) No error. A comma is not used between two verbs joined by *nor* (*know* nor *care*). Option (4) is incorrect because only *nor* can be paired with *neither.*

5. (2) The original sentence is a fragment. Inserting the helping verb *is* makes the verb phrase complete. Options (3), (4), and (5) are illogical.

Many people think of their country as the center of the world and see all the other countries revolving around them. The British, for example, don't consider the American Revolution to be a major historical event and don't give it much space in their schoolbooks. To them, it was an event that interfered with the much more important relationship they had with France. Brazil has developed a huge amount of industry in recent years and has joined the world market. Most Americans neither know of this economic development nor care. Both France and the United States ignored the history of Vietnam and so became involved in a difficult conflict there. The world is getting smaller. Every country could benefit from teaching its people history from a world view.

Connecting Other Verb Forms
(page 58)

6. (1) *They tried to cure sickness by satisfying the gods or driving the spirits away.* Option (1) is the only choice that has two parallel verbals. *Satisfying* and *driving* have the same ending.

7. (2) Option (2) is the best combination of sentences 5 and 6 because it has two parallel verbs (*study* and *experiment*). It is not necessary to repeat *to* in front of *experiment.* Options (4) and (5) create fragments.

8. (5) *Leading to the germ theory of disease* is a fragment. Option (5) is the best choice because it adds the verbal phrase to sentence 7 with the fewest words. In option (4), the *and* is not necessary.

9. (5) *First vaccinations and then antibiotics were developed.* The two subjects (*vaccinations* and *antibiotics*) are related in time order. Because of this relationship, they can share the same verb *(were developed).*

Health care has taken an interesting turn. In the beginning humans believed sickness was caused by angry gods or evil spirits. They tried to cure sickness by satisfying the gods or driving the spirits away. Eventually humans began to rely on natural remedies such as herbs and plant extracts to relieve illness. Then people began to study the human body and experiment with new medicines and surgery. Bacteria were discovered in the 1600s, leading to the germ theory of disease. First vaccinations then antibiotics were developed for various diseases. Technology such as X rays, EEGs, EKGs, and artificial organs followed. Some people, however, have begun to believe that modern medicine can neither cure every ill nor answer every need. They have returned to more traditional solutions such as herbal remedies, acupuncture, and even simple faith.

KEEPING TRACK
Top Score = 9

Your Score = ☐

5 Making Lists

Writing About Three or More
(page 62)

1. (4) *Having, raising,* and *getting* are parallel verbals. Options (1), (2), (3), and (5) do not make the three items in the list parallel in form.

2. (2) There are four things listed here that cause stress. A comma must separate each item. Option (4) makes the list not parallel.

3. (1) *After learning more about the harmful effects of stress* is an introductory group of words that needs a comma between it and the rest of the sentence.

4. (3) *Help* is a plural verb and does not match with the singular subject *book.* Option (1) is incorrect because you don't need a comma to separate two subjects *(movie, book)* joined by *or.*

5. (5) *Such mini-vacations let you step back and take a fresh look at your life.* The two verbs *let* and *take* are parallel in form and share the same subject *(mini-vacations).*

Excess stress is taking a toll on human health today. Having a job, raising a family, and just getting through each day can cause a certain amount of stress. Stress can also come from frustration, anger, grief, and a loss of control. After learning more about the harmful effects of stress, more and more adults are beginning to take measures to reduce the stress in their lives. There are many ways to take a daily vacation from stress. Either an exciting movie or a good book helps you get your mind off the stressful aspects of your life. Exercising or taking a nap can provide welcome relief too. Such mini-vacations let you step back and take a fresh look at your life.

KEEPING TRACK
Top Score = 5

Your Score = ☐

6 Combining Complete Thoughts

Using Commas and Connecting Words
(pages 66–67)

1. (4) The idea in the second part of the sentence gives an example of an enclosed space. The idea in the second part of the sentence is not in addition to the idea in the first part. Therefore, these ideas cannot be joined by *and.*

2. (5) Option (5) makes the verbs in the list parallel. The comma is needed after *chest* because it is one of the listed items.

3. (1) *People with agoraphobia are afraid to be in open places, so they often cannot leave their own homes.* Using the connecting word *so* shows the relationship between having agoraphobia and not leaving home. The first thing causes the second.

4. (4) *These phobias do not involve a loss of contact with reality, yet they may severely limit a person's life. Yet* is the only connecting word given in the options that correctly shows the contrast between the two ideas in sentence 9.

5. (5) No error. Option (1) creates a fragment.

A phobia is a strong fear that has no basis in reality. There are many types of such unreasonable fears. For example, claustrophobia is the extreme fear of enclosed places. A person suffering from claustrophobia could not stand being in an elevator. Inside the elevator, the person would feel tightness in the chest, have a rapid pulse, or even faint. People with agoraphobia are afraid to be in open places, so they often cannot leave their own homes. Acrophobia is the fear of heights. Acrophobic people often experience vertigo, or dizziness, when they are up off the ground. These phobias do not involve a loss of contact with reality, yet they may severely limit a person's life. Some therapists treat phobias by gradually exposing the individual to the thing that he or she fears. This treatment is fairly painless and often effective.

Using Semicolons
(pages 70–71)

6. (4) *Fast-food restaurants are popular and handy; however, some people feel that fast food is not the most healthful you can buy. However* logically expresses the relationship between two contrasting ideas.

7. (1) Remember to use a comma before *but* when it connects two complete sentences. *And* and *so* do not express the relationship between the ideas in the two sentences.

8. (4) Commas are not used to separate subjects and verbs. Option (3) is incorrect because a semicolon can only connect two complete thoughts. *Potatoes, chicken, and even fruit pies* is not a complete sentence.

9. (2) *With salt* needs to be connected to the first sentence. Ending sentence 6 with *loaded* does not complete the idea.

10. (3) *Soda pop and creamy shakes may look cool and refreshing, yet they are sure to contain either sugar or artificial sweeteners. Yet* is used here to show that the two ideas contrast with one another.

Fast-food restaurants are popular and handy; however, some people feel that fast food is not the most healthful you can buy. Think about a meal you have had at a fast-food restaurant. It may have been tasty, but chances are at least some of the items were deep-fried. Potatoes, chicken, and even fruit pies take a dunk in sizzling oil. Ketchup, relish, and dressings are also loaded with salt, yet salt is already overused by many. With all that salt and oil, you need something to drink. Soda pop and creamy shakes may look cool and refreshing, yet they are sure to contain either sugar or artificial sweeteners. Oil, salt, and sugar don't appear on the fast-food menu, but they are most likely in the fast food.

KEEPING TRACK
Top Score = 10
Your Score = ☐

7 Combining Unequal Ideas

Placing a Secondary Idea at the Beginning
(page 75)

1. (1) *Because of its ladle-like appearance* is an introductory dependent phrase and must be followed by a comma. Therefore, options (2) and (5) are incorrect. A connecting word such as *and* or *so* is not needed because the connecting word *Because* is already present.

2. (2) *According to a legend of the Iroquois Indians, the three stars that make up the tail of the bear are remnants of a mighty hunting party.* Options (3) and (4) are not logical. *Because* and *consequently* cannot be used to connect the ideas in the two sentences. Option (5) does not identify the source of the legend *(the Iroquois Indians).*

3. (5) When two subjects *(bear* and *Indians)* are joined by *and,* you must use a plural verb *(were). Even though* cannot be used as a connecting word in this sentence because *even though* is used to show that one idea is in spite of another.

4. (2) Semicolons are not used before *and.* A comma is used before *and* when *and* connects two complete thoughts. Therefore, options (3), (4), and (5) are incorrect.

5. (3) *Blood then drips from the bear, tinting the leaves and giving us our fall colors every year. Tinting* and *giving* are parallel because they both end in *-ing.*

Today's astronomers have charted 88 star patterns, or constellations. Because of its ladle-like appearance, one such constellation is called the Big Dipper. However, the Big Dipper has also been known as the Greater Bear and as the Great Bear and Hunters. According to a legend of the Iroquois Indians, the three stars that make up the tail of the bear are remnants of a mighty hunting party. After the party was attacked by stone giants, the great bear and the three surviving Indians were carried to the sky by invisible hands. There the Indians still chase the bear today. The first Indian carries a bow, and the second carries a kettle. The third carries sticks to make a fire for cooking the bear when he is slain. Blood then drips from the bear, tinting the leaves and giving us our fall colors every year.

Placing a Secondary Idea at the End
(pages 78–79)

6. (2) *Our physical abilities and their limits are not entirely known.* Option (2) gets rid of unnecessary words by combining the two related subjects.

7. (5) If you read sentence 4 to yourself, you don't hear a pause after *impossible. Although* does not express the relationship of the ideas in this sentence.

8. (4) *The child would be crushed unless the man lifted the pipe. Unless* is the only connecting word that logically expresses the relationship of the ideas in the sentence.

9. (2) *Even though* shows the exact relationship between the two ideas. The man lifted the pipe in spite of the fact that it weighed 400 pounds.

10. (3) *Even though* expresses the same kind of relationship as the one found in question 9. None of the other options show this relationship.

Humans are capable of remarkable feats of strength and courage. Our physical abilities and their limits are not entirely known. Sometimes people are able to do things that seem impossible, in spite of their limitations. One man saw a child trapped under a heavy pipe. The child would be crushed unless the man lifted the pipe. He ran forward and lifted it off the child, even though the pipe weighed 400 pounds. Another man crossed a field, crawled through a hedge, and climbed stairs to save a drowning baby, even though he had lost his legs in Vietnam. People like these are almost superhuman in the moment when they act.

KEEPING TRACK
Top Score = 10
Your Score = ☐

8 Placing Information Within Sentences

Using Dependent Thoughts to Identify Nouns
(page 82)

1. (3) Did you remember that semicolons join two complete thoughts? *Especially a hot mug of tea on a cold winter's day* is not a complete thought but a phrase added on to the end of sentence 1. Options (1) and (2) create fragments.

2. (3) *Whether you drink black tea or herbal tea* is an introductory dependent thought and needs a comma placed after it. Options (2) and (4) are not logical. Option (5) creates a fragment.

3. (3) *Such water is full of oxygen and will bring out the full flavor of the tea.* Option (3) pairs two related verbs with a common subject.

4. (5) *Who* cannot refer to a thing *(teapot).* Therefore, option (5) is correct. Option (2) creates a fragment.

5. (4) *If you brew the tea longer than that, it will be too bitter to enjoy.* This revision gets rid of a vague subject-verb combination *(It is important)* and puts a specific subject-verb in its place *(you brew).* Options (1), (2), and (5) are incorrect because you usually don't use a connecting word after an introductory dependent thought.

Americans are becoming more and more fond of drinking tea, especially a hot mug of tea on a cold winter's day. Whether you drink black tea or herbal tea, the goal of every tea drinker is to brew the perfect pot of tea. To perform this feat, first fill a teakettle with cold tap water. Such water is full of oxygen and will bring out the full flavor of the tea. Bring the water to a full rolling boil. Next, fill the china cup or teapot that will be used to brew the tea with some of the water to warm it. Let the water sit for a few minutes, pour it out, and then add your favorite teabags or loose tea. Pour the boiling water over the top of your tea, and let it brew for the recommended time. If you brew the tea longer than that, it will be too bitter to enjoy.

Using Dependent Thoughts to Give More Information
(page 85)

6. (2) *Former exchange students, who number in the hundreds of thousands, look back on their experiences fondly.* A verb is needed to pair with the subject *students.* The only verb in the options is *look.*

7. (4) *Differences between cultures and homesickness at times overwhelmed students.* In option (4), two related subjects *(differences* and *homesickness)* share a common verb.

8. (4) Remember that *who* refers to people. Option (1) is incorrect because a comma is used before a dependent thought only when you hear a pause.

9. (1) The dependent phrase *who take part in overseas study programs* is necessary to identify *Those people.* Therefore, option (2) is not correct because of the comma. A comma signifies that the dependent phrase is not needed to identify the subject.

Living abroad is totally different from reading about or even visiting a foreign country. Foreign exchange students, who number in the hundreds of thousands, look back on their experiences fondly. However, most are also quick to say that living in another country was demanding and challenging. Differences between cultures and homesickness at times overwhelmed students. They began to succeed when they began to make new friends, who helped them find their way in new surroundings and a new language. It seems that being an exchange student and living with a host family mean much more than just stepping into a scene from a travel poster. Those people who take part in overseas study programs not only master other languages and make new friends. They also learn about themselves and their ability to cope.

Using Noun Phrases to Give More Information
(page 88)

10. (5) Dependent thoughts that give additional information should be separated from the rest of the sentence with commas. Therefore, option (1) is incorrect. Options (2) and (4) do not make sense when used in sentence 1.

11. (5) *And* always connects two words, phrases, or sentences that are similar. Since *Several parks have five or more roller coasters* is a complete sentence, option (5) is correct because it makes *each one is wilder than the next* a complete sentence too.

12. (4) Commas are used to separate items in a list. The *Beast* is one of these items. Options (2) and (3) create a fragment.

13. (1) *Carrying you twenty turns in eleven seconds, the Jetscream at Six Flags over Mid-America is a very exciting ride.* Option (2) creates a fragment. Option (5) is incorrect because there is no cause-and-effect relationship in the sentence.

14. (1) *The mighty Canadian Mine Buster, a roller coaster in Toronto, is as thrilling as any ride in the United States.* Option (2) is incorrect because *who* cannot refer to a thing *(Buster).* Option (4) leaves out needed information by substituting the pronoun *It* for the name of the roller coaster.

Roller coasters, the most frightening rides at amusement parks, also have the longest lines of riders. Several parks have five or more roller coasters, and each one is wilder than the next. The excitement of the rides is suggested by the names of the more popular coasters, such as the Beast, the Demon, and the Screaming Eagle. The Bat, at Kings Island near Cincinnati, was the first roller coaster with the cars suspended under the tracks. When the cars turn a corner, they swing from side to side. Carrying you twenty turns in eleven seconds, the Jetscream at Six Flags over Mid-America is a very exciting ride. At Great America near Chicago, you can ride the American Eagle and reach a top speed of sixty miles an hour. The Mighty Canadian Mine Buster, a roller coaster in Toronto, is as thrilling as any ride in the United States.

KEEPING TRACK

Top Score = 14

Your Score = ☐

9 Going Too Far

Run-On Sentences
(page 93)

1. (3) Because *As the sun moves farther north in the sky* is an introductory dependent thought, you must place a comma after *sky.* Options (2) and (5) would apply only if two complete independent thoughts were being connected.

2. (1) *Early European people used to light the largest log they could find for Yarol, their god of light and warmth.* Option (3), *he was their god of light and warmth,* creates a run-on.

3. (1) Sentences 6 and 7 are both independent thoughts. Thus, option (1) is correct. Option (2) creates a run-on. The connecting words *but, nevertheless,* and *even when* do not logically express the relationship between the two sentences.

4. (3) The original wording is a run-on of two thoughts—a semicolon effectively separates them. Option (1) changes the first complete thought into a fragment *(Jewish people who celebrate the Feast of Lights at this time).*

5. (4) *Having deep religious meaning, these celebrations serve another purpose as well.* The revised sentence is smoother and uses fewer words than the original.

In the Northern Hemisphere, there have long been celebrations in late December. As the sun moves farther north in the sky, people have celebrated its return and the lengthening of the days. Early European people used to light the largest log they could find for Yarol, their god of light and warmth. They were trying to get the sun to rise high in the sky so that it would catch fire from the log and warm the earth again. It seemed to work every year. This ritual became the Christmas celebration of burning the Yule (Yarol) log. Jewish people celebrate the Feast of Lights at this time; they are celebrating a miracle in their temple long ago. Having deep religious meaning, these celebrations serve another purpose as well. Remembering that the days are growing longer helps people stay cheerful in the frigid days of January.

Comma Splices
(page 97)

6. (2) *Bombarded daily by food ads* is followed by a comma because it is a descriptive phrase that comes at the beginning of the sentence. Option (3) creates a fragment. Options (4) and (5) are not logical.

7. (2) Commas are not used to separate two verbs *(knows* and *uses).* Option (1) creates a fragment.

8. (4) The original wording is a run-on. Option (4) is the best choice since the connecting word *because* shows why the product food label is a reliable source of information. The connecting words in (3) and (5) don't show the correct relationship between the two thoughts.

9. (3) The original wording is a comma splice. Adding *but* before *federal* logically expresses the contrast between the two independent thoughts.

10. (5) *In addition, some manufacturers include nutritional information on the label, such as the vitamin, mineral, fat, and fiber content of the food.* Options (5) and (2) are similar. Using *they* as the subject is unclear writing. The reader may not be able to tell who or what the pronoun *they* refers to.

Bombarded daily by food ads, many consumers often find it difficult to make sensible, nutritious choices. The wise shopper knows about nutrition and uses that knowledge to plan healthful menus. One of the most reliable sources of information on food can be the product label itself because it often lists the food's ingredients. The label may also tell the consumer how long the food has been on the shelf and the date by which it must be sold. In some instances, such information is put there voluntarily by the manufacturers, but federal law requires it in other cases. The amount of information varies, but all food labels must contain at least the name of the product, the net weight, and the name and location of the manufacturer, packer, or distributor. On canned food, the net weight includes the liquid in which the product is packed. In addition, some manufacturers include nutritional information on the label, such as the vitamin, mineral, fat, and fiber content of the food.

KEEPING TRACK
Top Score = 10
Your Score = ☐

Keeping Track

Here's a chart for you to enter your scores from the Keeping Track boxes. Compare your scores with the top scores.

	Top Score	Your Score
Lesson 1 Sentence Sense	4	______
Lesson 2 Adding Details	5	______
Lesson 3 Pairing Subjects	9	______
Lesson 4 Pairing Verb Forms	9	______
Lesson 5 Making Lists	5	______
Lesson 6 Combining Complete Thoughts	10	______
Lesson 7 Combining Unequal Ideas	10	______
Lesson 8 Placing Information Within Sentences	14	______
Lesson 9 Going Too Far	10	______
TOTAL	76	______

Did you get a top score in any of the lessons? Are there any lessons that you didn't do so well in? You might want to review the answer explanations for any lesson you had trouble with. Practice the skill taught in that lesson as well by writing your own sentences. Then sharpen your skills on the Extra Practice that follows.

Extra Practice in Writing Sentences

Directions: The following items are based on a paragraph that contains numbered sentences. Some of the sentences contain errors in sentence structure, usage, or mechanics. A few sentences, however, are correct as written. Read the paragraph and then answer the items based on it. For each item, choose the answer that would result in the most effective writing of the sentence or sentences. The best answer must be consistent with the meaning and tone of the rest of the paragraph.

(1) More than six million burglaries committed in houses and apartments each year. (2) If you live in an apartment, there are a few precautions you can take so that you make things harder for a burglar. (3) Use the security that your building already offers, some buildings have special features such as alarm buttons. (4) Your building may have one of those. (5) If it does, be sure you know where the button is. (6) Lighting should be sufficient in stairwells laundry rooms, and parking lots, as well as around the exterior of the building, so report burnt-out lights to the manager. (7) If the outside door has a lock, don't prop it open just becawse a friend is coming over. (8) Installing a dead-bolt lock on the door of your own apartment is also a good idea. (9) If you go on vacation, tell a friend or the building supervisor where you are going and when you will return. (10) Security in your building can be improved by getting to know your neighbors and working with them. (11) Many large apartment buildings have organized tenant patrols. (12) These groups help the police and themselves since they watch for crime in and around their buildings.

1. Sentence 1: **More than six million burglaries committed in houses and apartments each year.**

   What correction should be made to this sentence?

   (1) replace More with Although more
   (2) change committed to are committed
   (3) change committed to being committed
   (4) insert a comma after committed
   (5) no correction is necessary

   ① ② ③ ④ ⑤

2. Sentence 2: **If you live in an apartment, there are a few precautions you can take so that you make things harder for a burglar.**

   If you rewrote sentence 2 beginning with

   If you live in an apartment, you can make things harder for a burglar

   the next word should be

   (1) there
   (2) by
   (3) take
   (4) and
   (5) you

   ① ② ③ ④ ⑤

3. Sentence 3: **Use the security that your building already offers, some buildings have special features such as alarm buttons.**

   Which of the following is the best way to write the underlined portion of this sentence? If you think the original is the best way, choose option (1).

   (1) offers, some
   (2) offers, and some
   (3) offers, so some
   (4) offers. Some
   (5) offers some

   ① ② ③ ④ ⑤

4. Sentences 4 and 5: **Your building may have one of those. If it does, be sure you know where the button is.**

   The most effective combination of sentences 4 and 5 would include which of the following groups of words?

   (1) of those, so if it does
   (2) Be sure you know where your
   (3) Be sure your building
   (4) Maybe your building has
   (5) If your building has one,

   ① ② ③ ④ ⑤

5. Sentence 6: **Lighting should be sufficient in stairwells laundry rooms, and parking lots, as well as around the exterior of the building, so report burnt-out lights to the manager.**

   What correction should be made to this sentence?

   (1) remove the word should
   (2) insert a comma after stairwells
   (3) remove the comma after rooms
   (4) replace so with and
   (5) change report to reporting

   ① ② ③ ④ ⑤

6. Sentence 7: **If the outside door has a lock, don't prop it open just becawse a friend is coming over.**

   What correction should be made to this sentence?

   (1) replace If with Even if
   (2) remove the comma after lock
   (3) insert a comma after open
   (4) change the spelling of becawse to because
   (5) change is coming to are coming

   ① ② ③ ④ ⑤

7. Sentence 9: **If you go on vacation, tell a friend or the building supervisor where you are going and when you will return.**

   Which of the following is the best way to write the underlined portion of this sentence? If you think the original is the best way, choose option (1).

   (1) vacation, tell
   (2) vacation, and tell
   (3) vacation. Tell
   (4) vacation tell
   (5) vacation; tell

   ① ② ③ ④ ⑤

8. Sentence 10: **Security in your building can be improved by getting to know your neighbors and working with them.**

   If you rewrote sentence 10 beginning with

   Know your neighbors and

   the next word should be

   (1) working
   (2) to work
   (3) getting to work
   (4) work
   (5) works

   ① ② ③ ④ ⑤

9. Sentence 12: **These groups help the police and themselves since they watch for crime in and around their buildings.**

   If you rewrote sentence 12 beginning with

   By watching for crime in and around their buildings,

   the next words should be

   (1) the police
   (2) and helping
   (3) themselves
   (4) these groups
   (5) since they

   ① ② ③ ④ ⑤

Answers to Extra Practice in Writing Sentences begin on page 226. Record your score on the Progress Chart on the inside back cover.

Writing Essays

The second part of the GED Writing Skills Test consists of an essay. You may not think that writing an essay has much to do with your life, but actually the *skills* you need to write an essay are skills that can be used in everyday life. They involve thinking, organizing, expressing, and improving.

After you complete the multiple-choice questions on the conventions of English, you'll be given *one* essay topic to write about. (Your topic may appear in a list with others, but you will be told which one to write on.) The topic won't require any special knowledge or research on your part. In fact, the people who make up the GED Test make sure that the topic will be familiar to the average adult living in today's society. They even include a little background information. Below is an example of such an essay topic.

> Personal, or home, computers became available on a wide scale in the 1970s. Millions of consumers have since bought them.
>
> Why do many people buy home computers? Detail your thoughts about the reasons a person might have in an essay of about 200 words. Be specific, and give examples.

To write an essay on that topic, you need to do a number of things. First, you have to take the time to think about the topic so that you have a number of good ideas to include in your essay. You'll be given 45 minutes for the essay section of the GED Writing Skills Test, and that is enough time for you to take the first five minutes or so to think. It may sound funny, but there are different ways you can use to think of ideas. Lesson 10 in this section will explain some of them.

Once you've thought of ideas, you need to organize them in a way that will help the GED essay scorers see the logic of your ideas. There are also different ways to organize ideas; you'll study and practice them in Lesson 11.

All this thinking and organizing comes before you actually begin to write your essay. For that reason, this first step in the process of writing an essay is sometimes called the prewriting, or planning, stage.

Once you've planned your essay, you begin writing your first version of it. At this stage of the writing process, you expand all the ideas you thought of into sentences, and you put your sentences into paragraphs. As you write, you may think of one or two more ideas to include, or you may decide to omit some. Good examples of your ideas may come to you. The important thing to remember at this stage is that you don't have to write perfectly. The goal at this step is to get something down on paper that you can work to improve. Lessons 12–16 in this section will help you develop the writing skills you use at this stage.

Improving your essay comes in the next step. Improving writing is usually called revising. Revising is a step that many people—letter writers, students, businesspersons—neglect to do, but it is a necessary step. Turning in a GED essay without revising it would be like serving your family a half-cooked meal or handing your boss a half-completed job. When you revise, you correct or improve sentence structure and think of even better ways to express your ideas. You make sure your essay as a whole will give the GED scorers the correct, the *best,* impression of you and your writing skills. Lesson 17 will give you tips on how to revise.

LESSON 10

Prewriting: Getting Ideas

Suppose you buy a car and a friend asks, "How do you like it?" You'd probably be quick to give him an answer. "It's terrific. It gets good gas mileage, it rides smoothly, and it looks so sporty. But I wish I had a little more room inside. And I worry about what would happen if a bigger car ever hit me."

It would be easy to *tell* your friend all the good and bad points about the car. But if you were asked to *write* about your car, would it be so easy?

If you're like many people, you may be afraid that you will walk in to take the GED Test, look at the blank page in front of you, and think, "I don't have anything to write about." That's a frightening feeling, but you can overcome it if you learn how to make a plan before you start to write an essay. There are actually a number of ways you can use to think of a plan. One way is to think carefully about the topic and list your ideas. That is what you were doing in the last part of each Warm-up exercise in the first section of this book. A few other ways are explained on the following pages. You can practice them and then choose the way that works best for you.

Brainstorming

Maybe you can't readily think of good ideas to list about a topic, so you think that you don't know much about it. But if you brainstorm, you'll probably be surprised. Brainstorming is a way to find out *all* the ideas, facts, and feelings you have about a topic. To brainstorm, you put the topic you are going to write about at the top of a sheet of paper. Then, for a certain amount of time, you jot down on that paper *every* idea that comes into your mind about the topic. Keep writing down ideas; don't be concerned if some seem boring or silly or unrelated. Thoughts will set off other thoughts you might have hidden in your mind about the topic.

Also, don't worry about writing in sentences at this point; just use words and phrases. Don't even worry about being neat. Your purpose is to create a "storm in your brain" so that all you know about a topic will be swept up and blown right out onto your list. You can sort through the ideas and pick the best ones later.

Here's an Example

With the topic of fast foods, a GED student brainstormed the following list of ideas.

Fast Foods

greasy
fattening
ice cream
fries
teenagers
pickles
straws
favorite-root beer
birthday celebrations
help to parents
BIG profit
diet
workers like
shakes
quick
chicken lickin'
drive-in convenience
great for lunches
kids like
friends meet
pizza parlor
onions
soda
T.V. commercials
cheese-burgers
teens' jobs
fish fry
after movies
deserve a break

Did you notice that the ideas seem to be written down in no special order? Some ideas, such as TV commercials, don't even seem to relate to the topic too well. But a list of many ideas about the topic has been developed. It's a starting point.

Try It Yourself

Below are some brainstormed ideas about the topic of swimming. Very quickly, see if you can add five ideas of your own to the list.

	Swimming	
fun	cooling	tanned people
hot sun	lessons	bathing suits
uses muscles	noseplugs	salt water

Did you think of such ideas as waves, good exercise, swimming pool, beach, picnic, sunglasses, diving board, backstroke, races, Olympics? They are the kinds of ideas that may have occurred to you. Or maybe you came up with others. That's good—the more ideas, the better.

Warm-up

Now see if you can brainstorm for all the possible ideas hidden in your brain about the topic of birthdays. Take three minutes. Remember to jot down *all* your ideas, whether they seem silly, boring, good, or useless. Then compare your ideas with the Sample Warm-up Answers below.

Asking Questions

Remember the conversation about the car in the last section? A friend asked one question: "How do you like your new car?" The answer included a number of good ideas.

Sometimes you can come up with ideas about a topic by pretending you are talking with a friend about that topic. Imagine the questions he or she might ask you. What would be your answers to those questions? Your imaginary answers should provide you with ideas and facts to write about your topic.

Here's an Example

If you were conducting an imaginary "question and answer" session to get ideas about the topic of fast foods, it might go something like the dialogue in the next column.

Friend: **Who** likes fast foods?
You: little kids, teenagers, mothers who are tired, people in a hurry, workers on their lunch hours
Friend: **What** do they like about fast foods?
You: They're quick and hot and good tasting, but they're often high in calories and sometimes greasy. They are a meal-in-one, like pizza, hamburgers with lettuce, tomatoes, and french fries, or salad bars.
Friend: **When** do people go to fast-food restaurants?
You: when they're on their way somewhere, when they're in a hurry, when they want to eat cheaply, when they want to meet with friends, when they need someplace convenient
Friend: **Where** do you find fast-food restaurants?
You: everywhere—shopping malls, downtown, near major highways, in small towns, at tourist sites, even at zoos
Friend: **Why** are they so popular?
You: They offer good, fast, cheap food.
Friend: **How** do fast-food restaurants manage to put out good, fast, cheap food?
You: They have efficient work routines. They hire mostly young people who don't expect to earn high wages.

Did you notice the ideas that come out in that imaginary "conversation"? Some were different from the ones that came out in brainstorming.

The "five *w* and an *h*" questions—*who, what, when, where, why, how*—are good ones to ask to get ideas about a topic. In fact, they are the same ones that newspaper reporters ask when investigating a story.

Try It Yourself

Suppose you are asked to write about clothes and fashion. Here are some questions that could be asked about that topic. How would you answer them?

Friend: **Who** is most concerned about clothes and fashion?
You:
Friend: **What** kinds of clothes are there?
You:
Friend: **When** are people most concerned with the way they are dressed?
You:
Friend: **Where,** if any place, are people uncon-

Sample Warm-up Answers
Here are just a few sample ideas that could be brainstormed about the topic of birthdays. If you had trouble coming up with many, use these as a starting point and try again: candles on a cake, ice cream, presents, forget sometimes, husband always remembers, one year older, thirtieth coming up, sixteenth was best.

cerned about the way they are dressed?
You:
Friend: **Why** are many people concerned with fashion?
You:
Friend: **How** do a person's clothes reflect his or her personality?
You:

Did your answers to the questions give you ideas about the topic of clothes? Perhaps you thought that businesspeople are most concerned about the way they dress. Or perhaps you answered that a person's clothes reveal how much he or she values appearances. As long as you came up with ideas, the question-and-answer session was successful.

Warm-up

Now use the topic of movies. List six questions that could be asked about movies, and then write your answers to those questions. You don't have to answer in complete sentences; you can just list ideas if that's easier. Also, remember that it is easy to make up questions if you use the words *who, what, when, where, why,* and *how.* However, you don't *have* to use those question words.

Selecting

Once you have come up with a list of all the ideas you have thought of through brainstorming or questioning, you need to select the ones that will be most useful to you in writing about the topic. (Even if you have thoughtfully made a list of your ideas, you may find that some don't quite relate to the topic after a second look. That's all right; now is the chance to sort them out.) Pick out the ideas you think you can use, and cross out the ones that don't seem to fit in.

Once you have narrowed down your storehouse of ideas, look at your new, smaller list and add any ideas that come to you. Then you can put the ideas in some logical order.

Sample Warm-up Answers
These aren't sample *answers,* but they are sample *questions* that you can use to ask yourself if you had trouble coming up with your own: Who goes to movies? What kinds of movies are there? When are movies at their best? Where do people watch movies? Why do people watch movies? How have movies changed over the years?

Here's an Example

Below are the ideas about fast food that the GED student brainstormed. In looking at his list of ideas, he decided to zero in on the narrowed-down idea that fast-food restaurants are popular. The ideas that did not fit in with that aspect of the topic were crossed out. He decided to use the remaining items for writing an essay on the popularity of fast-food restaurants.

Fast Foods

~~greasy~~ ~~fattening~~
ice cream fries
teenagers pickles
~~straws~~ ~~favorite root beer~~
birthday celebrations
help to parents ~~BIG profit~~
~~diet~~
workers like
quick shakes
~~chicken lickin'~~
drive-in convenience great for lunches
kids like friends meet
pizza parlor onions
soda
~~T.V. commercials~~
teens' jobs cheese-burgers
after movies
fish fry deserve a break

The student thought of two more ideas to add to the list.

inexpensive many locations

Then he saw how the ideas fell into three groups. He used the remaining items on the list as reasons that fast-food places are popular with families, with workers, and with teenagers.

Families' Reasons

inexpensive
birthday celebrations
help to parents
quick
drive-in convenience
kids like it
gives a break from cooking

Workers' Reasons

quick
inexpensive
great for lunches
many locations

Teenagers' Reasons

popular foods (cheeseburgers, pizzas, soda)
teens' jobs
friends meet
after movies
inexpensive

Try It Yourself

Suppose you have to write about the mental and physical benefits of running. Read the following list of ideas on the topic of running. Cross out all the ideas from the list that don't seem to fit in with that narrowed-down topic.

time to think	figure out problems
builds strength	accomplish a goal
listen to music	alone
helps lungs	dogs chase you
good shoes	roads
tiring	feels good
builds muscles	lose weight
pretty scenery	sweat
relaxing	

Now list the ideas you have left in your list under these headings: *Mental Benefits of Running* and *Physical Benefits of Running.*

The ideas that don't seem too relevant to either one of the headings are these: listen to music, good shoes, tiring, pretty scenery, alone, dogs chase you, roads, and sweat. Under the mental benefits, you probably listed these ideas: time to think, relaxing, figure out problems, and accomplish a goal. Under physical benefits, these ideas fit best: builds strength, helps lungs, builds muscles, feels good, and lose weight.

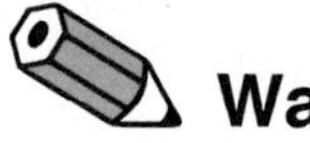

Warm-up

Look back at your brainstormed list of ideas about birthdays from the first Warm-up in this lesson. Read over the items, and then list the ones that you think you might use in an essay on the topic.

Now see if you can group the ideas from this new, shorter list into some logical order, perhaps memorable birthdays or people, places, and things that you relate to birthdays.

Now go back and do the same for the ideas you listed as answers to your questions on movies in the second Warm-up. Select the ones you would include in an essay, and group them.

LESSON 11

Prewriting: Organizing Ideas

A construction company needs certain materials to start building a house, and it needs a blueprint to follow as it builds. A blueprint is the plan of the house.

The same is true of "building" an essay. Your ideas are the materials you'll use. Before you start to build, you have to draw up a blueprint, or plan of organization.

Outlining

One kind of blueprint you can use for writing is an **outline.** An outline helps you organize your groups of ideas. It lists in order the main headings of each group and, under each heading, the specific ideas, or details, that belong in that group. When you begin to write, your outline will remind you of what you want to say and in what order you want to say it.

Coming to Terms

outline a plan for an essay that shows the groups of ideas that will be written about

Here's an Example

Another adult student was practicing writing an essay on physical fitness. Here are the groups of ideas she came up with.

Eating
always eat breakfast
avoid snacks
no junk food
eat at regular times
eat from four basic food groups

Exercise
aerobics
love to swim
take kids to pool at the Y

Well-being
no drugs
enough sleep
avoid harmful things
"beauty rest"

Below is the outline that the student made from these ideas. The main headings are numbered, and the specific ideas are lettered.

1. Eat properly
   a. eat from the four basic food groups
   b. eat meals at regular times; few snacks
   c. avoid junk food
2. Exercise
   a. aerobics class
   b. family swim at the Y
3. Take care of well-being
   a. try to get enough sleep each night
   b. avoid harmful substances—alcohol, drugs

Notice how some specific ideas were combined. Notice too that one of the specific ideas has examples listed after it. Two examples of harmful substances—alcohol and drugs—are included on the woman's outline so that she'll remember to include them in her essay. In that way, she'll get her idea across more clearly to her reader.

Try It Yourself

Go back to the ideas on fast foods that the GED student grouped on page 114. See if you can make an outline from those. Some ideas you may want to combine; others you may want to add examples to.

Your numbered headings should be "Families' reasons," "Workers' reasons," and "Teenagers' reasons." Did you see any ideas that might be combined? For example, you could have combined "quick" with "convenient" and "help to parents" with "break from cooking." That is what the student did with his ideas. Here is his outline. How does it compare with yours?

1. Families' reasons
   a. quick and convenient
   b. inexpensive
   c. help to parents; a break from cooking
   d. treat for the kids
   e. good idea for birthday celebrations
2. Workers' reasons
   a. great for lunches
   b. quick
   c. inexpensive
   d. easy to get to; many locations
3. Teenagers' reasons
   a. serve popular foods—cheeseburgers, pizzas, soda, and so on
   b. inexpensive
   c. good place to meet friends; after school, after movies
   d. source of jobs

Warm-up

In *each* column below, put a check mark in front of the idea that is more general and could be used as a heading over the other, more specific ideas in the group.

A	B
___ nurses	___ omelets
___ lab technicians	___ sausages
___ health careers	___ pancakes
___ doctors	___ eggs
___ X-ray technicians	___ breakfast foods

C	D
___ jazz	___ books
___ music	___ letters
___ rock	___ written communication
___ soul	___ newspapers
___ classical	

Check your answers with the Warm-up Answers below. Then see if you can fill in this outline with appropriate ideas.

Careers for a Person Interested in Helping Others

1. ______________________________

a. nurse's aide
b. doctor
c. paramedic
d. ______________

2. ______________________________

a. teacher
b. teacher's aide
c. cafeteria worker

3. Community careers

a. fire fighter
b. ______________

On the Springboard

Go back to your grouped ideas on birthdays from the last Warm-up in Lesson 10. Make up an outline with them. Then do the same with your grouped notes on movies from the same exercise.

Warm-up Answers
A. health careers **B.** breakfast foods **C.** music **D.** written communication **1.** Health careers **1d.** *sample answer:* lab technician **2.** School careers **3b.** *sample answer:* garbage collector

Mapping

Sometimes it's difficult to organize your ideas in a list or outline form. You can't quite "picture" where general ideas and specific details fit into the overall plan of the essay. In that case, you can try another type of "blueprint," a method of organizing ideas called **mapping.**

Mapping is, in some ways, even more like a house blueprint than an outline is because mapping creates a picture of your plan for your essay.

To map out your essay plan, you write your topic in the middle of a sheet of paper and circle it. From that circle, you draw branches on which you write the main headings for each group of ideas. From those branches, you draw smaller ones on which you write the details that belong with each heading.

Coming to Terms

map a diagram of the grouping of ideas for an essay

Here's an Example

Look at the map at the top of page 117. It is a map of the same ideas about keeping fit that you saw outlined earlier on page 115.

Try It Yourself

Here are groups of ideas about ways that adults learn outside school. How would you map them?

Reading	**Television**	**Experiences**
newspapers	news	traveling
magazines	science programs	museums
books	historical miniseries	observing people

What would you put in the middle circle? Since learning outside school is the topic, that should be in the middle. The three main lines drawn from it should have the three main headings: Reading, Television, and Experiences. In turn, each of those headings should have three lines drawn from it with a specific idea about that heading listed on each.

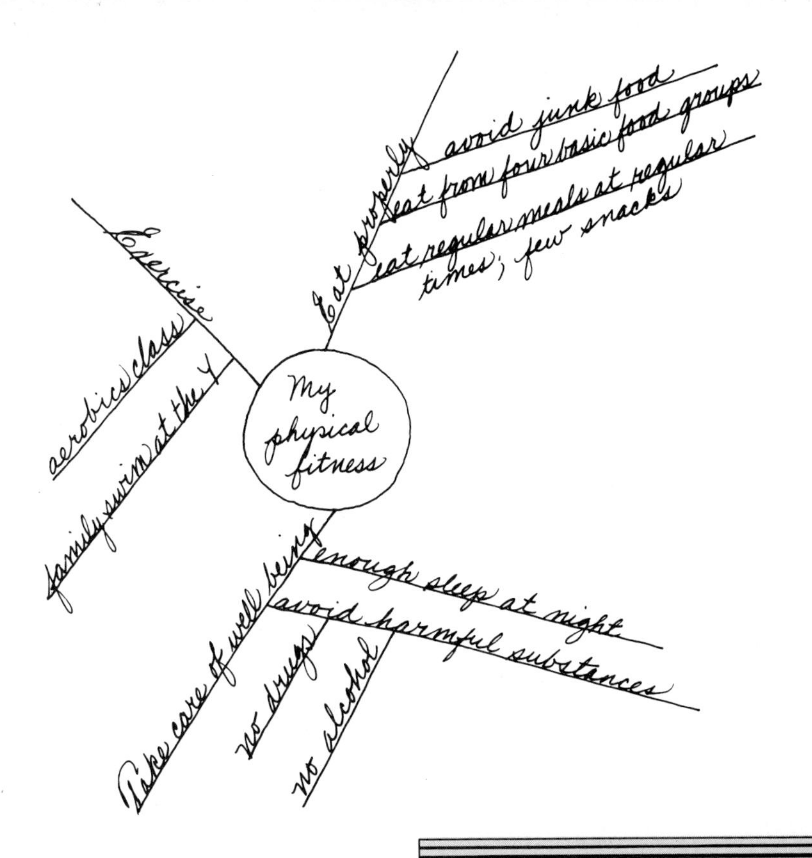

Warm-up

Fill in the blank parts of this map on the topic of enjoying the seasons.

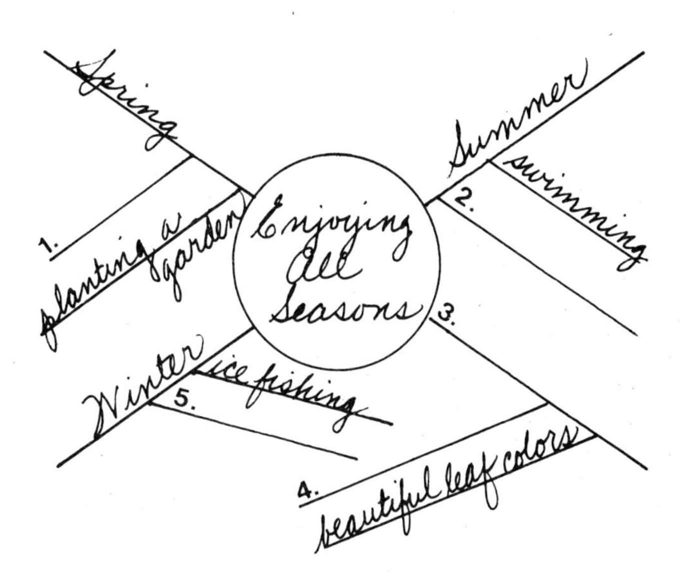

Compare your ideas with those in the Sample Warm-up Answers below. Your answers will most likely be different, but each should belong in the appropriate group.

Sample Warm-up Answers
1. return of warm weather **2.** concerts in the park
3. Autumn (or Fall) **4.** football **5.** Christmas

On the Springboard

Suppose you want to write an essay on all the activities you do in an average week. Use the technique you like best to come up with ideas. Then make a map to organize your ideas for the essay on your busy life. Be sure to include different factors that make your life so busy. Indicate on the map specific examples of each of those factors when you can.

A Test-Taking Tip

On the GED Writing Skills Test, you *will* be given scratch paper. Remember to use it for writing down your ideas and then mapping or outlining them.

LESSON 12

Writing Paragraphs

Once you know the ideas you want to include in your essay and have drawn up some kind of plan for them, you're ready to begin writing. Each group of ideas on your outline or map will become one **paragraph** in your essay. A paragraph is a group of sentences that all relate to one general idea. That general idea is the heading of the group. It is often expressed in a **topic sentence** somewhere in the paragraph. The rest of the sentences tell about the specific ideas that belong in the group under the heading.

Coming to Terms

paragraph a group of sentences that expresses one general idea

topic sentence the sentence in a paragraph that clearly states the general idea of the paragraph

Writing a Topic Sentence

When you have a group of ideas headed by one general idea, you want to state that general idea in a sentence. That sentence will be the topic sentence of your paragraph. It will also indicate your attitude toward, opinion of, or reaction to the general idea. In other words, it will summarize what you are saying about the general idea in the rest of the paragraph. For this reason, it is sometimes called your main idea.

The topic sentence *usually* will be the first sentence of the paragraph. All the other sentences in the paragraph will give details, reasons, examples, or incidents to support the main idea stated in the topic sentence.

Here's an Example

Suppose you have an essay topic of sports. You've listed your ideas and organized them in outline form, and one group looks like this.

1. The fun of winter sports
   a. ice skating
   b. playing hockey
   c. cross-country skiing
   d. downhill skiing; like to watch on TV

The topic sentence should tell about the main heading of winter sports and include your general thought about it. For example, it might be something like this.

- Winter sports can be fun to watch on TV and even more fun to do yourself.

In the following topic sentences, the general idea is *italicized* and the writer's attitude, opinion, or reaction to it is in **bold.** Together, they make up the main idea.

- *Changing a flat tire* **is something every driver should know how to do.**
- *My wedding* **turned out to be one of the funniest experiences of my life.**
- *Earning a high-school diploma* **is an important step in getting a better job.**

Try It Yourself

Read this group of ideas and write a topic sentence for a paragraph about them.

1. Buying a car
   a. determine your price range
   b. decide on features—color, make, number of doors, engine size
   c. consider the availability of parts and service
   d. arrange for financing

What would be a good topic sentence for the paragraph? It should state the general idea—buying a car. And it should summarize what all the specific ideas deal with, for that is what the writer wants to say about buying a car. Since each idea tells one thing that has to be done when someone buys a car, the topic sentence should say something like, "Buying a car is a detailed process" or "Buying a car is not a simple, one-step act" or "A person has to do several things when he or she wants to buy a car." Your topic sentence should have been something like that.

Warm-up

For each of the outlines below, write an appropriate topic sentence.

1. Caring for a child
   a. keep the child on a routine
   b. feed the child nutritious meals
   c. teach the child to behave well
   d. let him know you love him

   Topic sentence: ______________________

   ____

2. Traveling by train
   a. have no driving worries
   b. can get up and move around
   c. enjoy the scenery
   d. meet other people

   Topic sentence: ______________________

   ____

3. Learning to drive
   a. find a patient teacher
   b. hold the steering wheel with both hands
   c. stay alert
   d. do not panic

   Topic sentence: ______________________

   ____

Compare your topic sentences with those in the Sample Warm-up Answers.

Read each set of ideas listed below. Write a general heading for them. Then think of an appropriate topic sentence for a paragraph that would include the set of ideas.

4. ______________________
   a. take notes
   b. study regularly
   c. review periodically
   d. stick to it

   Topic sentence: ______________________

   ____

5. ______________________
   a. tell dog to sit
   b. if he does, give treat
   c. if not, push rear end down gently
   d. continue until he obeys all the time

   Topic sentence: ______________________

   ____

6. ______________________
   a. some movies take you far away
   b. some put you in different time
   c. romantic movies let you forget troubles
   d. adventure movies let you travel with handsome hero or beautiful heroine

   Topic sentence: ______________________

   ____

See how your answers compare with the samples given below.

Now read the following paragraph. Then write a good topic sentence for the paragraph on the line.

7. ______________________

One kind of annoying person is the person who talks constantly. He won't let anyone say one word in the conversation and thinks that only what he has to say is important. Another type that bothers me is the super-neat person who is constantly picking up or cleaning off everything. But the person who bothers me the most is the one who constantly gossips about others. I can't help thinking that he gossips about me when I'm not around. I wish these kinds of people would just stay away from me.

Supporting Details

You have written a topic sentence for a group of ideas. Now your reader will think, "Prove that to me" or "Tell me why you think that way." In the rest of your paragraph, it is up to you to do just that, to support what you've said in the topic sentence. How do you do that? By expanding the specific ideas into sentences. Because these ideas help support the topic sentence, they are sometimes called supporting details.

Sample Warm-up Answers
1. Child care involves more than just watching over a child. **2.** Train travel has advantages over travel by car. **3.** If you are learning how to drive, keep in mind the following things. **4.** Good study habits; *topic sentence:* Successful learners follow these good study habits. **5.** Training a dog; *topic sentence:* Training a dog to sit involves a few careful steps. **6.** What movies do for you; *topic sentence:* Movies can take you away from the routine of everyday life. **7.** Certain kinds of people truly annoy me.

Here's an Example

Here is a set of ideas that an adult student thought of for a paragraph on gifts.

1. match gifts with receiver
   a. reader—book, magazine subscription
   b. hunter—bow and arrows, hunting vest
   c. bicyclist—gloves, helmet
   d. baby—teddy bear, squeeze toy

The man's topic sentence became "Gifts should be bought with the receiver in mind." Because his specific ideas were examples, he started out his first supporting detail with the phrase *for example* to show his reader that his next idea would be just that.

■ For example, a reader would love to get a book or a magazine subscription.

Look at how he finished his paragraph by expanding his specific ideas into sentences.

■ A hunter, however, would prefer a bow and arrow or a hunting vest. A bicyclist wouldn't have much use for either of those kinds of gifts, but gloves, a helmet, or a waterbottle would be appreciated. And a teddy bear or squeeze toy would suit a baby just fine.

When you write supporting details for your paragraphs, you don't *have* to write one sentence for each idea. As you write, you may want to explain one particular idea in two or three sentences or combine two ideas into one. Examples of your ideas may come to you as you write, and you'll want to include them. (Notice that the student added the waterbottle to the list of the bicyclist's gifts.) But the set of ideas you developed in your plan is a great help in guiding your writing. By following it, you'll be much more likely to say everything you want to say in a clear, logical order.

Now read the man's paragraph from start to finish.

■ Gifts should be bought with the receiver in mind. For example, a reader would love to get a book or magazine subscription. A hunter, however, would prefer a bow and arrow or a hunting vest. A bicyclist wouldn't have much use for either of those kinds of gifts, but gloves, a helmet, or a waterbottle would be appreciated. And a teddy bear or squeeze toy would suit a baby just fine.

Try It Yourself

Suppose you were given the assignment to write about why people should stop smoking. You've thought carefully and come up with the following set of ideas.

1. Reasons to stop smoking
   a. injures your lungs
   b. causes cancer
   c. stains your teeth
   d. offends other people

First you write this topic sentence: "People should stop smoking for several reasons." Now you need to write the rest of the paragraph. What would you do?

The first idea is an important one, so maybe you decided to say that in your first supporting detail: "Most important, smoking injures your lungs." It would be a good idea to explain how serious injured lungs are; you could add a second sentence to make that clear: "Damaged lungs make breathing difficult."

What about the second specific idea? It too is important, and you probably want to tell your reader that there is evidence to support it: "There is also strong evidence that smoking tobacco causes cancer."

The next two reasons aren't quite as harmful to the smoker, so a good way to write about them would be to combine them into one: "If these two major reasons aren't quite enough to persuade a smoker to quit, perhaps the facts that smoking stains teeth and offends other people are enough to tilt the balance in favor of quitting."

Of course, your sentences don't have to be exactly like those. As long as they explained the specific details in complete sentences that helped support the topic sentence, they are fine. Now take a look at the sample completed paragraph.

"People should stop smoking for several reasons. Most important, smoking injures your lungs. There is also strong evidence that smoking tobacco causes cancer. If these two major reasons aren't quite enough to persuade a smoker to quit, perhaps the facts that smoking stains teeth and offends other people are enough to tilt the balance in favor of quitting."

Warm-up

For each of the topic sentences below, think of three or four ideas that could be used to support it. Then write a paragraph about them.

1. You can usually tell a person's feelings by the look on his face.
2. Some people love to live dangerously.
3. Things don't always work out for the best.

There are sample paragraphs given below. Notice how the details are written in complete sentences and support the topic sentence. Make sure yours do too.

On the Springboard

Choose as many topics below as you can. For each one you choose, think of several specific ideas. Then write a topic sentence. Finally, write a paragraph that expands the specific ideas into complete, supporting sentences.

how the weather affects people
coping with a divorce
choosing a name for your child
why some people are dishonest
the best place to be on a hot summer day
my idea of a romantic evening
the worst habits to have
what money is good for
how to deal with a pushy salesperson
the feeling of riding a motorcycle
planting a garden
how to search for the best buy
how to show someone you love them

Sample Warm-up Answers
1. You can usually tell a person's feelings by the look on his face. A smile is a clue that the person is happy or at least amused. Knitted brows mean either worry or deep thought. Tears, of course, usually tell of sadness or pain.
2. Some people love to live dangerously. There are people, for example, who travel around the world climbing mountains. Others like the danger of speed, either legally on a racetrack or illegally on the freeway. Still others risk sharks in the ocean or rocket into space to find their thrills.
3. Things don't always happen for the best. Plans can go wrong, and disappointment results. Unemployment or disability can cause financial hardship. Sickness, death, and pain are realities. None of these conditions is ever really for the best, yet mature people accept that they exist and try to make the best of them.

LESSON 13

From Paragraph to Essay

Usually when you write, you think of more than one group of related ideas and so need more than one paragraph to explain them. That is especially true of the essay topic on the GED Writing Skills Test.

A paragraph is a group of closely related sentences explaining one main idea. An essay is a group of closely related *paragraphs* explaining the writer's views on one topic.

In a paragraph, the topic sentence states the main idea of the paragraph. In an essay, the **controlling idea** contains the main idea of the entire essay, and the individual topic sentence of each paragraph states the main idea of that supporting paragraph.

You state the controlling idea in a sentence or short paragraph at the start of your essay. You support it by writing paragraphs that help explain it. Then you conclude your essay by summarizing what you've just written.

Diagram of an Essay

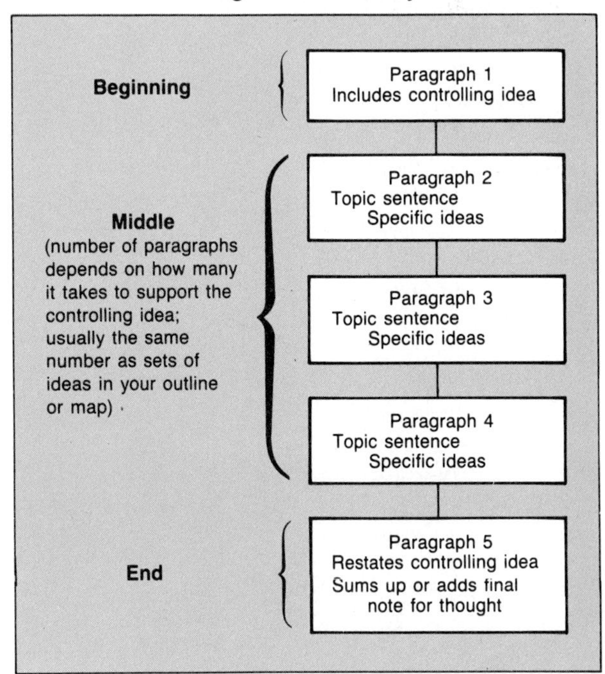

Notice how important the controlling idea is in each part.

Coming to Terms

controlling idea the main idea of an entire essay. The controlling idea states the topic and what the writer is going to say about it.

Writing a Beginning

There is an old Irish proverb that says, "A good beginning is half the work." When you are writing an essay, that is a fine piece of wisdom to follow. The beginning of your essay gets you off to a good, strong start. It has one important purpose: to state the controlling idea of the whole essay. The controlling idea must be broad enough to include all the ideas you will present in the other paragraphs of your essay. In many ways, writing the controlling idea for an essay is like writing a topic sentence for a paragraph.

Here's an Example

Do you remember the GED student from Lesson 10 who was preparing an essay on fast foods? Here again is the outline for that essay.

The Popularity of Fast Foods

1. Families' reasons
   a. quick and convenient
   b. inexpensive
   c. help to parents; gives a break from cooking
   d. treat for the kids
   e. good idea for birthday celebrations
2. Workers' reasons
   a. great for lunches
   b. quick
   c. inexpensive
   d. easy to get to; many locations
3. Teenagers' reasons
   a. serve popular foods—cheeseburgers, pizzas, soda, and so on
   b. inexpensive
   c. good place to meet friends; after school, after movies
   d. source of jobs

In order to write the beginning of his essay, the man looked at the topic and at the general headings for his groups of ideas. He wrote this sentence to summarize those ideas.

■ Fast-food restaurants are popular because they don't appeal to just one group.

That sentence stated the controlling idea of his essay because all the general and specific ideas relate to it. However, after reading the sentence, the man felt it was a little too abrupt to open his essay that way. He decided to split the sentence into two and added a little more introductory information.

■ The popularity of fast-food restaurants in our society is undeniable. It is also understandable because they don't appeal to just one group.

The student felt that was a satisfactory beginning because it stated his controlling idea and was interesting to read. He was right.

Try It Yourself

Here is an outline for an essay about friendship. Consider that topic, look at the general headings, and try to write a beginning for the essay. Make sure the beginning includes the controlling idea.

True Friends

1. Are trustworthy
   a. share secrets
   b. give honest opinions
   c. can be depended on for favors
2. Are sensitive
   a. understand feelings
   b. won't consciously do anything to hurt you
3. Are there when you need them
   a. won't let inconvenience stand in the way
   b. will share in good and bad

What do the general headings tell you? They list qualities that true friends have. The controlling idea should therefore include that message about the topic of friendship, perhaps in a sentence like this: "True friends must have several important qualities."

That sentence in itself is fine as a statement of the controlling idea. If you wanted to, you could also add to the beginning of the essay. Since the essay's topic is *true* friends, you might want to point out to your reader that many people don't make the distinction between true friends and other people they know. That will help the reader understand that the essay will explain the distinction. A little background information such as the following sentences would be a good idea: "When asked who their friends are, many people begin to name dozens. However, they are probably confusing friends with acquaintances. True friends must have several important qualities."

Your beginning most likely didn't use those words or perhaps even that exact background idea, but if it introduced the essay with some background information and gave the controlling idea, it should be all right.

A Test-Taking Tip

You may have heard that the way to start an essay is with a statement that grabs the reader's attention: perhaps a shocking statement or a funny quote. If you can readily think of such an opener for your GED essay, fine. But don't waste your time trying to think of a catchy opening line. Instead, concentrate on writing a good, strong controlling idea. That is a necessary ingredient for any good essay, and it will stick in the GED scorers' minds. Even the catchiest opener is a mistake if it isn't followed by a controlling idea.

Warm-up

Read the following outline. Then write a controlling idea for the essay that will be based on the outline. If you feel the opening needs some background information, add that as well.

The Human Body

1. The skeleton
   a. strong framework supports the body
   b. protects the insides of the body
   c. joints allow bending and moving
2. The respiratory system
   a. takes in needed oxygen
   b. gets rid of waste gas
3. The circulatory system
   a. 60,000 miles of tubing carry blood
   b. brings oxygen and food to the rest of the body
   c. fights disease
4. The nervous system
   a. coordinates the body's activities
   b. perceives the outside world
5. The muscular system
   a. makes movement possible
6. The digestive and excretory systems
   a. take in nourishment
   b. get rid of waste

Beginning of essay (including the controlling idea):

Compare your beginning with the sample given below. Then read the following essay. On the lines provided, write a good beginning for it. Remember to include the controlling idea.

From the time we are little, we know what it's like to enjoy a birthday party. Five- and six-year-olds love the cake and ice cream, balloons, and games that are part of this type of party. Teenagers celebrate birthdays with pizza, music, and talk. Even adults enjoy celebrating a birthday with ice cream and cake, drinks and snacks, talk, and jokes about "old age."

Even more often, adults have "no special occasion" parties. Drinks, snacks, and sometimes even dinner are served. The partiers visit with other guests and listen or dance to music.

Finally, there is the party with a purpose. This could be a shower to help an engaged couple furnish their new home or to help an expectant mother outfit her new arrival. Sometimes it's a party to celebrate a special occasion, such as retirement from a job or a fiftieth wedding anniversary. Parties such as this include special guests and gifts.

So if you are a "party person," take your pick. There are many kinds of parties with which to fill your life.

Compare your essay beginning with the one given under Sample Warm-up Answers below. If you'd like even more practice, look back at the outlines you created in Lesson 11 for the general topics of birthdays and movies. Write an essay beginning for each.

Sample Warm-up Answers

The human body is an amazing combination of complex systems. Each system performs at least one vital function.

Everyone loves a party, or it seems at least almost everyone does. Different kinds of parties take place often throughout people's lives.

A Test-Taking Tip

On the GED Writing Skills Test, you are actually given a little help in writing a controlling idea for your essay. The topic you are given in the essay assignment is a specific one. You are also given some background information with it. You can use the words in the essay assignment not only to help guide your thinking and organizing but also to help you write the beginning of your essay. You can often write your controlling idea by restating the essay assignment. For example, here is how one woman used an essay assignment to write the beginning of her essay.

Essay assignment: Television is still a relatively new invention, yet it has had profound effects on America and on Americans' lives. Write about 200 words discussing the effects that television has. You can write about the good effects, the bad effects, or both.

Essay beginning: Television has profoundly affected both the way we spend our time and what we know about the world. Some of the effects have been good, yet others have made our lives worse.

Writing the Middle

The middle of your essay is the part where you explain or prove your controlling idea. You do that by writing a paragraph about each of the groups of ideas in your outline or map. The general heading of each group becomes the topic sentence of a paragraph, and each specific idea is explained in one or more sentences, just as you would do if you were writing a single paragraph.

When you write your middle, supporting paragraphs, you again may find that you want to add specific ideas, combine others, or change the order in which the ideas were listed on your outline or map. That's perfectly all right as long as such changes improve your essay.

In addition, and this may surprise you, don't worry too much about making mistakes in spelling, grammar, or punctuation when you begin to write your middle paragraphs. In fact, don't be too concerned about making your sentence structure absolutely correct.

When you begin to write your middle paragraphs, you are actually writing the **first draft** of your essay. Your main goal at this point is to get your ideas down on paper in an organized way. You'll have the chance to fix any errors you may make later.

Coming to Terms

first draft the first version of an essay

Here's an Example

Look back at the outline for the fast-food essay on page 122. Below are the three paragraphs that the GED student wrote about the three groups of ideas in the outline. Compare the paragraphs with the outline. The topic sentence of each paragraph is in *italics.* See how the topic sentences relate to the general headings on the outline. The specific ideas from the outline are in **bold.** Notice how he sometimes changed their wording and how he added details.

■ *Fast-food restaurants make sense to families for a number of reasons.* They are **quick and convenient.** They are also relatively **inexpensive,** so families on tight budgets can still enjoy them. Dinner at a fast-food restaurant is a **help to parents** because it gives them a **break from cooking.** It's a **treat for the kids** too. In fact, kids love fast-food restaurants so much that many of these restaurants now offer special **birthday celebrations.**

Families are not the only ones who go to fast-food restaurants. *Workers also find good reasons to eat at them.* Fast-food restaurants are **good lunch spots** for workers who **don't have much time** before getting back to the office. The **low cost** of the food is important to workers too. In addition, fast-food restaurants are quite often **easy to get to** because there are so many of them at so **many different locations.** Very few businesses are far from one.

Teenagers as a group seem especially attracted to fast-food restaurants. The restaurants **serve popular foods** such as cheeseburgers, pizza, soda pop, and milk shakes. Like everyone else, teenagers like the **low cost.** Even those who don't have much spending money can afford fast food. Fast-food restaurants have become almost a home away from home for many teenagers because they are a **good place to meet**

friends after school or **after the movies.** Perhaps most important to teenagers are the **jobs** that fast-food restaurants offer them. For many people, being a fast-food cook or checkout person was their first job.

Try It Yourself

Turn back to page 122, and study the outline about true friends again. On your own sheet of paper, write middle paragraphs for an essay based on the outline. Remember that the beginning of the essay will start out something like this: "When asked who their friends are, many people begin to name dozens. However, they are probably confusing friends with acquaintances. True friends must have several important qualities." Write that beginning or your own at the top of the paper, and then write your middle paragraphs.

If you've written your first draft of the essay about friends, you can compare yours with the one that follows. Because there are three sets of ideas in the outline, you should have written three paragraphs. The topic sentence of each paragraph should include the meaning of the general heading for that set of ideas. The specific ideas should be explained in sentences. If your paragraphs look something like the following, you did a good job.

"True friends must be trustworthy. If you tell them a secret, you know that they won't tell it to anyone else. If you talk to them about your problems, you can trust them to give their honest opinion. When you ask a real friend to do a favor for you, you know it will be done, not forgotten.

"In addition to being worthy of your trust, true friends must be sensitive. They must try to understand how you feel. In fact, sometimes they will know how you feel even before you tell them. When you are upset, they will make every effort to understand why. They would never consciously do anything to hurt you.

"True friends must also be there when you need them. They won't say that it's not convenient to talk with you or to come over. They share in the good times and in the bad."

Can you match the ideas in your paragraphs with the ideas on the outline in the same way that the ideas in the paragraphs above do? If so, you wrote a good first draft of the middle of an essay.

Warm-up

Below are the beginning and end of an essay about reasons for getting married, as well as an outline of ideas for the middle of the essay. On your own paper, write a first draft of the middle of the essay.

Beginning:

Today's high rate of divorce is often a topic of discussion, yet wedding bells continue to ring. Why do many people still choose to marry? Men and women marry for many reasons.

Outline:

Reasons for Marrying

1. For love
   a. humans need to care and be cared for
   b. marriage vow to love for the rest of one's life—leads to security, stability
   c. contentment and happiness can result
2. For companionship
   a. marriage fights loneliness
   b. go places and do things together; share good and bad times
3. For practical reasons
   a. two together live more cheaply—share rent or mortgage, food, etc.
   b. become helpmates—share duties and responsibilities

Ending:

Marriage, then, fulfills our needs for love and companionship while also meeting several practical needs. It is no wonder that people continue to march down the aisle.

You can compare your middle paragraphs with the sample ones below. Then you might want to use your outlines about birthdays and movies and write middle paragraphs for them as well.

Sample Warm-up Answers

Marriage fulfills our need for love. Human beings have the need to care and be cared for. When people get married, they promise to give each other that caring love. They vow to do so for the rest of their lives. This promise gives each a sense of security and stability. By fulfilling each other's need for love, a married couple can make each other happy and content.

A second reason people marry is for companionship. Loneliness is a frightening thing. To come home every night to someone you love is much better than coming home to a lonely apartment. To go places and do things with someone you love makes your life more enjoyable. Having someone to share good times and bad times with is comforting.

There are practical reasons for marrying too. Two people living together can live more cheaply than two living apart. A couple shares the rent or mortgage, food, and utility bills. They also become helpmates to each other and so share duties and responsibilities. Often what the husband cannot do, the wife can, and vice versa.

A Test-Taking Tip

When you write your GED essay, you may find that you want to write about the idea in, say, the third paragraph of your essay before the idea in the second. Perhaps it's easier for you to write about one idea before another; you feel your words can flow more easily and quickly. If that happens, go ahead and do it. Write what comes easiest first, and then go back and fill out the rest.

Writing an Ending

The ending of an essay is a short paragraph that restates the controlling idea. It helps summarize, or wrap up, the meaning of the entire essay for the reader. Since your ending is the last "look" at your essay that the GED scorers will have, you want to make your ending as strong and impressive as possible.

Here's an Example

Here is the GED student's complete essay—beginning, middle, and end—about fast food. Notice how the ending changes some of the wording but keeps the meaning of the controlling idea that is stated in the beginning paragraph.

■ The popularity of fast-food restaurants in our society is undeniable. It is also understandable because they don't appeal to just one group.

Fast-food restaurants make sense to families for a number of reasons. They are quick and convenient. They are also relatively inexpensive, so families on tight budgets can still enjoy them. Dinner at a fast-food restaurant is a help to parents because it gives them a break from cooking. It's a treat for the kids too. In fact, kids love fast-food restaurants so much that many of these restaurants now offer special birthday celebrations.

Families are not the only ones who go to fast-food restaurants. Workers also find good reasons to eat at them. Fast-food restaurants are good lunch spots for workers who don't have much time before getting back to the office. The low cost of the food is important to workers too. In addition, fast-food restaurants are quite often easy to get to because there are so many of them at so many different locations. Very few businesses are far from one.

Teenagers as a group seem especially attracted to fast-food restaurants. The restaurants serve popular foods such as cheeseburgers, pizza, soda pop, and milk shakes. Like everyone else, teenagers like the low cost. Even teenagers who don't have much spending money can afford fast food. Fast-food restaurants have become almost a home away from home for many teenagers because they are a good place to meet friends after school or after the movies. Perhaps most important to teenagers are the jobs that fast-food restaurants offer them.

For many people, being a fast-food cook or checkout person was their first job.

Fast-food restaurants, then, are successful because they offer something to just about everyone. Because of this wide appeal, their popularity will probably continue.

Try It Yourself

Refer back to the beginning and middle paragraphs that you wrote about friendship. Think of a good ending for the essay. Make sure your ending restates the controlling idea that you wrote at the beginning.

The controlling idea of the essay is "True friends must have several important qualities." For that reason, your ending should include a restatement of that idea. It could also summarize what the qualities are, in a sentence such as this: "True friends are, therefore, special people who are trustworthy, sensitive, and there when you need them."

You could also use the background information from the beginning paragraph to add a final note to the essay: "People probably have far fewer friends than they at first believe. In fact, if a person has just one true friend, he or she is very lucky."

Read your entire essay about friendship from beginning to end. Does the end "wrap up" the essay in an interesting way? Would someone else be able to read your essay, put it aside, and then tell you what it said about friendship? If so, your essay and its ending are satisfactory.

Warm-up

After you read the following beginning and middle paragraphs, write an end for this essay.

Almost no one can resist the crunch of a potato chip. Most people, however, give hardly a thought to what makes this popular food so distinct from others.

To begin with, the potato chip is entirely American. In 1853 at an expensive restaurant in Saratoga Springs, New York, a dissatisfied customer complained about the french-fried potatoes. The chef became so upset with the complaints that he kept cutting the potatoes into thinner and thinner slices. Then he dipped them in hot oil and sprinkled them with salt. The result was what we know today as the potato chip. From this humble beginning, two more important distinctions helped make the chip the popular food that it is today.

The taste and texture of the potato chip distinguish it from other foods. The potato chip is crispy, crunchy, and salty. Its flavor provides a nice contrast to the bland or sweet taste of so many of our foods today. Its texture stands out against all the soft food we eat.

Unlike many other foods, chips are also convenient. They are small and easy to take along with you in a box or bag. They even fit inside a lunch box. Potato chips are easy to handle as finger foods at any party or get-together.

Now write an ending paragraph for this essay.

____

____

____

____

At the bottom of this page is a sample ending for the essay. Compare yours with it.

Now put the final touch on the first drafts of your essays about birthdays and movies. Write an ending for each.

On the Springboard

Below is the essay assignment for "The Real Thing" that follows. Prepare to write the essay by prewriting. First get ideas for your essay by using whichever technique—making a list, free writing, brainstorming, or asking questions—that works best for you. Then organize your ideas by outlining or mapping them.

For more than twenty years, the dangers of smoking have been well known. Yet recent surveys show that more than 40 million Americans continue to smoke cigarettes or cigars.

Why do people smoke? Detail your thoughts on this question in an essay of about 200 words.

Sample Warm-up Answer

For these reasons, the potato chip is more than just another popular snack. It is distinct for its American origin, its taste and texture, and its convenience.

A Test-Taking Tip

Some people make the mistake of not quite "addressing the issue" when they write an essay. In other words, they don't write on the topic they've been assigned. Instead, they get sidetracked by the background information that is given with the topic, or they let themselves wander off on another topic that they prefer to write on.

Don't let that happen to you when you take the GED Writing Skills Test. Read the background information you are given, but then focus on the topic itself and read it *several times.* Restate that topic as a controlling idea and jot it down at the top of your scratch paper before you begin to think of ideas. That will help keep your writing focused. Remember: If you write on a topic other than the one you're assigned, your essay will be scored a 0.

 The Real Thing 

Directions: This is a test to find out how well you write. The test has one question that asks you to present an opinion on an issue or to explain something. In preparing your answer for this question, you should take the following steps:

1. Read all of the information accompanying the question.
2. Plan your answer carefully before you write.
3. Use scratch paper to make any notes.
4. Write your answer.
5. Read carefully what you have written and make any changes that will improve your writing.
6. Check your paragraphing, sentence structure, spelling, punctuation, capitalization, and usage, and make any necessary corrections.

You will have 45 minutes to write on the question you are assigned. Write legibly and use a ballpoint pen.

For more than twenty years, the dangers of smoking have been well known. Yet recent surveys show that more than 40 million Americans continue to smoke cigarettes or cigars.

Why do people smoke? Detail your thoughts on this question in an essay of about 200 words.

You will find a sample essay on page 156.

Transitions

When you build a house, you need to use nails to hold together the boards that make up the framework of the house. The parts of an essay need to be "nailed" together also so that your piece of writing will be seen as one whole.

You can bridge the gaps between the sentences and paragraphs of your writing by using **transition** words and phrases. A transition is a move from one thing to another. Transition words and phrases help your reader move from one sentence or paragraph to another by showing the relationship between the ideas in them. You've already used some transition words when you combined ideas in sentences. Below are those and others you can use to tie your essay together.

When you are adding similar information—

along with	in addition
also	moreover
and	not only . . . but also
as well as	too
furthermore	

When you are introducing an example—

for example	such as
for instance	to illustrate

When you are emphasizing an idea—

indeed	of course
in fact	

When you are explaining time relationships—

after	next
at the same time	not long after
at times	now that
before	once
during	since then
finally	then
first (second, etc.)	to begin with
following	when
last	while
meanwhile	until

When you are discussing causes and effects—

as a result	nevertheless
because	since
consequently	so
for that reason	so that
if . . . then	therefore

When you are comparing things—

also	similarly
likewise	too
not only . . . but also	

When you are contrasting things—

although	nevertheless
as opposed to	on the contrary
but	on the other hand
despite	still
even though	unless
except	whereas
however	while
in contrast	yet

When you are concluding your essay—

finally	then
in conclusion	

Other phrases can signal transitions to your readers too. Sometimes even whole sentences serve as transitions.

Coming to Terms

transition a move from one thing to another. Transition words and phrases can be used to signal your reader that you are moving from one idea to another.

Here's an Example

Take one last look at the fast-food essay. The transitions are in **bold.** Some of them were included in the student's first draft. Others were added when he reread his essay and realized he could signal some of his transitions better.

■ The popularity of fast-food restaurants in our society is undeniable. It is **also** understandable **because** they don't appeal to just one group.

Fast-food restaurants make sense to families for a number of reasons. They are quick and convenient. They are **also** relatively inexpensive, **so** families on tight budgets can still enjoy them. Dinner at a fast-food restaurant is a help to parents **because** it gives them a break from cooking. It's a treat for the kids **too. In fact,** kids love fast-food restaurants so much that many of these restaurants now offer special birthday celebrations.

Families are not the only ones who go to fast-food restaurants. Workers **also** find good reasons to eat at them. Fast-food restaurants are good lunch spots for workers who don't have much time **before** getting back to the office. The low cost of the food is important to workers **too. In addition,** fast-food restaurants are quite often easy to get to **because** there are so many of them at so many different locations. Very few businesses are far from one.

Finally, teenagers as a group seem especially attracted to fast-food restaurants. The restaurants serve popular foods **such as** cheeseburgers, pizza, soda pop, and milk shakes. Like everyone else, teenagers like the low cost. Even teenagers who don't have much spending money can afford fast food. **Of course,** fast-food restaurants have become almost a home away from home for many teenagers **because** they are a good place to meet friends after school or after the movies. Perhaps most important to teenagers are the jobs that fast-food restaurants offer them. For many people, being a fast-food cook or checkout person was their first job.

Fast-food restaurants, **then,** are successful **because** they offer something to just about everyone. **Because** of this wide appeal, their popularity will probably continue.

Did you notice how the entire first sentence of the third paragraph served as a transition? It told you, the reader, that you were now going to read about a second group that liked fast-food restaurants.

Try It Yourself

Here are two paragraphs from an article about sleep. As you read them, think of good transitional phrases you could use to relate ideas in two or three places. Concentrate especially on a transitional phrase that would best lead from the first paragraph to the second.

■ Different persons have differing daily cycles of activity and sleep. Some people rise early and cheerfully in the morning. These "morning larks" have daily cycles that rise quickly to a midmorning peak.

About 10 percent of the people are "night owls." They work best at night and like to sleep late in the morning. It takes night owls longer to get started after they wake up. It takes them longer to go to sleep.

If the sentences in those paragraphs sounded short and choppy to you, it is precisely because they lacked transitional words and phrases. Since the second sentence is an example of the idea mentioned in the first, you could use a phrase such as *for instance* or *for example* to introduce it: "Different persons have differing daily cycles of activity and sleep. For example, some people rise early and cheerfully in the morning."

The second paragraph begins a new and opposite example from the one discussed in the first paragraph. For that reason, a phrase showing contrast, such as *in contrast* or *on the other hand,* could be used to let the reader know that: "On the other hand, about 10 percent of the people are 'night owls.' "

The last sentence gives additional information about the sleeping habits of night owls. Perhaps you decided to show the transition by rewriting the last sentence like this: "It takes night owls longer to get started after they wake up. In addition, it takes them longer to go to sleep."

Of course, you probably didn't choose those exact transitions. Read the paragraphs again with the transition words and phrases you chose to use. Do the sentences flow more smoothly? Are the relationships between ideas clearer? Do you as a reader know when one idea is leading into another? If so, your choice of transition words or phrases was good.

Warm-up

The following essay needs transition words and phrases to tie its sentences and paragraphs smoothly together. On the lines, write the words or phrases that you feel will best tie together the ideas before and after the lines.

Life in the city is very different from life in the country. City people, **(1)** ____________, love city living; country people, **(2)** ____________, would never consider leaving the country. Both lifestyles have their advantages.

(3) ____________ city living is exciting and fast-paced, life in the country is calm and relaxing. The city offers theaters, restaurants, sports, and museums; **(4)** ____________, the country offers wide-open spaces and beautiful scenery.

(5) ____________ does the city have many places for entertainment, **(6)** ____________ it has many places to find a job. **(7)** ____________, the country is limited in nearby places to work. **(8)** ____________, people often must travel far to their jobs.

(9) ____________ the differences between city and country life, both are satisfying places for people to live.

You can compare your choice of transition words and phrases with the ones in the Sample Warm-up Answers. Many transition words and phrases mean nearly the same thing, so your choices may not match those exactly.

Now take the time to go back to your essays on true friends, birthdays, and movies. Notice the places where you already used transition words and phrases. See if there are other places where you could add them.

On the Springboard

Below is the essay assignment for "The Real Thing" that follows. Prepare to write the essay by prewriting. First get ideas for your essay by using whichever technique—making a list, freewriting, brainstorming, or asking questions—that works best for you. Then organize your ideas by outlining or mapping them.

Large companies employ hundreds, even thousands, of people, sometimes in more than one location. Small companies, on the other hand, employ only a few people and usually have limited, intimate office space.

Compare and contrast working for a big company with working for a small company. Write down your ideas in a composition of about 200 words. Be specific with your details.

The Real Thing

Directions: You have 45 minutes to write on this question. Write legibly and use a pen.

Large companies employ hundreds, even thousands, of people, sometimes in more than one location. Small companies, on the other hand, employ only a few people and usually have limited, intimate office space.

Compare and contrast working for a big company with working for a small company. Write down your ideas in a 200-word composition. Be specific with your details.

You will find a sample essay on page 156.

Sample Warm-up Answers
1. of course **2.** on the other hand **3.** Whereas **4.** in contrast **5.** Not only **6.** but also **7.** However **8.** Consequently **9.** Despite

LESSON 14

Relating Ideas

When you think of being related to other people, you might think of being your father's child, or your husband's wife, or your sister's brother. You are related to all the people in your family, but each relationship is a little different.

Your ideas are related to each other too. And like your differing relationships with the members of your family, ideas fit together in different ways. Some ideas fit together according to the way they happened in time. Some relate according to the order of their importance. Others fit together in a cause-and-effect relationship. Still others are connected because they are similar or are different.

So just as you can see yourself as a son or a wife or a brother, you can look at the relationships of your ideas in different ways. When you write your GED essay, you must make these relationships clear to the scorers. The organization of your ideas in your outline or map is one way to make the relationships clear. The use of transitional words and phrases is another.

Time Order

One way ideas can be related to each other is by time. Often something that happens occurs in a step-by-step order: first one thing, then another, and then another.

If you are writing an essay about a process (that is, how to do something or how something works) or about a series of events, put your ideas and facts in time order. By putting your ideas in your outline or map following a time order, your essay will then show your readers how the ideas are related.

Here's an Example

The essay in the next column shows the series of events that a repair person goes through on an average day. Notice how the transition words and phrases, together with the order of the ideas themselves, help show the time order.

■ My usual work day follows a pleasant routine. When I first get up in the morning, I put on a pot of coffee. Then I take a nice hot shower to wake me up. After that, I get dressed for work and go to the kitchen to make some breakfast. While I eat breakfast and have my morning coffee, I read the morning newspaper and relax before starting off on another day.

Not long after eight o'clock, I leave for work. When I arrive there, I look at my schedule of jobs and plan my day. First, I get together all my equipment and tools. Second, I pack all these things into the company van. Finally, I start off to my first service stop of the day.

Throughout the day, I visit homes and businesses to repair electrical appliances. Before each visit, I check my work order and make sure I have the correct address of the customer. During each visit, I try to be pleasant and efficient. When the job is finished, I make out a bill for the customer, and then go on to my next client.

After my service calls are completed, I return to my company and complete a report of my day's work. Finally, I drive home to a well-deserved rest.

Try It Yourself

Read the following paragraph on giving a dog a bath. Decide how you would rewrite the paragraph. Pretend that you are going to outline the ideas, and jot down the numbers of the sentences in the order in which you would put them.

■ (1) Rub him dry thoroughly with a big, thick towel. (2) Get the dog wet by spraying him with a hose or pouring buckets of water over him. (3) If you have followed these steps, you should end up with a nice, clean dog. (4) Sprinkle flea powder all over his dry, clean coat, and rub it in well. (5) Get out all the supplies you will need: water, soap, towels, and flea powder. (6) Rinse the soapy dog thoroughly with water from the hose or from a bucket. (7) Giving a dog a bath is an easy process. (8) Rub the soap on his wet coat, and scrub him all over.

You should have realized that sentence 7 was the topic sentence because it stated the main idea of the entire paragraph; therefore, a good place for it would be right at the beginning. Sentence 5 is the first step in the process of bathing a dog. Sentences 2, 8, 6, and 1 describe the sequence of wetting, soaping up, rinsing, and drying the dog. Sentence 4 is the last step in the process. Sentence 3 is a good conclusion for the whole paragraph.

Now read the paragraph again, this time with the sentences in the correct order. As you read, think of transition words that could be used to reinforce the time order:

"Giving a dog a bath is an easy process. Get out all the supplies you will need: water, soap, towels, and flea powder. Get the dog wet by spraying him with a hose or pouring buckets of water over him. Rub the soap on his wet coat, and scrub him all over. Rinse the soapy dog thoroughly with water from the hose or from a bucket. Rub him dry thoroughly with a big, thick towel. Sprinkle flea powder all over his dry, clean coat, and rub it in well. If you have followed these steps, you should end up with a nice, clean dog."

As you read, you probably thought of using such terms as *first, next,* and *after that* to help lead from one idea to the next. That would make the organization of the ideas even easier to understand.

Warm-up

Write a composition about the process of writing the first draft of an essay. Tell the steps you have studied so far. Make notes showing the order of the steps. Use transition words and phrases between sentences and, if necessary, paragraphs.

Sample Warm-up Answer

Writing the first draft of an essay is a process. That means there are steps involved that must be followed if you want to write a successful essay.

First, you must think. With the essay topic in front of you, you must take the time to think about it. A number of techniques can be used at this step to produce a list of ideas to write about.

Next, you select the ideas you want to include and group them. If you think of more ideas at this time, feel free to add them. You can then organize your grouped ideas in an outline or a map, whichever way works best for you.

Once your ideas are organized, you can begin to write your first draft. The controlling idea goes at the beginning, along with some background information. Then you write your middle paragraphs, using your outline or map to guide you. Finally, add an ending paragraph that restates the controlling idea and wraps up the essay.

After you've followed these steps, you'll most likely have a good first draft of an essay.

A Test-Taking Tip

The directions for the essay on the GED Writing Skills Test will not directly tell you to "prewrite." They will probably say something like "plan your essay" and "make notes," and those instructions mean the same thing as "prewrite." Be sure to follow them. Use the scratch paper that will be provided to prewrite your essay.

On the Springboard

Write about an average weekday in *your* life. Make notes of your ideas in time order, and follow that order when you begin to write. Use transition words and phrases to help show the order. If you need more than one paragraph, make sure you use a good transition between the paragraphs.

The Real Thing

Directions: You have 45 minutes to write on this question. Write legibly and use a pen.

Television has been a part of modern American society for several decades. It has undergone changes just as society has.

Think about the television shows of today and how they have changed from the time you first began watching television. Write a composition of about 200 words that discusses those changes.

You will find a sample essay on page 156.

Order of Importance

If you had to list the ten most important things in your life, would you put your stereo ahead of your mother on the list? Or if you had one hour left to live, would you spend forty-five minutes playing pool and fifteen minutes talking to your family and friends?

For some essay topics, you need to decide what is the most important and what is the least important idea in your explanation. Then you need to decide if it will be better to organize your ideas in a most important to least important order or in a least important to most important order.

You put the most important ideas first when you want to give a straightforward explanation. In that way you present your readers with the items of the greatest impact quickly. That is the way newspaper reporters write their stories. They put the most important facts in the first few paragraphs of a story and then the facts of less importance farther down the page. Sometimes, however, you may want to be dramatic in an explanation. You build up to the most exciting point by presenting the least important ideas first and the most important idea last.

Here's an Example

In this first essay, the ideas are discussed from most important idea to least important.

■ On fall weekends, I don't have to put on layers of clothing, get stuck in a traffic jam, and spend an arm and a leg to see my favorite football team. I prefer being an "armchair quarterback."

The best thing about watching a game at home is that I can sit in a comfortable chair in my warm living room with a snack and a drink and enjoy the game. No rain or snow falls on my head. No wind blows in my face. No cold bites at my hands and feet.

Sitting in my easy chair, I have a great view of all the players and all their moves on the field. Unlike the fans in the stands, I can also see the expressions on the faces of the players and coaches. On the television, I can even see instant replays.

From my armchair, I can hear the announcer call all the plays, just as the fans in the stands hear it. In addition, the TV announcer gives me information about the players' backgrounds and about other games going on at the same time.

Let someone else root in the stands for the Giants or the Broncos. I'll sit at home and enjoy football every weekend.

Now look at that same essay with the order of the ideas reversed. In this essay, the most important idea comes last.

■ On fall weekends, I don't have to put on layers of clothing, get stuck in a traffic jam, and spend an arm and a leg to see my favorite football team. I prefer being an "armchair quarterback."

From my armchair, I can hear the announcer call all the plays, just as the fans in the stands hear it. In addition, the TV announcer gives me information about the players' backgrounds and about other games going on at the same time.

Even better, I have a great view of all the players and all their moves on the field. Unlike the fans in the stands, I can also see the expressions on the faces of the players and coaches. On the television, I can even see instant replays.

Best of all, however, I can sit in a comfortable chair in my warm living room with a snack and a drink and enjoy the game. No rain or snow falls on my head. No wind blows in my face. No cold bites at my hands and feet.

Let someone else root in the stands for the Giants or the Broncos. I'll sit at home and enjoy football every weekend.

Try It Yourself

Here are three groups of ideas about the topic of keeping drunk drivers off the road. Suppose you were going to write an essay and wanted to order your paragraphs starting with the most important. In which order would you write about the groups?

Reasons to Keep Drunk Drivers off the Road

Will save money
- a. lower insurance rates due to fewer accidents
- b. less cost of accident cleanup

Will save lives
- a. thousands of innocent victims of drunk drivers
- b. the drunk drivers themselves
- c. the heartbreak of families, both the victims' and the drivers'

Will save time
- a. time and work by police
- b. traffic and criminal court time

Which of those groups of ideas deals with the most important reason to stop people from driving when they are drunk? Most people would agree that the loss of lives is the most tragic result of drunk driving. Therefore, an essay written in order from most important idea to least important would most likely discuss the second group of ideas after the beginning paragraph.

The next paragraph would probably be about the first group of ideas—the three main ways that money would be saved. The final paragraph would discuss saving time, since that appears to be the least important reason for stopping drunk drivers.

Warm-up

Plan an essay entitled "The Things That Mean the Most to Me." Imagine that floodwaters are nearing your home and you can bring only five things with you when you evacuate. You want to build up the suspense in the essay, so that the reader will wonder what is the most important thing to you. Therefore, you want to write about your fifth choice first and the item of most importance to you last. List the items you would save in order of least important to most important.

1. ______________________________
2. ______________________________
3. ______________________________
4. ______________________________
5. ______________________________

On the Springboard

Use your list of important items from the Warm-up. Then write an essay about the five things you would bring with you if you had to evacuate your home.

The Real Thing

Directions: You have 45 minutes to write on this question. Write legibly and use a pen.

The radio is one of the most popular inventions of the last 100 years. From transistor to boom box, its uses are many.

Discuss the different ways people use the radio in their daily lives. Detail your thoughts in a composition of about 200 words. Be specific and clear.

You will find a sample essay on page 157.

Cause and Effect

What causes alcoholism? What are the effects of smoking on people? What happens when pregnant women don't get good medical care? These are serious ideas that you probably have thought about.

Why won't the car start? Why is the baby crying? These are everyday questions that you may have asked yourself.

All these ideas have to do with causes and effects. Sometimes, when you write about certain ideas, you can find a connection between them because one idea causes the other to occur. Often several causes will produce one effect; for example, many reasons could combine to produce a losing baseball season for a team. Sometimes, too, several effects are brought about by a single cause; for example, moving to a new area may result in a different home, new friends, a different job. Often an essay assignment will come right out and ask you to write about the causes or the effects of a particular event.

Here's an Example

The following personal essay talks about three positive effects of a diet.

■ My friends sighed when they heard I was on another diet. Once more, I had decided to try to lose the extra 25 pounds I had been carrying around for the last five years. This diet, however, worked for me. Within three months, I was 25 pounds lighter! With my new figure came many changes.

First of all, all my clothes were falling off my new thin body. I had to buy a whole new wardrobe. That made a giant dent in my budget, but it was a satisfying dent.

Then I had to get used to all the flattering comments people gave me. I was embarrassed at first, but soon learned to be pleased and flattered with their compliments. It was nice to be told how good I looked.

The best result of all was the feeling I now had about myself. I looked good, and therefore I felt good about myself. My self-confidence increased. My outlook on life brightened, and the "new me" was just plain happy.

Try It Yourself

A cause makes something else happen. What might be the causes, or reasons, for a person's depression?

Perhaps you've felt depressed at times, or a friend or family member has. You may even have read magazine or newspaper articles about depression. Use those personal experiences to think of as many causes of depression as you can.

The loss of a loved one or a job usually makes a person feel depressed. Money problems often do too. Does divorce or the breakup of a relationship come to your mind? What about the general low self-esteem of a person who feels he has never really succeeded at anything? Often such a person becomes depressed.

If you mentioned any of those ideas (as well as any other things that can result in depression), you have the start of an essay on the causes of depression. You could then organize those ideas and write your essay.

Now try looking at the other side of the coin. Think about results, or effects. What are the effects of falling in love?

What happens when people fall in love? Again, think of your personal experiences; television shows and movies are also good sources of ideas.

When a person first realizes he or she is in love, sometimes a pleasant, light-hearted feeling results. Often a long-term relationship develops in which both people try to learn more about each other and become closer to one another. Eventually, they may even think about marrying. Those are just some of the effects of falling in love. Are they ones that you thought of?

Warm-up

Consider the following situation:

A man is very successful at his job.

What might be some causes of, or reasons for, his success?

1. ______________________

2. ______________________

3. ______________________

What might be some effects, or results, of his success?

1. ______________________

2. ______________________

3. ______________________

Using the ideas that you just listed, write two *paragraphs.* The first one should be about the reasons a person is successful on a job. The second paragraph should tell about the effects of job success. You can compare your lists and paragraphs with the samples given under Sample Warm-up Answers below.

Sample Warm-up Answers
Causes: **1.** hard worker **2.** knows what he or she is doing **3.** is good at office politics *Effects:* **1.** makes good money **2.** has self-respect **3.** has the respect of others

What makes a person successful at his or her job? Hard work, of course, is one factor. The dedication of working hard pays off. Yet hard work is not the only way to job success. A person must also know what he or she is doing; he or she must produce quality work. In addition, the successful worker must know how to work with others and even how to maneuver around certain co-workers. Such office politics is essential to success on the job.

Most people desire success on the job for the results that it brings. First in many people's minds, of course, is the money that job success usually involves. Most companies these days realize that they must reward their successful workers with good pay in order to keep them with the company and, therefore, to keep the company itself successful. In addition, people respect themselves when they know they are a success. They also enjoy the respect of others. For many people, such respect is just as important a result of job success as money.

On the Springboard

Choose one of the topics you just wrote a paragraph about. Expand your list of ideas for that topic by adding more details under each idea. In that way, each idea becomes a general heading for a group of specific ideas. Then, using the outline that you just created, write an *essay* about the reasons for or the effects of job success.

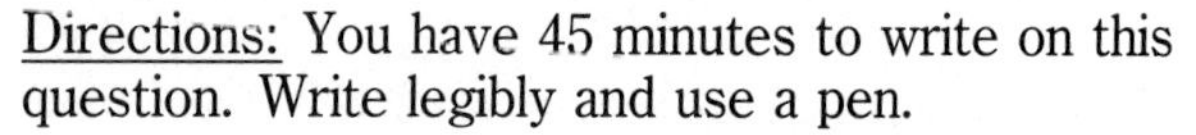

The Real Thing

Directions: You have 45 minutes to write on this question. Write legibly and use a pen.

The atomic bomb was first dropped in 1945. In the more than four decades since that date, its presence has affected the world, individual countries, and individual persons.

How has the bomb changed our lives? Analyze the effects of the bomb and write about them in an essay of about 200 words.

You will find a sample essay on page 157.

Compare and Contrast

When you look at two brothers or two sisters, you usually notice their similarities and their differences very quickly. You might compare the two and see that they both have the same deep-set brown eyes. However, then you notice that one has a turned-up nose that is different from the other's straight nose. You can compare and contrast the two in many ways.

Comparing and contrasting people, things, or ideas is another way of relating your ideas in writing. Essay topics often ask you to do just that.

Here's an Example

Look at how one man structured an essay in which he compared and contrasted himself with his father.

■ "Like father, like son" is an old saying. Like many old sayings, it's true—part of the time.

My father was always a friendly man. He loved to take walks and talk with the neighbors and the local shopkeepers. When he was at home, my dad enjoyed peace and quiet. His idea of relaxing was to sit in his easy chair and read the newspaper and his sports magazines. I can still picture my father with his curly brown hair, light blue eyes, and high cheek bones.

I, on the other hand, am not quite as outgoing as my father. I like people but sometimes feel uncomfortable with new people in a new situation. When I want to relax, I lie on the floor, prop my legs up, and, with headphones on, blast my rock music. I am especially like my father, though, in at least one respect. I see my dad when I look in the mirror at my hair and eyes and cheeks. I see, in myself, my father as he looked twenty-five years ago.

In that essay, the ideas were organized like this.

1. My father
   a. approach to people
   b. idea of relaxation
   c. appearance
2. Me
   a. approach to people
   b. idea of relaxation
   c. appearance

Notice that each paragraph contains the same points of comparison (that is, approach to people, idea of relaxation, and appearance) presented in the same order. All the information about the father is presented in one paragraph; then all the information about the son is presented in the next.

Another way the man could have arranged his ideas was by alternating them, like this.

1. Approach to people
   a. my father's
   b. mine
2. Idea of relaxation
   a. my father's
   b. mine
3. Appearance
   a. my father's
   b. mine

With this arrangement, each point of comparison (for example, approach to people) is the topic of its own paragraph. A comparison or contrast of that point is made. Then you go on to the next point (for example, relaxation) and make the comparison or contrast of that point. Here is the man's essay rearranged along those lines.

■ "Like father, like son" is an old saying. Like many old sayings, it's true—part of the time.

My father and I have somewhat different approaches to people. My father was always a friendly man. He loved to take walks and talk with the neighbors and the local shopkeepers. I, on the other hand, am not quite as outgoing as my father. I like people but sometimes feel uncomfortable with new people in a new situation.

On ideas of relaxation, too, we differ. When he was home, my dad enjoyed peace and quiet. His idea of relaxing was to sit in his easy chair and read the newspaper and his sports magazines. When I want to relax, I lie on the floor, prop my legs up, and, with headphones on, blast my rock music.

I am especially like my father, though, in at least one respect. I can still picture him with his curly brown hair, light blue eyes, and high cheek bones. I see my dad when I look in the mirror at my own hair, eyes, and cheeks. I see, in myself, my father as he looked twenty-five years ago.

Both those arrangements are good. Did you have a preference when you read them?

Try It Yourself

Below is part of an outline for an essay that compares and contrasts running a household with running a business. The first two points of comparison in each group are similarities; the last is a difference. How would you complete the outline?

1. Running a household
   a. money management—you need income and to keep account of expenses; what's left is savings
   b. divide up household work among family members
   c. ______________________________
2. Running a business
   a. money management—you need income and to keep track of expenses; what's left is profit
   b. ______________________________
   c. profit is the driving force

What idea would you list as 1c? It is a point of contrast from 2c, which is the driving force behind running a business. What is the driving force behind running a household? For many people, it is love and the high value they place on keeping the family close. If you thought of an idea similar to that for 1c, you were correct.

Now what about 2b? It is a point of comparison that has to do with the division of labor. In a family, members often share the work. What happens in a business? The work is divided up among the workers at all different levels. That is the idea that belongs on 2b.

Warm-up

Here are the same ideas about running a household and running a business. In this outline, the ideas are arranged differently. Each paragraph will discuss one point of comparison or contrast. How would you complete the outline using the ideas from Try It Yourself?

1. Money management
   a. ______________________________
   b. ______________________________
2. Division of work
   a. ______________________________
   b. ______________________________
3. Driving force
   a. ______________________________
   b. ______________________________

You can compare your outline with the one given below under Sample Warm-up Answers.

If you'd like more practice with comparing and contrasting ideas, why not write an essay using the ideas about running a household and running a business? Choose whichever arrangement of ideas you like best. You can also choose one of the following topics to write about. Think of points of comparison and contrast and arrange them the way *you* think is most effective.

two athletes
two car models
two bosses you've had
two movies or TV shows you've seen
two of your children

Sample Warm-up Answers

1. Money management
   a. in a household—you need income and to keep account of expenses; what's left is savings
   b. in a business—you need income and to keep account of expenses; what's left is profit
2. Division of work
   a. in a household—among family members
   b. in a business—among workers
3. Driving force
   a. in a household—love and the value placed on the family
   b. in a business—desire for profit

On the Springboard

Look back at the essays in Here's an Example in which a man compared and contrasted himself with his father. Write a similar essay in which you compare and contrast yourself with your mother or father, or with a sister or brother. Don't forget to prewrite by thinking of ideas and organizing them before you begin your first draft.

The Real Thing 

Directions: You have 45 minutes to write on this question. Write legibly and use a pen.

Once most people lived in the country on farms or in small villages. Today large cities and their surrounding suburbs are the main centers of population.

Compare and contrast life in a city with life in a small, rural town and with life in a suburb. Write your ideas in a composition of about 200 words. Be specific.

You will find a sample essay on page 157.

LESSON 15

Backing Up Your Ideas

Did you ever hear this old exchange between a parent and child?

"Where did you go?"

"Out."

"What did you do?"

"Nothing."

It is meant to show the frustration parents feel when their children don't communicate well with them. The child gives an answer to each question, but the answers don't give *enough* information to be satisfying to the parent.

When you write, you give information to support your controlling idea and the topic sentence of each paragraph. You need to supply *enough* information to satisfy your reader's interest in your ideas.

Backing up your ideas with a mere list of details is not enough. You need to expand on your supporting information by giving specific details that will give your reader a vivid picture of exactly what you mean. He or she won't be left with questions. Your writing will also be more interesting because of all the precise details you've given.

Give Examples

One good kind of specific detail to use in backing up your ideas is an example. The example might be a person, place, thing, or incident. It should be exact rather than general, and you should describe it precisely to make the greatest effect on your reader.

What examples do you use to back up an idea? Ask yourself exactly what it is you need to prove or explain it. Are you talking about people? about places? about things? about events?

Once you have decided just what it is you need for examples, what can you say about each example? Ask yourself the questions a reader might ask you about your example: Who? What? When? Where? Why? How? Keep asking yourself those questions, or other ones you can think of, until you have enough supporting information to satisfy even you.

Here's an Example

Read the following two compositions about an afternoon at a football game. The first one gives ideas (the rain, the loss, the fall) to support the topic sentence, but the details are not expanded upon.

■ Attending the football game last Saturday turned into a disastrous event. It rained during the entire game. We were soaked since we didn't have any raincoats. Our team lost by a score of 31–30. The other team scored a field goal in the last minute of the game. Finally, I fell off the bleachers and broke my wrist as I was getting ready to leave. All in all, the day was terrible.

Now read this next composition about the same experiences. Notice how it expresses the same ideas, but the writer has expanded upon each with examples to give a clear impression to you, the reader. These examples help you picture the scene and answer questions you would want to ask the writer.

■ Attending the football game last Saturday turned into a disastrous event.

It rained during the entire game. We were soaked because we didn't have any raincoats. The players were not only soaked, but also so mud-covered that we could hardly tell who was on which team. At one point in the game, even the players couldn't tell which player was which. One of the players on the opposing team handed off the ball to one of our players. He couldn't tell, with all the mud-covered uniforms, that it wasn't his teammate.

Even worse was the fact that our team lost by a score of 31–30. With two minutes to go in the game, our defense held them on our five-yard line and kept them from scoring. But with less than a minute to go, we fumbled and they got the ball. Then they kicked a field goal with twenty seconds left in the game.

The final disaster of the day occurred when I was climbing down from the bleachers. I slipped on a wet step and fell. It wasn't bad enough that I managed to break my wrist in the fall, but I crashed into two little kids as well.

All in all, my day at the football game was terrible!

Try It Yourself

Suppose that you have decided to write an essay starting with this controlling idea: "Sitting in a bus station for an hour teaches you many things about the way people use their time." What examples could you use to show how people use their time?

First, choose two or three people you had seen in a bus station as examples to explain your controlling idea. Then tell how each one spent the time there.

For each person that you decide to use as an example, you might first ask yourself these questions:

Who is the person? (Since you probably don't know names, you could describe the person in some way.)

What is the person doing?

When does he or she do these things?

Where is he or she doing these things?

Why do you suppose he or she is doing these things?

How does he or she go about doing these things?

If you give specific answers to each of the questions, you could come up with quite a bit of specific information to explain your examples precisely.

Warm-up

Now suppose that you are going to write an essay based on this controlling idea: "Some people work hard to make life better for others." Since you are discussing people, and because you want specific supporting information, you need to choose two or three people you are familiar with to use as examples of your statement.

Examples: **1.** ______________________

2. ______________________

3. ______________________

Your idea about these people is that they work hard to help others. Jot down answers to each of the following questions for *each* of your example people:

1. Who has had their lives improved by this example person?
2. What does your example person do to make other people's lives better?
3. When does the example person do these things?
4. Where does the example person do these things?
5. Why does the example person work to make people's lives better?
6. How does the example person make people's lives better?

If you answered all the questions, you probably came up with quite a bit of specific supporting information to back up your ideas.

On the Springboard

Write an essay about people you know who have helped other people improve their lives. Use your ideas from the previous Warm-up. Outline them or map them; then write a first draft of an essay.

"The Real Thing"

Directions: You have 45 minutes to write on this question. Write legibly and use a pen.

A hero is someone who is looked up to and admired. In times past, heroes were kings, soldiers, cowboys, politicians, scientists, and athletes.

Are there heroes in our time? If so, who are they, and why are they considered heroes? If not, why not? Detail your thoughts on this topic in a 200-word essay. Give specific examples.

You will find a sample essay on page 158.

Use Facts and Opinions

Another good way to back up your ideas in your essay is with a combination of **facts** and **opinions.** The facts give concrete evidence to back up your ideas, and the opinions tell your personal reactions. Both facts and opinions help you make your ideas clearer and more precise.

Be sure that you can tell the difference between facts and opinions. You can prove a fact by referring to reliable sources of evidence. You can agree or disagree with an opinion, but you cannot prove or disprove it. Some opinions can be supported by facts, and some are just a matter of your own preference.

Coming to Terms

fact a statement that can be proved

opinion a statement of belief or preference

Here's an Example

The following two pieces of writing are about the sea. This first one gives details to support the controlling idea, but it does not expand on the details.

■ Although the surface of the ocean looks the same all over to us, it really is not. The ocean surface is divided into sections made up of different kinds of water. The deep sea is blue. The water nearer land is green, yellow, gray, or brown. Sometimes there are even sections of reddish water. They look very strange to us.

There are other differences in the sea water besides color. Some parts of the ocean are saltier than others. Some parts are warmer or colder than other parts. The sea is really much more complex than it seems at first sight.

After reading that passage, did you have a clear impression of the differences in the ocean? Or did you still have questions in your mind about the topic? For example, did you wonder what caused the different colors in the ocean? Did you want to know why some parts of the sea are saltier than others? Or why some parts are warmer or colder than others? Did you wonder why the red part seemed strange?

The passage on the complex nature of the ocean includes details but does not really explain them in any depth. If the details had been expanded upon with facts and opinions, the passage might have developed into something like the following essay.

■ Although the surface of the ocean looks the same all over to us, it really is not. The ocean surface is divided into sections made up of different kinds of water.

The deep sea is blue. This water contains very little life. The water is clear and sunlight can go far down into the water here, making the color appear blue. It is the most beautiful since the color is such a deep shade and contrasts sharply with the sky. The water nearer land is green, yellow, gray, or brown. These colors are caused by an abundance of plant life and by minerals deposited in these areas by rivers. Sometimes there are even sections of reddish water. To me, these parts seem strange, almost gruesome, because it makes me think of blood in the water. The red color, however, is caused by a large number of plants or animals with red pigment living in a certain area. The Red Sea got its name because of the huge quantity of red plankton living there.

There are other differences in the sea water besides color. Some parts of the ocean are saltier than others. Parts of the ocean in areas of intense heat are the saltiest because the heat causes such quick evaporation. The Red Sea is the saltiest ocean in the world; it is 4 percent salt. River water, melting ice, or an abundance of rain or snow makes parts of the sea less salty. The water temperature is also influenced by the sun's intensity in an area. The ocean's temperature varies from 28° F in polar seas to 96° F near the equator.

The sea is really much more complex than it seems at first sight. Perhaps that is why it is so fascinating.

Try It Yourself

See if you can pick out the facts and opinions that support the ideas in the following composition by a GED student.

■ Our visit to New York City was an exciting adventure. First, my husband and I went up to the top of the Empire State Building. It is 102 stories high, and from the observation deck, you can see almost all of the city. It was breathtaking, like looking out the window of an airplane.

Another great spot we visited was Yankee Stadium, a place I had always dreamed of seeing. It is where Babe Ruth, Joe DiMaggio, and Reggie Jackson played ball. The place was just filled with excitement when the game between the Yankees and the Red Sox began.

Finally, we went to the United Nations Building, where people from countries all over the world meet to try to keep the world peaceful. We saw diplomats from the Soviet Union, Greece, and Kenya when we were there. Seeing the UN made us both stop and think. I hope that the men and women there can help keep world peace.

Visiting these places in New York was very interesting. I hope we can go there again sometime.

Did you notice the main ideas of the supporting paragraphs? They backed up the controlling idea that visiting New York was an exciting adventure. They were visiting the Empire State Building, seeing a game at Yankee Stadium, and going to the UN Building.

Then there were facts to back up those ideas: The height of the Empire State Building enables you to see almost all the city. Yankee Stadium is the place where Babe Ruth, Joe DiMaggio, and Reggie Jackson played. The UN Building is where diplomats from countries all over the world meet to try to keep the world peaceful.

The woman gave opinions too, in order to back up her ideas. The "breathtaking" view from the Empire State Building, the "great" Yankee Stadium, and the hope "that the men and women there can help keep world peace" are all examples of the writer's personal reactions to the things she saw.

Warm-up

Label each statement *fact* or *opinion.*

__________ **1.** Honda motorcycles are the best bikes you can buy.

__________ **2.** Water makes up the largest part of your body.

__________ **3.** Studying for the GED Test is difficult.

__________ **4.** The Golden Gate Bridge is in San Francisco.

__________ **5.** Ann's new outfit is attractive.

__________ **6.** Ann's boyfriend thinks that Ann's new outfit is attractive.

Check below to see whether you correctly chose which statements were facts and which were opinions.

Now suppose you are planning an essay on the dangers of drug abuse. Which of the following statements could you use as facts in your essay? Mark them with an *F.* Which could you use as opinions? Mark them with an *O.* Mark any statement that is irrelevant (that is, it doesn't have anything to do with the danger of drugs) with an *I.*

______ **7.** People who deal drugs should receive stiff prison sentences.

______ **8.** John Belushi, Judy Garland, Janis Joplin, and basketball star Len Bias were all celebrities who died from drug overdoses.

______ **9.** Some drugs stay in the body for days and even weeks, so it is not necessary to take drugs every day for an overdose to occur.

______ **10.** Some drugs are legal, prescription drugs; others are not.

______ **11.** Drugs give you a temporary high, but they are not worth the risk.

______ **12.** If a pregnant woman abuses drugs, her child may be born with a birth defect.

See if you were able to detect the facts, opinions, and irrelevant statements by checking the Warm-up Answers below.

Warm-up Answers
1. opinion **2.** fact **3.** opinion **4.** fact **5.** opinion **6.** fact
7. O **8.** F **9.** F **10.** I **11.** O **12.** F

Think about the part of the country where you live. Do you think it's a good place to live or not? List both facts and opinions to back up the ideas you might use in an essay with this controlling idea: "This part of the country is a good place to live." (Or "not a good place to live," if that's what you believe.)

1. Weather

   Facts: ______________________________

   ____

   ____

   Opinions: ______________________________

   ____

   ____

2. Places to visit

   Facts: ______________________________

   ____

   ____

   Opinions: ______________________________

   ____

   ____

3. Things to do:

   Facts: ______________________________

   ____

   ____

   Opinions: ______________________________

   ____

   ____

4. Kinds of jobs available

   Facts: ______________________________

   ____

   ____

   Opinions: ______________________________

   ____

   ____

On the Springboard

Use the facts and opinions you listed in the Warm-up exercise to write an essay telling whether the part of the country where you live is a good place or not. You may want to add details or reorganize the groups of ideas before you begin to write your first draft. Don't forget to write a beginning and an end also.

"The Real Thing"

Directions: You have 45 minutes to write on this question. Write legibly and use a pen.

> Fast-food restaurants have become overwhelmingly popular in the past few decades. They do billions of dollars' worth of business each year.
>
> Consider the advantages that fast-food restaurants offer, the disadvantages, or both. Write down your ideas in a 200-word essay. Be specific, and back up your ideas.

You will find a sample essay on page 158.

LESSON 16

Choosing Your Words

When a carpenter goes to work, he takes with him all the tools he will need to do a good job. When you go about writing an essay, you need to bring all your best tools with you too. Your tools in writing are the words you use to communicate your ideas. Without those tools, your ideas would never take the shape of an essay.

The words you use must be the best ones you can choose for the job of communicating each particular idea. You want to use the most precise and accurate words possible so that your final product, your essay, will be clear and effective.

What are the "best" words to use? They are the ones that give the clearest idea and the most vivid picture.

Be Precise

When an archer shoots his arrows, he aims to hit the bull's-eye. When you write an essay, you want to be on target too. You want every word to mean precisely what *you* mean so that you communicate your ideas in the most exact way you can.

Here's an Example

Read the following two paragraphs about the same picnic. The first one tells about the event in vague, general words.

■ On the Fourth of July, we went to a very good party. It was held in a very big park with lots of nice green grass. We had lots of food to eat. We had great meat, nice salad, and good fruit. There were all kinds of drinks. We all felt very good. There was only one really sad part of the day. It had to come to an end.

Notice all the common general words such as *good, big, lots of, nice,* and *great.* Notice also how many times the writer used the word *very.* Those words are so general that they just don't have a precise meaning. They don't help you picture the picnic at all.

Now read the following version of the same picnic. Notice how this writer used words that are similar in meaning to terms like *good* and *big,* but they are much more specific.

■ On the Fourth of July, we went to a fantastic party. It was held in a spacious park with acres of rolling, green lawns where we could play horseshoes and volleyball as well as just sit at picnic tables and visit. We had a huge variety of delicious foods to eat: mouth-watering hamburgers, hot dogs, and spicy Italian sausages, crispy salad, and cold, juicy oranges, peaches, pears, and grapes. There was also a wide selection of drinks. We all felt relaxed and sociable. There was only one sad part of the day. It had to come to an end.

Because the writer used specific words, you can picture the scene in your mind. In fact, the writer deliberately used words that appeal to your senses to help you do just that. Couldn't you almost see the park and taste the food?

Try It Yourself

Some words in the following sentences help give you a clear, precise impression of what the writer was trying to say. Can you identify them?

■ The wailing squad car squealed around the hairpin curve in the road.

■ Slimy snakes hiss when they are disturbed.

■ The mob surged forward, pressing closer to the police lines.

What words in the first sentence help you picture the scene? *Wailing* helps you "hear" the siren of the squad car, *squealed* helps you "hear" the tires against the road, and *hairpin* helps you "see" the sharpness of the curve. Look how dull and imprecise the sentence would be with more general words: "The loud squad car drove around the sharp curve in the road."

What words did you choose in the second sentence? *Slimy* is a good, precise, descriptive word, and *hiss* helps you "hear" precisely what the snake sounds like.

What about the third sentence? Descriptive words are not the only words that can be precise. Nouns and verbs can be specific and precise too. *Mob* is more specific than *group* or even *crowd; surged* and *pressing* are much more precise than *moved* or *moving* would be.

Warm-up

Fill in three specific words similar in meaning to each of the following general words but more precise. You can use a dictionary or even a thesaurus if you need to.

1. say ________ ________ ________
2. walk ________ ________ ________
3. fat ________ ________ ________
4. sadness ________ ________ ________
5. old ________ ________ ________

Compare your answers with those given under Sample Warm-up Answers. Some of yours will probably be different; there are often many precise words for each general word.

Now substitute a specific word or words for each of the **bold** words or phrases in the sentences below.

6. Ice cream tastes **very good** on a **hot** day.

____

7. The **sound** of the fire relaxed us.

____

8. **A lot of** cars were skidding on the **cold road.**

____

9. Workers **walk** into the **building** every day.

____

10. That group's **music** really makes me feel **good.**

____

See how your rewritten sentences compare with the samples given.

Finally, write a sentence about each of the following things. If you need to, use the senses indicated in parentheses to help you find words to give a precise impression.

11. air pollution (the sight and smell of it)

____

12. popcorn (the smell and taste of it)

____

13. the wind (the feel and sound of it)

____

14. a baby (the sight and sound of it)

____

15. a jet taking off (the sight and sound of it)

____

On the Springboard

Below is the topic assignment from "The Real Thing" that follows. Do some prewriting activities to develop a list of precise words that will help you communicate your ideas about it.

> Many couples are deciding not to have children these days, and of those who are, many are having only one. Families with three or more children are increasingly unusual.
>
> What effects will this situation have on children? Compare and contrast being an only child with having brothers or sisters. Write a 200-word essay about this topic. Be specific.

Use whichever technique—making a list, free writing, brainstorming, or asking questions—that works best for you. Try to remember what it was like to be an only child or to grow up with brothers or sisters. Think *precisely,* not in general terms.

Sample Warm-up Answers

1. state, remark, demand **2.** stroll, march, lope **3.** plump, swollen, obese **4.** sorrow, grief, anguish **5.** antique, outdated, ancient

6. Ice cream tastes especially refreshing on a sultry day. **7.** The crackle of the fire relaxed us. **8.** Hundreds of cars were skidding on the icy freeway. **9.** Workers trudge into the factory every day. **10.** That group's hard, driving rock really makes me feel alive.

11. Settling thick and white on the city, the smog burns people's eyes and wrinkles their noses with its stink of car exhaust. **12.** Movie popcorn, with its buttery smell and salty crunch, is one of my favorite foods. **13.** The soft summer breeze whispered into my ear. **14.** The tiny, wrinkled newborn wailed in its crib for food. **15.** Taking off, a supersonic jet looks like a huge silver bird and roars like a lion.

“The Real Thing”

Directions: You have 45 minutes to write on this question. Write legibly and use a pen.

Many couples are deciding not to have children these days, and of those who are, many are having only one. Families with three or more children are increasingly unusual.

What effects will this situation have on children? Compare and contrast being an only child with having brothers and sisters. Write a 200-word essay about this topic. Be specific.

You will find a sample essay on page 158.

Avoid Slang

You, as well as most other people, probably use slang terms such as *hassle, bummer,* or *cool it* when talking to others. **Slang** is any word or phrase used in a new way in informal speech. People know what you're saying when you use these informal, modern terms.

However, although slang is often easy to understand in informal conversation, it is not a good idea to use it in any piece of writing except, perhaps, in a personal letter to a good friend. For one thing, slang becomes dated fairly quickly. For another, it is often as imprecise as general words. Slang in a GED essay will certainly hurt its score.

By improving your vocabulary to include as many precise words as possible, you'll also increase your ability to avoid slang and use more specific, informative, and therefore effective words.

Coming to Terms

slang a word or phrase used in a new way in informal speech

Here's an Example

The following paragraph is fine as part of a letter from one friend to another, but not as part of a formal essay. The slang words are in **bold.**

■ Last night was a **bummer.** My good friend, Jim, got **plastered** and started to **hassle** me when I told him to **cool it** and sober up. He **blew his top** and told me to stop being a **downer.** I told him that I had no **hang-ups** about partying, but **getting crocked** was not my idea of **having a ball** and if he didn't **lay off,** I was going to **cut out.**

Try It Yourself

Read this pair of sentences. Decide which sentence avoids slang and so would be clearer and more effective in a formal writing situation like the GED essay test.

■ We tried to play ball with the company, but our plan was a bust.

We tried to do business with the company, but our plan failed.

Which terms are used in informal situations? *Play ball* is slang (when it doesn't refer to a ball game, of course). So is the term *a bust.* The second sentence, on the other hand, uses the terms *do business* and *failed,* which are good, acceptable ways to communicate those ideas. The second sentence, therefore, would be best for a formal piece of writing.

Try one more before you go on to the Warm-up.

■ He was so relaxed that he never panicked when things went wrong.

He was so laid back that he never pushed the panic button when things screwed up.

Which terms are likely to become dated, and which are standard, formal English? You could probably tell that *relaxed* was better than *laid back, panicked* better than *pushed the panic button,* and *went wrong* better than *screwed up.* The first sentence avoids slang.

Warm-up

Rewrite each of the following sentences. Change the slang terms used into standard, formal terms. Sample answers appear below.

1. His figures were in the ball park, but we needed to know exact numbers up front.

____

2. Some private eyes on the tube give me the creeps.

____

3. The head honcho always hollers his head off at the hard hats on the job.

____

4. When someone hassles you, it is a real bummer.

____

5. Use your head when you go to take the test; don't let the situation get to you.

____

6. The two-bit robber spent time in the slammer.

____

7. People with problems sometimes go to a shrink.

____

8. I had a ball at the party and didn't hit the sack until three.

____

On the Springboard

Write an essay about a time that you went out to enjoy yourself and ended up having a not-so-enjoyable time. Remember to prewrite and then write a first draft. Be sure you avoid using slang.

Sample Warm-up Answers
1. His figures were approximate, but we needed to know exact numbers in advance. **2.** Some detectives on television make me feel uneasy. **3.** The foreman always yells at the construction workers on the job. **4.** When someone causes you trouble, it is an unfortunate situation. **5.** Think when you go to take the test; don't let the situation unnerve you. **6.** The petty thief spent time in prison. **7.** People with problems sometimes go to psychiatrists. **8.** I had a fun, enjoyable time at the party and didn't go to bed until three.

The Real Thing 

Directions: You have 45 minutes to write on this question. Write legibly and use a pen.

> The telephone is little more than 100 years old, yet it has become a seemingly necessary means of communication in the world today.
> Think about what life would be like in today's society if the telephone had never been invented. Write a 200-word composition that gives specific examples of the changes.

You will find a sample essay on page 159.

Make Sure Every Word Is Necessary

When people give you advice on the best way to live your life, they often say, "Make every minute count." Similar advice holds true for writing: "Make every word count."

Readers do not want to wade through extra words to find out what you are trying to say. They want you to be concise. When you're concise, you use as few words as possible to convey your message clearly. You can be concise if you—

1. reduce the number of extra words used to express an idea
2. avoid repeating ideas

Here's an Example

Read these two compositions about a man who moved from modern society into the wilderness. Notice that the first one is very wordy but the second one is worded concisely.

■ Charles Finn was a person who was happy. He lived in an area of beautiful mountains. In spite of the fact that he was poor, Charles found great joy in the way he chose to live his life. The goal that he had in life was to enjoy nature and lead a simple life in a simple manner. He bought only what was absolutely essential to survive in this day and age.

Charles rose each day at six a.m. in the morning. He engaged in working in his garden most of the day. In the event that it rained, he stayed inside and read books of a wildlife nature that he prized. Each and every evening he took a long walk in the outdoors to engage in the study of nature. When he came home, he went to bed a happy man.

Now read the concise version all the way through once. Then read it again, comparing each sentence with the wordy one above.

■ Charles Finn was a happy person. He lived in a beautiful mountainous area. Although he was poor, Charles found great joy in living. His goal was to enjoy nature and to lead a simple life. He bought only what was essential for survival today.

Charles rose each day at six. He worked in his garden most of the day. If it rained, he stayed inside and read his prized wildlife books. Every evening he took a long walk outdoors to study nature. When he came home, he went to bed a happy man.

Some people think that phrases such as "in spite of the fact that" and "in this day and age" make their writing sound important and formal. Actually, phrases like that are wordy and just bog a reader down. Crisp, concise writing is always best.

Try It Yourself

Each of the following sentences is wordy. Think of ways in which you could make each more concise.

■ At this point in time, he wants a technical kind of job.

How could that sentence be shortened and still get its message across? A quicker and still-effective way to say "at this point in time" is "now" or "currently." "A technical kind of job" takes five words to say what "a technical job" says in three. Perhaps you thought of rewriting the sentence along these lines: "He now wants a technical job."

Consider this sentence.

■ I think that it is probable that I will go on to college.

You seldom have to write "I think" because your reader *knows* that he or she is reading your ideas. You don't write about others' ideas unless you specifically state that with words such as "some people think." Also, "it is probable" is a stuffy way to say "probably." The sentence would be more effective and concise if it were written something like this: "I will probably go on to college."

Now try one last wordy sentence.

■ The goal that I am working for is to save five hundred dollars.

There is nothing wrong with "the goal that I am working for," but you probably realized that it is just as easy to write and therefore read "my goal": "My goal is to save five hundred dollars."

Warm-up

Change each of the phrases below to make it less wordy.

1. in the area of the Rocky Mountains

____

2. in a secret manner

____

3. the idea that I am thinking about

____

4. in spite of the fact that she is upset

____

5. a mechanic in the field of automobiles

---

6. visible to the eye

Sample answers are given below. How do yours compare with them?

Now rewrite each of the following sentences to make it concise.

7. We haven't decided the issue as to whether we should leave today or tomorrow.

---

8. He refuses to discuss any topic that is of a political nature.

---

9. Due to the fact that it is cold, the house paint will not dry.

---

10. The company's headquarters are in a downtown building that is large in size and square in shape.

You can compare your rewritten, concise sentences with those under Sample Warm-up Answers.

Finally, rewrite the following essay. Make the wording more concise by doing away with or shortening any wordy expressions. Feel free to drop as many words as you think necessary or to change the wording as you like, but keep the same meaning.

At this particular point in time, I personally think that people who commute back and forth to a city to work have a day that is long and tiring. Each and every day, some have to ride about approximately three hours on the train or in a car. Due to this fact, their day expands to eleven hours away from home. They repeat this again five times every week.

To solve this kind of problem, these people who work could decide as to whether they should move to the near vicinity of the city where they work, or whether they should find a job nearer to the area of their present homes. Since it's the case that either change would cut down on the number of hours they would have to travel, I personally believe that the change would benefit their lives.

If people want lives that are relaxing and family-centered, they should live near the place where they work.

On the Springboard

Think of a person you like very much. Think of all the precise words and phrases you could use to explain the kind of person he or she is. Determine the most positive things you could say about a person.

Then think of a person you dislike very much. Think of all the words and phrases you could use to describe his or her behavior or personality. Determine the most negative things you could say about a person.

Write an essay about the best words you could use to describe someone, the worst words, or both.

“The Real Thing”

Directions: You have 45 minutes to write on this question. Write legibly and use a pen.

Some people continue to read books, magazines, and newspapers, but many more people turn to television rather than reading for their entertainment as well as information.

Why do many people prefer television to reading? Discuss your answer to that question in an essay of about 200 words. Give clear, specific examples.

You will find a sample essay on page 159.

Sample Warm-up Answers

1. in the Rocky Mountains **2.** secretly **3.** my idea **4.** even though she is upset **5.** an automobile mechanic **6.** visible **7.** We haven't decided whether we should leave today or tomorrow. **8.** He refuses to discuss anything political. **9.** Because it is cold, the house paint will not dry. **10.** The company's headquarters are in a large, square downtown building.

Commuters have a long and tiring day. Every day some ride approximately three hours on the train or in a car. Consequently, their day expands to eleven hours away from home. They repeat this five times every week.

To solve this problem, these workers could consider either moving closer to the city or finding a job nearer their homes. Since either change would cut down on the number of hours they would have to travel, the change would benefit them.

If people want relaxing, family-centered lives, they should live near their work.

LESSON 17

Revising

Improving Your Essay

In the last few lessons, you've been writing first drafts of essays. Remember that a first draft is the first version of a piece of writing. No professional writer would ever turn in a first draft to a publisher because he or she knows that a first draft is not a final, finished product. It is never the best work that a professional writer can do, and it won't be your best work either.

When you write a first draft, you are getting your ideas down on paper in a way that enables you to sit back, take a good, hard look at your ideas, and improve them. That is the goal of the next step in the writing process: after prewriting and then writing a first draft, you improve, or **revise,** your writing.

Actually, you may revise bits and pieces of your sentences and paragraphs even as you write your first draft. That happens with many writers. Even so, revision work demands one step all to itself. In fact, there are actually two phases, or parts, to revising your writing.

To help you revise your writing, you might want to learn a few of the marks that professional writers and editors use. Here's a chart showing the most common and useful marks.

Revision Marks

Mark	Meaning
∧	insert the words or punctuation written above
(delete mark)	delete
—	delete; replace with any words or punctuation written above
≡	make a capital letter (m becomes M)
/	change to a small letter (M becomes m)
(loop with arrow)	move to the place shown
. , :	(draw in any punctuation you want to add)

Coming to Terms

revise to improve your writing by making necessary changes in a first draft

Here's an Example

Here is the first draft of a paragraph with some revision marks showing how the writer decided to improve her writing.

■ Several years ago I was in a car accident and suffered a concussion and a broken arm and had to spend several days in the hospital. When my husband left me there that first night I began to feel a little lonely and to be depressed. Then a man from the lab came and took blood out of my arm. Then a nurse came in and gave me a shot. She said it would put me to sleep. I didn't fall asleep for quiet a while, and all I could hear were people softly moaning and ambulance sirens. When a few hours later, I awoke, there was a woman in the other bed in my room. She had tubes sticking out of all parts of her body. I'll never forget that hospital stay as long as I live.

You can practice using these marks on your own writing as you work through the next two sections of this lesson.

Checking Your Organization

When you are part of a team, you know that all the team members have to be organized and work together for the good of the whole team. Each person has to do his or her part within that organization. If that happens, then the team will work as one and be able to do a successful job.

In an essay too, all the parts must work together to make the essay an organized whole. Only then will the essay do a successful job of communicating your ideas. Your first job in revising your essay is to make sure it achieves this organization and unity by checking the following items.

1. The controlling idea is clear.
2. Every sentence and paragraph supports the controlling idea.
3. The ideas tie smoothly together with transitions.
4. There is a clear beginning, middle, and end.

Here's an Example

The following is an example of a GED-like essay topic.

■ Personal, or home, computers became available on a wide scale in the 1970s. Since that time, millions of consumers have bought them.

Why have many people purchased home computers? Detail your thoughts about the reasons a person might buy one in an essay of about 200 words. Be specific, and include details.

Here is an essay that a GED student wrote on that topic as practice. Notice how she revised parts of her essay to improve its organization and unity.

■ Millions of consumers have bought home computers since they first came on the market. If a survey taker asked each one, "What does your computer mean to you?", the owner might call it a tool, an advantage, a toy, or a status symbol.

The most straightforward reason for buying a home computer is to get a job done. People who keep detailed financial records can get the job done faster and better with a computer. People who write a lot can too. Equipment that provides access to computerized information services can also be very useful.

In addition,

¶ Having a home computer at home can give a student important advantages providing help with papers, computer classes, or spelling, for example. Young children can use special programs too.

Some people are not interested in the work or school benefits that a computer offers. For such people,

¶ The computer is a very, very expensive toy. Computer games are popular with children and adults alike. Some people even program their own games. ~~Other people, however, don't find these games enjoyable at all.~~

Still other buyers

~~Many people~~ get computers merely because they are a status symbol. All the "in" people have one. Many of these people never even turn the machine on.

A home computer owner, therefore, may own such a machine for a number of reasons. The makers of personal computers have obviously been successful in marketing their product to different kinds of people.

~~These are the reasons people have these machines.~~

She felt her beginning and its statement of the controlling idea were fine, and she was right. However, she decided to make some of her transitions clearer. She also found one idea that didn't truly relate to the controlling idea, so she crossed it out. And she felt her ending could be strengthened. Can you see the improvement that her revision work brought?

Try It Yourself

How would you revise the organization of this essay? If this is your own book or if you can photocopy this page, use the revision marks. Check the beginning, middle, and end as well as the transitions. Here's a clue: there is also one unrelated idea that should be crossed out.

■ Playing games is one way that people enjoy spending their leisure time.

First, there is card playing. Cards have been around for hundreds of years and are still popular. Little children enjoy games like Old Maid and Fish. Adults play games such as poker and rummy. Moreover, many adults join card clubs that play bridge or canasta.

Board games are popular. Children start out with games like Candy Land and Chutes and Ladders because they don't have to be able to read directions to play them. Once children are older, they move on to play games such as Monopoly, Parcheesi, checkers, and chess. Monopoly was created during the Great Depression of the 1930s. Adults as well as children spend many leisure hours playing these same board games.

Finally, there is the outdoor athletic game. Before they even start school, children play tag, hide and seek, and hopscotch. Soon they learn how to play dodgeball, softball, and other organized, group sports. This interest carries over into adulthood. Many men and women belong to local sports teams that play games such as softball, basketball, or bowling.

Games have been popular for centuries. They will probably always be a way for adults and children alike to spend their hours away from work or school.

What did you think of the beginning of that essay? It was fairly weak because it was only one sentence long and didn't give a strong statement of the controlling idea for the entire essay. Since the middle of the essay details three kinds of games, that information could also go into the beginning paragraph in a sentence such as this: "People of all ages seem to like three different kinds of games."

The middle paragraphs support that controlling idea except for this detail in the third paragraph: "Monopoly was created during the Great Depression of the 1930s." That little bit of history may be interesting, but it isn't related to the controlling idea. It should have been the sentence that you chose to cross out.

The ending is a strong conclusion that wraps up the essay. But what about transitions throughout the essay? "First" in the second paragraph and "Finally" in the fourth help lead the reader into new ideas. However, the first sentence of the third paragraph is abrupt. Did you want to add a transition term such as "second" or "also" or "another popular kind of game" to that sentence? If so, you revised the spot that needed a better transition.

Warm-up

Here is a GED-like essay assignment. Prewrite and then write a first draft about the topic. You'll revise your first draft in the next exercise.

Credit is a key way of doing business in today's society. Millions of customers routinely use bank or store credit cards to buy everything from clothes to plane tickets. Others make major purchases such as carpeting or furniture "on time" by signing credit agreements in which they agree to make monthly payments. Interest on credit purchases is high.

What are some of the advantages and disadvantages of using credit rather than paying cash? Write a composition of about 200 words detailing your thoughts on this issue. Be specific.

On the Springboard

Take the first draft of the essay that you wrote for the Warm-up exercise. Improve its organization by checking for the following items. Use the revision marks on your essay if necessary.

1. The controlling idea is clear.
2. Every sentence and paragraph supports the controlling idea.
3. The ideas tie smoothly together with transitions.
4. There is a clear beginning, middle, and end.

Checking Your Details

Once you've worked on the organization and unity of your essay and revised it if necessary, you need to take a second look at your writing. This time, concentrate on the details found in the individual sentences. Make sure that the following qualities are present in your writing. If they are not, use the revision marks to improve your essay.

1. Specific examples help support your details.
2. A variety of sentence structures makes your writing flow and sound smooth.
3. The structure of each sentence is correct and will be clear to your reader.
4. The expression of your ideas is clear because you've used concise, precise, and standard words.

Here's an Example

Here again is the student's essay on the reasons for buying a computer. In this second step of the revision process, she used the revision marks to improve the details in her writing.

■ Millions of consumers have bought home computers since they first came on the market. If a survey taker asked each one, "What does your computer mean to you?", the owner might call it a tool, an advantage, a toy, or a status symbol.

The most straightforward reason for buying a home computer is to get a job done.

or who write a lot

People who keep detailed financial records ^

accomplish their work

can ^ ~~get the job done~~ faster and better with a computer. ~~People who write a lot can too.~~

Equipment that provides access to comput-

erized information services can also be ~~very~~ useful.

In addition, having a ~~home~~ computer at home can give a student important advantages *by* providing help with papers, computer classes, or spelling, for example. Young children can use special programs ~~too.~~ *to improve their reading, writing, and number work.*

Some people are not interested in the work or school benefits that a computer offers. For such people, the computer is ~~a~~ *an extremely* ~~very, very~~ expensive toy. Computer *chess and video* games are popular with children and adults alike. Some people even program their own games.

Still other buyers ~~get~~ *purchase* computers merely because they are a status symbol. All the "in" people have one. Many of these people never even turn the machine on.

A home computer owner, therefore, may own such a machine for a number of reasons. The makers of personal computers have obviously succeeded in marketing their product to different kinds of people.

In two spots the writer added examples to help get her meaning across. She also fixed several sentences and improved her choice of words in several places. Her revision work succeeded in improving her essay.

Try It Yourself

Check the following composition for its details. Add examples if you think of any; make sure the sentence structures are correct and varied; improve any unclear expression. Use the revision marks if you can.

■ Soap operas seem to be one of the most popular kinds of television program. Viewers love to see their favorite characters have wonderful heights of success and terrible depths of despair. Soap operas make viewers think that their own lives are dull and routine. Soap operas also give the viewers a taste of excitement. They let their fans escape from the everyday work of real life for a little while to a fantasy. People find that getting involved in a world of money, glamour, and high fashion is a fun and relaxing way to spend an hour or two. The soap operas probably will continue to draw big audiences since they provide a little "get-away" from work and routine.

Perhaps you thought of specific soap operas to name or common soap-opera plots to detail. The third and fourth sentences could be combined or varied in some other way so that they both don't start out with "Soap operas" and then a verb. The choice of words is basically effective but could be improved in a spot or two: "characters *experience* wonderful heights of success" and "draw *huge* audiences," for example. In the fifth sentence, the phrase "for a little while" seems better placed after "let their fans escape" than after "real life."

Did you think of some of these revisions? Did you think of others? Make sure your revision marks truly improved the writing.

On the Springboard

Finish revising your essay on consumer credit by checking its details. Review the essay for these qualities. If it needs improvement, use the revision marks.

1. Specific examples help support your details.
2. A variety of sentence structures makes your writing flow and sound smooth.
3. The structure of each sentence is correct and clear to your reader.
4. The expression of your ideas is clear because you've used concise, precise, and standard words.

A Test-Taking Tip

Just as the directions for the GED essay will not tell you directly to "prewrite," they also won't tell you to "revise." Instead, they will say something like, "Read carefully what you have written and make any changes that will improve your writing." That is precisely what revising is. Be sure to revise first your organization and then your sentences and details. Use the revision marks if you need to; they won't bother the GED scorers. In fact, the marks will show the scorers that you know revising is an important and necessary step in writing an essay.

The Real Thing

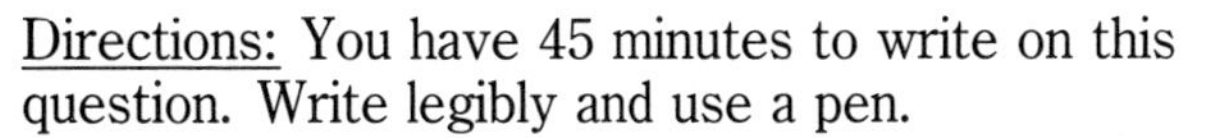

Directions: You have 45 minutes to write on this question. Write legibly and use a pen.

People in many countries around the world are seeking, in one way or another, a voice in their governments through the right to vote. Every election day in this country millions exercise their voting rights, yet millions more do not.

Why do many people choose not to vote? Write a composition of about 200 words discussing this question. Include specific details.

You will find a sample essay on page 159.

Answers: "The Real Thing"

Here are sample essays that you can compare with your own.

13 From Paragraph to Essay
(page 128)

Daily the public is warned that smoking can cause lung cancer, heart disease, and damage to unborn children. Yet 40 million Americans continue to smoke. Why? Most smokers continue their habit for two main reasons: it brings them pleasure, and giving it up causes pain.

Although people may take up smoking to please their friends or defy their parents, they soon find other benefits. Smoking seems to calm frazzled nerves and clear the mind. It may help a person get a grip on angry feelings or calm down after an unpleasant encounter. The cigarette or cigar pleases the mouth and hands. To a smoker, the smoke actually tastes and smells good.

In contrast, giving up smoking often causes severe mental tension and anxiety. A withdrawing smoker is usually bad-tempered. The result can be strained relationships with friends, family, and co-workers.

Still, the pain of tobacco withdrawal does not last forever. On the other hand, lung cancer is almost incurable, and death *is* forever. Smokers enjoy the short-term rewards of smoking and try to ignore the long-term penalties. They quit only when they cannot ignore them any longer.

Transitions
(page 130)

Working for a large company that employs thousands of people may seem glamorous because you are part of an organization that everyone has heard of. If you work for the small company around the corner that employs only five people, you have no such identity. Yet each kind of employment has its advantages and drawbacks.

A big company offers possibilities. Through transfers and promotions, an employee may be able to learn new skills and get ahead. Besides good pay, large companies usually offer fringe benefits such as profit sharing and pensions, excellent medical insurance, or a subsidized cafeteria.

A big company, though, tends to be impersonal. An employee may feel lost in the shuffle; he or she may even be assigned an employee "number." If a layoff is necessary, people are simply let go. No one can really take sole credit for success or responsibility for failure, since too many people are involved in any single project.

In contrast, a small company is more like a family. Employees often know more about one another's lives and care for one another's welfare. Each person has a role, and if something does not get done, the responsibility is apparent. On the other hand, a person can take credit for a good piece of work. Yet pay and the chances for promotion are usually limited in a small company.

In this country there are job opportunities in both big and small companies. Often people can weigh the advantages and disadvantages of each and then choose which kind of employer is best for them.

14 Relating Ideas

Time Order
(page 132)

To make a profit, commercial television has to appeal to a large audience. The American public has changed with the times, and TV programming has changed as well.

Some changes have reflected shifts in the family, the role of women, and sexual morality. When I first began watching television in the 1950s and 1960s, many hit programs were about middle-class families who lived comfortable lives, had minor problems, and resolved them in half an hour. Then, in the 1970s, such programs as "All in the Family" began to show more realistic people with more realistic problems, conflicts, and even prejudices. Single-parent families have more recently appeared on television shows, and lately there have been competent career women. Special dramas that deal with such touchy issues as wife beating and the sexual abuse of children also began to appear in recent years and now are aired almost routinely.

Over the years the amount of violence has increased on TV. Even war dramas, which were popular in the 1960s, seldom showed violence openly. As violence increased in the world, it increased in television shows as well. Today fistfights and gunplay are common on detective shows and police dramas.

Curiously, reruns of many older programs now air on many local television stations. The popularity of some of these shows perhaps means that some people also prefer the society of twenty or thirty years ago.

Like our society itself, then, television changes. To a degree, it has mirrored social changes in the family, our willingness to discuss sexual matters, and increased acceptance of violence.

Order of Importance
(page 134)

Whether working or playing, waking or going to sleep, traveling or homebound, people often have a radio nearby. People find as many different uses for the radio as there are things to do during the day.

If there were no radios, how would teenagers learn the latest hits? Radios provide a beat for dance music and set the mood for a romantic evening.

Radio relieves boring routine. Almost every driver stalled in rush-hour traffic tunes to radio to ease the frustration. Although most parents refuse to believe so, a little background music can make studying go better as well.

Radios are also companions for the lonely. Night workers tune in to the phone-in programs for reassurance that others also are up and about. The runner's companion is the radio plugged into his ears. Hospital patients and invalids pass the time with their favorite show.

Millions of people depend on radios to wake them in the morning. They bring us the news and weather reports throughout the day. In fact, perhaps radio's most important function is that it can bring us news and weather bulletins almost immediately. Radios are much more accessible than TV sets, so they are a more effective means of communication during emergencies. Radio is like an old friend; it is there when we want it and there when we need it. Its many uses prove what an invaluable friend it is.

Cause and Effect
(page 136)

For more than four decades, world leaders have had the power to destroy the world as we know it through the use of atomic weapons. The atomic age marked a turning point in the way the world works—militarily, politically, economically, and emotionally.

For fear of self-destruction, the major powers have not fought a war with one another since nuclear weapons came on the scene. Instead, they have backed wars in smaller countries throughout the world—Vietnam, Afghanistan, Nicaragua. Much of the struggle has taken place secretly (for example, through terrorism and espionage) or peacefully (through foreign aid and economic competition).

The presence of the bomb has divided the world politically into the United States and its allies on one side, with the Soviet Union and its allies on the other. Less powerful "Third World" countries have banded together to protect their own interests.

The enormous cost of building and maintaining nuclear arsenals in various countries has hurt economic growth in some cases. The United States, Europe, Russia, and China have spent on weapons huge sums that could have gone to housing, food, or medical care.

Hardest to measure is the effect in people and their outlook on life. Knowing that the world could be destroyed creates a stress that may lurk quietly in the background. One result may be a desire for quick rewards instead of planning for future generations.

We all know of the immediate effects that the atomic bomb had in 1945. Its long-range effects have been varied and just as serious.

Compare and Contrast
(page 138)

Whether people live in a city, a suburb, or a small, rural town, chances are they think their way of life is best. Each way of life has advantages and disadvantages.

People from cities say they like the excitement and variety their life has to offer. Big-league sports teams, famous entertainers, theater, and art exhibits are all available. In a city, one rubs shoulders with people from all sorts of backgrounds, and the mix can be exciting.

In a small, rural town, people may not have easy access to entertainment, but they can readily enjoy outdoor recreation such as fishing, hunting, and hiking. The air is pure, and the stars shine brightly at night. People know their neighbors and have probably known them for years. When your friends know your life history, they can judge you for what you really are, and not just by outward appearances.

People in the suburbs believe they have the best of both worlds. They can reach the excitement of the city; they also have trees and yards and family neighborhoods. They have more stability and longer relationships with neighbors than city people, but more variety than a rural area seems to offer.

In many ways, though, the three ways of life are not as different as they might seem. In all three, people care for family and friends; they work and make a living; they look for ways to play and relax. The ingredients for a good life can be found in a city, a suburb, and a small town, if a person looks for them.

15 Backing Up Your Ideas

Give Examples
(page 140)

Today as in other times, there are both celebrities and heroes. Celebrities gain fame by some behavior that attracts the public's attention. Although some people imitate celebrities, heroes are the people who set an example of real worth.

Heroes can be found in many fields of endeavor, but they have some features in common. They dedicate themselves to a value and pursue it with unusual courage. Some heroes, such as Mother Theresa or Martin Luther King, Jr., advance social justice. Some, like Franklin Roosevelt or Winston Churchill, give their nation courage in time of war. Others, like Anwar Sadat, work for peace when war is popular.

People who dedicate themselves to advance our knowledge of science and medicine are heroes. Jonas Salk's discovery of penicillin has helped saved thousands of lives. The first organ transplant recipients risked their lives to help further our medical technology and so increased the chances for future recipients, who could be you or I. The astronauts on the ill-fated space shuttle *Challenger* actually gave their lives in the cause of space exploration.

Even anonymous people can be heroes if they display great courage in an important cause. For example, a man or woman who rescues someone else from a burning building, an icy river, or an armed attacker is also a hero.

Heroes, therefore, do exist in the world today. It is certainly for the benefit of all of us that they do.

Use Facts and Opinions
(page 143)

The billions of dollars' worth of business that fast-food restaurants do each year is proof of their popularity. That popularity is due to a number of advantages such restaurants offer, but they have their drawbacks as well.

One major advantage of fast-food restaurants is that they *are* fast. Whereas dinner at a regular restaurant can take an hour or more, dinner at a fast-food place takes only minutes. With today's time pressures, that speed can be important. Getting to the restaurant can be quick as well—fast-food restaurants are nearly everywhere, and formal dress is not required. When a person is traveling, the predictability of fast-food restaurants is reassuring. They look the same as their "cousin" at home, the menu is identical, and the quality of the food is predictable. Wholesale buying keeps prices under control.

The very predictability of a fast-food place can also be a drawback, however. The same menu everywhere becomes boring. Even in such different places as New Mexico and Boston, a Whopper is a Whopper. Fast-food restaurants also promote eating on the run; the family meal around the kitchen table is unheard of in some homes, and that situation is unfortunate. Nutritionists have warned that most fast food is not especially healthful; it tends to be high in sodium and fat.

Fast-food restaurants do serve a useful purpose, therefore. But for the sake of both health and variety, one should not make them a steady diet.

16 Choosing Your Words

Be Precise
(page 146)

Big families are out of style. In fact, many consider them impractical. With the world's population multiplying and cars shrinking, with women working and prices rising, raising an only child is becoming the norm. The only child enjoys some distinct blessings, yet is denied other experiences that only a person with a brother or sister can enjoy.

Only a few years ago, an only child was commonly thought to be spoiled and lonely. Now we read that they are likely to be well-adjusted individuals and high achievers. An only child is the focus of all the parents' hopes for the future. For a single chlld, more can be spent on necessities such as education and food as well as on extras such as music lessons and family trips. The child spends much time with adults and consequently learns their mature vocabulary and viewpoint. All these experiences may indeed give the only child important advantages in the competition of life.

However, people with brothers and sisters have some important advantages too. They learn to live with peers, to settle problems, to share their belongings, and to learn from one another. When they grow up, brothers and sisters are often true friends. No one else can understand each other with the same depth.

Whatever the advantages and disadvantages, none of us chooses to be an only child or to have brothers and sisters. Luckily, there are advantages either way.

Avoid Slang
(page 147)

If the telephone had never been invented, people would have to work harder to get in touch with each other. Most people would merely be inconvenienced, but our way of doing business would be severely changed.

On the personal level, most people today don't write letters often; they pick up the phone instead. But without the telephone, letter writing would be a necessity. To keep in touch with friends, to place an order, or to plan a party, pen and paper would be needed.

Without a phone, people would have to get out and go places. For a social visit, they would have to meet. To check on a particular item, they would have to go to a store and take a look.

Business would definitely suffer. The speed with which orders could be placed, goods shipped, and problems solved would decrease severely. The economy as a whole would no doubt slow down.

On the other hand, there would be some definite advantages to life without a phone. It would not stop ringing *just* as a person came in the door. No one would rush from the shower, dripping wet, to answer the phone and hear "Sorry, wrong number." Obscene calls would be unknown.

Life without a phone would be inconvenient and economically jarring. However, it could also be more peaceful than life as we know it.

Make Sure Every Word Is Necessary
(page 149)

People spend years in school learning to get information and fun from reading. But in their leisure time, they generally turn to television for both news and entertainment. Why has television become such a central part of people's lives?

Perhaps the most important reason is that television *depicts* life, while books translate it into marks on paper. A person experiences television directly, but complex mental processes are required to translate the printed word into events and emotions. Watching television, one not only hears words but sees people and their actions. Printed descriptions provide only the words. Even if the magazine or book has illustrations, there are relatively only a few.

Watching television seems more sociable than reading a book. People watch television together and chat while they listen. Later, one can also discuss a show with friends who have seen it. It is much more difficult to share the printed page.

Since there are thousands of books and magazines available, one must make choices about what to read. Choices about TV are simpler.

To go beyond the surface, to delve into complex issues, to hear unpopular opinions, books and magazines are still necessary. For day-to-day enjoyment, though, television is a convenient option.

17 Revising
(page 155)

All of us have heard repeatedly that a democracy can operate properly only if people participate. Participation means voting. Going to the polls requires only a few hours a year at most. Yet many people never make it. The reason is a mixture of laziness and discouragement.

The laziness often starts with voter registration. People don't know where to go to register and don't bother to find out. If they do know where to register, they may make the excuse that the registration office is not open at convenient hours. Perhaps they put off registering until just before an election but wait too long; it becomes too late to register for that election. Then they procrastinate again until it is too late for the next election.

Even people who are registered to vote often do not. To vote before work means getting up early; to vote after work means getting home late. However, admitting these motivations means admitting to being lazy. As a result, other excuses are offered: "My one vote won't make any difference." (But what if everyone said that?) "I don't understand the issues." (Why not make the effort to learn?) "I don't like either candidate." (Then choose the lesser of two evils or write in someone else's name.)

Some people are truly discouraged about the election process. Members of minorities often feel that their vote doesn't count because they don't feel much in control of their lives to begin with. Such people don't realize that one vote *can* make a difference, and that if enough of them began to vote, they would form a voting bloc and thereby begin to make their wishes heard.

Reasons for not voting don't exist; excuses do. Once people overcome their laziness or discouragement, they will begin to exercise this valuable right and privilege.

Now go on and do the Extra Practice in Writing Essays that follows to sharpen your essay-writing skills for the GED Test.

Extra Practice in Writing Essays

Directions: This is a test to find out how well you write. Each topic assignment below asks you to present an opinion on an issue or to explain something. In preparing your answer, you should take the following steps:

1. Read all of the information accompanying each question.
2. Plan your answer carefully before you write.
3. Use scratch paper to make any notes.
4. Write your answer.
5. Read carefully what you have written and make any changes that will improve your writing.
6. Check your paragraphing, sentence structure, spelling, punctuation, capitalization, and usage, and make any necessary corrections.

You will have 45 minutes to write on each question. Write legibly and use a ballpoint pen.

1. Millions of dollars are spent each year by people attending baseball games, football games, soccer games, basketball games, and numerous other sports. In addition, millions of dollars' worth of advertising money is spent on commercials during televised games.

   Why are spectator sports so popular in this society? Answer that question in an essay of about 200 words. Give specific examples.

2. People are living longer and longer. Senior citizens are making up an increasingly larger portion of the population.

   Think about the lives of senior citizens in today's world. What are their needs and interests, and how do they differ from younger persons'? Answer that question in a composition of about 200 words. Give clear examples.

3. More and more people are working at home these days. Computers, the telephone, express delivery services—these and other goods and services help make home business possible and even practical.

   What would be the effects of working at home? Write about the effects on the individual, on society, or on both. Detail your thoughts in a 200-word essay.

4. Unrequested mail, or "junk mail" as it is sometimes called, often greets the individual reaching into his or her mailbox. Junk mail can be advertising, charity requests, or political information.

   Think about unrequested mail. Write about the positive aspects of such mail, the negative aspects, or both in a 200-word essay.

5. Most full-time workers these days receive two or three weeks' paid vacation as part of their job benefits. Some people like to travel on their vacation, while others enjoy staying at home.

   Compare and contrast spending a vacation traveling with spending one at home. Present your ideas in a composition of about 200 words. Be specific.

Sample essays appear on pages 226–228.

Editing Your Work

Once you've prewritten, written, and revised your GED essay, you need to take one last step to produce your best possible piece of work. You need to edit your writing for style and for errors in grammar and usage, such as subject-verb agreement or verb times. You also edit to spot and correct mistakes in the mechanics of English—spelling, punctuation, and capitalization. These mechanical parts are just as necessary to make your essay read smoothly as nuts, bolts, and wires are to make a car or motorcycle run smoothly.

Editing is similar to combing your hair or straightening your tie. It helps you put the best possible appearance on a part of you—your essay. In addition to editing your own work on the GED Writing Skills Test, you'll need to edit passages and answer multiple-choice questions about them. Of those questions, 35 percent will involve errors in usage, and 30 percent errors in the mechanics.

Most of the questions that test your editing skills will take this form.

> If you throw a dart at a map of california, the chances that it will strike a spot representing a desert are one in four.
>
> What correction should be made to this sentence?
>
> (1) insert a comma after dart
> (2) change california to California
> (3) remove the comma after california
> (4) change the spelling of desert to dessert
> (5) change are to is
>
> 

Notice that the options cover different areas. Two concern punctuation, one capitalization, one spelling, and one verb usage. Half the time the fifth option for a question like this will be "no correction is necessary," and sometimes that will be the correct answer. In this case, however, a correction *is* necessary. California is the name of a state, so it should be capitalized. Option (2) is the correct answer to that item.

Another kind of editing item will take this form.

> Half of the people who live in California today was not born there.
>
> Which of the following is the best way to write the underlined portion of this sentence? If you think the original is the best way, choose option (1).
>
> (1) was
> (2) is
> (3) were
> (4) are
> (5) be
>
> 

This kind of item, you may remember from the first section, is also used to test your knowledge of sentence structure. With this kind of test question, the options will cover only one general area. In this case, it's the use of the correct verb form. Since the subject of the sentence is plural (half of the people), the verb needs to be plural. Since the time that the sentence is talking about is the past, the verb needs to show the past time. Option (3) is the only right verb form you could use in that sentence: "Half of the people who live in California today were not born there."

The lessons in the following section will help you improve your editing skills concerning usage, the mechanics, and even sentence structure. Spelling breaks will give you clues on learning to spell problem words. In addition, the Style Guide near the back of this book will be a great help if you want a stronger background in verb forms, word usage, and rules for punctuation and capitalization. Refer to it whenever you feel the need.

SPELLING BREAK 1

Spelling Techniques

The people at the GED Testing Service have assembled a list of more than 800 words that writers frequently misspell. (The list is near the back of this book.) The words that are tested on the GED Writing Skills Test will come from that list.

If you are a good speller, you can practice editing for spelling mistakes when you do the "The Real Thing" exercises in this section. If you know that you have trouble spelling, the Spelling Breaks in this section will give you helpful techniques and practice in learning to spell the GED words and other words.

Many GED candidates think that they have to be "natural-born spellers" or else they can never learn to spell. That's not true. Most words in the English language follow definite spelling patterns. These patterns can be learned. The words that don't follow a pattern, the exceptions, can be memorized.

A good dictionary will be a great spelling aid to you. A dictionary can show you the following things about a word: its pronunciation, its spelling, its meanings, and how to divide it into parts. (It's easier to learn the spelling of a long word if you divide it into parts and memorize them.) In addition, knowing the meaning can help you become more familiar with the word and remember it the next time you see it.

Experts have pinpointed the main causes of spelling errors. Becoming aware of these problem areas will also help you avoid spelling problems:

1. *Not seeing the letters:* Take the time to read words carefully and correctly.
2. *Mispronouncing:* If you mispronounce a word, chances are you will also misspell it. Use a dictionary to help you with a word's correct pronunciation.
3. *Not listening carefully:* "Tuning in" to a word's sound will help you learn to spell it.

Here is a list of study aids for mastering the GED Spelling List and your own Target List from the next page.

1. Divide the GED Spelling List into groups. Study a group at a time. Put missed words on your Target List on the next page.
2. Write problem words several times. Spell them aloud as you write them. Hearing the correct spelling is one of the best ways for it to "stick with you."
3. Avoid careless errors. Make it a habit to proofread everything you write for spelling errors.
4. Divide a word into parts and learn to spell it part by part.
5. Pair similar words. Learn the differences between these pairs (for example, *accept* and *except*).
6. Write similar words in the same sentence.
7. Write the words from your Target List in sentences.
8. If possible, make a tape recording of the words on your Target List. Practice writing the words as you play back the tape.

With some effort, you should be able to develop a sensitivity to words and thus improve your spelling.

Warm-up

Proofread the following sentences carefully. Can you find spelling errors? Circle the misspelled words you find.

1. Alot of people install an auxilary battery in their trucks. They can use this extra to run equipement while camping without running down the truck's main battery.

2. With the increase in numbers of obese Americans, it is evidant that sugar is the cause of many weight problems. Dieters are now expearimenting with ways to cut sugar amounts in recipees by at least halve.

Use any of the spelling techniques mentioned in this Spelling Break to master these words from the GED Spelling List.

acknowledge	eligibility	perpendicular
ascend	environment	privilege
beautiful	inoculate	significant
believe	miscellaneous	therefore
courageous	negligence	undoubtedly
distinction	parallel	Wednesday

Warm-up Answers
1. A lot; auxiliary; equipment **2.** evident; experimenting; recipes; half

Target Word List

It is important to know the words you tend to misspell in your own writing, whether they are on the GED Spelling List or not. As you proofread your work, write any misspelled words you find on this Target Word List or on a sheet of paper of your own. Divide them into parts if that will help you remember their spelling, or write them in sentences. As you work through the Spelling Breaks in this book, add words that you have trouble spelling to your list.

LESSON 18

Verb Times

Telling Time with Verbs

You've been using verbs to tell the action or condition in your sentences. The verb in each sentence also tells the *time* the action or condition takes place. There are five main types of time that a verb can show: present, future, and three different kinds of past.

Look at the five main times of a verb below. In each case, you can use different forms to tell the same time.

- *Present event:* My car's engine **is** finally in tune. It **is running** well.
- *Future event:* My car's engine **will run** better after the tune-up. It **will be running** like a dream by the weekend.
- *Past event:* My car's engine **made** funny noises last week. It **was clanking** all the way to work.
- *Past and continuing event:* For the past few days, the engine and the belts **have made** strange noises. In general, my car **has been acting** like a lemon.
- *Past event before another past event:* I **had had** no trouble with it before yesterday. It **had been running** extremely well for an old car.

Notice that verb phrases can be used to show certain times. *Will* is used to help show the future, and *has, have,* and *had* help show the past. You can use these and other helping verbs to show different variations on verb times: for example, "I *could have been* a star" or "The car *is being tuned* up right now." Those sentences sound very natural because you use such verb phrases all the time in your speech.

In general, though, the five main verb times shown above are the ones you use most often in speaking and writing. When you edit your writing, you need to make sure that each verb is showing the right time. Determine when the action or condition takes place, and see whether the verb matches that time.

☑ A Test-Taking Tip

On the GED Writing Skills Test, you must know if the times of the verbs are correct in your essay and in the paragraphs with multiple-choice questions. Words and phrases like those below can help you determine which time a verb should show.

currently	yesterday
in the 1990s	today
last summer	tomorrow
a month ago	formerly

Here's an Example

You can tell that the verb in this sentence is right because the phrase *last year* shows you that the action took place in the past.

- The price of haircuts **rose** greatly **last year.**

On the other hand, you can tell that the verb in this sentence is wrong because *next month* shows you that the action will take place in the future.

- My hairdresser has increased the price of haircuts next month.

Try It Yourself

Read the paragraph below. Notice the verbs in **bold** type. Can you tell if each verb is in the correct time?

- The race-to-space **begins** in 1957, when the Russians successfully launched Sputnik I. The first American in space **was** Alan B. Shepard, who was launched in 1961. The United States space program took off after that. In 1969, U.S. astronauts **were** the first Earthlings on the moon. Since the sixties, the Russians and Americans **will launch** many vehicles capable of carrying more people and equipment than earlier flights. In the future, space stations **were built** so people can set up factories in space and use the space stations as bases for further exploration.

Begins is incorrect because it describes a present event. The time clue in the sentence is *in 1957.* The launching of Sputnik I is a past event. Therefore, the sentence should read,

"The race-to-space *began* in 1957, when the Russians successfully launched Sputnik I."

In the next two sentences, *was* and *were* are correct because they describe past events. *In 1961* and *In 1969* are the time clues.

Will launch describes a future event. *Since the sixties* introduces a past action. The corrected sentence should read, "Since the sixties, the Russians and Americans *have launched* many vehicles capable of carrying more people and equipment than earlier flights."

Finally, the phrase *In the future* is the clue that the verb should be telling of a future event: "In the future, space stations *will be built* so people can set up factories in space and use the space stations as bases for further exploration."

A Test-Taking Tip

When you edit your essay for mistakes in verbs and other errors, you can use the same marks that you used to revise. For example, if you want to change the form of a verb, just cross it out and write the correct form above it.

Warm-up

Change each of these verbs so that it describes a present event. Then write a sentence using the new verb.

1. have raised ______________________

____

____

2. had influenced ______________________

____

____

Compare your answers with those given under Sample Warm-up Answers below.

Now change each of these verbs so that it describes a future event. Then write a sentence using the new verb.

3. precede ______________________

____

____

4. offer ______________________

____

____

Compare your answers with the Sample Warm-up Answers below.

Change each of these verbs so that it describes a past event. Then write a sentence using the new verb.

5. borrow ______________________

____

____

6. repeat ______________________

____

____

Again, compare your sentences with the sentences under Sample Warm-up Answers.

Change each of these verbs so that it describes a past and continuing event. Then write a sentence using the new verb.

7. discover ______________________

____

____

8. realize ______________________

____

____

Sample answers for 7 and 8 appear below.

Sample Warm-up Answers

1. raise, raises, is raising, OR are raising; The governor raises taxes after every election. **2.** influence, influences, is influencing, OR are influencing; A father influences his children tremendously.

3. will precede OR will be preceding; The bridesmaids will precede the bride down the aisle next Saturday. **4.** will offer OR will be offering; Our store will be offering a 20-percent discount on that sofa next week.

5. borrowed, was borrowing, OR were borrowing; We borrowed several hundred dollars from my in-laws last year.

6. repeated, was repeating, OR were repeating; When the president did not answer, the reporter repeated her question.

7. has discovered, have discovered, has been discovering, OR have been discovering; Researchers have discovered many causes of cancer but no guaranteed cure. **8.** has realized, have realized, has been realizing, OR have been realizing; She has been slowly realizing that her marriage has problems.

Change each of these verbs so that it describes a past event that came before another event. Then write a sentence using the new verb plus another verb showing past time.

9. congratulate ______________________

____

____

10. proceed ______________________

____

____

Before you go on, see how your answers compare with those given below.

The following paragraph contains errors in the times of all but two verbs. Edit the paragraph, and correct all the errors. Either cross out and correct the verbs on this page or a copy of it, or rewrite the paragraph on your own paper.

George Goodbody begins studying for his GED Test two months ago. He will take a course at the community college that helped him learn to study. He receives high marks on every practice test. These results encouraged him to schedule a date for his GED Test.

A sample answer appears below.

On your own paper, write a paragraph that describes how you currently feel about the value of an education. Then rewrite the paragraph so that it describes how you felt about the value of an education when you left school.

Watching Sequence

When you are writing a paragraph or an essay, you should generally keep your verbs in the same time. However, sometimes the meaning of one or two individual sentences requires you to use verbs in different times.

When you edit your writing, pay attention to the piece of writing as a whole as well as to the meanings of the individual sentences. If things happen at the same time, make sure the verbs show that. If things happen before or after others, make sure the verbs reflect that time order.

Here's an Example

Look at the following sentences. According to the meaning of the sentences, the verbs are used correctly.

- The Social Security Act **was passed** in 1935. Even though the Social Security Benefits Reform Act **was passed** in 1985, it **is** still a controversial issue between politicians and voters.

However, if you were editing the following pair of sentences, you would need to cross out the verb *are* in the second sentence and change it to *will be,* since the time *of that sentence* is in the future.

- You **are invited** to a christening on September 21. Both sets of grandparents **are** there.

A Test-Taking Tip

Here is a common error in verb times that you will come across on the GED Writing Skills Test.

- After Sherlock Holmes assembled all the clues, he solves the mystery of "The Speckled Band."

The sentence describes a past event, but both verbs are not in the same time. To answer a question about a sentence like that, choose the option that places both verbs in the same time.

- After Sherlock Holmes *assembled* all the clues, he *solved* the mystery of "The Speckled Band."

Try It Yourself

When you read this paragraph, decide whether it should generally be told in the past or present time. Then see if all the verbs are in the right time. (Here's a hint: one verb should be in a time different from the others. A word clue will help you see which one.)

Sample Warm-up Answers

9. had congratulated OR had been congratulating; I had congratulated Julia on the promotion before I realized I was talking to her twin sister. **10.** had proceeded OR had been proceeding; We had proceeded with caution until we got your okay on the matter.

George Goodbody began studying for his GED Test two months ago. He took a course at the community college that helped him learn to study. He received high marks on every practice test. These results encouraged him to schedule a date for his GED Test.

■ When I arrived at the VFW meeting last night, I knew something exciting was about to happen. Four television reporters come in with their cameras and lights. Two policemen are standing at the door. All the VFW members were crowded in a corner of the room whispering. Soon it became obvious what is going to happen. Someone had heard that the governor was coming to talk to us. To have such an important man in our small town is always news, and last night was no different. Everyone wanted to be part of the excitement.

In general, that paragraph should be written in the past since it says that the event happened "last night." Therefore, in the second sentence the verb *came* is needed. For that same reason, *were standing* should be the verb in the third sentence. What about "what is going to happen" in the fifth sentence? Did you see that *is* should be changed to *was?* The rest of the verbs are all right. Even though *is* in the next-to-last sentence is a present verb, the word *always* is a clue that the verb should show a present, continuing time.

☑ A Test-Taking Tip

On the GED Writing Skills Test, you will have several questions that require you to take account of the time of the *entire* paragraph in order to choose the right verb time for a particular sentence. So if you have options that involve a change in the time of a verb, insert each choice in the original sentence and see if it makes sense. *Then check the entire paragraph* to make sure the time of that verb fits with the time of the paragraph.

Warm-up

Each of the following sentences contains a verb that's in the wrong time. Rewrite each sentence so that the verbs are used correctly.

1. My grandmother auditions eight times for a talent scout and finally got a part in a Bigger Burger commercial.

____

____

____

2. Last Sunday our preacher invites me to read the Bible in church.

____

____

3. When I went to the dentist for my checkup last week, she asks me if I floss every day.

____

____

____

Check your sentences against those under Sample Warm-up Answers before you go on.

Now edit this movie and book review so that it is *generally* told in the present time. Edit it on this page or on a copy of it, or rewrite the paragraph on another sheet of paper.

I liked the movie *Of Mice and Men* so much that I actually went back and read the book. It tells a very interesting story. In it, two ranchhands, George and Lennie, go to work on a ranch in California. Lennie, a big, strong man, does good work, but he is slow-minded. When the boss's son, Curley, saw Lennie, he picked a fight with him just to prove how tough he is. George told Lennie not to fight, but when Curley kept hitting Lennie, George finally told Lennie to hit back. Lennie didn't realize his strength and breaks Curley's hand. Lennie immediately felt terrible that he had hurt someone, but Curley begins to hate Lennie and causes trouble for him later in the story.

Sample Warm-up Answers
1. My grandmother auditioned eight times for a talent scout and finally got a part in a Bigger Burger commercial. **2.** Last Sunday our preacher invited me to read the Bible in church. **3.** When I went to the dentist for my checkup last week, she asked me if I floss every day.

I liked the movie *Of Mice and Men* so much that I actually went back and read the book. It tells a very interesting story. In it, two ranchhands, George and Lennie, go to work on a ranch in California. Lennie, a big, strong man, does good work, but he is slow-minded. When the boss's son, Curley, sees Lennie, he picks a fight with him just to prove how tough he is. George tells Lennie not to fight, but when Curley keeps hitting Lennie, George finally tells Lennie to hit back. Lennie doesn't realize his strength and breaks Curley's hand. Lennie immediately feels terrible that he has hurt someone, but Curley begins to hate Lennie and causes trouble for him later in the story.

On the Springboard

Directions: Read this paragraph carefully and then answer the questions that follow it.

(1) Many film buffs have seen the movie "Casablanca" numerous times. (2) Its portrayal of the love story between Rick and Ilsa, played by Humphrey Bogart and Ingrid Bergman, makes this movie popular for years. (3) The context of World War II gives the love story an interesting, added dimension. (4) Because it was filmed in 1942, "Casablanca" also shows the struggle between Nazi Germany and the world it tries to conquer. (5) "Casablanca" has finally been released on videocassette. (6) Now future generations have been able to enjoy this classic film and thrill to the line, "Here's looking at you, kid."

1. Sentence 2: **Its portrayal of the love story between Rick and Ilsa, played by Humphrey Bogart and Ingrid Bergman, makes this movie popular for years.**

   Which of the following is the best way to write the underlined portion of this sentence? If you think the original is the best way, choose option (1).

   (1) makes
   (2) has made
   (3) had made

   (1) (2) (3)

2. Sentence 4: **Because it was filmed in 1942, "Casablanca" also shows the struggle between Nazi Germany and the world it tries to conquer.**

   What correction should be made to this sentence?

   (1) change was to is
   (2) change shows to showed
   (3) change tries to tried

   (1) (2) (3)

3. Sentence 6: **Now future generations have been able to enjoy this classic film and thrill to the line, "Here's looking at you, kid."**

   Which of the following is the best way to write the underlined portion of this sentence? If you think the original is the best way, choose option (1).

   (1) have been able
   (2) will be able
   (3) are able

Choose a movie, television show, or book that you especially like. Write a paragraph or an essay telling what happens in the story. First write about the events as if they are happening in the present. Then rewrite your paragraph or essay, changing the time to the past. Don't forget to prewrite, write a first draft, and revise.

You can find the answers to the Springboard multiple-choice questions on page 216.

Did you get all three Springboard items right? If so, try your skill with verbs on "The Real Thing." If you are having trouble with the times of verbs, review this lesson and practice writing paragraphs in one time and then another.

The Real Thing

Directions: Read the paragraph and then answer the items based on it.

(1) Have you ever heard the phrase "use it or lose it"? (2) New research by brain experts will show that continued mental challenges lead to healthier brain cells and more efficient thinking. (3) Previously, experts beleived that senility was a natural outgrowth of aging. (4) A recent thirty-year study has shown that older people who maintain a high level of interaction with their environment do not decline mentally in their old age. (5) Eighty-five percent of all people over 65 do not have any significant memory loss or other forms of mental disabilities. (6) Researchers also have found that previously noted behavioral and mental changes in the elderly may have resulted from improper medication, depression, or other treatable conditions. (7) As a result, new educational programs are being offered in which par-

ticipants learn ways to maintain or restore intellectual skills. (8) They are taught that a flexible attitude and a willingness to explore new ideas will help them remain mentally active. (9) In addition, learning how to make their lives more stimulating is taught. (10) Lillian Rabinowitz, 75, founder of the San Francisco chapter of the Gray Panthers, says, "I think persons have a lifelong capability to learn, and to me that is my greatest treasure."

1. Sentence 2: **New research by brain experts will show that continued mental challenges lead to healthier brain cells and more efficient thinking.**

   Which of the following is the best way to write the underlined portion of this sentence? If you think the original is the best way, choose option (1).

   (1) will show (2) shows
   (3) showed (4) has shown
   (5) will have shown

   ① ② ③ ④ ⑤

2. Sentence 3: **Previously, experts beleived that senility was a natural outgrowth of aging.**

   What correction should be made to this sentence?

   (1) change beleived to beleive
   (2) change the spelling of beleived to believed
   (3) change was to will be
   (4) change the spelling of natural to natrual
   (5) no correction is necessary

   ① ② ③ ④ ⑤

3. Sentence 6: **Researchers also have found that previously noted behavioral and mental changes in the elderly may have resulted from improper medication, depression, or other treatable conditions.**

   Which of the following is the best way to write the underlined portion of this sentence? If you think the original is the best way, choose option (1).

   (1) have found (2) will find
   (3) had found (4) find
   (5) finding

   ① ② ③ ④ ⑤

4. Sentence 8: **They are taught that a flexible attitude and a willingness to explore new ideas will help them remain mentally active.**

   What correction should be made to this sentence?

   (1) change are to were
   (2) change are to had been
   (3) change will help to helped
   (4) change will help to helping
   (5) no correction is necessary

   ① ② ③ ④ ⑤

5. Sentence 9: **In addition, learning how to make their lives more stimulating is taught.**

   If you rewrote sentence 9 beginning with

   They also

   the next word(s) should be

   (1) learn
   (2) learned
   (3) will learn
   (4) will be learning
   (5) had learned

   ① ② ③ ④ ⑤

Directions: You have 45 minutes to write on this question. Write legibly and use a pen.

Large companies employ hundreds, even thousands, of people, sometimes in more than one location. Small companies, on the other hand, can employ only a few people and usually offer limited, intimate office space.

Compare and contrast working for a big company with working for a small company. Write down your ideas in a composition of about 200 words. Be specific with your details.

Check your answers, read the sample essay, and record your score on page 218.

SPELLING BREAK 2

Plurals

Most names for persons or things in our language have two forms. One form—the singular—names one person or thing *(tractor, key, branch).* The other form—the plural—names more than one person or thing *(tractors, keys, branches).* For most words, you just need to add *-s* to form the plural. But some words require more. The rules that follow will help you learn to spell these words.

1. Add *-es* if a word ends in *ch, sh, s, x,* or *z.*

   church/church**es** bush/bush**es**
   gas/gas**es** box/box**es**
   buzz/buzz**es**

2. Add *-es* if a word ends in *o.*

   potato/potato**es** hero/hero**es**

   Music terms ending in *o* are usually exceptions to this rule.

   alto/alto**s** piano/piano**s** solo/solo**s**

3. Add *-ves* after dropping the *f* in most words that end in *f.*

   loaf/loa**ves** wife/wi**ves**
   thief/thie**ves**

   Some common exceptions to this rule are these.

   chief/chief**s** roof/roof**s**
   belief/belief**s**

4. Add *-ies* after dropping the *y* in words that end in *y.*

   company/compan**ies**
   emergency/emergenc**ies**

5. Add only *-s* if words end in *ay, ey,* or *oy.*

   holiday/holiday**s**
   valley/valley**s** decoy/decoy**s**

6. You need to change the basic spelling of some words rather than add *-s* or *-es.*

   emphas**i**s/emphas**e**s
   wom**a**n/wom**e**n

7. For some words, one form of the word is both singular and plural.

   one **deer** or two **deer**
   one **series** or two **series**

Warm-up

Edit this paragraph. Find five misspelled words.

Some libaries have reference sections staffed by people who can answer inquirys from the public. Do you need to know how many misteries were written by Agatha Christie? Do you want to know what profecies Jeanne Dixon has for the new year? Call the reference people; their fact-finding abilitys are amazing.

Check your answers with the Warm-up Answers below.

Find the spelling errors in these sentences. Rewrite each sentence. Even some singular words are misspelled.

1. The playrights buried themselfs in their work.

____

____

2. The cafateria at work serves cold mashed potatos at least three times a week.

____

____

3. When the platoon is on manuvers, the cook's responsibitys include making pots and pots of coffee.

____

____

4. To Dagwood Bumstead, happyness is a sandwhich stacked a foot high.

____

____

5. Charitys often don't have the funds to build fancy facilitys.

____

____

Warm-up Answers
You should have corrected these words: *libraries, inquiries, mysteries, prophecies,* and *abilities.*

6. The hospidal's labratory lost my blood sample.

____

____

7. Jane was greatful for the warmth of the whirlpool after an hour of weight lifting and exsercises.

____

____

8. Docters and nurses are trained to handle several emergencys at once.

____

____

The correct way to write sentences 1–8 is shown below.

Write a sentence using each of the following GED Spelling List words in its plural form.

9. factory ______________________________

10. holiday ______________________________

11. view ______________________________

12. secretary ______________________________

13. bicycle ______________________________

14. address ______________________________

15. similarity ______________________________

16. university ______________________________

17. tendency ______________________________

18. dozen ______________________________

19. chief ______________________________

20. article ______________________________

21. controversy ______________________________

22. loaf ______________________________

23. monkey ______________________________

24. match ______________________________

Correct spellings of the plural forms of these words are listed below.

---

1. The *playwrights* buried *themselves* in their work. **2.** The *cafeteria* at work serves cold mashed *potatoes* at least three times a week. **3.** When the platoon is on *maneuvers,* the cook's *responsibilities* include making pots and pots of coffee. **4.** To Dagwood Bumstead, *happiness* is a *sandwich* stacked a foot high. **5.** *Charities* often don't have the funds to build fancy *facilities.* **6.** The *hospital's laboratory* lost my blood sample. **7.** Jane was *grateful* for the warmth of the whirlpool after an hour of weight lifting and *exercises.* **8.** *Doctors* and nurses are trained to handle several *emergencies* at once.

Your sentences should contain the plural forms spelled this way: **9.** factories **10.** holidays **11.** views **12.** secretaries **13.** bicycles **14.** addresses **15.** similarities **16.** universities **17.** tendencies **18.** dozens **19.** chiefs **20.** articles **21.** controversies **22.** loaves **23.** monkeys **24.** matches

LESSON 19

Verb Forms

Regular Verbs

You might have noticed in Lesson 18 that verbs in the past time are spelled differently from verbs in the present or future. They usually have a *d* sound at the end.

■ Today I believe he is innocent; yesterday I believed he was guilty.

So many verbs follow this form that they are called **regular verbs.** You probably don't have much trouble using regular verbs. In fact, if you have any problem at all, it's most likely in spelling them. When you edit your GED essay or any other writing, make sure you've followed these rules.

1. For a regular verb ending with a silent *e,* just add *-d.*

   dance   danced   have danced

2. For a regular verb ending with a vowel *(a, e, i, o, u)* and a consonant (any other letter), add *-ed.*

   repeat   repeated   have repeated
   travel   traveled   have traveled

3. For a verb ending with two consonants, add *-ed.*

   affect   affected   have affected

4. For a regular verb ending with a consonant-vowel-consonant pattern that has one vowel sound (for example, *jog*) or that is stressed on the final part (for example, *omit*), double the final consonant and add *-ed.*

   jog   jogged   have jogged
   omit   omitted   have omitted

5. For a regular verb ending with a consonant and *y*, change the *y* to *i* and add *-ed.*

   spy   spied   have spied
   study   studied   have studied

6. For a regular verb ending with a vowel and *y,* add *-ed.*

   play   played   have played

If you want to use the *-ing* form of any verb, you follow the same rules as before, with these two exceptions.

1. For a verb ending with a silent *e,* drop the *e* before you add *-ing.*

   dance   is dancing

5. For a verb ending with a consonant and *y,* just add *-ing.*

   spy   was spying
   study   were studying

Coming to Terms

regular verb a verb that forms the past time by adding *-d* or *-ed*

Here's an Example

Look how one GED student edited a piece of his writing so that the regular verbs were spelled correctly.

■ My job is much more pleasant than it used to be. My former boss was always yelling and ~~orderring~~ ordering everyone about nonstop from eight until four. He sometimes accused people of loafing on the job. We workers ~~refered~~ referred to him behind his back as "Sarge" because he reminded us of an army drill sergeant. We tried to please him but could not. I've ~~enjoied~~ enjoyed work so much more since he has retired.

The student corrected *ordering* so that it followed the second rule, *referred* so that it followed the fourth rule, and *enjoyed* so that it followed the sixth rule. These regular verbs were all written correctly in his first draft: *used* (rule 1), *yelled* (rule 3), *accused* (rule 1), *reminded* (rule 3), *tried* (rule 5), and *retired* (rule 1).

Try It Yourself

Read the paragraph below. Edit it for verb spelling. Are the *italicized* verbs spelled correctly?

■ As a teenager, I often *defyed* my parents. When I was *restricted* for my rebellion, my friends all *pityed* me. I *planed* many ways of *escapeing* restriction, but my conscience always *controled* me in the end. I *liked* my freedom and often *regreted* my behavior.

Since *defy* and *pity* end with a consonant and *y*, you should have decided to change the *y* to *i* and add *-ed*. The correct spellings would be *defied* and *pitied*. *Restricted* and *liked* are both spelled correctly. *Plan, control,* and *regret* all end with a consonant-vowel-consonant pattern. *Plan* has only one vowel sound, and you stress the last part of the words *control* and *regret* when you say them aloud. Therefore, you must double the final consonant and add *-ed* to these verbs. They are spelled *planned, controlled,* and *regretted*. Finally, *escapeing* has had *-ing* added to the word *escape*. Since *escape* ends with a silent *e*, you should have decided to drop the second *e* and spelled the word *escaping*.

Warm-up

Rewrite each sentence, inserting the simple past form of the regular verb in parentheses.

1. (ache) After studying without my glasses for the GED Test, my head ______ for a while.

____

____

2. (collect) When the instructor ______ the exams, he let us go home early.

____

____

3. (transfer) Since I ______ into this department, my morale has improved.

____

____

4. (breathe) He ______ a sigh of relief after the job interview.

____

____

5. (hurry) I ______ home to watch the Super Bowl.

____

____

Warm-up Answers
1. ached **2.** collected **3.** transferred **4.** breathed **5.** hurried

Here are two lists of words from the GED Spelling List. Write ten complete sentences using a subject and a verb from each list. Be creative, but don't use the same list word twice.

SUBJECTS	REGULAR VERBS
amateur	analyzing
heroes	benefited
daughter	congratulated
business	persuading
optimist	stretching
soldier	apologized
playwright	conquered
visitor	eliminated
governor	depositing
government	balanced

Irregular Verbs

If all verbs were regular, a writer's life would be much easier. However, some verbs don't follow any particular rules when you change them from the present to the past.

■ Today compact discs and tapes **bring** people musical pleasure. In years past long-playing records **brought** our parents and grandparents musical pleasure. Over the centuries live performances **have brought** people musical pleasure.

These kinds of verbs are called **irregular** because they don't follow any pattern. In fact, some even have two different forms for the different kinds of past time. There's one for the simple past—

■ Today is the day I **give** forty dollars to the United Way at work.

Last year I **gave** thirty dollars.

And one for the past and continuing event or the past event before another past event—

■ I **have given** money to the United Way every year for the past five years.

I **had given** money to individual charities before that time.

There is one rule you can memorize about this kind of irregular verb: the second past form is *always* used as part of a verb phrase. In other words, it is always used with a helping verb like *has* or *have*.

Being able to tell which verb form to use in a particular sentence is part of the editing job.

Coming to Terms

irregular verb a verb that doesn't follow any pattern when you change it from present to past

Here's an Example

This man has just witnessed a "fender bender." The police officer wants his version of what happened. Read his account aloud. *Listen* to the way he uses verbs.

■ "I seen it, officer. I been here the whole time. This first car run the red light."

Can you hear the mistakes he made in using verbs? Now *look* at the eyewitness's report to the police officer. Remember that the second past form can never stand alone as a single-word verb.

"I seen it" contains an error because *seen* needs to be used in a verb phrase. He could say, "I have seen it." But it would be more appropriate in this case to use the simple past form and say, "I saw it."

In the second sentence, *been* is used in error. Again, *been* should be used in a verb phrase. The witness should say, "I have been here the whole time."

"This first car run the red light" is also incorrect. He should use the simple past form, *ran.* So his report should be "I saw it, officer. I have been here the whole time. This first car ran the red light."

If you know right now that you have trouble speaking and writing the correct forms of irregular verbs, spend some time studying the verb chart in the Style Guide near the back of this book. Say the verb forms aloud until they begin to sound right to you. Once you are able to "trust your ear" in writing and editing, using the right verb becomes easy.

Try It Yourself

After winning a fierce battle, Julius Caesar uttered the now famous words "I came. I saw. I conquered." Of course, his original words were spoken in Latin, but they are written here in English using the simple past forms of two irregular verbs and one regular verb. Now think about this: Would Caesar have been just as correct to say, "I come. I seen. I conquered"?

"I conquered" is fine because *conquer* is a regular verb. But saying "I come" when you are indicating something that happened in the past is incorrect. He would have needed to add a helping verb and say "I have come." Saying "I seen" is also incorrect. *Seen* is the second past form of *see,* so it too needs an extra verb with it. Caesar would have had to say "I have seen."

Here's what Caesar's famous quote would have been if he had used the second past forms of those three verbs: "I have come. I have seen. I have conquered."

Now ask yourself this: What do the *italicized* verbs in these sentences have in common?

■ I *have drank* the iced tea.

I *have ran* the race.

I *had wrote* the letter.

All three verbs have a helping verb in front of them. Yet all three verbs—*drank, ran,* and *wrote*—are simple past forms of the verbs *drink, run,* and *write.* They don't need any extra help. To make them correct, you can take away the extra verb and write, "I drank the iced tea. I ran the race. I wrote the letter." Or you can leave the extra verbs in and use the third part of each verb: "I have drunk the iced tea. I have run the race. I have written the letter."

Warm-up

Rewrite each sentence, inserting the correct past form of the verb in parentheses.

1. (go) After soaking in the hob tub, the soreness in my muscles was ______.

2. (do) Her sudden outburst of singing was ______ to get attention.

3. (speak) Several union representatives ______ at the yearly workers' meeting.

4. (choose) My daughter ______ to take gymnastics rather than ballet.

5. (become) The coast of Florida's Panhandle has ______ a favorite winter vacation spot for many Canadians.

6. (forget) How could you have ______ our anniversary?

7. (break) Janet ______ with family tradition at Christmas by going to the beach.

8. (eat) Have you really ______ a gallon of ice cream in just two days?

9. (see) The exterminator ______ termites in the basement.

10. (be) When he ______ a puppy, my dog preferred steak scraps for dinner.

Check your sentences with the answers given under Warm-up Answers. If you got any wrong, study the verb chart in the Style Guide before you go on.

Many of the sentences in the following passage contain errors in using both regular and irregular verbs. Edit the passage. Cross out the wrong verbs and write correct ones on this page or a copy of it, or rewrite the passage on your own paper.

Ben Franklin's formal schooling ended when he be ten, but his curiosity and intelligence made him one of our most famous founders. He spended most of his life as a printer or diplomat. In his spare time, he studyed languages and science. He begun the first circulating library in America and become postmaster general of the U.S. Post Office. Franklin was elected to help frame the Declaration of Independence, which was actually wrote by Thomas Jefferson, but which was corrected by Ben Franklin. He died at the age of 84 after devoting the last months of his life writing essays to encourage the abolition of slavery.

Warm-up Answers
1. gone **2.** done **3.** spoke **4.** chose **5.** become **6.** forgotten **7.** broke **8.** eaten **9.** saw **10.** was

Ben Franklin's formal schooling ended when he was ten, but his curiosity and intelligence made him one of our most famous founders. He spent most of his life as a printer or diplomat. In his spare time, he studied languages and science. He began the first circulating library in America and became postmaster general of the U.S. Post Office. Franklin was elected to help frame the Declaration of Independence, which was actually written by Thomas Jefferson, but which was corrected by Ben Franklin. He died at the age of 84 after devoting the last months of his life writing essays to encourage the abolition of slavery.

On the Springboard

Directions: Read this paragraph carefully and then answer the questions that follow it.

(1) Edgar Allan Poe was the writer of such eerie tales as "The Fall of the House of Usher" and "The Tell-Tale Heart." (2) During his lifetime, he received very little pay for his writing. (3) He had wrote some of the best poetry in the nineteenth century, yet he was not well liked by other poets. (4) What begun as a promising career ended in tragedy. (5) Many people think Poe drank himself to death, but research has proved that he was not an alcoholic. (6) Poe's genius has never been doubted, but he was a man with many problems.

1. Sentence 3: **He had wrote some of the best poetry in the nineteenth century, yet he was not well liked by other poets.**

   What correction should be made to this sentence?

   (1) change had wrote to had written
   (2) change had wrote to writed
   (3) change was to be

   (1) (2) (3)

2. Sentence 4: **What begun as a promising career ended in tragedy.**

   What correction should be made to this sentence?

   (1) change begun to began
   (2) change the spelling of career to carreer
   (3) change ended to ends

   (1) (2) (3)

3. Sentence 5: **Many people think Poe drank himself to death, but research has proved that he was not an alcoholic.**

   What correction should be made to this sentence?

   (1) change drank to drunk
   (2) remove the comma after death
   (3) no correction is necessary

   (1) (2) (3)

"My Most Unforgettable Character" was a popular type of story in *Reader's Digest* magazine. Authors of this kind of story wrote about relatives, friends, or other people who made a lasting impression on them. Who would *you* consider to be memorable characters in your life? Choose one memorable character from your past to write about in an essay. Plan, write, and revise your essay. Then edit it for verb times, verb forms, and spelling.

Check your multiple-choice answers for On the Springboard on page 216. Did you get all three correct? If so, move on to "The Real Thing." If you are still having problems with verb forms, review the chart in the Study Guide. Listen to the sounds of the correct verb forms. Then write sentences with the ones you have trouble with.

"The Real Thing"

Directions: Read the paragraph and then answer the items based on it.

(1) The contributions of immigrants have added a tremendous richness to American culture. (2) One man who came from England in 1914 became one of Hollywood's biggest stars. (3) His trademarks were a gentlemanly black bowler, an oversized jacket, and a bamboo cane. (4) He was the classic silent movie clown known as the Little Tramp, his real name was Charlie Chaplin. (5) Before coming to America at the age of 25, Chaplin had spent most of his life in poverty. (6) Within a year and a half of his movie debut in 1914, he earned $12,844 a week. (7) One year later, he signed a multimillion-dollar movie contract. (8) Taxes at that time took only a small amount of a person's annual income. (9) Movies had became such a part of Chaplin's life that he wrote, directed, and starred in his own films. (10) As a director, Chaplin was a perfectionist he shot a scene over and over until he was satisfied with it. (11) Although there been no radio or television publicity in those early days of technology, his movies were instant hits. (12) Many movie buffs believe him to have been the most creative movie genius of this century.

1. Sentence 4: **He was the classic silent movie clown known as the Little Tramp, his real name was Charlie Chaplin.**

   Which of the following is the best way to write the underlined portion of this sentence? If you think the original is the best way, choose option (1).

   (1) Tramp, his (2) Tramp. His
   (3) Tramp his (4) Tramp, since his
   (5) Tramp and his

   (1) (2) (3) (4) (5)

2. Sentence 8: **Taxes at that time took only a small amount of a person's annual income.**

   What correction should be made to this sentence?

   (1) change the spelling of Taxes to Taxs
   (2) change took to had took
   (3) change took to had taken
   (4) insert a comma after amount
   (5) no correction is necessary

   (1) (2) (3) (4) (5)

3. Sentence 9: **Movies had became such a part of Chaplin's life that he wrote, directed, and starred in his own films.**

   What correction should be made to this sentence?

   (1) change became to become
   (2) change wrote to written
   (3) change wrote to had wrote
   (4) change the spelling of starred to stared
   (5) no correction is necessary

   (1) (2) (3) (4) (5)

4. Sentence 10: **As a director, Chaplin was a perfectionist he shot a scene over and over until he was satisfied with it.**

   Which of the following is the best way to write the underlined portion of this sentence? If you think the original is the best way, choose option (1).

   (1) perfectionist he shot
   (2) perfectionist shot
   (3) perfectionist, shooting
   (4) perfectionist he shoots
   (5) perfectionist he had shot

   (1) (2) (3) (4) (5)

5. Sentence 11: **Although there been no radio or television publicity in those early days of technology, his movies were instant hits.**

   What correction should be made to this sentence?

   (1) replace Although with Before
   (2) change the spelling of Although to Altho
   (3) change been to be
   (4) change been to was
   (5) remove the comma after technology

   (1) (2) (3) (4) (5)

Directions: You have 45 minutes to write on this question. Write legibly and use a pen.

By the time the average child turns eighteen, he or she has spent 20,000 hours watching television.

Discuss the advantages television offers to children, the disadvantages, or both. Write a 200-word essay detailing your views. Give specific examples.

Check your answers, read the sample essay, and record your score on pages 218–219.

SPELLING BREAK 3

Troublesome Letters

You know how to double a final consonant when adding *-d, -ed,* or *-ing* onto a verb. In addition, some English words have double consonants within them that might cause spelling problems because you don't hear a double sound.

a**cc**omplish   bri**ll**iant   po**ss**ible

Other words have totally silent letters.

ai**s**le   colum**n**   dou**b**t

You may mispronounce still other words and incorrectly spell them the way you pronounce them.

acros**s** (not acrost)
math**e**matics (not mathmatics)
bach**e**lor (not bachlor)

If you develop your ear for sounds as people speak and your eye for letters as you read, words with double letters, silent letters, or frequently mispronounced letters won't present too much of a problem.

Warm-up

Find and edit the eight misspelled words in the book review below. You can check the GED Spelling List near the back of this book if you need to.

Last Febuary, the Asociation for the Advancement of Star Research published a beautifull book that belongs on evry astronomy buff's bookshelf. The book details the birth, life, and death of a star. (The tempratures involved in this evolution are staggering.) Many multicolored drawings and photographs acompany the explanations. In genral, the ideas put forth in this book comunicate the need for scientists around the world to cooperate in further star research.

Check your edited version with the Warm-up Answers to see whether you caught and corrected all the spelling mistakes.

For numbers 1 through 10, one word in each group is misspelled. Rewrite *each* word, correcting the misspelled word. All these words are from the GED Spelling List in one form or another.

1. abundance, carefull, coffee

____

2. maintainance, congratulating, sudden

____

3. conceivible, positive, measure

____

4. tremendous, changeable, committment

____

5. appearance, allmost, unnecessary

____

6. disease, muscle, aquaintance

____

7. refered, fatigue, occasional

____

8. interfering, language, excellant

____

9. assistent, embarrass, friend

____

10. attendance, benefitted, exhausting

____

See how many words you spelled correctly by checking the Warm-up Answers on the next page.

Now find the spelling errors in these sentences. Rewrite each sentence correctly.

11. The dissapointed audience got a refund when the play's performance was cancelled.

____

____

12. By the time the thunder claped, we had allready seen the lightening flash.

____

____

13. It's silly to be quarelling over that TV show, since it's really a matter of personal preferrence.

____

____

14. Sevral tornadoes occured along the storm front.

Now check your rewritten sentences with those at the end of this Spelling Break.

Here are five words with double letters, silent letters, or frequently mispronounced letters. Write a sentence with each word.

15. propeller

16. guidance

17. assistant

18. quantity

19. different

Sample sentences are given below.

Now combine your spelling and verb-use skills. Find the spelling and verb errors in the following sentences. Rewrite each sentence, correcting any errors that you find.

20. He brung flowers to the cemtery where his wife is buryed.

Warm-up Answers
You should have corrected these words in the book review: *February, Association, beautiful, every, temperatures, accompany, general,* and *communicate.*

These are the words that had been misspelled: **1.** careful **2.** maintenance **3.** conceivable **4.** commitment **5.** almost **6.** acquaintance **7.** referred **8.** excellent **9.** assistant **10.** benefited

11. The *disappointed* audience got a refund when the play's performance was *canceled.* **12.** By the time the thunder *clapped,* we had *already* seen the *lightning* flash. **13.** It's silly to be *quarreling* over that TV show, since it's really a matter of personal *preference.* **14.** *Several* tornadoes *occurred* along the storm front.

Sample sentences: **15.** Pilots needed someone to begin spinning their propellers on early planes. **16.** Family guidance is available from numerous sources in the community. **17.** She doesn't want to be just an assistant anymore. **18.** That food store is cheaper than the rest because it buys goods in quantity. **19.** It's funny, but I don't feel any different today.

21. Possesive people prefer piles of possesions.

22. Her holesome apearance made Doris Day a big star in the 1950s and '60s.

23. After the earthquake, rescuers seen considrable damage in the center of the city.

24. In the future, rebelions be handled by the goverment militia.

25. Tire chains are indispensible when travelling in winter in the higher elevations.

26. Last Sunday, the Thompsons had drove through the housing developement to see the new models.

27. Work on our new kichen celing begun yesterday.

28. You have the right temperment for dealing with angery customers.

Rewritten sentences with correctly spelled words and verb forms appear below.

---

20. He *brought* flowers to the *cemetery* where his wife is *buried.* **21.** *Possessive* people prefer piles of *possessions.* **22.** Her *wholesome appearance* made Doris Day a big star in the 1950s and '60s. **23.** After the earthquake, rescuers *saw considerable* damage in the center of the city. **24.** In the future, *rebellions will be* handled by the *government* militia. **25.** Tire chains are *indispensable* when *traveling* in winter in the higher elevations. **26.** Last Sunday, the Thompsons *drove* through the housing *development* to see the new models. **27.** Work on our new *kitchen ceiling began* yesterday. **28.** You have the right *temperament* for dealing with *angry* customers.

LESSON 20

Subject-Verb Agreement

Matching Verbs with Subjects

You learned in Lesson 18 that the time of verbs often must match. In this lesson you will learn more about making subjects and verbs match.

You already know that subjects can be singular or plural. The basic rules are (1) if the subject is singular, use a singular verb, and (2) if the subject is plural, use a plural verb. In addition, you've learned from your work with combining sentences that if there is more than one subject and they are connected by *and,* you use a plural verb. If they are connected by *or, either . . . or,* or *neither . . . nor,* you match the verb with the closest subject.

In writing a first draft, it's easy to mismatch subjects and verbs. One goal of editing, then, is to check that subjects and verbs agree.

Here's an Example

Below is a paragraph from the first draft of a newspaper article. Notice how the reporter went back and edited his subjects and verbs.

■ Some dentists have a new motto: Have drill, will travel. This special health-care group brings dentistry to homebound patients. Either the dentist or a dental assistant take^s X rays and clean^s teeth. Even cavities are filled at home. Records and equipment ~~is~~ *are* packed into suitcases that fit into a car's trunk. Often the dentists base~~s~~ their fees on the patient's ability to pay. This new service ~~are~~ *is* helpful to the very ill, the handicapped, and the elderly.

The subject-verb pairs "dentists have" and "cavities are filled" match because the subjects and verbs are plural. "Group brings" matches because both are singular. (A word like *group* is usually considered singular because it most often refers to all the members as *one* whole, as it does in the sentence here.)

The subjects *dentist* and *dental assistant* were connected with *either . . . or,* so the paired verbs needed to match with the closest subject, which is singular. *Records* and *equipment* were paired with *and,* so he changed the verb to be plural.

"Dentists bases" was not a match because *dentists* is plural and *bases* is singular. (Remember that verbs that end in *s* are usually singular, not plural.) Finally, *service* is a singular word. (Some people might think *service* is plural because it ends with an *s* sound, but the sound in this case has nothing to do with the matter.) "Service is" matches.

Can you see how the reporter correctly edited his story?

Try It Yourself

Read and edit the first draft of another article below. Mark the necessary changes on this page or a copy of it, or write the correct verbs on your own paper.

■ Whether people work indoors or out, they need to protect their skin. Outside, sun and wind dries skin and damages hair. Hats protects skin and hair from these elements, as do moisturizing sunscreens. Inside, both heating and air-conditioning rob skin of moisture. A room humidifier ease the dryness in office or home air.

Which verbs did you decide to change? "Sun and wind" need the plural verb *dry* because they are two subjects connected with *and. Hats* is plural, and so its verb should be too: "Hats protect." Because *heating* and *air-conditioning* are connected with *and,* the plural verb *rob* is right in that sentence. But because *humidifier* is singular, its verb should be the singular *eases,* not the plural *ease.*

Warm-up

Rewrite each sentence. Choose the verb that matches the subject.

1. John, Paul, George, and Ringo (was, were) the Beatles.

2. A hammer and a wrench (makes, make) a lot of repairs possible.

3. Neither his one friend nor his many enemies (has, have) anything good to say about Frank's job performance.

4. Neither money nor talent (was, were) lacking in Marla, but a kind heart was.

5. Elephants (forget, forgets) that they don't really like peanuts.

6. (Is, Are) your family well?

7. That mechanic (doesn't, don't) know how to replace a muffler.

8. Either your dogs (goes, go) or I do!

Check your answers with those at the end of this Warm-up.

Sentences 9 through 11 contain singular subjects and verbs. Make each subject plural. Then rewrite the sentence with a matching verb.

9. The retiree is planning a trip in his new motorhome.

10. The salad dressing was left on the kitchen counter last night.

11. One weekend every fall, our bowling team hunts for deer in Maine.

Check your answers before you go on.

Sentences 12 through 14 contain plural subjects and verbs. Make each subject singular. Then rewrite the sentence. Make sure the verb matches the new subject.

12. Chesapeake Bay retrievers make excellent hunting dogs.

13. The consumer agencies were pleased with the results of the investigation.

14. Weather forecasters don't care if it rains.

Before you go on, take the time to check your answers to the last three sentences.

Finally, edit these sentences for mismatched subjects and verbs. Either mark the corrections within the sentences, or rewrite the sentences on your own paper. Not all the sentences have errors.

15. Credit cards gives you the freedom to buy on time.

16. The Little League mothers and fathers is expected to attend the meeting.

17. Old quilts and an antique sampler hang on my bedroom walls.

18. Absence make the heart grow fonder.

19. Neither the bus nor the train go to Bountiful any longer.

Warm-up Answers
1. were **2.** make **3.** have **4.** was **5.** forget **6.** Is **7.** doesn't **8.** go

9. The retirees are planning a trip in their new motorhome. **10.** The salad dressings were left on the kitchen counter last night. **11.** One weekend every fall, our bowling teams hunt for deer in Maine.

12. A Chesapeake Bay retriever makes an excellent hunting dog. **13.** The consumer agency was pleased with the results of the investigation. **14.** A weather forecaster doesn't care if it rains.

15. change *gives* to *give* **16.** change *is* to *are* **17.** no error **18.** change *make* to *makes* **19.** change *go* to *goes*

On the Springboard

Directions: Read this paragraph carefully and then answer the questions that follow it.

(1) Computers are becoming indispensable in allmost every aspect of your life. (2) They can even help you change the way you look. (3) If you want to redesign your face, a computer imaging system can take some of the guesswork out of plastic surgery. (4) In the past, you would have needed a photograph of your dream face, or a plastic surgeon would sketch changes on your photograph. (5) Now a camera, a screen, a computer, and an electronic stylus helps you and your doctor predict the results of surgery. (6) This new technology is not picture-perfect, but at least it will take the "byte" out of your suspense over the surgical results.

1. Sentence 1: **Computers are becoming indispensable in allmost every aspect of your life.**

   What correction should be made to this sentence?

   (1) change are to is
   (2) remove the word are
   (3) change the spelling of allmost to almost

   (1) (2) (3)

2. Sentence 5: **Now a camera, a screen, a computer, and an electronic stylus helps you and your doctor predict the results of surgery.**

   What correction should be made to this sentence?

   (1) remove the comma after camera
   (2) change helps to help
   (3) change helps to helped

   (1) (2) (3)

Do you have very definite opinions about your appearance? Do you hate your naturally curly hair or love your long, artistic fingers? If you are like most people, you try to accent your best features and hide your worst ones.

What do you consider your best physical feature? What feature do you especially try to hide or play down?

Write an essay in which you tell about your best physical feature and about your worst. Don't forget to prewrite, write a first draft, and revise your essay. Then edit it for any incorrect verbs and for spelling mistakes.

Check your multiple-choice answers for On the Springboard on page 216. If all your answers were correct, move on to "The Real Thing." If subject-verb agreement is still causing you difficulty, go back and review this lesson.

"The Real Thing"

Directions: Read the paragraph and then answer the items based on it.

(1) If you had lived in ancient Rome, you might have relieved the symptoms of the common cold by sipping an onion broth. (2) In colonial America, you might have relied on pennyroyal tea or an herbal concoction made from plants such as buckthorn, coltsfoot, and bloodroot. (3) In your grandmother's time, lemon and honey were used to cure colds, or in extreme cases, a hot toddy laced with rum was prepared. (4) Today, if you don't have a family remedy to rely on, you probably take one of literally thousands of drug preparations available without perscription. (5) Some remedies contains ingredients that remind you of the folk medicine of the past; others are formulated with fancy chemical creations. (6) Old or new, simple or fancy, many will relieve some of the familiar cold symptoms. (7) However, not a single one will prevent, cure, or even shorten the course of the common cold. (8) That is according to a panel of nongovernment experts who reported to the Food and Drug Administration about the safety, effectiveness, and accuracy of claims made on the labels of some 50,000 drug products. (9) The panel indicates that proper use of over-the-counter drugs can help relieve cough, sinus congestion, and a runny nose. (10) Yet it also made clear that allthough these products may relieve certain symptoms, they do not cure the cold itself.

1. Sentence 3: **In your grandmother's time, lemon and honey were used to cure colds, or in extreme cases, a hot toddy laced with rum was prepared.**

Which of the following is the best way to write the underlined portion of this sentence? If you think the original is the best way, choose option (1).

(1) were used
(2) was used
(3) is used
(4) were being used
(5) were using

(1) (2) (3) (4) (5)

2. Sentence 4: **Today, if you don't have a family remedy to rely on, you probably take one of literally thousands of drug preparations available without perscription.**

What correction should be made to this sentence?

(1) change don't to doesn't
(2) remove the comma after on
(3) change the spelling of probably to probly
(4) change take to takes
(5) change the spelling of perscription to prescription

(1) (2) (3) (4) (5)

3. Sentence 5: **Some remedies contains ingredients that remind you of the folk medicine of the past; others are formulated with fancy chemical creations.**

What correction should be made to this sentence?

(1) change contains to contained
(2) change contains to contain
(3) change the semicolon to a comma
(4) change are to is
(5) change are to be

(1) (2) (3) (4) (5)

4. Sentence 9: **The panel indicates that proper use of over-the-counter drugs can help relieve cough, sinus congestion, and a runny nose.**

Which of the following is the best way to write the underlined portion of this sentence? If you think the original is the best way, choose option (1).

(1) indicates
(2) indicated
(3) done indicated
(4) will indicate
(5) indicate

(1) (2) (3) (4) (5)

5. Sentence 10: **Yet it also made clear that allthough these products may relieve certain symptoms, they do not cure the cold itself.**

What correction should be made to this sentence?

(1) change made to make
(2) change the spelling of allthough to although
(3) change may relieve to relieves
(4) remove the comma after symptoms
(5) change the spelling of itself to itsself

(1) (2) (3) (4) (5)

Directions: You have 45 minutes to write on this question. Write legibly and use a pen.

Commercials are broadcast on most television stations. They appear every five to ten minutes during regularly scheduled programming and are used to advertise a wide range of products and services.

Discuss the positive aspects of commercials, the negative aspects, or both. Write a 200-word essay detailing your thoughts.

Check your answers and read the sample essay on page 219.

Interrupting Phrases

Often words and phrases come between the subjects and verbs in your sentences. Then you might find matching them a little more difficult. The farther apart the subject and verb are, the closer you must look at the way they match.

Sometimes an added thought comes between the subject and verb. Look at the following list of words. When one of these words begins an added thought that comes between the subject and verb, be careful not to mismatch them.

like	together with
plus	as well as
with	along with
including	in addition to
accompanied by	

Sometimes a descriptive phrase comes between the subject and verb. In other sentences, a noun phrase or dependent thought that gives more information about the subject comes between the subject and the verb. Don't be fooled into thinking a word in the phrase or thought is the main subject of the sentence. It never is.

Here's an Example

Notice that the added thoughts in the following sentences don't affect the relationship between the subjects and verbs (in **bold**).

■ **Erosion** (plus poor farming practices) **ruins** large farm areas.

Bad eating **habits,** together with a lack of exercise, **ruin** the health of many people.

Salt—accompanied by baking soda—**makes** a good substitute for toothpaste.

Such added thoughts are very often separated from the rest of the sentence by punctuation: parentheses, commas, or dashes. Even if they are not, don't let them get in the way of your choosing the correct verb.

Now look at the paragraph below. Each subject and verb match. Notice the groups of words coming between the subjects and verbs.

■ **One** of Eleanor Huitt's many hobbies **is** basketweaving. **Eleanor,** an Appalachian woman, **learned** this skill from her grandmother. Together with her two sisters, **she** also **sells** all kinds of split-oak baskets. Their **shop,** which is a popular stop for visitors to this region, **is** the place to go for baskets and other mountain crafts.

☑ A Test-Taking Tip

On the GED Writing Skills Test, you will need to know how to match subjects and verbs. If you can mentally place parentheses, commas, or dashes around anything that comes between the subject and its verb, then you will be successful in correctly answering subject-verb items.

Try It Yourself

Look at each pair of sentences below. In one sentence, the subject and verb match. But in the other sentence, the writer was confused by the words coming between the subject and verb; therefore, the subject and verb do not match. Can you tell which sentence is correct?

■ Queen Mary, with her ladies in waiting, were imprisoned in the Tower of London.

The tax bill, as well as its written congressional interpretations, is a thick document.

Perhaps you noticed the error in the first sentence because commas separate the added thought "with her ladies in waiting" from the rest of the sentence. If you remove this phrase, the sentence would read, "Queen Mary were imprisoned." By rearranging the sentence, it is easier to see the error. The corrected sentence is "Queen Mary, with her ladies in waiting, was imprisoned in the Tower of London."

Now try this pair.

■ Our side, the Giants, is ahead.

The book containing all the wedding pictures are on the bottom shelf.

Pictures is not the subject of the second sentence because it is part of the descriptive phrase "containing all the wedding pictures." Many people might think that *pictures* is the subject because it is so close to the verb. The corrected sentence is "The book containing all the wedding pictures is on the bottom shelf."

Warm-up

Rewrite each of these sentences. Choose the correct verb in parentheses.

1. Deborah, as well as Carole, (enjoys, enjoy) bowling in a league.

2. The load of steel girders, together with the specially manufactured rivets, (was, were) delivered on time.

3. The general public, plus members of the entertainment industry, (chooses, choose) the outstanding program of the year.

4. Bandages soaked with antiseptic often (prevents, prevent) infection in a wound.

5. Beverages such as coffee and tea (was, were) served at the committee meeting.

You can check your rewritten sentences against the verbs in the Warm-up Answers below.

Write a sentence in the present time using each of these phrases as the subject. Be careful to match your verb and subject.

6. The list of government officials

7. A catalog of special deals

8. My mother, as well as my grandmother,

9. An hour of these exercises

10. Three of the dollar bills

Sample sentences appear under Warm-up Answers at the end of this exercise.

The paragraph below contains some mismatched subjects and verbs. Edit the paragraph. Cross out and correct the errors on this page, or rewrite the paragraph on your own paper.

Americans every year spends billions of dollars on products that do nothing for them. Consumers do so because they, like people since ancient times, wants to believe in miracles. All of us, at one time or another, has seen or heard about a product that can easily solve our worst problem. If the promise in the ad sound too good to be true, however, it probably is. Few treatments sold through the mail delivers on their promises. Not all advertisements for health products is totally false, of course. But when people try quack remedies instead of getting effective medical help, their illnesses progress, sometimes beyond the treatable stage.

Warm-up Answers
1. enjoys **2.** was **3.** chooses **4.** prevent **5.** were

Sample sentences: **6.** The list of government officials contains the name of the spy. **7.** A catalog of special deals is available from the marketing department. **8.** My mother, as well as my grandmother, goes to the family reunion every year. **9.** An hour of these exercises takes too much out of me. **10.** Three of the dollar bills are counterfeit.

Americans every year *spend* billions of dollars on products that do nothing for them. Consumers do so because they, like people since ancient times, *want* to believe in miracles. All of us, at one time or another, *have* seen or heard about a product that can easily solve our worst problem. If the promise in the ad *sounds* too good to be true, however, it probably is. Few treatments sold through the mail *deliver* on their promises. Not all advertisements for health products *are* totally false, of course. But when people try quack remedies instead of getting effective medical help, their illnesses progress, sometimes beyond the treatable stage.

On the Springboard

Directions: Read this paragraph carefully and then answer the questions that follow it.

(1) Some office workers, afraid of computer technology, thinks that computers are too complicated. (2) Actually, operating a computer is easy once a person learns how. (3) Many companies now offer training courses to help their employees learn that working with computers is fun and is a more efficient way to organize an office. (4) A worker with computer skills is also more likely to be promoted.

3. Sentence 1: **Some office workers, afraid of computer technology, thinks that computers are too complicated.**

   What correction should be made to this sentence?

   (1) remove the comma after technology
   (2) change thinks to think
   (3) change are to is

   (1) (2) (3)

4. Sentence 4: **A worker with computer skills is also more likely to be promoted.**

   Which of the following is the best way to write the underlined portion of this sentence? If you think the original is the best way, choose option (1).

   (1) is (2) was (3) are

   (1) (2) (3)

How do you feel about computers? Do you enjoy the new technology and look foward to using the latest computer-related gadget? Do you hate the thought of computers sending you mail and calling you on the phone? Or are you tired of all the talk about computers and feel that you couldn't care less?

Write an essay telling how you feel about computers in your life. Think of ideas and organize them, write a first draft, and revise it. Then edit it for the usage and spelling problems you've studied so far.

You can check your answers to the Springboard multiple-choice questions on page 216.

Did you get both correct? If so, try your subject-verb matching skills on "The Real Thing." If you're still having problems, practice writing your own sentences and paragraphs with interrupting phrases between subjects and verbs.

The Real Thing

Directions: Read the paragraph and then answer the items based on it.

(1) During cold weather, dogs and cats needs to be protected from ice, snow, and low temperatures. (2) Don't walk your dog near rock salt or other ice-melting chemicals because these chemicals stick to your pet's paws. (3) Excessive licking of a paw's underside or redness on or between the footpads are a sign of pain or irritation. (4) After walking your dog through ice and snow, wipe his paws, top and bottom, with a damp cloth. (5) Your pet, if he stays outdoors or in a chilly garage, also need a doghouse. (6) The doghouse should be close to your dog's size when he lies down, without too much air space overhead. (7) That way his body heat provided warmth to his special home. (8) Small, short-haired dogs, like chihuahuas, should be outside only for a few minutes. (9) Larger and shaggier dogs can be let out for longer periods of time. (10) If you have a cat that likes to spend the night out, check under your hood or blow your horn before starting your car. (11) Cats love to curl up under the hood because they love to be near the warmth of the engine.

6. Sentence 1: **During cold weather, dogs and cats needs to be protected from ice, snow, and low temperatures.**

   What correction should be made to this sentence?

   (1) insert a comma after dogs
   (2) change needs to need
   (3) remove the comma after ice
   (4) change the spelling of temperatures to tempratures
   (5) no correction is necessary

   (1) (2) (3) (4) (5)

7. Sentence 3: **Excessive licking of a paw's underside or redness on or between the footpads are a sign of pain or irritation.**

   Which of the following is the best way to write the underlined portion of this sentence? If you think the original is the best way, choose option (1).

   (1) are
   (2) is
   (3) was
   (4) were
   (5) have been

   (1) (2) (3) (4) (5)

8. Sentence 5: **Your pet, if he stays outdoors or in a chilly garage, also need a doghouse.**

   Which of the following is the best way to write the underlined portion of this sentence? If you think the original is the best way, choose option (1).

   (1) need
   (2) needs
   (3) needed
   (4) be needing
   (5) should need

   (1) (2) (3) (4) (5)

9. Sentence 7: **That way his body heat provided warmth to his special home.**

   What correction should be made to this sentence?

   (1) insert a comma after heat
   (2) change provided to will provide
   (3) change provided to providing
   (4) change the spelling of special to speshul
   (5) no correction is necessary

   (1) (2) (3) (4) (5)

10. Sentence 11: **Cats love to curl up under the hood because they love to be near the warmth of the engine.**

    If you rewrote sentence 11 beginning with

    Loving to be near the engine's warmth, cats often

    the next word(s) should be

    (1) curl
    (2) curls
    (3) curling
    (4) curled
    (5) had curled

    (1) (2) (3) (4) (5)

Directions: You have 45 minutes to write on this question. Write legibly and use a pen.

Some people think that people's attitudes toward work and service have changed over the last few decades.

Do you feel that people no longer believe in working hard and serving others on their jobs? Write a 200-word essay giving your views on this topic. Be specific; give examples to support your views.

Check your answers and read the sample essay on pages 219–220.

Inverted Sentences

In most of your sentences, the subject comes before the verb. But sometimes an effective sentence is not written this way. In certain kinds of sentences, the verb comes before the subject. When you write or edit such sentences, you have to be especially careful that the subjects and verbs match.

Here's an Example

When you write a sentence that asks a question, the verb usually comes first. Sometimes the subject comes between two verb parts.

■ Why **are you** angry?
Does the **volume** of my radio **bother** you?

You also frequently place the verb before the subject in a sentence that begins with *here* or *there.* In such sentences, *here* and *there* are introductory words; they are *never* the subject.

■ Here **is** the latest **list** of GED spelling words. (The subject is *list,* not *Here.*)

There **are** twelve **months** in a year. (The subject is *months,* not *There.*)

Often the phrase *here is* is shortened to *here's,* and *there is* is shortened to *there's.* When you see or write these shortened expressions, don't forget that the singular verb *is* lies within them.

Sometimes, for emphasis, the word order in a sentence is changed to place the verb before the subject.

■ **Included** in the collection **are** three rare **stamps.**

If it were not inverted, this sentence would read, "Three rare **stamps are included** in the collection."

■ Among the coach's faults **is** his **tendency** to lose his composure at critical moments.

If rewritten in normal subject-verb order, the sentence would read, "His **tendency** to lose his composure at critical moments **is** among the coach's faults.

Try It Yourself

Which of these sentences has an error in subject-verb agreement?

■ There are many ways to give a party.

What time in the morning do your sons wake up?

Along storm-swept Cape Hatteras lies many old hulls of wrecked ships.

Were you able to sort out the subjects and verbs in the sentences? In the first sentence, the word *ways* is the subject: "Many ways are there to give a party." So the plural verb *are* is correct.

In the second sentence, the word *sons* is the subject: "Your sons do wake up at what time in the morning?" So the plural verb *do wake* is correct.

In the third sentence, however, the subject is *hulls:* "Many old hulls of wrecked ships *lie* along storm-swept Cape Hatteras." The verb needs to be plural in that sentence.

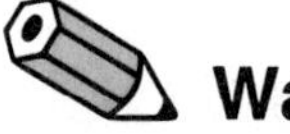

Warm-up

Edit these sentences by marking these pages or by rewriting them on another sheet of paper. Make the subjects and verbs match.

1. What is the earliest samples of printing?

2. There were a Chinese book printed between 971 and 983 that required the carving of 130,000 wooden blocks.

3. Less popular in Chinese communities were the printing of paper money using wooden blocks.

4. When were wooden movable type first used by the Chinese?

5. Here's some examples of the way the Chinese printed books.

6. Does you know who invented the printing press?

7. Less well known is the efforts of a Dutch printer named Laurens Coster.

8. There's different theories about the invention of printing.

9. How popular were the output of early printing presses?

10. Why was the books of a fifteenth-century printer more expensive than books printed today?

On the Springboard

Directions: Read this paragraph carefully and then answer the questions that follow it.

(1) Perhaps most popular among new sports is BMX racing, which began just a few years ago in California. (2) BMX stands for bicycle motocross. (3) On some tracks, racers go over jumps called whoop-de-doos, ride around banked curves called berms, and even fly off a jump called a tabletop. (4) There is certain safety precautions a racer must take. (5) A safety helmet, as well as elbow pads and knee pads, are required at many BMX race tracks.

5. Sentence 1: **Perhaps most popular among new sports is BMX racing, which began just a few years ago in California.**

   Which of the following is the best way to write the underlined portion of this sentence? If you think the original is the best way, choose option (1).

   (1) is
   (2) are
   (3) was

   (1) (2) (3)

6. Sentence 4: **There is certain safety precautions a racer must take.**

   What correction should be made to this sentence?

   (1) change is to are
   (2) change the spelling of certain to sertain
   (3) change take to taken

   (1) (2) (3)

7. Sentence 5: **A safety helmet, as well as elbow pads and knee pads, are required at many BMX race tracks.**

   What correction should be made to this sentence?

   (1) change are to is
   (2) remove the word are
   (3) no correction is necessary

   (1) (2) (3)

Everyone has problems—sometimes major ones, sometimes minor ones. Pick a problem that you have now, and write an essay about it. Be specific about what the problem is, and include different ways to solve it if you think of some. You can write your essay as if someone in particular you know is going to read it, or as if someone you don't know at all is going to read it. You choose. Remember to prewrite, write, revise, and edit.

Check your Springboard multiple-choice answers on pages 216–217.

A score of three correct answers means you're ready to go on to "The Real Thing." If you got one or more wrong, review this section and then get in a little more practice with writing inverted sentences before you move on.

Warm-up Answers
1. change *is* to *are* **2.** change *were* to *was* **3.** change *were* to *was* **4.** change *were* to *was* **5.** change *Here's* to *Here are* **6.** change *Does* to *Do* **7.** change *is* to *are* **8.** change *There's* to *There are* **9.** change *were* to *was* **10.** change *was* to *were*

“The Real Thing”

Directions: Read the paragraph and then answer the items based on it.

(1) “Take two aspirin and call me in the morning.” (2) Often heard from busy doctors is that familiar prescription. (3) Aspirin is the most popular drug in the United States. (4) Americans take more than 80 million aspirin a day. (5) These are enough to cure about 15 billion headaches a year. (6) Aspirin was first marketed in Germany in 1899, but its history really began 2,300 years ago in ancient Greece. (7) Hippocrates, the father of modern medicine, found that chewing on willow leaves reduced pain. (8) For the next 1,600 years, willow leaves and willow bark was used as folk medicine cures. (9) It wasn't until 1853 that a German researcher combined the chemicals from the willow and other plants to produce acetylsalicylic acid, or aspirin. (10) Since that time, thousands of studies of the properties of aspirin has been done to discover how aspirin works. (11) In 1982, British pharmacologist John Vane discovered that aspirin blocks the manufacture of hormonelike chemicals. (12) These chemicals trigger pain fever, and inflammation. (13) For his work, Vane won the Nobel prize.

11. Sentence 2: **Often heard from busy doctors is that familiar prescription.**

    What correction should be made to this sentence?

    (1) change the spelling of heard to herd
    (2) insert a comma after doctors
    (3) change is to are
    (4) change the spelling of familiar to familer
    (5) no correction is necessary

    (1) (2) (3) (4) (5)

12. Sentences 4 and 5: **Americans take more than 80 million aspirin a day. These are enough to cure about 15 billion headaches a year.**

    The most effective combination of sentences 4 and 5 would include which of the following groups of words?

    (1) taking enough to cure
    (2) Americans cure about
    (3) Americans take enough
    (4) a day, which are
    (5) a day, since these

    (1) (2) (3) (4) (5)

13. Sentence 8: **For the next 1,600 years, willow leaves and willow bark was used as folk medicine cures.**

    Which of the following is the best way to write the underlined portion of this sentence? If you think the original is the best way, choose option (1).

    (1) was used (2) were used
    (3) will be used (4) are used
    (5) is used

    (1) (2) (3) (4) (5)

14. Sentence 10: **Since that time, thousands of studies of the properties of aspirin has been done to discover how aspirin works.**

    Which of the following is the best way to write the underlined portion of this sentence? If you think the original is the best way, choose option (1).

    (1) has been done
    (2) would have been done
    (3) are done
    (4) is done
    (5) have been done

    (1) (2) (3) (4) (5)

15. Sentence 12: **These chemicals trigger pain fever, and inflammation.**

    What correction should be made to this sentence?

    (1) change trigger to triggered
    (2) insert a comma after pain
    (3) remove the comma after fever
    (4) replace and with or
    (5) no correction is necessary

    (1) (2) (3) (4) (5)

Directions: You have 45 minutes to write on this question. Write legibly and use a pen.

Happiness is something most people try to attain. The Declaration of Independence even goes so far as to state that people have the *right* to “the pursuit of Happiness.” Yet many people's pursuits of happiness differ because they view happiness in different ways.

What are some of the ways different people define happiness? Answer that question in an essay of about 200 words.

Check your answers, read the sample essay, and record your score on pages 220–221.

SPELLING BREAK 4

Homonyms

Have you ever seen this bumper sticker in a hospital parking lot or on the road?

You might not have realized it, but that saying involves homonyms—words that are pronounced the same way but are different in spelling and meaning. The bumper sticker makes a play on the word *patients*. Nurses usually have *patience* (that is, they are calm and uncomplaining) as they care for their *patients,* people who need medical care. You can see that although the two words sound alike, they mean very different things.

Sound-alike words are frequently misused in writing. When you write your GED essay, pay close attention to words that sound the same but are spelled differently. These words always have different meanings, and the people who evaluate your essay won't find their misuse amusing.

Read over this list of sound-alike pairs from the GED Spelling List. If you have trouble with any particular pairs, look up each word in that pair in a dictionary and jot down the words and their definitions on your Target List. Use the list to help you with the other exercises in this Spelling Break.

board/bored	role/roll
brake/break	sight/site
capital/capitol	stationary/stationery
coarse/course	week/weak
council/counsel	weather/whether
principal/principle	

Warm-up

Read the following paragraph and write the correct word in the blank before each homonym pair.

Economic experts are predicting an increase in home-based small businesses from now until the year 2000. Many people have become ______________ (*board* or *bored*?) with commuting to their jobs. They have decided to ______________ (*brake* or *break*?) with tradition and take on the ______________ (*role* or *roll*?) of an entrepreneur, a person who takes on all the responsibilities of a business. The ______________ (*principal* or *principle*?) concern of new entrepreneurs is always where to find the ______________ (*capital* or *capitol*?) to finance the businesses they start. Of ______________ (*coarse* or *course*?), a new businessperson should seek the advice of a legal ______________ (*council* or *counsel*?) before deciding ______________ (*weather* or *whether*?) or not to take in partners or stockholders.

Check your answers against the Warm-up Answers below.

Each of the following sentences contains at least one error in using sound-alike pairs. Rewrite each sentence, correcting any errors.

1. Scientists found pottery fragments in the coarse gravel at the archaeological digging sight.

____

____

2. Our new business stationery will be ready in about a weak.

____

____

Warm-up Answers
You should have written the following words in the blanks: *bored, break, role, principal, capital, course, counsel,* and *whether.*

3. The new whether satellite will be in stationery orbit over the United States.

4. The Commissioners' Counsel held its annual meeting in the bored room of the capital building.

Check your corrected spellings with the Warm-up Answers below before you go on.

The next five sentences are a little more difficult. They contain one error in using sound-alike pairs *and* one general spelling error. Find both errors and rewrite each sentence.

5. To perpare for his roll as a college student, the actor lived on a campus for two weeks.

6. Newton accidentaly discovered the principal of gravity when he noticed apples falling from a tree.

7. The site of snow-covered pine trees in December brings back plesant memories of Christmases past.

8. According to scientiffic observation, gravity breaks the speed of meteors entering earth's atmosphere.

9. The captane and his crew were week after spending five days in the life raft.

Check your answers for the last five sentences before going on.

In the last lesson, you learned about matching subjects and verbs. Numbers 10 through 14 contain spelling errors, mismatched subjects and verbs, or both. Edit the sentences on this page, a copy of it, or your own paper.

10. The principle and her teachers has gone to the in-service about teaching adults.

11. The puppies and their mother is week from lack of proper care.

12. The patient's apetite improved when he smelled the freshly baked rolls on his supper tray.

13. Either the hankerchief or the gloves is a good gift for my son's kindergarden teacher.

14. The corperal and his sergeant attended a Department of Defense semenar.

Warm-up Answers

1. Scientists found pottery fragments in the coarse gravel at the archaeological digging *site.* **2.** Our new business stationery will be ready in about a *week.* **3.** The new *weather* satellite will be in *stationary* orbit over the United States. **4.** The Commissioners' *Council* held its annual meeting in the *board* room of the *capitol* building.

5. To *prepare* for his *role* as a college student, the actor lived on a campus for two weeks. **6.** Newton *accidentally* discovered the *principle* of gravity when he noticed apples falling from a tree. **7.** The *sight* of snow-covered pine trees in December brings back *pleasant* memories of Christmases past. **8.** According to *scientific* observation, gravity *brakes* the speed of meteors entering earth's atmosphere. **9.** The *captain* and his crew were *weak* after spending five days in the life raft.

10. The *principal* and her teachers *have* gone to the in-service about teaching adults. **11.** The puppies and their mother *are weak* from lack of proper care. **12.** The patient's *appetite* improved when he smelled the freshly baked rolls on his supper tray. **13.** Either the *handkerchief* or the gloves *are* a good gift for my son's *kindergarten* teacher. **14.** The *corporal* and his sergeant attended a Department of Defense *seminar*.

SPELLING BREAK 5

Easy-to-Confuse Words

Sometimes it seems as if the English language is full of pitfalls. Not only do you have to learn the difference between sound-alike words, but you must also learn the difference between words that *almost* sound alike or look alike. Some pairs of words on the GED Spelling List look or sound alike, but they have very different meanings. Sometimes careful pronunciation will help you spell these words. A few of the pairs are made up of a word that is a verb and a word that is a noun: *advise* (verb)/*advice* (noun); *breathe* (verb)/*breath* (noun). Learning the difference between the two forms will help you use each one correctly.

Here is a list of easy-to-confuse words from the GED Spelling List. If you have trouble with any particular group of words, look up each word in a dictionary and jot down the word and its definition on your Target List. Use the list of words to do the exercises in this Spelling Break.

absence/absent
accept/except
advice/advise
affect/effect
angel/angle
breadth/breath/breathe
choose/chose
conscience/conscious
descend/descent
desert/dessert
formal/former
later/latter
loose/lose
moral/morale
personal/personnel
precede/proceed
quality/quantity
quiet/quite
seige/seize
thorough/through

Warm-up

Write one of the words below in the blanks in the paragraph. Use your Target List if you need definitions.

accept/except *later/latter* *desert/dessert*
loose/lose *formal/former* *moral/morale*
choose/chose *quiet/quite*
absence/absent

Our **1** __________ invitation for the fund-raising **2** __________ party arrived in a gilt-edged envelope today. It certainly will be **3** __________ an occasion because all our city officials **4** __________ one will be there. This **5** __________ official, the **6** __________ animal control commissioner, was not invited because he once **7** __________ to "arrest" the prize pet poodle of our hostess. While on its daily walk, the poodle broke **8** __________ and ran away. Its owner **9** __________ found it in a cage at the animal shelter, cuddled up in the corner with a flea-bitten mutt of the opposite sex. The owner was never **10** __________ the same after her pampered prize poodle presented her with three new family members. The **11** __________ of this story is "Pursue a prize poodle and you'll never be in the dog's house."

Make sure you chose the right words by checking your answers with the Warm-up Answers before going on.

Write one sentence for each word pair below. Write each sentence so that a reader will know that you thoroughly understand the meaning of the spelling list word.

12. accept __________
except __________

13. affect __________
effect __________

14. precede __________
proceed __________

Compare your sentences with the sample sentences given below.

Warm-up Answers
1. formal **2.** dessert **3.** quite **4.** except **5.** absent **6.** former **7.** chose **8.** loose **9.** later **10.** quite **11.** moral

12. She would not accept the gift. They liked the movie except for the ending. **13.** The noise does not affect his concentration. What effect will the rain have on the temperature? **14.** The bridesmaid will precede the bride down the aisle. Please proceed with your plans in spite of my absence.

There are two errors in each sentence below. One easy-to-confuse word from your list in this lesson will be used incorrectly. The other error will be either a verb-usage error or an error in matching subjects and verbs. Edit each sentence and correct all errors.

15. The walls of the castle and its moat was not enough to withstand the seize of the Norman invaders.

16. Tom, Dick, and Harry has asked for a second desert.

17. We had went to the Salvation Army store to chose a new couch for our apartment.

18. The descend into the mine shaft become dangerous after the power failure.

19. The price of former clothes for weddings are going up.

20. It were difficult to breath in the smoke-filled room.

21. One of the group activities are helping to improve the moral of the company personnel.

22. Are the leader of the gang bothered by a guilty conscious?

23. The lose pants, along with the purple hat and striped shirt, makes your clown costume unique.

Warm-up Answers
15. The walls of the castle and its moat *were* not enough to withstand the *seige* of the Norman invaders. **16.** Tom, Dick, and Harry *have* asked for a second *dessert.* **17.** We had *gone* to the Salvation Army store to *choose* a new couch for our apartment. **18.** The *descent* into the mine shaft *became* dangerous after the power failure. **19.** The price of *formal* clothes for weddings *is* going up. **20.** It *was* difficult to *breathe* in the smoke-filled room. **21.** One of the group activities *is* helping to improve the *morale* of the company personnel. **22.** *Is* the leader of the gang bothered by a guilty *conscience*? **23.** The *loose* pants, along with the purple hat and striped shirt, *make* your clown costume unique.

LESSON 21

Pronouns

You use **pronouns** in your speech and in your writing naturally. Pronouns are words such as *he, her, our, your,* and *its.* They stand in for the names of persons or things. You need to be concerned with three main skills when you use pronouns: (1) matching the pronoun to the noun it's standing for, (2) matching the pronoun to the verb and other pronouns, and (3) making sure your reader knows what the pronoun is standing for.

Coming to Terms

pronoun a word that stands in for a noun

Choosing the Right Pronoun

Pronouns are singular and plural just as nouns are. When you write, and especially when you edit, you have to make sure your pronouns match with the nouns they are standing for.

Here's an Example

In the passage below, the pronouns are *italicized.* Two of the pronouns do not match the names of the persons or things they are taking the place of.

■ If *you* have applied for credit, somewhere there is a file on *you. It* shows the companies *you* owe and how promptly *you* have paid *them.* The credit industry routinely keeps such files, and *they* do not necessarily keep the information confidential. If *one* is denied credit, *you* can request the nature, substance, and sources of the information collected about *you.*

It matches with *file,* and *them* matches with *companies.* However, *they* does not match with *credit industry* because one is singular and the other is plural. *One* is incorrect in this particular paragraph only because *you* is used everywhere else in the paragraph; to be consistent, *one is* should be changed to *you are.*

Try It Yourself

Can you figure out if the pronouns in this paragraph are used correctly?

■ Some cosmetic hair products may cling to one's hair shafts and make *it* seem thicker. However, no hair growth is actually involved. Nothing that one does to one's hair, once *it* has emerged from the scalp, will influence *its* growth. Permanent waving, shaving, and bleaching do not affect *your* hair *itself.*

It and *hair shafts* don't match because *it* is singular and *hair shafts* is plural. Also, *your hair* should be changed to *one's hair* because *one* and *one's* are used everywhere else. All the other pronouns are used correctly.

☑ A Test-Taking Tip

On the GED Writing Skills Test, you will have several questions that require you to take account of the pronouns used in the *entire* paragraph in order to choose the right pronoun for a particular sentence. So if you have options that involve a change in a pronoun, insert each choice in the original sentence and see if it makes sense. *Then check the entire paragraph* to make sure the pronoun you've chosen fits with the rest of the pronouns in the paragraph.

Warm-up

Choose the correct pronouns in parentheses. Then rewrite the sentences.

1. She or Vicki will lend you (her, their) sewing machine.

____

____

2. Great Britain is our ally, yet (they, it) sometimes disagreed with us.

____

____

3. All citizens should accept (his, her, their) responsibilities and vote.

____

____

4. Ask Ray and Julio for (his, their) opinions.

____

5. The army wants to buy more sophisticated weapons, but Congress may not give (it, them) the money.

____

____

____

6. You would be better off if (you, one) took a bus to the stadium.

____

____

Matching Pronouns with Verbs and Other Pronouns

You've already learned how to match pronouns and nouns. Once you have in mind the noun that a pronoun is standing for, it is usually not too difficult to match a verb or other pronoun with that pronoun. For example, if the noun is singular, so are the pronouns, and so too will be the verb.

One group of pronouns, however, often causes problems for writers. This group includes indefinite pronouns like *anyone, everybody, no one,* and *each.* These pronouns are called indefinite because they don't refer to any particular person or thing. Some words in this group are singular, and some are plural, while others can be either singular or plural. These three characteristics can make this group difficult to match to other words in a sentence.

Here's an Example

The words on the following list are usually singular.

anybody	everyone	nothing
anyone	everything	one
each	neither	somebody
either	nobody	someone
everybody	none	something

Warm-up Answers
1. her **2.** it **3.** their **4.** their **5.** it **6.** you

In each of the sentences below, the singular subject and the matching pronoun or verb are in **bold.**

■ **One** of the plants **was** dying.

Neither of the women called **her** son during the meeting.

Somebody has to see that the coffee maker is turned off.

These pronouns are always plural: *both, few, many, several.*

■ **Few** in the audience **were** interested in the movie.

Many in the audience **were** clapping **their** hands.

These pronouns may be either singular or plural, depending on their meaning in the sentence: *all, any, most, some.*

■ **Some** of the cargo **was** damaged.

Most of the books **were** brand new.

All of the students passed **their** GED Test.

Try It Yourself

In the paragraph below, several pronouns are *italicized.* Can you find the pronouns that don't match the other words in the sentences?

■ Do you have a favorite holiday? *Everyone* usually do. *Most* like Christmas or Hanukkah because both involve giving and receiving presents. *No one* have anything to say against Thanksgiving and their big turkey dinner either. Are *any* of your favorite holidays in the summer?

Everyone is considered singular, so it must match a singular verb *(does). Most* and *like* match, as do *both* and *involve,* because all are plural. *No one,* however, is singular, so you should have decided to change *have* to *has* and *their* to *his or her:* "No one has anything to say against Thanksgiving and his or her big turkey dinner either." *Any* is one of those special pronouns that can be matched with either *is* or *are.* In this case, *any* refers to the plural *holidays* and requires a plural verb *(are).*

Warm-up

Write each sentence, choosing the right pronoun or verb in parentheses.

1. Neither of my brothers (is, are) able to save (his, their) money.

____

____

2. Each of the women (is, are) going to contribute part of (her, their) paycheck to the relief fund.

____

____

3. A beginning runner learns soon enough to pace (himself, herself, himself or herself, themselves).

____

____

4. Many (is, are) called, but few (is, are) chosen.

____

____

5. Everything I have (is, are) yours.

____

____

Check your rewritten sentences against the correct pronouns and verbs listed under the Warm-up Answers below.

Warm-up Answers
1. is, his **2.** is, her **3.** himself or herself **4.** are, are **5.** is

The following passage contains errors in pronouns. Edit the passage on this page or a copy of it by crossing out the mistakes and writing in your corrections. Or rewrite the passage on your own sheet of paper.

Cooking vegetables is an art. Anybody who is anybody can read their cookbook to learn delicious ways to cook wonderful vegetable side and main dishes. Some of the cookbooks even provides a chapter about creating snazzy vegetable garnishes.

Everything about vegetables are interesting. One of the many nutritious facts about vegetables are that they retain more of their vitamins if cooked in its skin. You can enjoy an armchair adventure around the world by learning the origins of all the vegetables in one's local market. Each vegetable probably also has a fascinating history about their use in different parts of the world.

Cooking vegetables is an art. Anybody who is anybody can read *his or her* cookbook to learn delicious ways to cook wonderful vegetable side and main dishes. Some of the cookbooks even *provide* a chapter about creating snazzy vegetable garnishes.

Everything about vegetables *is* interesting. One of the many nutritious facts about vegetables *is* that they retain more of their vitamins if cooked in *their* skin. You can enjoy an armchair adventure around the world by learning the origins of all the vegetables in *your* local market. Each vegetable probably also has a fascinating history about *its* use in different parts of the world.

On the Springboard

Directions: Read this paragraph carefully and then answer the questions that follow it.

(1) Nothing makes banking more convenent than automated teller machines (ATMs). (2) Consumers can use these machines to do their banking without the assistance of a teller. (3) To use an ATM, a consumer must have a personal identification number. (4) This number will prevent unauthorized use of your account. (5) ATMs have many benefits; for example, you can make deposits or withdrawals twenty-four hours a day.

1. Sentence 1: **Nothing makes banking more convenent than automated teller machines (ATMs).**

   What correction should be made to this sentence?

   (1) change makes to make
   (2) change makes to made
   (3) change the spelling of convenent to convenient

   (1) (2) (3)

2. Sentence 5: **ATMs have many benefits; for example, you can make deposits or withdrawals twenty-four hours a day.**

   If you rewrote sentence 5 beginning with

   One of an ATM's many benefits

   the next word should be

   (1) are (2) is (3) was

   (1) (2) (3)

"The only thing we have to fear is fear itself." You've probably heard that saying before. Use it as the basis for an essay. If you agree with the idea, tell why. Think about how you overcame (or how you can overcome) fear. If you disagree with the idea, tell why. Tell what other things you fear.

Organize your ideas, write a first draft using them, and revise the draft. Then edit your essay for pronoun as well as verb use.

You'll find answers to the multiple-choice questions from On the Springboard on page 217.

If you didn't have any trouble getting the Springboard questions right, try getting "The Real Thing" questions that follow right too. If you're not yet ready for the GED-level questions, review the first two sections of this lesson and practice using pronouns before going on.

The Real Thing

Directions: Read the paragraph and then answer the items based on it.

(1) The sounds, rhythms, and moves of Kabuki make it the most popular of the traditional theater forms in Japan. (2) In Tokyo, they have a Grand Kabuki National Theater that houses a company of over two hundred actors who perform almost two hundred plays a year. (3) At the age of four, promising children begin their training. (4) Their training includes dancing and singing. (5) Traditionally, men perform all the roles in a Kabuki play. (6) Their faces are covered with a thick, white rice powder. (7) Straight eyebrows and tiny rosebud lips are painted on top of the powder. (8) Most Kabuki actors agree that movement are the most important element of their act. (9) Each one is always accompanied onstage by musicians and singers. (10) Kabuki is a highly stylized art form in which every movement and stance has meaning.

1. Sentence 2: **In Tokyo, they have a Grand Kabuki National Theater that houses a company of over two hundred actors who perform almost two hundred plays a year.**

   Which of the following is the best way to write the underlined portion of this sentence? If you think the original is the best way, choose option (1).

   (1) they have a Grand Kabuki National Theater that
   (2) it has a Grand Kabuki National Theater that
   (3) having a Grand Kabuki National Theater that
   (4) with a Grand Kabuki National Theater that
   (5) the Grand Kabuki National Theater

   (1) (2) (3) (4) (5)

2. Sentences 3 and 4: **At the age of four, promising children begin their training. Their training includes dancing and singing.**

   The most effective combination of sentences 3 and 4 would contain which of the following groups of words?

   (1) training and including
   (2) their training, which includes
   (3) that will also include
   (4) training, and their
   (5) training, dancing, and singing

   (1) (2) (3) (4) (5)

3. Sentence 8: **Most Kabuki actors agree that movement are the most important element of their act.**

   What correction should be made to this sentence?

   (1) change agree to agrees
   (2) change the spelling of agree to aggree
   (3) change are to is
   (4) replace their with there
   (5) no correction is necessary

   (1) (2) (3) (4) (5)

4. Sentence 9: **Each one is always accompanied onstage by musicians and singers.**

   What correction should be made to this sentence?

   (1) change is to are
   (2) change the spelling of always to allways
   (3) change the spelling of accompanied to acompanied
   (4) change the spelling of accompanied to accompanyed
   (5) no correction is necessary

   (1) (2) (3) (4) (5)

5. Sentence 10: **Kabuki is a highly stylized art form in which every movement and stance has meaning.**

   Which of the following is the best way to write the underlined portion of this sentence? If you think the original is the best way, choose option (1).

   (1) has
   (2) have
   (3) will have had
   (4) having
   (5) had

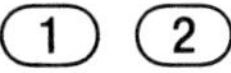

Directions: You have 45 minutes to write on this question. Write legibly and use a pen.

Cars have a number of different uses, and there is a wide variety of makes and models to accommodate the different needs of people. Yet some persons believe that the particular car an individual chooses reveals just as much about his or her personality as it does about his or her transportation needs.

Comment about the idea that a car is an extension of someone's personality. Back up your comments with specific details in an essay of about 200 words.

Check your answers and read the sample essay on page 221.

Making Your Reference Clear

As a writer, you can confuse your readers if you don't clearly show who or what a pronoun is referring to. You certainly don't want to confuse the GED essay readers. Therefore, when you edit your essay or any other piece of writing, make sure the noun that each pronoun is referring to is clear.

Here's an Example

What does *it* mean in the following sentence?

■ Bob replaced the clutch master cylinder and repaired the leak in the slave cylinder, but it still did not work properly.

What didn't work, the *clutch master cylinder* or the *slave cylinder?* This sentence is an example of unclear writing because it confuses the reader.

Sometimes, the confusing pronoun stands for a word in another sentence.

■ We met with the architect and the builder to discuss the blueprints of our new house. *They* were confusing.

Is it clear what *they* stands for? Who or what was confusing—the architect and the builder or the blueprints?

Often the best way to edit confusing pronouns is to just repeat the name of the person or thing.

■ Bob replaced the clutch master cylinder and repaired the leak in the slave cylinder, but the slave cylinder still did not work properly.

We met with the architect and the builder to discuss the blueprints of our new house. The blueprints were confusing.

Some misused pronouns refer to no noun at all. This group includes *it, you, they, this, that,* and *which.* Every time you use these words as a subject, a red flag should go up in your mind. Make sure the pronoun clearly refers to a noun in the sentence or paragraph.

■ *It* says in the encyclopedia that the Vikings had settlements in North America.

Who or what is *it?* A good writer would revise the sentence to read, "The encyclopedia says that . . . ."

- In the fall, they're scheduling a new class in consumer auto repair.

Who is scheduling the course? *They* does not refer to any specific people. One way to revise the sentence is "In the fall, a new class in consumer auto repair will be scheduled." Or: "In the fall, the park district is scheduling a new class in consumer auto repair.

Try It Yourself

In this paragraph, several pronouns are misused or are unclear. Once you have found the pronouns, think about how you would fix each sentence.

- Don't think about the GED Test if it makes you nervous. Some students worry so much that it makes them sick, which is the reason they usually don't do well on them. In many "How to Study" books it says that you should do something relaxing just before a test. They also say that you should get a good night's sleep before a test. As all nervous test takers already know, this is easier said than done!

This paragraph is filled with confusing substitute words. For example, in the second sentence the pronoun *which* is used, but there isn't even any noun for it to refer to. In the last sentence, the same is true for the pronoun *this.*

Here is *one* way to revise the paragraph so that the writer's meaning is clear to the reader: "Don't think about the GED Test if *the thought of* it makes you nervous. Some students worry so much that *they become sick. Because they become sick,* they usually don't do well on *the test. Many "How to Study" books say* that you should do something relaxing just before a test. They also say that you should get a good night's sleep before a test. As all nervous test takers know, *relaxing and sleeping before a test are* easier said than done!

Warm-up

Rewrite each of these nine confusing sentences. Compare your rewrites with the Warm-Up Answers at the bottom of this page.

1. Jack likes falling down and Jill likes carrying water, which is why they don't work well together.

____

____

2. This year, health insurance companies have raised the rates for women executives, and it's going to make insurance more expensive for them.

____

____

3. The overweight Marine ate less and exercised more; this helped him lose enough weight to fit into his dress blues again.

____

____

____

4. The good samaritan carried the injured man to his house.

____

____

5. My husband bought two kittens for our twin sons when they were five weeks old and barely able to leave their mother.

____

____

____

Sample Warm-up Answers
1. Because Jack likes falling down and Jill likes carrying water, they don't work well together. **2.** This year, health insurance companies have raised the rates for women executives. This increase will make insurance more expensive for the executives. **3.** The overweight Marine ate less and exercised more. This approach helped him lose enough weight to fit into his dress blues again. **4.** The good samaritan carried the injured man to the samaritan's house. (or to the injured man's house) **5.** My husband bought two kittens for our twin sons when the kittens were five weeks old and barely able to leave their mother. **6.** Manufacturers don't make cars the way they used to. **7.** Jennifer thinks writing is glamorous and hopes to be a writer. **8.** This pamphlet says that you have rights as a consumer. **9.** When the military attaché first arrived in Moscow, he met the ambassador.

6. They don't make cars the way they used to.

____

____

7. Jennifer thinks writing is glamorous and hopes to be one.

____

____

8. It says in this pamphlet that you have rights as a consumer.

____

____

9. The military attaché met the ambassador when he first arrived in Moscow.

____

____

On the Springboard

Directions: Read this paragraph carefully and then answer the questions that follow it.

(1) Scuba diving is deep-sea diving using equipment that is carried on the back of the diver. (2) Before the development of scuba equipment, they breathed air pumped down a long hose from the surface. (3) With scuba equipment, the diver receives air from the tanks through a rubber hose. (4) At the end of the hose is a demand regulator. (5) It keeps the pressure of the air in the diver's lungs equal to the pressure of the water, which is necessary to prevent serious lung damage.

3. Sentence 2: **Before the development of scuba equipment, they breathed air pumped down a long hose from the surface.**

   Which of the following is the best way to write the underlined portion of this sentence? If you think the original is the best way, choose option (1).

   (1) they
   (2) it
   (3) the divers

   (1) (2) (3)

4. Sentence 5: **It keeps the pressure of the air in the diver's lungs equal to the pressure of the water, which is necessary to prevent serious lung damage.**

   Which of the following is the best way to write the underlined portion of this sentence? If you think the original is the best way, choose option (1).

   (1) water, which (2) water, that
   (3) water; such regulation

   (1) (2) (3)

Think of your answers to these questions and jot them down on paper: Have you ever known someone who seemed to be a real "winner"? What characteristics do you think a winner has? Have you ever known a person who you would consider a real "loser"? What characteristics does a real loser have?

Write an essay that gives your definition of winners and losers. Back up your opinion with some real-life experiences of yours or of your family or friends. When you are finished prewriting, writing your first draft, and revising, edit your essay. Avoid any generalized statements that begin with "They say" or "This is" or other vague pronoun phrases.

Check your Springboard multiple-choice answers on page 217.

If you're confident in your skills with pronouns, try those skills on "The Real Thing." If not, practice writing your own sentences and paragraphs with pronouns before you go on.

“The Real Thing”

Directions: Read the paragraph and then answer the items based on it.

(1) “Generics” is a term that is heard frequently today, often in connection with consumer products that are sold without a brand name or fancy label. (2) What does it mean when used in reference to prescription drugs? (3) When a new drug is first developed, they usually patent and sell it exclusively under a single brand name. (4) Drug patents run seventeen years. (5) While this happens, the brand name of the first drug becomes well known. (6) Such original drugs are often referred to as “brand-name” drugs. (7) If there is no patent or after a patent has expired, other firms may manufacture and sell the drug either under different brand names or under the drug’s generic name. (8) These copies of the original drug are exact, and they are often called generic drugs. (9) Thus, every drug has a generic name and a brand name. (10) It is prominently used in advertising a drug to the medical profession, though the generic name must also appear in advertising and labeling in letters at least half as big as that of the brand name. (11) About 90 percent of all generic drugs are made by the major drug firms in the country, the ones who also develop “brand-name” drugs.

6. Sentence 2: **What does it mean when used in reference to prescription drugs?**

   What correction should be made to this sentence?

   (1) change does to do
   (2) replace it with the connection
   (3) replace it with this term
   (4) change the spelling of reference to referrence
   (5) no correction is necessary

   (1) (2) (3) (4) (5)

7. Sentence 3: **When a new drug is first developed, they usually patent and sell it exclusively under a single brand name.**

   Which of the following is the best way to write the underlined portion of this sentence? If you think the original is the best way, choose option (1).

   (1) they usually patent and sell it
   (2) they usually patented and sold it
   (3) usually patented, and sold,
   (4) it was usually patented and sold
   (5) it is usually patented and sold

   (1) (2) (3) (4) (5)

8. Sentence 5: **While this happens, the brand name of the first drug becomes well known.**

   What correction should be made to this sentence?

   (1) replace this with that
   (2) replace While this happens with During this time
   (3) remove the comma after happens
   (4) change becomes to become
   (5) no correction is necessary

   (1) (2) (3) (4) (5)

9. Sentence 8: **These copies of the original drug are exact, and they are often called generic drugs.**

   If you rewrote sentence 8 beginning with

   These exact copies of the original drug

   the next word should be

   (1) is
   (2) are
   (3) and
   (4) they
   (5) called

   (1) (2) (3) (4) (5)

10. Sentence 10: <u>It is</u> **prominently used in advertising a drug to the medical profession, though the generic name must also appear in advertising and labeling in letters at least half as big as that of the brand name.**

Which of the following is the best way to write the underlined portion of this sentence? If you think the original is the best way, choose option (1).

(1) It is
(2) The generic name is
(3) The brand name is
(4) That is
(5) Which is

<u>Directions:</u> You have 45 minutes to write on this question. Write legibly and use a pen.

Fewer people are having children these days, and those who do have fewer children. Many parents work and sometimes worry about their ability to care for their children. The word *parent* has become a verb in recent years, and how-to-parent books and magazines are popular.

What are the responsibilities of a parent in today's world? Answer that question in an essay of about 200 words. Be specific.

Check your answers, read the sample essay, and record your score on pages 221–222.

SPELLING BREAK 6

Adding -er and -est

You know that nouns can be either singular or plural. Their spelling usually changes—*effect/effects; category/categories; hero/heroes.* Descriptive words can also change their spelling. This change happens when you write about things in three degrees.

- Joan is *quiet.* (first degree—talking about one)
- Joan is *quieter* than Bob. (second degree—talking about two)
- Joan is the *quietest* person here. (third degree—talking about three or more)

Notice how *-er* and *-est* were added to *quiet.*

The rules that follow will help you form the three degrees of descriptive words. They are very similar to the rules for adding *-d* and *-ed* to *verbs.*

1. Add *-r* and *-st* to words that end in *e.*

hoarse, hoarse**r**, hoarse**st**

2. If a word ends in two consonants or in two vowels and a consonant, add *-er* and *-est.*

light, light**er**, light**est**
great, great**er**, great**est**

3. For a word that ends in a consonant-vowel-consonant pattern, double the final consonant before adding *-er* or *-est.*

hot, hot**ter**, hot**test**

4. For a word that ends in a consonant and *y,* change the *y* to *i* and add *-er* or *-est.*

heavy, heav**ier**, heav**iest**

5. For long words, add *more* or *most* in front of the word.

comfortable, **more** comfortable, **most** comfortable

If you are thinking in the other direction, add *less* or *least.*

comfortable, **less** comfortable, **least** comfortable

Here is a paragraph that contains six descriptive words from the GED Spelling List that are written in one of the three degrees. Notice how each **bold** word is spelled.

■ Did you know that something more than fashion is responsible for your wearing light colors in the summer and dark colors in the winter? The **healthiest** way to dress in hot weather is to wear **looser** and **lighter** clothes than you would wear in **cooler** weather. Your body's cooling system is **more efficient** when you substitute lightweight for **heavier** fabrics in the summer. Light colors are **more appropriate** for summer rather than winter wear because these colors reflect the sun's rays. In winter, dark colors are best because they absorb the sun's warmth.

To add *-est* to the list word *healthy,* you must first drop the *y* and add *i*—health*iest.* The same rule applies for adding *-er* to *heavy*—heav*ier.*

Since *loose* ends in *e,* you need only to add *-r*—loose*r. Light* and *cool* do not end in *-e,* so you must add *-er*—light*er* and cool*er.*

Because *efficient* and *appropriate* are rather long words, it is better to put *more* in front of them. Think how awkward it would be to say *efficienter* and *appropriater.*

Warm-up

Write a sentence using the degree shown for each descriptive word.

1. *coarse* (second degree) ______________

____

2. *easy* (third degree) ______________

____

3. *weak* (second degree) ______________

____

4. *strenuous* (third degree) ______________

____

5. *permanent* (second degree) ______________

____

Sample sentences appear under Warm-up Answers at the end of this Spelling Break.

Rewrite the passage below on another sheet of paper. Select the right degree for each word in parentheses.

6. World War II brought about many changes in women's wear. Wartime shortages of fabrics meant that dresses were (short) and (plain). As more women joined the work force, they needed (useful) clothes. The (likely) and (practical) outfit for the women of the forties was a suit. Because home-heating fuel was scarce, wool became (desirable) than silk for evening dresses.

Check your rewritten paragraph with the one under the Warm-up Answers at the end of this break.

The following five sentences contain spelling errors as well as errors in using pronouns and matching pronouns and verbs. Edit the sentences or rewrite them on your own paper.

7. Julio and Arthur consistantly recieved the highst marks on his GED practice essays.

8. Each GED student were encouragged to write in a journul every day in the quiettest place possible.

9. Few people was interesteder in selling their junk at the flea market than he.

10. The sign states that only quarders can be used in the washing machines and dryers.

11. Those bedding plants smell sweetter than the ones that borders your sidewalk.

12. No one are wierder than he is.

Warm-up Answers

1. This material is coarser than burlap. **2.** Mathematics may be the easiest subject to you, but not to me. **3.** The doctor appeared weaker but refused to be inoculated. **4.** Lifting an automobile would be a most strenuous experience. **5.** Alvin would like to find a more permanent livelihood.

6. World War II brought about many changes in women's wear. Wartime shortages of fabrics meant that dresses were *shorter* and *plainer.* As more women joined the work force, they needed *more useful* clothes. The *most likely* and *most practical* outfit for the women of the forties was a suit. Because home-heating fuel was scarce, wool became *more desirable* than silk for evening dresses.

7. Julio and Arthur *consistently received* the *highest* marks on *their* GED practice essays. **8.** Each GED student *was encouraged* to write in a *journal* every day in the *quietest* place possible. **9.** Few people *were more interested* in selling their junk at the flea market than he. **10.** The sign states that only *quarters* can be used in the washing machines and dryers. **11.** Those bedding plants smell *sweeter* than the ones that *border* your sidewalk. **12.** No one *is weirder* than he is.

LESSON 22

Capitalization

Knowing When to Capitalize

The main purpose of writing is to communicate your ideas clearly and concisely to your reader. Using capital letters incorrectly can distract your reader. Your goal as a writer is to get the reader to pay attention to what you have said and not to strange or creative uses of capital letters.

The rules for capitalization are given in the Style Guide on page 269 of this book. The practice exercises in this lesson will help you master those rules. Capital letters always start sentences, but you need to use them in other ways too.

Here's an Example

Read the following passage about an infamous European family and note the capitalized words.

■ Cesare Borgia and his sister, Lucrezia, were infamous for their ruthless pursuit of power in Renaissance Italy. At the age of 11, Lucrezia's father married her to a Spaniard, but the union was quickly annulled. When her father needed to acquire more power in Italy, he married her to an Italian nobleman. Five years later, Lucrezia's second marriage was also annulled. Her third husband was a handsome Italian duke called Bisceglie. Cesare Borgia felt that Bisceglie was a political threat and ordered him murdered. Her fourth and last marriage was also arranged for political reasons. At the ripe old age of 21, she married the Duke of Ferrara.

There are several capitalized words in the passage. For instance, the first sentence contains *Cesare Borgia, Lucrezia,* and *Renaissance Italy.* You probably already know that names of people and countries are capitalized, but you might not have realized that the names of historical periods are capitalized too. If you have trouble understanding why some words were capitalized in the passage, quickly read the section on capitalization in the Style Guide. Then reread the passage with the rules for capitalization in mind.

Try It Yourself

The following passage about the Lee family of Virginia is divided into two paragraphs. Only the first word in each sentence is capitalized in the paragraphs. Circle the words that should be capitalized, referring to the rules in the Style Guide if necessary. Some of the answers are given after *each* paragraph so that you can check your work as you go.

■ Henry lee was an american general who served in the war of independence. During the war, his reputation as a leader earned him the nickname of "light horse harry." When george washington died, it was light horse harry who delivered the famous phrase about washington, "first in war, first in peace, and first in the hearts of his countrymen."

Look at the words in the paragraph carefully and think about what they mean. The names of people and countries are always capitalized, so in the paragraph *Lee, George Washington, Washington,* and *American* have capital letters. You can apply this rule to Lee's nickname, Light Horse Harry, too. The War of Independence is an important historical event, so it must be capitalized. If you missed any, refer to the rules in the Style Guide before trying the next paragraph.

■ In february 1861, president abraham lincoln offered the command of the north's army to henry lee's son, robert e. lee. Lee respectfully declined the offer and volunteered his services to his home state of virginia. His brilliance as a military commander made him a strong opponent of general ulysses s. grant, whom lincoln ultimately chose for commander of the north's forces. After four years of bitter fighting, lee surrendered to grant on a spring day in 1865 at appomattox court house.

This paragraph had many capitalized words. Did you find them all? The names *February, Abraham Lincoln, Henry Lee's, Robert E. Lee, Virginia, Ulysses S. Grant, Lincoln, Lee, Grant,* and *Appomattox Court House* should be capitalized as well as *North's, General,* and *President.* How did you do?

Warm-up

Rewrite the following four sentences and correct the capitalization errors they contain.

1. My Cousin Amanda will perform for the San Francisco ballet company next sunday afternoon.

2. Last Winter, his scuba club traveled to the Great Barrier reef in australia.

3. In the United States, the east is more heavily populated than the west; therefore, people tend to move West because it is less crowded there.

4. As a child, I lived on crescent drive, which was just three blocks East of the Albany Drive-in theater.

In the Warm-up Answers you can find the words that should have been capitalized in these sentences and some words that should *not* have been capitalized.

The following passage contains no capital letters. Rewrite the passage and correctly add capital letters to the words that should be capitalized.

you may think that pigeons belong in central park, where you can feed them on saturday afternoons. but special pigeons, called carrier pigeons, have worked for a living for more than 5,000 years. they have transported everything from love letters to secret battle plans. during world war I in europe, they flew dangerous missions through clouds of poisonous gas. today on the northwest coast of france, carrier pigeons are used to transport blood samples to a central blood testing center. the forty veteran fliers travel every day of the year, except the three-month autumn hunting season. the average life span for new york city pigeons is about four years, but hard-working french carrier pigeons can live up to fifteen years.

Warm-up Answers
1. cousin, Ballet, Company, Sunday **2.** winter, Reef, Australia **3.** East, West, west **4.** Crescent Drive, east, Theater

You, Central Park, Saturday, But, They, During World War I, Europe, Today, France, The (forty), The (average), New York City, French

On the Springboard

Directions: Read this paragraph carefully and then answer the questions that follow it.

(1) Ansel Adams, a well-known photographer, became a friend to millions through his pictures of Yosemite National park. (2) He had a white beard and a broken nose, and he wore a Stetson hat and a hunting jacket. (3) To many, he looks like an old-timer from the early days of the West. (4) He spent over Sixty years trying to protect the forests and mountains from people. (5) His special interest was to protect the beauty of Yosemite. (6) His pictures let everyone know that Yosemite's beauty is worth saving.

1. Sentence 1: **Ansel Adams, a well-known photographer, became a friend to millions through his pictures of Yosemite National park.**

   What correction should be made to this sentence?

   (1) change became to become
   (2) change the spelling of friend to freind
   (3) change park to Park

   (1) (2) (3)

2. Sentence 3: **To many, he looks like an old-timer from the early days of the West.**

   What correction should be made to this sentence?

   (1) change looks to looked
   (2) change old-timer to Old-timer
   (3) change West to west

   (1) (2) (3)

3. Sentence 4: **He spent over Sixty years trying to protect the forests and mountains from people.**

   What correction should be made to this sentence?

   (1) change spent to spends
   (2) change Sixty to sixty
   (3) no correction is necessary

   (1) (2) (3)

Practice using capital letters. Write a paragraph or an essay about one or more of the following topics. Tell where you went and who you went with. Add details that will help your reader share the experiences with you.

1. What was your most memorable outing?
2. Did you ever take a trip that turned out to be a disaster or that turned out better than you thought it would?
3. What was the funniest or weirdest thing that ever happened to you on a trip?

You can check the answers to the multiple-choice items for On the Springboard on page 217.

If you need more practice with capitalization, refer to the section in the Style Guide and reread the lesson. If you had no trouble with the Springboard items, congratulations! You're ready to try the sample GED items in "The Real Thing."

☑ A Test-Taking Tip

Don't forget: You are not penalized for getting an answer wrong on the GED Writing Skills Test. Instead, you get points for getting answers right. And you can't get an answer right if you don't mark an option on the answer sheet. So if you've thought about a multiple-choice question and still don't know the answer, *guess*. Mark an answer on the sheet, and you'll have at least a one-in-five chance of getting it right.

“The Real Thing”

Directions: Read the paragraph and then answer the items based on it.

(1) You should choose a lawyer as you would a doctor, dentist, accountant, or anyone else which provides services. (2) The first and obvious step is to define the nature of your legal problem. (3) You will be wasting your time as well as an attorney's time if you bring a simple real estate transaction to a criminal defense specialist. (4) Once you have defined the problem, they're are a number of ways to find a lawyer to help you with it. (5) Most people seeking a lawyer begin by asking advice from a personal acquaintance or someone whose opinion they value, such as their banker, Minister, or another lawyer. (6) You can also find some answers in the public library in the *Martindale Hubbell Law Directory,* which for more than 100 years has published as complete a roster as possible of lawyers in the United States and Canada. (7) Most bar associations in larger cities have a Lawyer Referral and Information Service that can refer you to competent and reliable lawyers. (8) In numerous cities, Legal Aid And Defender offices assist without cost or at a nominal fee persons who cannot pay a lawyer. (9) Whenever you do decide to select a lawyer, it is always a good idea to keep in mind competence as well as accessibility and price. (10) Don't be embarrassed or reluctant to ask the attorney about his or her qualifications, experience, and continuing education.

1. Sentence 1: **You should choose a lawyer as you would a doctor, dentist, accountant, or anyone else which provides services.**

   What correction should be made to this sentence?

   (1) change choose to chose
   (2) change doctor to Doctor
   (3) replace which with who
   (4) change provides to provided
   (5) no correction is necessary

2. Sentence 4: **Once you have defined the problem, they're are a number of ways to find a lawyer to help you with it.**

   What correction should be made to this sentence?

   (1) change have to has
   (2) replace they're with their
   (3) replace they're with there
   (4) replace it with them
   (5) no correction is necessary

3. Sentence 5: **Most people seeking a lawyer begin by asking advice from a personal acquaintance or someone whose opinion they value, such as their banker, Minister, or another lawyer.**

   What correction should be made to this sentence?

   (1) change begin to began
   (2) replace advice with advise
   (3) replace personal with personnel
   (4) change the spelling of acquaintance to aquaintance
   (5) change Minister to minister

4. Sentence 6: **You can also find some answers in the public library in the *Martindale Hubbell Law Directory,* which for more than 100 years has published as complete a roster as possible of lawyers in the United States and Canada.**

   What correction should be made to this sentence?

   (1) change public library to Public Library
   (2) change the spelling of library to libary
   (3) replace which with who
   (4) change has to have
   (5) no correction is necessary

5. Sentence 8: **In numerous cities, Legal Aid And Defender offices assist without cost or at a nominal fee persons who cannot pay a lawyer.**

   What correction should be made to this sentence?

   (1) change the spelling of cities to citys
   (2) change And to and
   (3) change assist to assisting
   (4) change assist to assisted
   (5) replace who with which

   (1) (2) (3) (4) (5)

6. Sentence 9: **Whenever you do decide to select a lawyer, it is always a good idea to keep in mind competence as well as accessibility and price.**

   If you rewrote sentence 9 beginning with

   In selecting a lawyer,

   the next word(s) should be

   (1) keep
   (2) and keeping
   (3) and having kept
   (4) decide to keep
   (5) do remember to keep

Directions: You have 45 minutes to write on this question. Write legibly and use a pen.

In some elections, candidates begin to avoid presenting their own stands on issues and solutions to problems. Instead, they start to criticize and attack each other's positions.

In a composition of about 200 words, explain the reasons for such an election campaign and what possible effects it could have. Give specific examples.

Check your answers, read the sample essay, and record your score on page 222.

SPELLING BREAK 7

The Apostrophe

For such small punctuation marks, apostrophes (') can cause a lot of trouble. The best way to master them is to learn what they do: they show possession, and they show the omission, or dropping out, of letters.

1. Use *'s* to show that one person or thing has something else.

the recipe**'s** ingredients
my daughter**'s** dance lessons
Charles**'s** new truck

2. Use just the ' to show that more than one person or thing has something else.

your friend**s'** lawns
the heroe**s'** awards
the magazine**s'** covers

Exception: When a plural word does not end in *-s,* you must add *'s* to show possession.

the children**'s** room
the policemen**'s** training school

3. Don't use apostrophes when all you want to do is form the plural.

one business**'s** address
two businesses' address**es**

4. Apostrophes can show missing letters.

Who's (Who *i*s) there?
They're (They *a*re) here.
There's (There *i*s) no one here.

Learn words that sound like apostrophe words so you don't confuse them.

whose/who's their/they're/there
its/it's theirs/there's your/you're

5. Some pronouns that show possession and end in *-s* are not spelled with an apostrophe.

This coat is *yours.*
His is the blue one.
Hers is the red one.
The children are *ours*.

Notice the *italicized* words in the following passage. The words that show possession are spelled with an apostrophe. The words that are plural forms are spelled without one. The italicized pronoun is spelled without an apostrophe even though it shows possession.

■ *Hospitals* of one kind or another have been around for almost six thousand *years.* One function of *theirs* in the early Christian era was as a resting place for *travelers* and *victims* of disaster. A religious *community's duties* later expanded to include care for *lepers, cripples,* and the sick poor. A *nurse's* care became part of a *hospital's services* about the year 1155.

The following words are just plural; they don't show ownership: *hospitals, years, travelers, victims, duties, lepers, cripples,* and *services.* These words are possessives: *community's, nurse's,* and *hospital's*. They are singular words spelled with an *'s* . *Theirs* is a pronoun showing ownership, but it is not spelled with an apostrophe.

Warm-up

All but one of the *italicized* words in each passage below is wrong. Rewrite each passage with the correct spellings.

1. Have *your* ping-pong balls gone flat? *Its* easy to bring back *they're* bounce. Drop them in very hot water for fifteen *minutes'.* Now *who's* serve is it?

____

____

____

____

2. Female *spiders'* sure know how to attract *males'.* A female *release's* a perfume that is *her's* alone. Soon a male *show's* up and promptly *begin's* to wad the *female's* web into a ball.

____

____

____

____

You'll find correctly written passages in the Warm-up Answers in the next column.

Write a sentence that includes each phrase below.

3. whose black Chevette ______________

____

4. checking all the restaurants' ______________

____

5. automobile's license ______________

____

6. monkeys' quarreling ______________

____

Compare your sentences with the samples given under Warm-up Answers before you go on.

Edit each paragraph on this page or a copy of it, or rewrite the paragraphs on your own paper. Correct all spelling and verb errors.

7. According to the federal govment, Americas biggest workplace health problem be mental stress. This stress is cause by unsatisfactory work conditions. Boring job tasks', lack of control over working conditions, limited job opportunitys, and rotating shift work contributes to these health problems.

8. Check you're calender. If its Augusst, watch out for jellyfish at the beach. According to experts, if you exsperience a jellyfish's sting, you should relieve the discomfort as soon as possible. The applacation of an antiseptic will soon make you feel alright.

Warm-up Answers

1. Have your ping-pong balls gone flat? *It's* easy to bring back *their* bounce. Drop them in very hot water for fifteen *minutes.* Now *whose* serve is it? **2.** Female *spiders* sure know how to attract *males.* A female *releases* a perfume that is *hers* alone. Soon a male *shows* up and promptly *begins* to wad the female's web into a ball.

3. Whose black Chevette is parked outside? **4.** He enjoys checking all the restaurants' tables for carved initials. **5.** The automobile's license had expired five months ago. **6.** The monkeys' quarreling caused an uproar in the laboratory.

7. According to the federal *government, America's* biggest workplace health problem *is* mental stress. This stress is *caused* by unsatisfactory work conditions. Boring job *tasks,* lack of control over working conditions, limited job *opportunities,* and rotating shift work *contribute* to these health problems. **8.** Check *your calendar.* If *it's August,* watch out for jellyfish at the beach. According to experts, if you *experience* a jellyfish's sting, you should relieve the discomfort as soon as possible. The *application* of an antiseptic will soon make you feel *all right.*

LESSON 23

Punctuation

Knowing When and How to Punctuate

Without punctuation marks, you cannot communicate effectively as a writer. Punctuation marks are tools that are just as important to a writer as pen and paper. In *Writing Sentences,* you learned a lot about commas. In the last Spelling Break, you studied apostrophes. There are other useful marks of punctuation in addition to these. The punctuation section in the Style Guide will help you learn to use semicolons, colons, dashes, parentheses, and quotation marks.

Here's an Example

Read the passage below. It contains many kinds of punctuation marks. If you don't understand how the punctuation marks are used, review the rules in the Style Guide.

■ Backaches plague many people**.** Although theories vary as to the best treatment**,** most experts agree on the common causes**:** gradual wear and tear**,** stress **(**emotional and physical**),** and lack of proper exercise**.** Most back experts agree that the key to a pain**-**free back is strong muscles**,** particularly abdominal muscles**.** In the opinion of Leon Root**,** M**.**D**.,** many vague back maladies are due to disc problems**;** such problems are not developed enough to be diagnosed as such**.** **"**Most severe disc problems**,"** Dr**.** Root says**,** **"**got that way because they were neglected in the early stages**."** Dr**.** Root recommends a program of stretching and strengthening exercises for back problems**.** He says it is likely that **"**if you suffer from back pain**,** your condition is caused not by organic disease**,** but by muscles that are weak**,** tense**,** fatigued**—** or all three**."**

Try It Yourself

Each passage below is written without punctuation. Determine where you would put punctuation marks. Then compare your answers to those given after each passage.

■ Whether Im vacationing working or lounging around the house I must have the radio on The reasons are many I cant stand quiet I love to sing along with my favorite tunes and I can concentrate only when theres noise in the background

Edited passage: Whether I'm vacationing, working, or lounging around the house, I must have the radio on. The reasons are many: I can't stand quiet, I love to sing along with my favorite tunes, and I can concentrate only when there's noise in the background.

■ James T Kirk captain of the *Enterprise* is a graduate of the Starfleet Academy After piloting his ship around the television universe for three years Capt Kirk has made several movies In these movies he battles aliens and maniacs from the past Moreover he sees the death and rebirth of Spock his second in command

Edited passage: James T. Kirk, captain of the *Enterprise*, is a graduate of the Starfleet Academy. After piloting his ship around the television universe for three years, Capt. Kirk has made several movies. In these movies, he battles aliens and maniacs from the past; moreover, he sees the death and rebirth of Spock, his second in command.

Warm-up

The following eight sentences contain punctuation errors. You may have to add or remove punctuation marks. Identify the errors. Then rewrite each one so that it matches the Style Guide rules.

1. My birthday July 20, is also my parents anniversary.

___

___

2. The explorers breath came in ragged gasps; the hairs in his nose were crusted with ice crystals his toes were aching with frostbite.

____

____

3. On December 23 1986, Jeana Yeager and Dick Rutan set a record for flying around the world without stopping and without refueling.

____

____

4. "The sign over the country stores' door said, Live bait sold here."

____

____

5. "If you help me fix my car, Larry said, I'll take you hunting next weekend."

____

____

6. Romance novels such as *Springs Awakening,* and *Jenna's Choice* are my favorites.

____

____

7. You can order a booklet entitled How to Buy a Telephone, by writing to this consumer electronics group, in Washington D.C.

____

____

8. People walk for many reasons to enjoy the scenery, to rid themselves of tension to find solitude, or to get from one place to another.

____

____

Check your rewritten sentences against the ones in the Warm-up Answers.

Punctuation marks are missing from the following paragraph. Edit it by writing the marks on this page or a copy of it, or rewrite the paragraph on another sheet of paper.

His fame has lasted for fourteen centuries and brought him into the legends of our childhood Who is he He is King Arthur of course Using records of battles fought in the fourth century A D researchers have found references to a mighty warrior called Arthur No one however has been able to prove the existence of King Arthur of his castle at Camelot or of the famous Round Table Merlin his famous magician is a question mark too

A Test-Taking Tip

Just as the directions for the essay on the GED Writing Skills Test don't actually use the words *prewrite* or *revise,* they won't tell you directly to edit your writing. Instead, the directions will be similar to this: "Check your paragraphing, sentence structure, spelling, punctuation, capitalization, and usage, and make any necessary corrections." That means the same thing as "Edit your writing." So after you've prewritten, written a first draft, and revised, edit your essay to get the best possible score.

Warm-up Answers

1. My birthday, July 20, is also my parents' anniversary.
2. The explorer's breath came in ragged gasps; the hairs in his nose were crusted with ice crystals; his toes were aching with frostbite. **3.** On December 23, 1986, Jeana Yeager and Dick Rutan set a record for flying around the world without stopping and without refueling. **4.** The sign over the country store's door said, "Live bait sold here." **5.** "If you help me fix my car," Larry said, "I'll take you hunting next weekend."
6. Romance novels such as *Spring's Awakening* and *Jenna's Choice* are my favorites. **7.** You may order a booklet entitled "How to Buy a Telephone" by writing to this consumer electronics group in Washington, D.C. **8.** People walk for many reasons: to enjoy the scenery, to rid themselves of tension, to find solitude, or to get from one place to another.

His fame has lasted for fourteen centuries and brought him into the legends of our childhood. Who is he? He is King Arthur, of course. Using records of battles fought in the fourth century A.D., researchers have found references to a mighty warrior called Arthur. No one, however, has been able to prove the existence of King Arthur, of his castle at Camelot, or of the famous Round Table. Merlin, his famous magician, is a question mark too.

On the Springboard

Directions: Read this paragraph carefully and then answer the questions that follow it.

(1) In 1815, Walter Hunt created the first safety pin that worked well. (2) The idea of the pin, however is more than four thousand years old. (3) The Greeks Italians, and Sicilians used pins that looked something like the safety pins we now use. (4) These old pins were not designed well, so their uncovered points pricked the people who used them. (5) Hunt solved this problem by hiding the point. (6) Hunt earned four hundred dollars for his invention of a "safe pin."

1. Sentence 2: **The idea of the pin, however is more than four thousand years old.**

   Which of the following is the best way to write the underlined portion of this sentence? If you think the original is the best way, choose option (1).

   (1) pin, however is
   (2) pin, however, is
   (3) pin; however, is

   (1) (2) (3)

2. Sentence 3: **The Greeks Italians, and Sicilians used pins that looked something like the safety pins we now use.**

   What correction should be made to this sentence?

   (1) insert a comma after Greeks
   (2) remove the comma after Italians
   (3) insert a comma after Sicilians

   (1) (2) (3)

3. Sentence 4: **These old pins were not designed well, so their uncovered points pricked the people who used them.**

   Which of the following is the best way to write the underlined portion of this sentence? If you think the original is the best way, choose option (1).

   (1) well, so (2) well; so
   (3) well. And so

   (1) (2) (3)

What "roles" do you play in life? Do you have a job? Are you a citizen? If you buy things, you're a consumer. If you have children, you're a parent.

Write an essay about the various roles you have in this society. Write as if someone who doesn't know you at all will read your essay. That should help you be specific. Don't forget to prewrite, write, revise, and edit.

You can check your answer to the multiple-choice Springboard questions on page 217.

If you're confident of your knowledge about punctuation, read the tip that follows and then go on to the last "Real Thing." If you still have doubts, analyze some of the sentences in the instructional material in this book. Determine why punctuation was used where it was. Then practice on your own.

A Test-Taking Tip

Once you have prewritten, written, revised, and edited your GED essay, you need to take one last step: read your entire essay over from start to finish, the way the GED scorers will read it. This step is like looking yourself over in a full-length mirror before going out on a big date or for an important appointment. Are *you* impressed by what you see? You will be if you've followed the steps for writing an essay, and the GED scorers will be too.

“The Real Thing”

Directions: Read the paragraph and then answer the items based on it.

(1) Most would agree that trees are beautiful, but should you go out of your way to plant a tree? (2) The answer is yes. (3) Planting trees is a fine way to commemorate birthdays, anniversaries, reunions, graduations, and other special occassions. (4) Remember, too, that beauty is contagious, if you plant trees around your home, your neighbors may do the same. (5) Trees can help increase the value of your property. (6) A tree can be a natural air conditioner; the evaporation from a single large tree can produce the cooling effect of ten room-size air conditioners operating twenty hours a day. (7) A tree can also serve as a buffer against unpleasant noises. (8) Certain trees can help freshen the atmosphere with the trees' own natural, pleasant fragrances. (9) For example one cherry tree can perfume the air with 200,000 flowers, and their beauty can be breathtaking. (10) Planting and caring for a tree is really easy to do, and the tree will reward you many times with its beauty and shade.

1. Sentence 1: **Most would agree that trees are beautiful, but should you go out of your way to plant a tree?**

   What correction should be made to this sentence?

   (1) change agree to have agreed
   (2) change the spelling of beautiful to beautyful
   (3) remove the comma after beautiful
   (4) remove the word but
   (5) no correction is necessary

   ① ② ③ ④ ⑤

2. Sentence 3: **Planting trees is a fine way to commemorate birthdays, anniversaries, reunions, graduations, and other special occassions.**

   What correction should be made to this sentence?

   (1) change is to are
   (2) remove the comma after birthdays
   (3) insert a comma after other
   (4) change the spelling of occassions to occasions
   (5) no correction is necessary

   ① ② ③ ④ ⑤

3. Sentence 4: **Remember, too, that beauty is contagious, if you plant trees around your home, your neighbors may do the same.**

   Which of the following is the best way to write the underlined portion of this sentence? If you think the original is the best way, choose option (1).

   (1) contagious, if (2) contagious if
   (3) contagious, even if
   (4) contagious and if (5) contagious. If

   ① ② ③ ④ ⑤

4. Sentence 9: **For example one cherry tree can perfume the air with 200,000 flowers, and their beauty can be breathtaking.**

   What correction should be made to this sentence?

   (1) insert a comma after example
   (2) remove the comma after flowers
   (3) remove the word and
   (4) replace their with there
   (5) replace their with they're

   ① ② ③ ④ ⑤

5. Sentence 10: **Planting and caring for a tree is really easy to do, and the tree will reward you many times with its beauty and shade.**

   What correction should be made to this sentence?

   (1) insert a comma after Planting
   (2) change is to are
   (3) remove the comma after do
   (4) change will reward to has rewarded
   (5) replace its with it's

   ① ② ③ ④ ⑤

Directions: You have 45 minutes to write on this question. Write legibly and use a pen.

Much has been said and written in the last few decades about the changing role of women. Very little, however, has been devoted to the changes that men have experienced in that same time.

What are the roles of a man in today's society? Detail your thoughts about that topic in a composition of about 200 words.

Check your answers, read the sample essay, and record your score on page 223.

SPELLING BREAK 8

Adding *-ly*

You can add *-ly* to descriptive words to help them describe still other descriptive words. There are four basic rules for adding *-ly* to words.

1. For most descriptive words, just add *-ly*.

   apparent + *-ly* = apparent**ly**
   careless + *-ly* = careless**ly**
   awkward + *-ly* = awkward**ly**
   awful + *-ly* = awful**ly**

2. For words that end in *ble,* drop the *e* and add *-ly.*

   advisable + *-ly* = advisa**bly**
   comfortable + *-ly* = comforta**bly**

3. For words that end in *y,* change the *y* to *i* and add *-ly.*

   easy + *-ly* = eas**ily**
   day + *-ly* = da**ily**

4. If words already end with two *ll*'s, add only *-y.*

   full + *-ly* = full**y**

5. Memorize words that follow their own rules.

   whole + *-ly* = **wholly**
   true + *-ly* = **truly**

Warm-up

Add *-ly* to each of these GED Spelling List words. Then write a sentence with each *-ly* word.

1. necessary ____________________
2. peaceable ____________________
3. healthy ____________________
4. decisive ____________________

The correctly spelled words can be found in the Warm-up Answers at the end of this Spelling Break.

Add *-ly* to the word in front of each sentence. Then select a position for the word, and rewrite the sentence on your own paper.

5. (inevitable) All writers suffer from writer's block. **6.** (successful) Many experienced writers have managed to overcome writer's block. **7.** (intense) They sit down and make themselves write for thirty minutes about anything that pops into their heads.

Check your answers with those below.

The following three sentences contain two or more spelling errors. Edit each sentence here or on your own paper, correcting all the errors.

8. We anxsiously waited for the marryage counsellor to speak.

9. Will you have your wool clotheing proffessionally dry-cleaned?

10. After twellve weeks of boot camp, the new recruit desparately wanted to go home.

Check your answers with the answer section before going on.

Edit each of these short paragraphs for spelling and capitalization errors. Mark this page or a copy of it, or rewrite the paragraphs on your own paper.

11. The whether bullitin on the Television continusly warned of the aproaching hurricane. Residents along the gulf of Mexico were orderred to leave they're homes.

12. Driving thru the Rocky mountains in our old clunker was extremily nerve-wracking. Fortunatly, the car didn't break down until we had made it to Oklahoma city.

Warm-up Answers
1. necessarily **2.** peaceably **3.** healthily **4.** decisively

The position of your *-ly* words may be different, but they should be spelled the same as these:
5. All writers *inevitably* suffer from writer's block. **6.** Many experienced writers have managed to overcome writer's block *successfully.* **7.** They sit down and make themselves write intensely for thirty minutes about anything that pops into their heads.

8. We *anxiously* waited for the *marriage counselor* to speak.
9. Will you have your wool *clothing professionally* dry-cleaned?
10. After *twelve* weeks of boot camp, the new recruit *desperately* wanted to go home.

11. The *weather bulletin* on the *television continuously* warned of the *approaching* hurricane. Residents along the *Gulf* of Mexico were *ordered* to leave *their* homes. **12.** Driving *through* the Rocky *Mountains* in our old clunker was *extremely* nerve-wracking. *Fortunately,* the car didn't break down until we had made it to Oklahoma *City.*

Answers: On the Springboard

18 Verb Times

Telling Time with Verbs
(page 168)

1. (2) The movie was popular in the past, and it will continue to be popular, as the passage states. The only option that applies to both a past event and its continuation is (2).

2. (3) The time clue in this sentence is *1942.* Germany *tried* (in the past) to conquer the world.

3. (2) The time clue is *future generations.* The only option that expresses future time is (2).

Corrected passage:

Many film buffs have seen the movie "Casablanca" numerous times. Its portrayal of the love story between Rick and Ilsa, played by Humphrey Bogart and Ingrid Bergman, has made this movie popular for years. The context of World War II gives the love story an interesting, added dimension. Because it was filmed in 1942, "Casablanca" also shows the struggle between Nazi Germany and the world it tried to conquer. "Casablanca" has finally been released on videocassette. Now future generations will be able to enjoy this classic film and thrill to the line, "Here's looking at you, kid."

19 Verb Forms

Irregular Verbs
(page 176)

1. (1) The second part of a verb (*wrote*) is not used with a helping verb. *Written* is used with a helper like *had.*

2. (1) Because *begun* is the third part of the verb *begin,* it is never used alone. *Began* can be used without a helper.

3. (3) No error. If you chose option (1), keep in mind that *drunk* must always be used with a helping verb.

Corrected passage:

Edgar Allan Poe was the writer of such eerie tales as "The Fall of the House of Usher" and "The Tell-Tale Heart." During his lifetime, he received very little pay for his writing. He had written some of the best poetry in the nineteenth century, yet he was not well liked by other poets. What began as a promising career ended in tragedy. Many people think Poe drank himself to death, but research has proved that he was not an alcoholic. Poe's genius has never been doubted, but he was a man with many problems.

20 Subject-Verb Agreement

Matching Verbs with Subjects
(page 182)

1. (3) *Almost* is the correct spelling. *Computers are* matches because both words are plural.

2. (2) Sentence 5 has four subjects *(camera, screen, computer,* and *stylus).* Therefore, the verb must be plural *(help)* to match. Option (3) changes the verb from present to past. The time clue *now* tells you that the sentence is in present time.

Corrected passage:

Computers are becoming indispensable in almost every aspect of your life. They can even help you change the way you look. If you want to redesign your face, a computer imaging system can take some of the guesswork out of plastic surgery. In the past, you would have needed a photograph of your dream face, or a plastic surgeon would sketch changes on your photograph. Now a camera, a screen, a computer, and an electronic stylus help you and your doctor predict the results of surgery. This new technology is not picture-perfect, but at least it will take the "byte" out of your suspense over the surgical results.

Interrupting Phrases
(page 186)

3. (2) The subject of sentence 1 is plural *(workers). Workers think* matches. *Technology* is not the subject because it is part of the interrupting phrase *afraid of computer technology.*

4. (1) *Worker* and *was* match because they are both singular. But *was* shows past time. The passage is written in present time. Therefore, *worker is* is correct.

Corrected passage:

Some office workers, afraid of computer technology, think that computers are too complicated. Actually, operating a computer is easy once a person learns how. Many companies now offer training courses to help their employees learn that working with computers is fun and is a more efficient way to organize an office. A worker with computer skills is also more likely to be promoted.

Inverted Sentences
(page 189)

5. (1) The subject of this inverted sentence is *BMX racing.* The verb is in present time because the sport's popularity continues.

6. (1) *There* is never the subject of a sentence. The plural word *precautions* is the subject. Therefore, *are* is the correct verb choice.

7. (1) *Helmet,* not *knee pads,* is the subject of the sentence. Option (2) creates a fragment by removing part of the verb.

Corrected passage:

Perhaps most popular among new sports is BMX racing, which began just a few years ago in

California. BMX stands for bicycle motocross. On some tracks, racers go over jumps called whoop-de-doos, ride around banked curves called berms, and even fly off a jump called a tabletop. There are certain safety precautions a racer must take. A safety helmet, as well as elbow pads and knee pads, is required at many BMX race tracks.

21 Pronouns

Matching Pronouns with Verbs and Other Pronouns
(page 197)

1. (3) *Convenient* is the correct spelling. *Nothing makes* matches because they are both singular.

2. (2) *One of an ATM's many benefits is that you can make deposits or withdrawals twenty-four hours a day. One,* not *benefits,* is the subject.

Corrected passage:

Nothing makes banking more convenient than automated teller machines (ATMs). Consumers can use these machines to do their banking without the assistance of a teller. To use an ATM, a consumer must have a personal identification number. This number will prevent unauthorized use of your account. One of an ATM's many benefits is that you can make deposits or withdrawals twenty-four hours a day.

Making Your Reference Clear
(page 201)

3. (3) Using the pronoun *they* could mislead the reader into thinking that the *equipment breathed* air. It is clearer to write *the divers breathed.*

4. (3) Options (1) and (2) make a misleading reference to *the pressure of the water.* Using (3) correctly identifies the regulation of air and water pressures as the thing that prevents lung damage.

Corrected passage:

Scuba diving is deep-sea diving using equipment that is carried on the back of the diver. Before the development of scuba equipment, the divers breathed air pumped down a long hose from the surface. With scuba equipment, the diver receives air from the tanks through a rubber hose. At the end of the hose is a demand regulator. It keeps the pressure of the air in the diver's lungs equal to the pressure of the water; such regulation is necessary to prevent serious lung damage.

22 Capitalization

Knowing When to Capitalize
(page 207)

1. (3) *Park* is capitalized because it is part of the name *Yosemite National Park.*

2. (1) Because the passage is written about someone who lived in the past, the past form of *looked* is correct.

3. (2) There is no reason to capitalize *sixty. Spent* (1) is correct because it shows past time.

Corrected passage:

Ansel Adams, a well-known photographer, became a friend to millions through his pictures of Yosemite National Park. He had a white beard and a broken nose, and he wore a Stetson hat and a hunting jacket. To many, he looked like an old-timer from the early days of the West. He spent over sixty years trying to protect the forests and mountains from people. His special interest was to protect the beauty of Yosemite. His pictures let everyone know that Yosemite's beauty is worth saving.

23 Punctuation

Knowing When and How to Punctuate
(page 213)

1. (2) *However* is a word that interrupts the flow of the sentence and must have commas before and after it.

2. (1) *Greeks* is the first item in a list and must have a comma after it. No comma is needed after the last word in a series.

3. (1) No error. The independent thought *their uncovered points pricked the people who used them* is connected to the independent thought *these old pins were not designed well* with a connecting word *(so)* and a comma.

Corrected passage:

In 1815, Walter Hunt created the first safety pin that worked well. The idea of the pin, however, is more than four thousand years old. The Greeks, Italians, and Sicilians used pins that looked something like the safety pins we now use. These old pins were not designed well, so their uncovered points pricked the people who used them. Hunt solved this problem by hiding the point. Hunt earned four hundred dollars for his invention of a "safe pin."

Answers: "The Real Thing"

18 Verb Times

Telling Time with Verbs
(pages 168–169)

1. (2) *Will show* expresses future time. The passage mainly is about research that is occurring in present time. Therefore, *shows* is the correct choice because it is the only verb in the options that shows present time.

2. (2) *Believed* is the correct spelling. Remember the rule from grammar school "*i* before *e* except after *c*"?

3. (1) Option (5) creates a fragment. *Will find* shows future time, and *find* shows present time. *Have found* is correct because it shows a past and continuing event.

4. (5) No error.

5. (1) *They also learn how to make their lives more stimulating.* Again, because these programs take place in present time, *learn* is correct.

Corrected passage:

Have you ever heard the phrase "use it or lose it"? New research by brain experts shows that continued mental challenges lead to healthier brain cells and more efficient thinking. Previously, experts believed that senility was a natural outgrowth of aging. A recent thirty-year study has shown that older people who maintain a high level of interaction with their environment do not decline mentally in their old age. Eighty-five percent of all people over 65 do not have any significant memory loss or other forms of mental disabilities. Researchers also have found that previously noted behavioral and mental changes in the elderly may have resulted from improper medication, depression, or other treatable conditions. As a result, new educational programs are being offered in which participants learn ways to maintain or restore intellectual skills. They are taught that a flexible attitude and a willingness to explore new ideas will help them remain mentally active. They also learn how to make their lives more stimulating. Lillian Rabinowitz, 75, founder of the San Francisco chapter of the Gray Panthers, says, "I think persons have a lifelong capability to learn, and to me that is my greatest treasure."

KEEPING TRACK
Top Score = 5

Your Score = ☐

Sample essay:

Working for a big company may seem glamorous—one is part of an organization everyone has heard of. That doesn't happen if you work for the place around the corner that employs five people. Yet each kind of employment has its advantages and drawbacks.

Through transfers and promotions, an employee may learn new skills and get ahead in a big company. The fringe benefits may include training programs, excellent medical insurance, or a subsidized cafeteria. The workers at a big company are likely to have a union which looks out for their interests and charges dues.

A big company, though, tends to be impersonal. If a layoff is necessary, people are simply let go. Too many people are involved in any single project for any one person to be noticed for his or her work.

A small company is more like a family. Each person has a role, and if something does not get done, it is noticed. On the other hand, a person can take credit for good work. Employees often know more about each other's lives and care for each other's welfare.

In the United States there are many job opportunities in both big and small companies. Often people can choose which kind of employer is best for them.

19 Verb Forms

Irregular Verbs
(page 177)

1. (2) The original sentence is a comma splice. Option (3) is a run-on. Option (2) is correct because it separates the two independent thoughts with a period and a capital letter.

2. (5) No error.

3. (1) *Became* is a verb form that is used without a helping verb. *Had become* is correct. Option (3) is incorrect because *wrote* cannot be used with a helper.

4. (3) The original sentence is a run-on. Option (3) corrects this error by changing the second independent thought into a descriptive detail.

5. (4) *Been* must always be used with a helping verb. But *had been* would not be parallel with the verb *were* in the independent thought. *Before* does not logically express the relationship between the two ideas in the sentence.

Corrected passage:

The contributions of immigrants have added a tremendous richness to American culture. One man who came from England in 1914 became one of Hollywood's biggest stars. His trademarks were a gentlemanly black bowler, an oversized jacket, and a bamboo cane. He was the classic silent movie clown known as the Little Tramp. His real name was Charlie Chaplin. Before coming to America at the age of 25, Chaplin had spent most of his life in poverty. Within a year and a half of his movie debut in 1914, he earned $12,844 a week. One year later, he signed a multimillion-dollar movie contract. Taxes at that time took only a small amount of a person's annual income. Movies had become such a part of Chaplin's life that he wrote, directed, and starred in his own films. As a director, Chaplin was a perfectionist, shooting a scene over and over until he was satisfied with it. Although there was no radio and television publicity in those early days of technology, his movies were instant hits. Many movie buffs believe him to have been the most creative movie genius of this century.

KEEPING TRACK

Top Score = 5

Your Score = ☐

Sample essay:

For the most part, television offers children more disadvantages than advantages. Special shows do teach children reading and math skills in an entertaining way.

Many children come home from school before their parents come home from work. When this happens, watching television can help these children feel less lonely. Television, however, is too often used as a babysitter so parents can do other things rather than take care of the child.

Many children cannot entertain themselves unless they are in front of a TV. They don't read many books because they find reading dull compared to the excitement of a TV show.

Most television programs do not give a realistic view of life. Children may become frustrated because they want their families to be as smooth running as the television families seem to be. Children from poor families see things that television children have and wonder why they can't have the same things.

It is very difficult for some children to realize that many of the programs on television are make-believe. If parents keep using TV as a babysitter, who will teach a child about the realities of day-to-day life?

20 Subject-Verb Agreement

Matching Verbs with Subjects (pages 182–183)

1. (1) When two subjects (*lemon* and *honey*) are joined by *and,* they match with a plural verb.

2. (5) *Prescription* is the correct spelling.

3. (2) *Remedies* is plural and must match with a plural verb *(contain)*. The time clue in sentence 4 *(today)* tells you that a present time verb is needed in sentence 5.

4. (2) Sentence 8 states that the panel made its study in the past. Therefore, the verb *indicated* is correct.

5. (2) *Although* is the correct spelling.

Corrected passage:

If you had lived in ancient Rome, you might have relieved the symptoms of the common cold by sipping an onion broth. In colonial America, you might have relied on pennyroyal tea or an herbal concoction made from plants such as buckthorn, coltsfoot, and bloodroot. In your grandmother's time, lemon and honey were used to cure colds, or in extreme cases, a hot toddy laced with rum was prepared. Today, if you don't have a family remedy to rely on, you probably take one of literally thousands of drug preparations available without prescription. Some remedies contain ingredients that remind you of the folk medicine of the past; others are formulated with fancy chemical creations. Old or new, simple or fancy, many will relieve some of the familiar cold symptoms. However, not a single one will prevent, cure, or even shorten the course of the common cold. That is according to a panel of nongovernment experts who reported to the Food and Drug Administration about the safety, effectiveness, and accuracy of claims made on the labels of some 50,000 drug products. The panel indicated that proper use of over-the-counter drugs can help relieve cough, sinus congestion, and a runny nose. Yet it also made clear that although these products may relieve certain symptoms, they do not cure the cold itself.

Sample essay:

Commercials have positive and negative aspects. On the positive side, commercials sell products and this, in turn, provides jobs. Commercials also inform us of new products and often provide important public service information. They pay for our favorite television shows and give us a chance to run to the bathroom or kitchen.

There are negative aspects to commercials, though. Some people find them too loud and too one-sided. Commercials usually have one purpose: to sell a product. Commercials usually sell an image rather than the usefulness of a product. For example, most people buy a truck or car not for practical reasons but for the way they will look and feel while driving it.

We are influenced to buy what the product's company wants to sell. In effect, we are brainwashed to be like everyone else and wear a certain perfume, or use a particular shaving cream, or brush our teeth with a sexy toothpaste.

Sometimes commercials insult our intelligence by using talking fruit or people sailing around in toilet bowls to sell a product. As consumers, if we weren't swayed by all this nonsense, then commercials would probably become more practical and informative.

Interrupting Phrases (pages 186–187)

6. (2) *Dogs* and *cats* are both subjects. Therefore, the plural verb *need* is correct.

7. (2) The subjects *licking* and *redness* are connected by *or*, so the verb should match with the closest *(redness is).*

8. (2) Since *pet* is the subject of the sentence, it needs the singular verb. *Outdoors* and *garage* are part of the interrupting phrase *if he stays outdoors or in a chilly garage.*

9. (2) A verb showing future time is needed in sentence 7 because the doghouse has not been built yet.

10. (1) *Loving to be near the engine's warmth, cats often curl up under the hood. Cats* and *curl* match because they are both plural. You also need to use a verb in the present time.

Corrected passage:

During cold weather, dogs and cats need to be protected from ice, snow, and low temperatures. Don't walk your dog near rock salt or other ice-melting chemicals because these chemicals stick to your pet's paws. Excessive licking of a paw's underside or redness on or between the footpads is a sign of pain or irritation. After walking your dog through ice and snow, wipe his paws, top and bottom, with a damp cloth. Your pet, if he stays outdoors or in a chilly garage, also needs a doghouse. The doghouse should be close to your dog's size when he lies down, without too much air space overhead. That way his body heat will provide warmth to his special home. Small, short-haired dogs, like chihuahuas, should be outside only for a few minutes. Larger and shaggier dogs can be let out for longer periods of time. If you have a cat that likes to spend the night out, check under your hood or blow your horn before starting your car. Loving to be near the engine's warmth, cats often curl up under the hood.

Sample essay:

Service with a smile is hard to find. Just a generation ago, people believed the sayings "a good day's work for a good day's pay," and "any job worth doing is worth doing well."

It is really difficult now to find workers who are happy to help a customer. Shoppers must often stand around in a store for a long time hoping that a clerk will appear to answer their questions or ring up a sale. Full-service gas stations are almost a thing of the past.

Getting information from someone in a large company is often frustrating because the person who answers the phone is never the one who can answer your question. Instead, you are usually transferred from one person to another as each one fails to take any responsibility for helping you or for finding the right person to help you.

It could be that workers are so poorly paid that they are not motivated to work hard. There is no incentive to do your best when you are only making minimum wage. When a worker does go out of the way to give good service, it is a pleasant surprise.

Inverted Sentences
(page 190)

11. (5) No error.

12. (4) *Americans take more than 80 million aspirin a day, which are enough to cure about 15 billion headaches a year.* Sentences 4 and 5 are combined by making the second sentence into a dependent part. *Which are* refers to *aspirin.*

13. (2) *Willow leaves* and *willow bark* are two subjects joined by *and.* Therefore, a plural verb is needed. Options (1) and (5) are singular verbs.

14. (5) *Since that time, thousands of studies of the properties of aspirin have been done to discover how aspirin works.* The plural subject *thousands* must match with a plural verb. The action of the sentence takes place in the past.

15. (2) A word series is separated by commas.

Corrected passage:

"Take two aspirin and call me in the morning." Often heard from busy doctors is that familiar prescription. Aspirin is the most popular drug in the United States. Americans take more than 80 million aspirin a day, which are enough to cure about 15 billion headaches a year. Aspirin was first marketed in Germany in 1899, but its history really began 2,300 years ago in ancient Greece. Hippocrates, the father of modern medicine, found that chewing on willow leaves reduced pain. For the next 1,600 years, willow leaves and willow bark were used as folk medicine cures. It wasn't until 1853 that a German researcher combined the chemicals from the willow and other plants to produce acetylsalicylic acid, or aspirin. Since that time, thousands of studies of the properties of aspirin have been done to discover how aspirin works. In 1982, British pharmacologist John Vane discovered that aspirin blocks the manufacture of hormonelike chemicals. These chemicals trigger pain, fever, and inflammation. For his work, Vane won the Nobel prize.

KEEPING TRACK

Top Score = 15

Your Score = ☐

Sample essay:

Many people view happiness in two ways: what they possess makes them happy or how they feel about themselves makes them happy.

Unfortunately, many Americans are happy only when they are able to buy certain things. These things could be as expensive as a house in the "right" neighborhood or as inexpensive as the latest style of jeans.

Children as well as adults are caught up in this desire to own the best or to own what makes them feel a part of a group. There are designer clothes and shoes for children. Who doesn't know a child who has come home saying that he wanted a pair of expensive basketball shoes just like the other kids? And if he doesn't get them, he says that he'll be unhappy for the rest of his life.

Real happiness comes from how a person feels inside. To be happy, a person should feel confident and should feel a certain pride about how he or she deals with other human beings.

Having a good job and a loving family makes some people happy. Others do volunteer work in hospitals, with the Cub Scouts, or in adult literacy programs. Helping others gives these volunteers happiness.

21 Pronouns

Matching Pronouns with Verbs and Other Pronouns
pages 198–199

1. (5) The subject of the sentence is *Grand Kabuki National Theater.*

2. (2) *At the age of four, promising children begin their training, which includes dancing and singing.*

3. (3) *Movement is* matches.

4. (5) No error.

5. (2) *Movement* and *stance* require a plural verb because the two subjects are connected by *and.* Therefore, the plural verb *have* is correct.

Corrected passage:

The sounds, rhythms, and moves of Kabuki make it the most popular of the traditional theater forms in Japan. In Tokyo, the Grand Kabuki National Theater houses a company of over two hundred actors who perform almost two hundred plays a year. At the age of four, promising children begin their training, which includes dancing and singing. Traditionally, men perform all the roles in a Kabuki play. Their faces are covered with a thick, white rice powder. Straight eyebrows and tiny rosebud lips are painted on top of the powder. Most Kabuki actors agree that movement is the most important element of their act. Each one is always accompanied onstage by musicians and singers. Kabuki is a highly stylized art form in which every movement and stance have meaning.

Sample essay:

Some people think there is a life cycle of cars that parallels the life cycle of people. They say that for each kind of car there is a season.

The teenager adores his first jalopy. It gives him wheels—never mind that it clanks, smokes, and lurches. Still, if he starts to earn some "real money," he may get a "hot" car that can "lay a patch" of rubber on the pavement as it screeches out of intersections. The car shows that its owner is someone to reckon with.

As he matures, he may marry. Now responsible for the finances of a family, he trades the powerful, sporty car for a compact, economy vehicle that will go its daily rounds on almost no gasoline at all.

Should children join the family, the economy car's cramped seating is inadequate. The car is replaced by a station wagon, which is quickly filled with strollers and baseball bats and becomes a kind of extension of the family garage.

As years pass, the parents trade the wagon for a dignified, four-door sedan. Then there may be an interesting development: As the owner enters mid-life crisis, he finds that car stodgy and limiting. Throwing caution to the winds, our hero buys a snappier version of his younger self's speedster.

At last the sports car begins to seem a bit extreme and a sedan too large. The owner may purchase one more car—a more comfortable model of the economy car. With good care, that car may finally outlast its owner.

Making Your Reference Clear
(pages 202–203)

6. (3) *It* does not clearly refer to any one thing. Substituting *this term* for *it* makes the meaning of the sentence clear.

7. (5) The pronoun refers to *drug* (in the dependent thought that begins the sentence) so the pronoun must be singular. The present verb in the dependent thought indicates that a present verb should be used throughout the sentence.

8. (2) The *while this happens* is too vague because it does not refer to anything in particular. But *during this time* is specific.

9. (2) *These exact copies of the original drug are often called generic drugs. Copies* and *are* match because both are plural.

10. (3) In the original wording, can you tell what *it* refers to? Option (3) clearly shows that *the brand name* (not *the generic name*) is used in advertising.

Corrected passage:

"Generics" is a term that is heard frequently today, often in connection with consumer products that are sold without a brand name or fancy label. What does this term mean when used in reference to prescription drugs? When a new drug is first developed, it is usually patented and sold exclusively under a single brand name. Drug patents run seventeen years. During this time, the brand name of the first drug becomes well known. Such original drugs are often referred to as "brand-name" drugs. If there is no patent or after a patent has expired, other firms may manufacture and sell the drug either under different brand names or under the drug's generic name. These exact copies of the original drug are often called generic drugs. Thus, every drug has a generic name and a brand name. The brand name is prominently used in advertising a drug to the medical profession, though the generic name must also appear in advertising and labeling in letters at least half as big as that of the brand name. About 90 percent of all generic drugs are made by the major drug firms in the country, the ones who also develop "brand-name" drugs.

KEEPING TRACK
Top Score = 10
Your Score = ☐

Sample essay:

Parenting becomes more difficult when both parents need to work to keep their family going in this very expensive world. No special license is needed to be a parent. Almost anyone can become one.

Children don't come with instructions. There are certain responsibilities, though, that every parent should assume. Parents should love and nurture their children while recognizing that all children are not alike; they have different talents and strengths. The children in a family should not be measured against one another. The uniqueness of each child should be fostered.

This alone is a huge job for parents. But there is more to parenting. A child should feel safe and secure, physically as well as emotionally. Children should be taught to respect the privacy of others, to value education, to respect work, and to be an individual.

There's a fine line between wanting more for your children than you had and pushing your children beyond their limits. Parents should remember that not everyone grows up to be the president of the United States. Despite how-to-parent books and magazines, parenting remains one of the hardest and most rewarding jobs on earth.

22 Capitalization

Knowing When to Capitalize
(pages 208–209)

1. (3) The pronoun *who* is used to refer to people. *Who provides services* is correct. The passage is written in present time.

2. (3) *They're* stands for *they are.* It is not logical to write *they are a number. Their* shows ownership.

3. (5) Because it is not used with the name of a person in this sentence, *minister* is not capitalized.

4. (5) No error. *Public library* would only be capitalized when it is used with the library's name (for example, the *Springfield Public Library*).

5. (2) In titles, small words like *the, and,* and *of* are not capitalized unless they are the first word in the title. *Persons* and *who* match.

6. (1) *In selecting a lawyer, keep in mind competence as well as accessibility and price.* Options (2) and (3) are not logical. Options (4) and (5) contain too many unnecessary words.

Corrected passage:

You should choose a lawyer as you would a doctor, dentist, accountant, or anyone else who provides services. The first and obvious step is to define the nature of your legal problem. You will be wasting your time as well as an attorney's time if you bring a simple real estate transaction to a criminal defense specialist. Once you have defined the problem, there are a number of ways to find a lawyer to help you with it. Most people seeking a lawyer begin by asking advice from a personal acquaintance or someone whose opinion they value, such as their banker, minister, or another lawyer. You can also find some answers in the public library in the *Martindale Hubbell Law Directory,* which for more than 100 years has published as complete a roster as possible of lawyers in the United States and Canada. Most bar associations in larger cities have a Lawyer Referral and Information Service that can refer you to competent and reliable lawyers. In numerous cities, Legal Aid and Defender offices assist without cost or at a nominal fee persons who cannot pay a lawyer. In selecting a lawyer, keep in mind competence as well as accessibility and price. Don't be embarrassed or reluctant to ask the attorney about his or her qualifications, experience, and continuing education.

KEEPING TRACK
Top Score = 6
Your Score = ☐

Sample essay:

More and more political candidates find that it is easier not to take a stand on anything. After all, if they don't make any promises, then they don't have to worry about keeping them.

Some candidates might feel that presenting solutions to community problems could leave themselves open to criticism from an opponent. They may believe that the best defense is a good offense. Candidates who campaign this way may be unclear about their own political beliefs and feel insecure about stating their position on certain issues.

To win an election, a candidate must get a lot of publicity. Candidates who verbally attack one another usually do get better press coverage than candidates who quietly state facts about their own stands on issues. Mudslinging candidates may have a negative view of government and the people in it. If so, they may feel comfortable attacking other candidates.

Mud-slinging is certainly more interesting to listen to than sober statements about how a candidate would improve the quality of the city's water supply. The press and the public may be disillusioned by the political system. Therefore, they would rather hear about the dirt than empty campaign promises. So scandal, real or imaginary, becomes the campaign issue.

23 Punctuation

Knowing When and How to Punctuate
(page 214)

1. (5) No error.

2. (4) *Occasions* is the correct spelling.

3. (5) A comma cannot join two complete sentences.

4. (1) Use a comma after an introductory phrase like *for example.* Option (3) is incorrect because the comma and *and* join two independent thoughts.

5. (2) When two subjects *(Planting* and *caring)* are joined by *and,* they match with a plural verb *(are).*

Corrected passage:

Most would agree that trees are beautiful, but should you go out of your way to plant a tree? The answer is yes. Planting trees is a fine way to commemorate birthdays, anniversaries, reunions, graduations, and other special occasions. Remember, too, that beauty is contagious. If you plant trees around your home, your neighbors may do the same. Trees can help increase the value of your property. A tree can be a natural air conditioner; the evaporation from a single large tree can produce the cooling effect of ten room-size air conditioners operating twenty hours a day. A tree can also serve as a buffer against unpleasant noises. Certain trees can help freshen the atmosphere with the trees' own natural, pleasant fragrances. For example, one cherry tree can perfume the air with 200,000 flowers, and their beauty can be breathtaking. Planting and caring for a tree are really easy to do, and the tree will reward you many times with its beauty and shade.

KEEPING TRACK
Top Score = 5
Your Score = ☐

Sample essay:

What does a man do in this rapidly changing world of social rules? Does he open a door for a woman and risk being reminded nastily that she is capable of opening doors for herself? The roles of men and women are changing so much that no one knows how to act any more.

On a night out, should the man always pay? If the woman is making about the same salary, why shouldn't she pay for the dates? Some single men might be threatened by this kind of equality.

The roles of married men are also changing. With the rise of two-income families, some pressure has been taken off men to be the breadwinner. Many men would probably like to play a bigger role in bringing up their children, yet this nurturing side of men is not always encouraged in today's society.

Women say they want men who are tender and caring, yet masculine and easy to lean on. What is really expected of men? Should they be tender or tough? Should they be the traditional breadwinner, or should they stay home and raise the children?

This all seems confusing, but maybe the answer to these questions is really simple. Each man must develop his own game plan and stick with it. This kind of confidence can help to end the confusion about changing roles.

Keeping Track

You can record your scores from the Keeping Track boxes on the chart below. Compare your scores with the top scores.

	Top Score	Your Score
Lesson 18 Verb Times	5	______
Lesson 19 Verb Forms	5	______
Lesson 20 Subject-Verb Agreement	15	______
Lesson 21 Pronouns	10	______
Lesson 22 Capitalization	6	______
Lesson 23 Punctuation	5	______
TOTAL	46	______

Which lessons did you get top or close to top scores in? Are there lessons that gave you problems? If so, review those lessons now. Practice editing your own writing for the kinds of errors discussed in those lessons. Then use the Extra Practice that follows for just that—extra practice.

Extra Practice in Editing Your Work

Part I

Directions: The following items are based on a paragraph that contains numbered sentences. Some of the sentences contain errors in sentence structure, usage, or mechanics. A few sentences, however, are correct as written. Read the paragraph and then answer the items based on it. For each item, choose the answer that would result in the most effective writing of the sentence or sentences. The best answer must be consistent with the meaning and tone of the rest of the paragraph.

(1) Once flourishing in grassy marshlands, the whooping crane allmost disappeared as farms and cities altered its natural habitat. (2) In the late 1940s, only one flock of fewer than 20 whooping cranes was left in the World. (3) After a long search, scientists found the bird's nesting grounds in Canada's remote Wood Buffalo Park in 1954. (4) It was an important discovery, it enabled biologists to begin a comprehensive program to save the great white bird. (5) Efforts began to protect the crane's habitat all the way from their Canadian nesting grounds to its winter grounds on the Gulf coast of Texas, 2,600 miles away. (6) An education program to help save the remaining birds were launched to alert farmers and hunters to the crane's endangered status. (7) Then they set about building up the whooping crane population. (8) These many ways of helping the whooping crane have paid off because the scientists strictly protected the birds, they educated the public, and performed bold experiments. (9) The total number of whooping cranes has now climbed to over 100, and is continuing to grow.

1. Sentence 1: **Once flourishing in grassy marshlands, the whooping crane allmost disappeared as farms and cities altered its natural habitat.**

   What correction should be made to this sentence?

   (1) change the spelling of flourishing to florishing
   (2) remove the comma after marshlands
   (3) change the spelling of allmost to almost
   (4) change disappeared to will disappear
   (5) change the spelling of disappeared to dissappeared

   (1) (2) (3) (4) (5)

2. Sentence 2: **In the late 1940s, only one flock of fewer than 20 whooping cranes was left in the World.**

   What correction should be made to this sentence?

   (1) remove the comma after 1940s
   (2) change was to were
   (3) change was to is
   (4) change World to world
   (5) no correction is necessary

   (1) (2) (3) (4) (5)

3. Sentence 4: **It was an important discovery, it enabled biologists to begin a comprehensive program to save the great white bird.**

   Which of the following is the best way to write the underlined portion of this sentence? If you think the original is the best way, choose option (1).

   (1) discovery, it enabled
   (2) discovery it enabled
   (3) discovery, or it enabled
   (4) discovery; however, it enabled
   (5) discovery, enabling

   (1) (2) (3) (4) (5)

4. Sentence 5: **Efforts began to protect the crane's habitat all the way from their Canadian nesting grounds to its winter grounds on the Gulf coast of Texas, 2,600 miles away.**

   What correction should be made to this sentence?

   (1) change began to has begun
   (2) replace their with its
   (3) change the spelling of their to they're
   (4) change Canadian to canadian
   (5) change winter to Winter

   (1) (2) (3) (4) (5)

5. Sentence 6: **An education program to help save the remaining birds were launched to alert farmers and hunters to the crane's endangered status.**

   Which of the following is the best way to write the underlined portion of this sentence? If you think the original is the best way, choose option (1).

   (1) were launched
   (2) was launched
   (3) are launching
   (4) is launching
   (5) launched

   1 2 3 4 5

6. Sentence 7: **Then they set about building up the whooping crane population.**

   What correction should be made to this sentence?

   (1) replace they with wildlife biologists
   (2) replace they with the farmers and hunters
   (3) change set to will set
   (4) insert a comma after about
   (5) no correction is necessary

   1 2 3 4 5

7. Sentence 8: **These many ways of helping the whooping crane have paid off because the scientists strictly protected the birds, they educated the public, and performed bold experiments.**

   If you rewrote sentence 8 beginning with

   The combination of strict protection, public education, and

   the next words should be

   (1) bold experimentation
   (2) experimenting boldly
   (3) performing bold experiments
   (4) bold performance
   (5) to perform bold experiments

   1 2 3 4 5

8. Sentence 9: **The total number of whooping cranes has now climbed to over 100, and is continuing to grow.**

   What correction should be made to this sentence?

   (1) change has to have
   (2) change has to will have
   (3) remove the comma after 100
   (4) change is to are
   (5) change is to have been

Part II

Directions: This is a test to find out how well you write. The test has one question that asks you to present an opinion on an issue or to explain something. In preparing your answer for this question, you should take the following steps:

1. Read all of the information accompanying the question.
2. Plan your answer carefully before you write.
3. Use scratch paper to make any notes.
4. Write your answer.
5. Read carefully what you have written and make any changes that will improve your writing.
6. Check your paragraphing, sentence structure, spelling, punctuation, capitalization, and usage, and make any necessary corrections.

You will have 45 minutes to write on the question you are assigned. Write legibly and use a ballpoint pen.

Drug abuse is a problem in today's society. Workers, students, athletes—people in all walks of life drink too much alcohol or use illegal drugs. Some people have suggested drug testing as one way to help solve the problem.

Think about the consequences of drug testing. Write an essay of about 200 words discussing its advantages, its disadvantages, or both.

Answers to Extra Practice in Editing Your Work begin on page 228. Record your score on the Progress Chart on the inside back cover.

Answers: Extra Practice

Writing Sentences
(pages 108–109)

1. (2) The original wording is a fragment because it has only part of a verb. Option (2) adds the helping verb *are,* which completes the verb phrase.

2. (2) *If you live in an apartment, you can make things harder for a burglar by taking a few precautions.* The original wording is grammatically correct, but it is too wordy. Option (2) helps make the sentence clear and concise.

3. (4) The original wording is a comma splice. Remember that a comma alone cannot connect two independent thoughts. The connecting words in (2) and (3) do not logically connect the two thoughts.

4. (5) *If your building has one, be sure you know where the button is.* The revised sentence is a smooth combination of sentences 4 and 5 because it makes sentence 4 into an introductory dependent thought.

5. (2) *Stairwells* is the first item in a list and needs a comma placed after it.

6. (4) *Because* is the correct spelling.

7. (1) A comma is needed after an introductory dependent thought *(If you go on vacation).* Therefore, options (3), (4), and (5) are incorrect.

8. (4) *Know your neighbors, and work with them to improve security in your building.* The revised sentence is smoother and more concise. Also, the verb *Know* must be parallel in form with the verb in the second independent thought. *Know* and *work* are parallel.

9. (4) *By watching for crime in and around their buildings, these groups help the police and themselves. By watching for crime in and around their buildings* is an introductory descriptive phrase. It describes *these groups,* so that phrase should become the subject of the new sentence.

Corrected passage:

More than six million burglaries are committed in houses and apartments each year. If you live in an apartment, you can make things harder for a burglar by taking a few precautions. Use the security that your building already offers. Some buildings have special features such as alarm buttons. If your building has one, be sure you know where the button is. Lighting should be sufficient in stairwells, laundry rooms, and parking lots, as well as around the exterior of the building, so report burnt-out lights to the manager. If the outside door has a lock, don't prop it open just because a friend is coming over. Installing a deadbolt lock on the door of your own apartment is also a good idea. If you go on vacation, tell a friend or the building supervisor where you are going and when you will return. Know your neighbors, and work with them to improve security in your building. Many large apartment buildings have organized tenant patrols. By watching for crime in and around their buildings, these groups help the police and themselves.

Writing Essays
(page 160)

Sample essay 1:

Every year Americans spend millions of dollars attending sporting events and millions of hours watching them on television. No one pays them to be spectators, and they end up with nothing to show for their time. Yet they do it, because sports seem to meet many needs that people cannot easily fulfill in their daily lives.

Games lend excitement to days filled with routine; they provide a safe outlet for competitive feelings and tensions. In sports there are clear winners and losers, while in real life, most of us have few clearcut victories; we just hope to get along. People identify with "their" teams, and a victory makes the fans feel like winners as well. An entire city seems to think better of itself if its team wins the Super Bowl or the World Series.

Sports teams also provide examples of some characteristics our society values highly. We believe in teamwork, in persistence in the face of difficulty, in hard work and skill. Winning teams and winning individuals must have these traits.

No doubt there are also some less desirable reasons for being a sports spectator. Some people plant themselves at the stadium or in front of the television set in order to avoid dealing with family issues or to escape necessary work.

Still, most of us need some relaxation as well as a "get-away" from everyday routine and stress. Watching sports can be one of the better ways to get it.

Sample essay 2:

Persons of 65, 75, or 85 used to be few and far between; today the group called senior citizens makes up the fastest-growing segment of our society. People stay in good health longer, and many more are living to extreme old age.

Not only do people live longer, but far more of them are retired. Before the Social Security system was established, few people could afford to retire; they worked until they died or became disabled. Retired, healthy persons were almost unknown.

Healthy older people are able to look out for their own interests. Increasingly, they are becoming involved in political action groups to work on issues of retirement, pensions, and health care. Like the rest of us, they want dignity and security.

As long as their health holds up, older people have the time and energy for community volunteer work. Such programs as Senior Grandparents and Service Corps of Retired Executives channel this energy into good causes. More and more, the elderly are a valuable resource for our society.

Unfortunately, increasing numbers of retired persons are drawing so much money from Social Security and other pension plans that these systems may run out of money. In the future, it may again become necessary for people to work as long as they are able.

Sample essay 3:

Computers, the telephone, and express delivery services are enabling more and more people to work at home. Working somewhere besides the shop or office has both positive and negative consequences. Most have to do with interactions with other people, with commuting, and with independence.

People who work at home obviously see more of their family and less of their co-workers than most employees do. To some people, time with their children, spouse, or aging parents is very important, and working at home meets their needs. On the other hand, those who see their co-workers regularly can usually keep better informed about what is new in their field and what is going on at the company. This knowledge can help them get ahead.

Home workers obviously save the time and money usually spent on commuting. They may be able to live in their "dream" location, far from the source of their paycheck.

Many people who work at home especially like planning their own hours. They can work when they are most efficient, even if that time is early in the morning or late at night. They can schedule their work around their other responsibilities. On the other hand, self-discipline is required to keep at the work when there is no supervisor.

New technology will probably enable even more people to work at home. However, many employees will continue to prefer the companionship and stimulation of the office, and conventional jobs will still be best for them.

Sample essay 4:

You come home and look in the mailbox, hoping to find a letter from a friend or even an unexpected check—a sweepstakes prize, perhaps. There is mail for you, all right, but not quite what you'd hoped. There are two letters requesting charitable contributions, three trying to sell you something, and one from a politician running for office. How does this mail make you feel?

The charities are all doing good work. You wish them well. Can you afford to send them a check? No, right now you have too many bills to pay. Feeling guilty, you slip these letters into the wastebasket.

The sales letters are promoting a magazine subscription that sounds interesting, a set of luggage you wish you had, and some insurance you really ought to buy. Can you afford them? Or should you—feeling very poor—toss them out? In the waste basket they go.

The politician outlines his stands on the issues. You don't know what you think about most of these subjects. Should you study the letter or—feeling very stupid—discard it?

You decide to toss out all the mail. It has made you feel guilty, poor, and stupid. You feel all unrequested mail should be banned. Should it?

Probably not. Many people can and do donate to charities. Without their contributions, the good work would be cut back. Busy people often buy by mail order. And if politicians did not outline their opinions, voters would be even less informed than they are at present.

So tomorrow, when your mailbox contains no letters, no checks, and eight items of "junk mail," remember that it's not all junk. Among the "trash," there may be a treasure for you.

Sample essay 5:

The first day of a vacation is wonderful. For two whole weeks, or maybe three, the alarm clock will not ring at the same early hour to start a person on the same familiar route to the same familiar duties. What should a person do with such freedom? Stay home and relax? Stay home and catch up on chores? Visit faraway relatives? Or have a grand and glorious trip to the mountains, the ocean, or another part of the world? To answer those questions, a few matters need to be considered.

The first question to answer is how much money is available. Traveling, unfortunately, usually costs more than staying home, especially if the whole family is involved. If travel is affordable, most people would choose to go. Seeing other places provides new insights into how others live and what the world is like.

On the other hand, family vacations—especially long automobile trips—are all too likely to develop into family quarrels. Parents and children are simply not used to being together twenty-four hours a day.

Besides being less expensive than travel, staying home can actually be more fun. Many people visit the tourist attractions in distant cities but have never seen the sights near home. With the money saved by not traveling, some special splurges may be possible. Besides, people who relax at home don't need a vacation to rest up from their vacation.

Most of the time I would choose to travel on my vacation. But if I could not, I would try to make a stay-at-home vacation an adventure in itself.

Editing Your Work
(pages 224–225)

1. (3) *Almost* is correct.

2. (4) There is no reason to capitalize *world,* since it's not the name of anything.

3. (5) The original wording is a comma splice. The punctuation in options (3) and (4) is correct, but *or* and *however* do not show the right relationship between the two independent thoughts.

4. (2) *Crane's* is a singular possessive noun, not a plural noun, so the pronoun before *Canadian nesting grounds* should be singular (its), not plural (their).

5. (2) *Program* and *was launched* match because they are both singular. *To help save the remaining birds* is just an interrupting phrase between the subject and the verb.

6. (1) Telling what the pronoun *they* refers to is difficult. Logically, *they* does not refer to *farmers and hunters.* The wildlife biologists built up the whooping crane population.

7. (1) *The combination of strict protection, public education, and bold experimentation has paid off.* The original sentence is too wordy. Also, the elements of the sentence are not parallel. *Protection, education,* and *experimentation* are three nouns with the same endings.

8. (3) Don't use a comma to separate two verbs *(has climbed* and *is continuing).*

Corrected passage:

Once flourishing in grassy marshlands, the whooping crane almost disappeared as farms and cities altered its natural habitat. In the late 1940s, only one flock of fewer than 20 whooping cranes was left in the world. After a long search, scientists found the bird's nesting grounds in Canada's remote Wood Buffalo Park in 1954. It was an important discovery, enabling biologists to begin a comprehensive program to save the great white bird. Efforts began to protect the crane's habitat all the way from its Canadian nesting grounds to its winter grounds on the Gulf coast of Texas, 2,600 miles away. An education program to help save the remaining birds was launched to alert farmers and hunters to the crane's endangered status. Then wildlife biologists set about building up the whooping crane population. The combination of strict protection, public education, and bold experimentation has paid off. The total number of whooping cranes has now climbed to over 100 and is continuing to grow.

Sample essay:

Drug abuse is a matter of continuing concern in our society. Lately, police departments, other government agencies, and some private companies have been requiring employees to provide urine samples to be tested for drugs. If illegal substances are found, employees may be fired, suspended, or required to enter a drug rehabilitation program. There has been much public debate as to whether such testing is a good idea. As is often the case, there are two sides to the issue.

Those favoring the tests believe our public servants—especially police—must set an example of law-abiding behavior. Others raise the issue of public safety. If police or such private employees as airline pilots go to work under the influence of drugs, other people's lives are endangered.

People opposed to the tests believe they are often inaccurate and also violate employees' rights. Certain prescription medicines, for example, cause positive test results in persons who do not use illegal drugs. Injustice may result. Perhaps more important is the right to privacy. Is it an employer's business what an employee does off duty, as long as job performance remains satisfactory? What right does an employer have to compel donation of body fluids?

There are strong arguments on both sides of the issue. If we succeed in reducing drug use through education, perhaps in the future the issue of drug testing will no longer be relevant.

The Posttests

You are now ready to take the final step in your study for passing the GED Writing Skills Test. Both Posttests in this book resemble the actual GED Writing Skills Test in the number and kinds of questions asked and in the essay assignment. When taking each Posttest, take no more than the allotted time for one entire test. Remember to guess whenever you don't know an answer. To get the best possible score, don't leave a question unanswered.

Take the first Posttest. Figure your score using the Answer Key on page 248 and the Essay Scoring Checklist on page 249. You may want or need to take the second Posttest based on your score.

If possible, try to make arrangements to take the actual GED Writing Skills Test as soon as you can after achieving passing scores on the Posttests in this book. Your test-taking skills will be sharp, and you will feel more confident.

WRITING SKILLS POSTTEST A

Directions

The Writing Skills Posttest consists of 55 multiple-choice questions and an essay. It is intended to measure your ability to use clear and effective English. It is a test of English as it is usually written, not as it might be spoken. Specific directions are given at the beginning of each part. Read these directions carefully before you begin.

You should take approximately 75 minutes to complete the multiple-choice questions. There is no penalty for guessing. Try to answer as many questions as you can. Work rapidly but carefully, without spending too much time on any one question. If a question is too difficult for you, skip it and come back to it later.

For each answer, mark one space.

EXAMPLE

The intelligens of computers is different from that of human beings.

What correction should be made to this sentence?

(1) change the spelling of intelligens to intelligence
(2) change is to are
(3) change the spelling of different to diffrent
(4) insert a comma after that
(5) no correction is necessary

The correct answer is (1); therefore, answer space (1) has been marked.

You should take no more than 45 minutes to complete the essay section of the test. You can use a separate sheet of paper for your essay.

Explanations for the answers and a sample essay are on pages 245–248. Answers to the questions are in the Answer Key on page 248. Directions for scoring your essay appear on page 249.

Part I

Directions: The following items are based on paragraphs that contain numbered sentences. Some of the sentences contain errors in sentence structure, usage, or mechanics. A few sentences, however, are correct as written. Read each paragraph and then answer the items based on it. For each item, choose the answer that would result in the most effective writing of the sentence or sentences. The best answer must be consistent with the meaning and tone of the rest of the paragraph.

Items 1–9 refer to the following paragraph.

(1) Shortly after the outbreak of World War II, several carmakers designed a small four-wheel-drive vehicle that could easily maneuver on difficult terrain. (2) The resulting "general purpose" vehicle was called a jeep, named from their initials—G.P. (3) Because of its intended use as a reconnaissance vehicle it was originally called the "Peep." (4) The jeep proved to be so versatile. (5) That it was also used to carry field kitchens, supplies, and wounded soldiers. (6) Becoming a weapon of war, the jeep had machine guns and missiles mounted on it. (7) The british designed and made a flying jeep complete with wings that was towed behind a glider and used by airborne troops. (8) The jeep came with too interesting features as standard equipment. (9) Because of its open top, the jeep was equipped with an iron rod mounted on the hood. (10) This rod protected the driver from having his head cut off by wires strung across the road by the enemy. (11) The windshield wipers were hand-operated. (12) This design conjures up a rather comic picture of a harried soldier driving his jeep in a downpour, trying to steer, shift gears, and operate the wipers he also had to watch for the enemy. (13) By the end of the war in 1945, over 600,000 of these popular and useful vehicles will have been built.

1. Sentence 1: **Shortly after the outbreak of World War II, several carmakers designed a small four-wheel-drive vehicle that could easily maneuver on difficult terrain.**

   What correction should be made to this sentence?

   (1) insert a comma after outbreak
   (2) change the spelling of several to sevral
   (3) replace that with who
   (4) change the spelling of maneuver to manuever
   (5) no correction is necessary

   (1) (2) (3) (4) (5)

2. Sentence 2: **The resulting "general purpose" vehicle was called a jeep, named from their initials—G.P.**

   What correction should be made to this sentence?

   (1) change the spelling of general to genral
   (2) insert a comma after vehicle
   (3) change was to were
   (4) replace their with its
   (5) no correction is necessary

   (1) (2) (3) (4) (5)

3. Sentence 3: **Because of its intended use as a reconnaissance vehicle it was originally called the "Peep."**

   Which of the following is the best way to write the underlined portion of this sentence? If you think the original is the best way, choose option (1).

   (1) vehicle it
   (2) vehicle; it
   (3) vehicle, it
   (4) vehicle. It
   (5) vehicle and

   (1) (2) (3) (4) (5)

GO ON TO THE NEXT PAGE.

4. Sentences 4 and 5: **The jeep proved to be so versatile. That it was also used to carry field kitchens, supplies, and wounded soldiers.**

   Which of the following is the best way to write the underlined portion of these sentences? If you think the original is the best way, choose option (1).

   (1) versatile. That
   (2) versatile, which
   (3) versatile that
   (4) versatile, and that
   (5) versatile because

   (1) (2) (3) (4) (5)

5. Sentence 6: **Becoming a weapon of war, the jeep had machine guns and missiles mounted on it.**

   If you rewrote sentence 6 beginning with

   It became a weapon of war

   the next word should be

   (1) when
   (2) and
   (3) so
   (4) but
   (5) until

   (1) (2) (3) (4) (5)

6. Sentence 7: **The british designed and made a flying jeep complete with wings that was towed behind a glider and used by airborne troops.**

   What correction should be made to this sentence?

   (1) change british to British
   (2) insert a comma after designed
   (3) change was to were
   (4) insert a comma after glider
   (5) change airborne to Airborne

   (1) (2) (3) (4) (5)

7. Sentence 8: **The jeep came with too interesting features as standard equipment.**

   What correction should be made to this sentence?

   (1) change came to comes
   (2) replace too with two
   (3) change the spelling of interesting to intresting
   (4) insert a comma after features
   (5) change the spelling of equipment to equippment

   (1) (2) (3) (4) (5)

8. Sentence 12: **This design conjures up a rather comic picture of a harried soldier driving his jeep in a downpour, trying to steer, shift gears, and operate the wipers he also had to watch for the enemy.**

   Which of the following is the best way to write the underlined portion of this sentence? If you think the original is the best way, choose option (1).

   (1) wipers he also had to watch
   (2) wipers, he also had to watch
   (3) wipers, so he also had to watch
   (4) wipers while also watching
   (5) wipers and to watch

   (1) (2) (3) (4) (5)

9. Sentence 13: **By the end of the war in 1945, over 600,000 of these popular and useful vehicles will have been built.**

   What correction should be made to this sentence?

   (1) insert a comma after end
   (2) change war to War
   (3) remove the comma after 1945
   (4) replace and with or
   (5) change will have to had

   (1) (2) (3) (4) (5)

GO ON TO THE NEXT PAGE.

Items 10–18 refer to the following paragraph.

(1) Lightning has always scared people, yet the chances of your being hit by lightning is about 2 million to 1. (2) More than 100 Americans a year are killed by lightning, and one man the human lightning conductor, was struck seven times in 35 years. (3) Roy C. Sullivan, a ranger in Shenandoah National park, has had his eyebrows burned off, has had his hair catch fire twice, and has been blown clear of his car after being struck by lightning. (4) Most people who are hit by lightning are not as lucky. (5) Protecting yourself is easy, and experts have made suggestions about several precautions to take. (6) When there is lightning, stay away from beaches and umbrellas, don't stand under a tree, don't talk on the telefone a lot, don't touch metal fences or wires, and don't put your hands on the metal shell of a car. (7) You may enjoy golfing, swimming, or hiking; if so, you should get indoors when it rains. (8) Worldwide, lightning flashes are common, there are 100 lightning flashes per second, with flashes 300 feet to 20 miles long. (9) Lightning travels from 100 to 1,000 miles per second from the sky to the ground and 87,000 miles per second in the opposite direction. (10) Ben Franklin was lucky when he performed his famous kite experiment. (11) Depending on if a real lightning bolt had been attracted to the kite and the metal key suspended from it, he would have been killed or badly burned. (12) Most scientists agree that Ben Franklin felt only small charges of electricity that were bouncing around in the clouds.

10. Sentence 1: **Lightning has always scared people, yet the chances of your being hit by lightning is about 2 million to 1.**

What correction should be made to this sentence?

(1) change the spelling of always to allways
(2) remove the comma after people
(3) replace your with you're
(4) change is to are
(5) no correction is necessary

(1) (2) (3) (4) (5)

11. Sentence 2: **More than 100 Americans a year are killed by lightning, and one man the human lightning conductor, was struck seven times in 35 years.**

What correction should be made to this sentence?

(1) change Americans to americans
(2) change are to is
(3) insert a comma after man
(4) change was to is
(5) no correction is necessary

(1) (2) (3) (4) (5)

12. Sentence 3: **Roy C. Sullivan, a ranger in Shenandoah National park, has had his eyebrows burned off, has had his hair catch fire twice, and has been blown clear of his car after being struck by lightning.**

What correction should be made to this sentence?

(1) remove the comma after Sullivan
(2) change ranger to Ranger
(3) change park to Park
(4) remove the word and
(5) change has been blown to has blew

(1) (2) (3) (4) (5)

GO ON TO THE NEXT PAGE.

13. Sentence 5: **Protecting yourself is easy, and experts have made suggestions about several precautions to take.**

If you rewrite sentence 5 beginning with

To protect yourself, experts

the next word should be

(1) are suggesting
(2) suggest
(3) suggested
(4) will suggest
(5) had suggested

(1) (2) (3) (4) (5)

14. Sentence 6: **When there is lightning, stay away from beaches and umbrellas, don't stand under a tree, don't talk on the telefone a lot, don't touch metal fences or wires, and don't put your hands on the metal shell of a car.**

What correction should be made to this sentence?

(1) remove the comma after lightning
(2) change talk to be talking
(3) change the spelling of telefone to telephone
(4) change the spelling of a lot to alot
(5) replace your with you're

(1) (2) (3) (4) (5)

15. Sentence 7: **You may enjoy golfing, swimming, or hiking; if so, you should get indoors when it rains.**

If you rewrote sentence 7 beginning with

If you golf,

the next words should be

(1) enjoy swimming, or hike,
(2) swim, or hike,
(3) swimming, or hiking,
(4) enjoy swimming or hiking,
(5) to swim, or to hike,

(1) (2) (3) (4) (5)

16. Sentence 8: **Worldwide, lightning flashes are common, there are 100 lightning flashes per second, with flashes 300 feet to 20 miles long.**

Which of the following is the best way to write the underlined portion of this sentence? If you think the original is the best way, choose option (1).

(1) common, there
(2) common there
(3) common because there
(4) common whenever there
(5) common. There

(1) (2) (3) (4) (5)

17. Sentence 11: **Depending on if a real lightning bolt had been attracted to the kite and the metal key suspended from it, he would have been killed or badly burned.**

What correction should be made to this sentence?

(1) replace Depending on if with If
(2) change had to has
(3) insert a comma after kite
(4) remove the comma after it
(5) replace he with you

(1) (2) (3) (4) (5)

18. Sentence 12: **Most scientists agree that Ben Franklin felt only small charges of electricity that were bouncing around in the clouds.**

Which of the following is the best way to write the underlined portion of this sentence? If you think the original is the best way, choose option (1).

(1) Franklin felt
(2) Franklin feels
(3) Franklin feeling
(4) Franklin would have felt
(5) Franklin will feel

(1) (2) (3) (4) (5)

GO ON TO THE NEXT PAGE.

Items 19–27 refer to the following paragraph.

(1) Food additives have become so much a part of the American way of eating that most of us would find it difficult to put together a meal that did not include them. (2) Changing lifestyles in this Century have resulted in more additives than former generations could have imagined. (3) As Americans moved from farms to cities, there were a need for foods that could be mass produced. (4) Greater sophistication increased demand for year-round supplies of seasonal products greater buying power gave industry a bigger market to please. (5) So today you had a wider variety of foods available and more additives in all foods. (6) By broadest definition, a food additive is any substance that becomes part of a food product when added either directly or indirectly. (7) Today, some 2,800 substances are intentionally added to foods to produce desired effects. (8) As many as 10,000 others find their way into various foods during processing, while being packaged, or storage. (9) An additive is intentionally used in foods to maintain or improve nutritional value, maintain freshness, make food more appealing, or help in processing or preparation. (10) The food is affected in various ways. (11) It can be changed in body and texture, cooking or baking results, and moisture retention. (12) By far the most predominant additives are sugar, salt, and corn syrup. (13) These three, plus citric acid, baking soda, vegitable colors, mustard, and pepper, account for more than 98 percent by weight of all food additives used in this country.

19. Sentence 2: **Changing lifestyles in this Century have resulted in more additives than former generations could have imagined.**

What correction should be made to this sentence?

(1) change Century to century
(2) change have to has
(3) change have resulted to resulting
(4) replace former with formal
(5) no correction is necessary

① ② ③ ④ ⑤

20. Sentence 3: **As Americans moved from farms to cities, there were a need for foods that could be mass produced.**

What correction should be made to this sentence?

(1) change moved to move
(2) remove the comma after cities
(3) replace there with their
(4) change were to was
(5) insert a comma after foods

① ② ③ ④ ⑤

21. Sentence 4: **Greater sophistication increased demand for year-round supplies of seasonal products greater buying power gave industry a bigger market to please.**

Which of the following is the best way to write the underlined portion of this sentence? If you think the original is the best way, choose option (1).

(1) products greater
(2) products, greater
(3) products; and greater
(4) products in order that greater
(5) products. Greater

① ② ③ ④ ⑤

GO ON TO THE NEXT PAGE.

22. Sentence 5: **So today you had a wider variety of foods available and more additives in all foods.**

Which of the following is the best way to write the underlined portion of this sentence? If you think the original is the best way, choose option (1).

(1) you had
(2) you have had
(3) you have
(4) you will have had
(5) you will have

① ② ③ ④ ⑤

23. Sentence 6: **By broadest definition, a food additive is any substance that becomes part of a food product when added either directly or indirectly.**

What correction should be made to this sentence?

(1) remove the comma after definition
(2) change is to be
(3) replace that with who
(4) insert a comma after product
(5) no correction is necessary

① ② ③ ④ ⑤

24. Sentence 8: **As many as 10,000 others find their way into various foods during processing, while being packaged, or storage.**

What correction should be made to this sentence?

(1) insert a comma after others
(2) change find to finds
(3) change find to found
(4) replace their with they're
(5) change while being packaged to packaging

① ② ③ ④ ⑤

25. Sentence 9: **An additive is intentionally used in foods to maintain or improve nutritional value, maintain freshness, make food more appealing, or help in processing or preparation.**

Which of the following is the best way to write the underlined portion of this sentence? If you think the original is the best way, choose option (1).

(1) freshness, make
(2) freshness make
(3) freshness. Make
(4) freshness, making
(5) freshness; make

① ② ③ ④ ⑤

26. Sentences 10 and 11: **The food is affected in various ways. It can be changed in body and texture, cooking or baking results, and moisture retention.**

The most effective combination of sentences 10 and 11 would include which of the following groups of words?

(1) It is affected
(2) ways, and it can be
(3) The food can be changed
(4) ways changing body and texture
(5) The food is affected and changed

① ② ③ ④ ⑤

27. Sentence 13: **These three, plus citric acid, baking soda, vegitable colors, mustard, and pepper, account for more than 98 percent by weight of all food additives used in this country.**

What correction should be made to this sentence?

(1) remove the comma after acid
(2) change the spelling of vegitable to vegetable
(3) remove the comma after colors
(4) change account to accounts
(5) change account to accounting

① ② ③ ④ ⑤

GO ON TO THE NEXT PAGE.

Items 28–36 refer to the following paragraph.

(1) Deciding to be the youngest person at the age of sixteen to sail around the world alone, Robin Graham left on an around-the-world sailing trip. (2) Robin wanted to see the world, not just as a tourist sees it with one-night stopovers, but as a visiter who would live with local people, eat their food, and learn their ways. (3) The loneliness of sailing by himself was the hardest thing Robin had to cope with. (4) On the first leg of his trip, from Hawaii to south Africa, he did not have a two-way radio. (5) He did, however, have a battery-operated tape recorder on board that he talked to as if it were a person. (6) In one journal entry, he freely admitted that reading books kept him sane on the trip. (7) To help eliminate the awful loneliness, friends gave him two mischievous kittens for company and the National Geographic Society gave him a two-way radio. (8) The 24-foot sailboat was so small that he couldn't stand up in the cabin; only the cats have headroom. (9) A problem Robin did not anticipate was exhaustion. (10) Robin knew it was dangerous to sail through shipping lanes. (11) When he did sail through them, he would have to stay awake for days to watch for large ships. (12) Sailing alone meant discomfort and danger he survived gales, hurricanes, and falling overboard. (13) Five years and more than 30,000 nautical miles later, Robin achieved his goal and discovering that he could survive against the ocean's elements.

28. Sentence 1: **Deciding to be the youngest person at the age of sixteen to sail around the world alone, Robin Graham left on an around-the-world sailing trip.**

If you rewrote sentence 1 beginning with

At the age of sixteen,

the next words should be

(1) and deciding
(2) the youngest person
(3) Robin Graham left
(4) Robin Graham decided
(5) and sailing

(1) (2) (3) (4) (5)

29. Sentence 2: **Robin wanted to see the world, not just as a tourist sees it with one-night stopovers, but as a visiter who would live with local people, eat their food, and learn their ways.**

What correction should be made to this sentence?

(1) change wanted to wants
(2) replace but with or
(3) change the spelling of visiter to visitor
(4) replace who with which
(5) insert to before learn

(1) (2) (3) (4) (5)

30. Sentence 4: **On the first leg of his trip, from Hawaii to south Africa, he did not have a two-way radio.**

What correction should be made to this sentence?

(1) remove the comma after trip
(2) insert a comma after Hawaii
(3) change south to South
(4) change did to does
(5) no correction is necessary

GO ON TO THE NEXT PAGE.

31. Sentence 5: **He did, however, have a battery-operated tape recorder on board that he talked to as if it were a person.**

What correction should be made to this sentence?

(1) remove the comma after did
(2) replace board with bored
(3) replace that with who
(4) change talked to talks
(5) no correction is necessary

(1) (2) (3) (4) (5)

32. Sentence 7: **To help eliminate the awful loneliness, friends gave him two mischievous kittens for company and the National Geographic Society gave him a two-way radio.**

What correction should be made to this sentence?

(1) change the spelling of eliminate to elimanate
(2) change the spelling of awful to awfull
(3) change the spelling of mischievous to mischievious
(4) insert a comma after company
(5) change Society to society

(1) (2) (3) (4) (5)

33. Sentence 8: **The 24-foot sailboat was so small that he couldn't stand up in the cabin; only the cats have headroom.**

Which of the following is the best way to write the underlined portion of this sentence? If you think the original is the best way, choose option (1).

(1) cats have
(2) cats having
(3) cats has
(4) cats had
(5) cats will have

(1) (2) (3) (4) (5)

34. Sentences 10 and 11: **Robin knew it was dangerous to sail through shipping lanes. When he did sail through them, he would have to stay awake for days to watch for large ships.**

The most effective combination of sentences 10 and 11 would include which of the following groups of words?

(1) knew it was dangerous to have to stay awake
(2) knew that when he sailed through dangerous shipping lanes
(3) shipping lanes, and when he did
(4) Shipping lanes were dangerous, and Robin knew it
(5) Robin knew to watch for

(1) (2) (3) (4) (5)

35. Sentence 12: **Sailing alone meant discomfort and danger he survived gales, hurricanes, and falling overboard.**

Which of the following is the best way to write the underlined portion of this sentence? If you think the original is the best way, choose option (1).

(1) danger he
(2) danger, he
(3) danger because he
(4) danger, yet
(5) danger. He

(1) (2) (3) (4) (5)

36. Sentence 13: **Five years and more than 30,000 nautical miles later, Robin achieved his goal and discovering that he could survive against the ocean's elements.**

What correction should be made to this sentence?

(1) replace later with latter
(2) change the spelling of achieved to acheived
(3) insert a comma after goal
(4) change discovering to discovered
(5) change the spelling of against to aginst

(1) (2) (3) (4) (5)

GO ON TO THE NEXT PAGE.

Items 37–45 refer to the following paragraph.

(1) Once you buy a computer and some accompanying software, you should learn how to keep it in good working condition. (2) Static discharge can wipe out data and even damage circuits. (3) It should be avoided. (4) Occasionaly, wipe your keyboard with a clean, lint-free cloth. (5) Spraying the cloth, not the keyboard, with an antistatic cleaning fluid helps too. (6) Place a static-free dust cover over your computer equipment. (7) This you do when you are not using it. (8) Clean your disk drive with a head cleaning kit, follow the manufacturer's recommendations. (9) Keep your computer in a room with good circulation to reduce excess dust and heat. (10) Your computer may even require a fan if you add circuit boards, and for safety's sake, use correctly wired outlets for your system. (11) To avoid loss of data or damage to the computer due to sudden increases or decreases in voltage, use a surge protector, a device that can be found in most computer stores. (12) Finally, read the manufacturer's warranty carefully to avoid any misunderstanding with the manufacturer or your dealer.

37. Sentence 1: **Once you buy a computer and some accompanying software, you should learn how to keep it in good working condition.**

What correction should be made to this sentence?

(1) remove the comma after software
(2) replace you should with one should
(3) replace it with them
(4) change the spelling of condition to condishun
(5) no correction is necessary

(1) (2) (3) (4) (5)

38. Sentences 2 and 3: **Static discharge can wipe out data and even damage circuits. It should be avoided.**

The most effective combination of sentences 2 and 3 would include which of the following groups of words?

(1) discharge, which can wipe out
(2) and this static discharge, damaging
(3) To avoid wiping out
(4) wiping out data and damaging
(5) can and should be avoided

(1) (2) (3) (4) (5)

39. Sentence 4: **Occasionaly, wipe your keyboard with a clean, lint-free cloth.**

What correction should be made to this sentence?

(1) change the spelling of Occasionaly to Occassionaly
(2) change the spelling of Occasionaly to Occasionally
(3) remove the comma after Occasionaly
(4) change wipe to wiping
(5) replace your with you're

(1) (2) (3) (4) (5)

GO ON TO THE NEXT PAGE.

40. Sentence 5: **Spraying the cloth, not the keyboard, with an antistatic cleaning fluid helps too.**

Which of the following is the best way to write the underlined portion of this sentence? If you think the original is the best way, choose option (1).

(1) helps
(2) help
(3) helped
(4) had been helping
(5) be a help

(1) (2) (3) (4) (5)

41. Sentences 6 and 7: **Place a static-free dust cover over your computer equipment. This you do when you are not using it.**

The most effective combination of sentences 6 and 7 would include which of the following groups of words?

(1) equipment when you
(2) After covering your computer
(3) equipment, for this
(4) placing and covering
(5) To place a static-free

(1) (2) (3) (4) (5)

42. Sentence 8: **Clean your disk drive with a head cleaning kit, follow the manufacturer's recommendations.**

What correction should be made to this sentence?

(1) change Clean to Cleaning
(2) remove the comma after kit
(3) insert so after the comma
(4) change follow to following
(5) change the spelling of recommendations to reccomendations

(1) (2) (3) (4) (5)

43. Sentence 10: **Your computer may even require a fan if you add circuit boards, and for safety's sake, use correctly wired outlets for your system.**

Which of the following is the best way to write the underlined portion of this sentence? If you think the original is the best way, choose option (1).

(1) boards, and for
(2) boards and for
(3) boards; however, for
(4) boards; and for
(5) boards. For

(1) (2) (3) (4) (5)

44. Sentence 11: **To avoid loss of data or damage to the computer due to sudden increases or decreases in voltage, use a surge protector, a device that can be found in most computer stores.**

What correction should be made to this sentence?

(1) remove the comma after voltage
(2) remove the comma after protector
(3) change the spelling of device to devise
(4) replace that with who
(5) no correction is necessary

(1) (2) (3) (4) (5)

45. Sentence 12: **Finally, read the manufacturer's warranty carefully to avoid any misunderstanding with the manufacturer or your dealer.**

Which of the following is the best way to write the underlined portion of this sentence? If you think the original is the best way, choose option (1)

(1) Finally, read
(2) Finally read
(3) Finally reading
(4) Finally to read
(5) Finally after reading

(1) (2) (3) (4) (5)

GO ON TO THE NEXT PAGE.

Items 46–55 refer to the following paragraph.

(1) Americans spend aproximately $25 million a year on over-the-counter sleep aids, and additional millions are spent by the 8.5 million Americans who take prescription sleeping pills. (2) But what do you do? (3) If you don't want to take pills yet can't get a good night's sleep? (4) If you are having trouble sleeping, first get a thorough physical examination to make sure the insomnia, or sleeplessness is not related to some physical ailment. (5) With physical problems ruled out, you should examine your eating, drinking, exercise, and relaxation habits to see if it might be preventing good sleep. (6) Your main problem not the inability to sleep but the fear that you will not sleep. (7) You could be a person who dwells on sleeplessness. (8) Eight hours of sleep are not needed by everyone; in fact, researchers have proved this. (9) Because your body gets used to sleep at certain times, regular times of going to bed and awaking will help. (10) Caffeine acts as a stimulant for most people, and due to this fact you should avoid beverages that contain the stimulant caffeine. (11) Smokers should note that nicotine is also a stimulant and that many ex-smokers have reported considerabley improved sleep after quitting. (12) To be an informed consumer, explore the alternatives to drugs with expert medical advice for an effective, safe, long-lasting solution to insomnia.

46. Sentence 1: **Americans spend aproximately $25 million a year on over-the-counter sleep aids, and additional millions are spent by the 8.5 million Americans who take prescription sleeping pills.**

What correction should be made to this sentence?

(1) change spend to spending
(2) change the spelling of aproximately to approximately
(3) remove the comma after aids
(4) change are to is
(5) replace who with which

(1) (2) (3) (4) (5)

47. Sentences 2 and 3: **But what do you do? If you don't want to take pills yet can't get a good night's sleep?**

Which of the following is the best way to write the underlined portion of these sentences? If you think the original is the best way, choose option (1).

(1) you do? If
(2) you do if
(3) you do, if
(4) you do. If
(5) you do; if

(1) (2) (3) (4) (5)

48. Sentence 4: **If you are having trouble sleeping, first get a thorough physical examination to make sure the insomnia, or sleeplessness is not related to some physical ailment.**

What correction should be made to this sentence?

(1) replace If with After
(2) remove the comma after sleeping
(3) change the spelling of sure to shure
(4) insert a comma after sleeplessness
(5) change is to are

(1) (2) (3) (4) (5)

49. Sentence 5: **With physical problems ruled out, you should examine your eating, drinking, exercise, and relaxation habits to see if it might be preventing good sleep.**

What correction should be made to this sentence?

(1) replace you with one
(2) replace your with you're
(3) change drinking to what you drink
(4) replace it with they
(5) no correction is necessary

(1) (2) (3) (4) (5)

GO ON TO THE NEXT PAGE.

50. Sentence 6: **Your main problem not the inability to sleep but the fear that you will not sleep.**

What correction should be made to this sentence?

(1) replace your with you're
(2) insert may be after problem
(3) replace but with and
(4) insert is after fear
(5) replace that with which

① ② ③ ④ ⑤

51. Sentence 8: **Eight hours of sleep are not needed by everyone; in fact, researchers have proved this.**

If you rewrote sentence 8 beginning with

Researchers have proved that not everyone

the next word(s) should be

(1) will need
(2) should need
(3) needed
(4) need
(5) needs

① ② ③ ④ ⑤

52. Sentence 9: **Because your body gets used to sleep at certain times, regular times of going to bed and awaking will help.**

Which of the following is the best way to write the underlined portion of this sentence? If you think the original is the best way, choose option (1).

(1) times, regular
(2) times regular
(3) times. Regular
(4) times; regular
(5) times, and regular

① ② ③ ④ ⑤

53. Sentence 10: **Caffeine acts as a stimulant for most people, and due to this fact you should avoid beverages that contain the stimulant caffeine.**

If you rewrote sentence 10 beginning with

You should avoid beverages containing caffeine

the next word(s) should be

(1) due
(2) because
(3) acting as
(4) for
(5) and

① ② ③ ④ ⑤

54. Sentence 11: **Smokers should note that nicotine is also a stimulant and that many ex-smokers have reported considerabley improved sleep after quitting.**

What correction should be made to this sentence?

(1) change is to was
(2) change is to will be
(3) insert who after ex-smokers
(4) change have to has
(5) change the spelling of considerabley to considerably

① ② ③ ④ ⑤

55. Sentence 12: **To be an informed consumer, explore the alternatives to drugs with expert medical advice for an effective, safe, long-lasting solution to insomnia.**

Which of the following is the best way to write the underlined portion of this sentence? If you think the original is the best way, choose option (1).

(1) explore
(2) one can explore
(3) you will explore
(4) explored
(5) be exploring

① ② ③ ④ ⑤

GO ON TO THE NEXT PAGE.

Part II

Directions: This is a test to find out how well you write. The test has one question that asks you to present an opinion on an issue or to explain something. In preparing your answer for this question, you should take the following steps:

1. Read all of the information accompanying the question.
2. Plan your answer carefully before you write.
3. Use scratch paper to make any notes.
4. Write your answer.
5. Read carefully what you have written and make any changes that will improve your writing.
6. Check your paragraphing, sentence structure, spelling, punctuation, capitalization, and usage, and make any necessary corrections.

You will have 45 minutes to write on the question you are assigned. Write legibly and use a ballpoint pen.

Competition is common in our society. It exists and is even encouraged in school, in sports, and in the business world.

Think about the effects of competition. Write down your thoughts about the positive effects, the negative effects, or both in a 200-word essay. Be specific, and give examples.

END OF EXAMINATION

Answers: Posttest A

1. (5) No error. Careful pronunciation will help you spell *several* correctly.

2. (4) *Their* refers to *jeep. Their* and *jeep* do not agree because *their* is substituted for words meaning more than one. Therefore, *its* is the correct pronoun for *jeep.*

3. (3) In this sentence, its dependent part comes first and needs a comma after it. *Because of its intended use as a reconnaissance vehicle* cannot stand alone as a sentence. Therefore, option (4) is incorrect.

4. (3) Logically, both these sentences cannot be considered complete. The first sentence leaves you hanging. *That* is used in the second sentence to introduce a dependent part. The best revision is to write them as one smoothly flowing sentence.

5. (1) *It became a weapon of war when machine guns and missiles were mounted on it.* Using the connecting word *when* shows that one event (mounting guns and missiles) came before another (becoming a weapon of war.)

6. (1) *British* is the name of a group of people. *British* is always capitalized.

7. (2) *Too* means "in addition to" or "also."

8. (4) This is an example of a run-on. Option (4) is the best choice because it gets rid of extra words and substitutes *had to watch* with *watching.*

9. (5) *Will have* suggests that the jeeps were never built.

Corrected passage:

Shortly after the outbreak of World War II, several carmakers designed a small four-wheel-drive vehicle that could easily maneuver on difficult terrain. The resulting "general purpose" vehicle was called a jeep, named from its initials—G.P. Because of its intended use as a reconnaissance vehicle, it was originally called the "Peep." The jeep proved to be so versatile that it was also used to carry field kitchens, supplies, and wounded soldiers. It became a weapon of war when machine guns and missiles were mounted on it. The British designed and made a flying jeep complete with wings that was towed behind a glider and used by airborne troops. The jeep came with two interesting features as standard equipment. Because of its open top, the jeep was equipped with an iron rod mounted on the hood. This protected the driver from having his head cut off by wires strung across the road by the enemy. The windshield wipers were hand-operated. This design conjures up a rather comic picture of a harried soldier driving his jeep in a downpour, trying to steer, shift gears, and operate the wipers while also watching for the enemy. By the end of the war in 1945, over 600,000 of these popular and useful vehicles had been built.

10. (4) *Lightning* is not the subject of *is. Chances* is the subject. Don't be tricked by the words that come between the subject and the verb.

11. (3) *The human lightning conductor* gives additional information about *one man.* The whole phrase must have commas around it. Therefore, option (3) is correct.

12. (3) *Park* should be capitalized because it is part of the name of the park.

13. (2) *To protect yourself, experts suggest taking several precautions. Suggest* correctly shows an action that takes place now. Options (3) and (5) show a past action. Option (4) shows an action that has not yet taken place.

14. (3) *Telephone* is not spelled the way it sounds. *A lot* is always spelled as two words.

15. (2) *If you golf, swim, or hike, you should get indoors when it rains.* The original sentence contains too many extra words. Option (2) is correct because the verbs *golf, swim,* and *hike* match. Options (1), (3), (4), and (5) are incorrect because the three verbs do not match endings.

16. (5) The original wording is a comma splice. Remember that a comma cannot join two complete sentences.

17. (1) *If* correctly shows that a real lightning bolt would have killed or burned Ben Franklin.

18. (1) The action in the sentence took place in the past. *Feels, would have felt,* and *will feel* do not show past actions.

Corrected passage:

Lightning has always scared people, yet the chances of your being hit by lightning are about 2 million to 1. More than 100 Americans a year are killed by lightning, and one man, the human lightning conductor, was struck seven times in 35 years. Roy C. Sullivan, a ranger in Shenandoah National Park, has had his eyebrows burned off, has had his hair catch fire twice, and has been blown clear of his car after being struck by lightning. Most people who are hit by lightning are not as lucky. To protect yourself, experts suggest taking several precautions. When there is lightning, stay away from beaches and umbrellas, don't stand under a tree, don't talk on the telephone a lot, don't touch metal fences or wires, and don't put your hands on the metal shell of a car. If you golf, swim, or hike, you should get indoors when it rains. Worldwide, lightning flashes are common. There are 100 lightning flashes per second, with flashes 300 feet to 20 miles long. Lightning travels from 100 to 1,000 miles per second from the sky to the ground and 87,000 miles per second in the opposite direction. Ben Franklin was lucky when he performed his famous kite experiment. If a real lightning bolt had been attracted to the kite and the metal key suspended from it, he would have been killed or badly burned. Most scientists agree that Ben Franklin felt only small charges of electricity that were bouncing around in the clouds.

19. (1) There is no reason to capitalize *century* because it does not name a specific thing.

20. (4) *There* is not the subject of sentence 3. *A need* is the subject, and it agrees with *was.*

21. (5) The original wording is a run-on. Option (2) is a comma splice. Option (3) is incorrect because a semicolon and a connecting word *(and)* are not used to join two complete sentences.

22. (3) The time clue *(today)* shows that the action in this sentence takes place in present time. *Had* and *have had* show a past action. *Will have had* and *will have* show actions that have not taken place.

23. (5) No error.

24. (5) *Packaging* is a thing and matches the two other things in the list (*processing* and *storage*).

25. (1) Commas are needed to separate items in a list. Also, the verbs in the list must match *(maintain, improve, maintain, make, help).* In option (4) *making* does not match the other verbs.

26. (3) *The food can be changed in body and texture, cooking or baking results, and moisture retention.* In the revised sentence, the subject of the first sentence *(food)* is combined with the verb in the second sentence *(can be changed).* This combination gets rid of repeated information.

27. (2) *Vegetable* is the correct spelling.

Corrected passage:

Food additives have become so much a part of the American way of eating that most of us would find it difficult to put together a meal that did not include them. Changing lifestyles in this century have resulted in more additives than former generations could have imagined. As Americans moved from farms to cities, there was a need for foods that could be mass produced. Greater sophistication increased demand for year-round supplies of seasonal products. Greater buying power gave industry a bigger market to please. So today you have a wider variety of foods available and more additives in all foods. By broadest definition, a food additive is any substance that becomes part of a food product when added either directly or indirectly. Today, some 2,800 substances are intentionally added to foods to produce desired effects. As many as 10,000 others find their way into various foods during processing, packaging, or storage. An additive is intentionally used in foods to maintain or improve nutritional value, maintain freshness, make food more appealing, or help in processing or preparation. The food can be changed in body and texture, cooking or baking results, and moisture retention. By far the most predominant additives are sugar, salt, and corn syrup. These three, plus citric acid, baking soda, vegetable colors, mustard, and pepper, account for more than 98 percent by weight of all food additives used in this country.

28. (4) *At the age of sixteen, Robin Graham decided to become the youngest person to sail around the world alone.* The original sentence contains repeated information *(to sail around the world* and *left on an around-the-world sailing trip).*

29. (3) *Visitor* is the correct spelling.

30. (3) *South* is capitalized because it is part of a geographical name *(South Africa).*

31. (5) No error.

32. (4) When *yet, and, or, for, so* or *but* join two sentences, a comma is needed before the connecting word.

33. (4) *Have* is a verb form that shows present action. *Cats had* correctly expresses a past action.

34. (2) *Robin knew that when he sailed through dangerous shipping lanes he would have to stay awake for days to watch for large ships.* The original sentences contain repeated information *(to sail through shipping lanes* and *when he did sail through them).*

35. (5) The original wording of the sentence is a run-on.

36. (4) *Achieved* and *discovering* do not have matching endings. Therefore, option (4) is correct.

Corrected passage:

At the age of sixteen, Robin Graham decided to become the youngest person to sail around the world alone. Robin wanted to see the world, not just as a tourist sees it with one-night stopovers, but as a visitor who would live with local people, eat their food, and learn their ways. The loneliness of sailing by himself was the hardest thing Robin had to cope with. On the first leg of his trip, from Hawaii to South Africa, he did not have a two-way radio. He did, however, have a battery-operated tape recorder on board that he talked to as if it were a person. In one journal entry, he freely admitted that reading books kept him sane on the trip. To help eliminate the awful loneliness, friends gave him two mischievous kittens for company, and the National Geographic Society gave him a two-way radio. The 24-foot sailboat was so small that he couldn't stand up in the cabin; only the cats had headroom. A problem Robin did not anticipate was exhaustion. Robin knew that when he sailed through dangerous shipping lanes he would have to stay awake for days to watch for large ships. Sailing alone meant discomfort and danger. He survived gales, hurricanes, and falling overboard. Five years and more than 30,000 nautical miles later, Robin achieved his goal and discovered that he could survive against the ocean's elements.

37. (3) Option (3) is correct because *them* refers to *a computer* and *software. Them* always refers to more than one thing, while *it* refers to only one thing.

38. (1) *Static discharge, which can wipe out data and even damage circuits, should be avoided.* The original wording contains repeated information. The revision gets rid of these extra words by changing most of sentence 2 into a dependent thought.

39. (2) *Occasionally* is the correct spelling.

40. (1) Since *Spraying* and *helps* are both singular, they match. The passage is written in the present time. Therefore, options (3), (4), and (5) are incorrect.

41. (1) *Place a static-free dust cover over your computer equipment when you are not using it.* In the original wording *This* does not refer to anything specific. The revision gets rid of this vague pronoun by making the second sentence into a dependent thought.

42. (4) The original wording is a comma splice. Option (4) corrects the error by making the second independent thought into an explanatory phrase. Option (2) creates a run-on. *So* is not logical as a connecting word because there is no cause-and-effect relationship.

43. (5) *And* does not logically connect the two independent thoughts because they are not closely related. The best revision is (5) because it makes the thoughts into two separate sentences.

44. (5) Remember that commas are placed around phrases that give additional information.

45. (1) If you read sentence 12 to yourself, you will hear the pause after the introductory word *Finally.*

Corrected passage:

Once you buy a computer and some accompanying software, you should learn how to keep them in good working condition. Static discharge, which can wipe out data and even damage circuits, should be avoided. Occasionally, wipe your keyboard with a clean, lint-free cloth. Spraying the cloth, not the keyboard, with an antistatic cleaning fluid helps too. Place a static-free dust cover over your computer equipment when you are not using it. Clean your disk drive with a head cleaning kit, following the manufacturer's recommendations. Keep your computer in a room with good circulation to reduce excess dust and heat. Your computer may even require a fan if you add circuit boards. For safety's sake, use correctly wired outlets for your system. To avoid loss of data or damage to the computer due to sudden increases or decreases in voltage, use a surge protector, a device that can be found in most computer stores. Finally, read the manufacturer's warranty carefully to avoid any misunderstanding with the manufacturer or your dealer.

46. (2) *Approximately* is the correct spelling.

47. (2) *But what do you do?* is an incomplete thought. *If* introduces a dependent thought, and no comma is needed before *if.*

48. (4) *Or sleeplessness* is an interrupting phrase that gives further information about *insomnia.* Therefore, option (4) is correct because it adds the comma after the interrupting phrase.

49. (4) The pronoun *it* refers to one thing. *They* is correct because it refers to several things *(eating, drinking, exercise,* and *habits).*

50. (2) The original wording is a fragment because it lacks a main verb.

51. (5) *Researchers have proved that not everyone needs eight hours of sleep. Everyone* is a singular subject and matches with the singular verb *needs. Need* is plural, *needed* shows a completed action, and *will need* shows a future action.

52. (1) The comma in option (1) correctly separates the introductory dependent thought from the independent thought.

53. (2) *You should avoid beverages containing caffeine because caffeine acts as a stimulant for most people.* The connecting word *because* shows the cause-and-effect relationship between the two ideas.

54. (5) When you add *-ly* to a word ending in *e,* you usually drop the final *e* before adding *-ly. Considerably* is the correct spelling.

55. (1) Option (2) is incorrect because *one* does not follow through with the use of *you* in the passage. Options (3) and (4) give verbs in the future and past time rather than the present.

Corrected passage:

Americans spend approximately $25 million a year on over-the-counter sleep aids, and additional millions are spent by the 8.5 million Americans who take prescription sleeping pills. But what do you do if you don't want to take pills yet can't get a good night's sleep? If you are having trouble sleeping, first get a thorough physical examination to make sure the insomnia, or sleeplessness, is not related to some physical ailment. With physical problems ruled out, you should examine your eating, drinking, exercise, and relaxation habits to see if they might be preventing good sleep. Your main problem may be not the inability to sleep but the fear that you will not sleep. You could be a person who dwells on sleeplessness. Researchers have proved that not everyone needs eight hours of sleep. Because your body gets used to sleep at certain times, regular times of going to bed and awaking will help. You should avoid beverages containing caffeine because caffeine acts as a stimulant for most people. Smokers should note that nicotine is also a stimulant and that many ex-smokers have reported considerably improved sleep after quitting. To be an informed consumer, explore the alternatives to drugs with expert medical advice for an effective, safe, long-lasting solution to insomnia.

Sample essay:

Competition crops up everywhere in human life and in nature too. Plants want their place in the sun. Tiny, cunning kittens fight over the mother cat's milk. Whenever anything important is in short supply, there will be competition.

In people, competition often brings out the best. For the glory of winning a race, athletes train their bodies to perfection. When running for public office, candidates may spend hours practicing speech making and powers of persuasion.

Competitive efforts may benefit society as well. To make a profit and grow, a business must offer the consumer a good product at a fair price. Competition often leads to useful new products—for example, improved stereo sound systems that make music more exciting than ever.

The results of competition are not always positive, however. Where there is a winner, there will be a loser. If people fail too often, they may give up trying to improve their lives, and they may even turn to drinking or drugs. Companies driven by competition have knowingly sold dangerous products.

The United States is a highly competitive society. Our challenge is to preserve the benefits of competition while avoiding the damage that it can do, to both individuals and organizations.

Finding Your Score

To find your score on the multiple-choice section of Posttest A, use the Answer Key below. Cross out the numbers of all the questions you answered incorrectly or did not answer at all. Then count how many questions you answered correctly. The checklist on the next page gives directions on scoring your essay. Once you have the number of correct multiple-choice answers and the score on your essay, refer to the Progress Chart on the inside back cover.

Answer Key

1. (5)
2. (4)
3. (3)
4. (3)
5. (1)
6. (1)
7. (2)
8. (4)
9. (5)
10. (4)
11. (3)
12. (3)
13. (2)
14. (3)
15. (2)
16. (5)
17. (1)
18. (1)
19. (1)
20. (4)
21. (5)
22. (3)
23. (5)
24. (5)
25. (1)
26. (3)
27. (2)
28. (4)
29. (3)
30. (3)
31. (5)
32. (4)
33. (4)
34. (2)
35. (5)
36. (4)
37. (3)
38. (1)
39. (2)
40. (1)
41. (1)
42. (4)
43. (5)
44. (5)
45. (1)
46. (2)
47. (2)
48. (4)
49. (4)
50. (2)
51. (5)
52. (1)
53. (2)
54. (5)
55. (1)

Scoring Your Essay If you're in a GED class, your teacher will be able to score your essay holistically, the way the GED Testing Service will have it scored.

If you're studying by yourself, on the other hand, you will again need someone to help score your essay. It could be the same person who scored your Skills Survey essay. The person you choose will not be able to score your Posttest essay holistically because holistic scoring requires a period of training and guidance by an expert. However, if the two of you use the following method, you should be able to determine a score for your essay that will come close to what a holistic score would be.

First have your scorer preview the checklist below before you give him or her your essay to score.

Essay Scoring Checklist

To the scorer: Preview this entire checklist before you read and score the essay.

Read the essay topic on page 244 or 264. Next, read the essay written on that topic *quickly*. Try to achieve an overall impression of the writing. Then put the essay aside and, without referring back to it, rate it using the following checklist and scale. Six represents the highest score, one the lowest.

	1	2	3	4	5	6
Message— the presence of a clear, controlling idea	☐	☐	☐	☐	☐	☐
Details— the use of examples and specific details to support the message	☐	☐	☐	☐	☐	☐
Organization— a logical presentation of ideas	☐	☐	☐	☐	☐	☐
Expression— the clear, precise use of language to convey the message	☐	☐	☐	☐	☐	☐
Mechanics— knowledge of the conventions of standard English (grammar, punctuation, and so on)	☐	☐	☐	☐	☐	☐

Now take the checklist and find the score using this method: For each mark in a column, add the number of points at the top of the column. Your total should be from 5 to 30. Then multiply that total by $\frac{2}{5}$. That will give you your final essay score on a scale of from 2 to 12. Now find that score and your score on the conventions of English section on the chart on the inside back cover.

WRITING SKILLS POSTTEST B

Directions

The Writing Skills Posttest consists of 55 multiple-choice questions and an essay. It is intended to measure your ability to use clear and effective English. It is a test of English as it is usually written, not as it might be spoken. Specific directions are given at the beginning of each part. Read these directions carefully before you begin.

You should take approximately 75 minutes to complete the multiple-choice questions. There is no penalty for guessing. Try to answer as many questions as you can. Work rapidly but carefully, without spending too much time on any one question. If a question is too difficult for you, skip it and come back to it later.

For each answer, mark one space.

EXAMPLE

The intelligens of computers is different from that of human beings.

What correction should be made to this sentence?

(1) change the spelling of intelligens to intelligence
(2) change is to are
(3) change the spelling of different to diffrent
(4) insert a comma after that
(5) no correction is necessary

The correct answer is (1); therefore, answer space (1) has been marked.

You should take no more than 45 minutes to complete the essay section of the test. You can use a separate sheet of paper for your essay.

Explanations for the answers and a sample essay are on pages 265–268. Answers to the questions are in the Answer Key on page 268. Directions for scoring your essay appear on page 249.

Part I

Directions: The following items are based on paragraphs that contain numbered sentences. Some of the sentences contain errors in sentence structure, usage, or mechanics. A few sentences, however, are correct as written. Read each paragraph and then answer the items based on it. For each item, choose the answer that would result in the most effective writing of the sentence or sentences. The best answer must be consistent with the meaning and tone of the rest of the paragraph.

Items 1–9 refer to the following paragraph.

(1) A Child Safety Day (CSD) is an event that attracts attention to the tragedy of missing children and educates the community about the problem. (2) A Child Safety Day provides parents and guardians with preventive information. (3) It also arms them with materials that can be provided to authorities to assist them if they ever have a missing child. (4) Perhaps most important, a CSD can open the lines of communication between parent, and child. (5) When children, in the company of their parents, receive safety tips and information, they learn to be safety conscience. (6) Any community, regardless of size, can organize a Child Safety Day with the cooperation of local civic organizations and volunteers. (7) A CSD is held at a public facility such as a town hall, shopping mall, civic center, fire house, school, church, or libary. (8) Volunteers can perform all types of duties. (9) Volunteers can assist parents in completing forms that record vital statistics. (10) They can also take photographs that are provided to the parents. (11) Volunteer dentists prepare a dental chart of each child law enforcement agents or trained volunteers fingerprint the children. (12) Child Safety Days bringing about greater community awareness of the growing problem and stress, "It can happen to the children of this community." (13) With this new awareness, communities made a commitment that the safety of every child is a responsibility of every adult in the community.

1. Sentence 1: **A Child Safety Day (CSD) is an event that attracts attention to the tragedy of missing children and educates the community about the problem.**

   What correction should be made to this sentence?

   (1) change Day to day
   (2) replace that with who
   (3) change the spelling of attention to atention
   (4) change the spelling of tragedy to tradgedy
   (5) no correction is necessary

   (1) (2) (3) (4) (5)

2. Sentence 3: **It also arms them with materials that can be provided to authorities to assist them if they ever have a missing child.**

   Which of the following is the best way to write the underlined portion of this sentence? If you think the original is the best way, choose option (1).

   (1) if they ever have a missing child
   (2) if the parents or guardians ever miss a child
   (3) if ever there be a child missing
   (4) if the parent or guardian ever has a missing child
   (5) if a child ever be missing by them

   (1) (2) (3) (4) (5)

GO ON TO THE NEXT PAGE.

3. Sentence 4: **Perhaps most important, a CSD can open the lines of communication between parent, and child.**

   What correction should be made to this sentence?

   (1) change the spelling of Perhaps to Peraps
   (2) remove the comma after important
   (3) change can open to opened
   (4) remove the comma after parent
   (5) no correction is necessary

   ① ② ③ ④ ⑤

4. Sentence 5: **When children, in the company of their parents, receive safety tips and information, they learn to be safety conscience.**

   What correction should be made to this sentence?

   (1) remove the comma after children
   (2) insert a comma after tips
   (3) remove the comma after information
   (4) replace they with the parents
   (5) replace conscience with conscious

   ① ② ③ ④ ⑤

5. Sentence 7: **A CSD is held at a public facility such as a town hall, shopping mall, civic center, fire house, school, church, or libary.**

   What correction should be made to this sentence?

   (1) change is to are
   (2) change the spelling of facility to facillity
   (3) change town to Town
   (4) change the spelling of libary to library
   (5) change the spelling of libary to libery

   ① ② ③ ④ ⑤

6. Sentences 8 and 9: **Volunteers can perform all types of duties. Volunteers can assist parents in completing forms that record vital statistics.**

   The most effective combination of sentences 8 and 9 would include which of the following groups of words?

   (1) duties, and volunteers
   (2) can perform by assisting
   (3) Volunteers and parents can perform
   (4) Volunteers can complete
   (5) duties, including assisting

   ① ② ③ ④ ⑤

7. Sentence 11: **Volunteer dentists prepare a dental chart of each child law enforcement agents or trained volunteers fingerprint the children.**

   Which of the following is the best way to write the underlined portion of this sentence? If you think the original is the best way, choose option (1).

   (1) child law
   (2) child, law
   (3) child, while law
   (4) child, yet law
   (5) child; and law

   ① ② ③ ④ ⑤

8. Sentence 12: **Child Safety Days bringing about greater community awareness of the growing problem and stress, "It can happen to the children of this community."**

   What correction should be made to this sentence?

   (1) change bringing to bring
   (2) change bringing to brings
   (3) change bringing to brought
   (4) change stress to stressing
   (5) change stress to stresses

   ① ② ③ ④ ⑤

9. Sentence 13: **With this new awareness, communities made a commitment that the safety of every child is a responsibility of every adult in the community.**

   Which of the following is the best way to write the underlined portion of this sentence? If you think the original is the best way, choose option (1).

   (1) communities made
   (2) communities make
   (3) communities makes
   (4) communities had made
   (5) communities be making

   ① ② ③ ④ ⑤

GO ON TO THE NEXT PAGE.

Items 10–18 refer to the following paragraph.

(1) What should you wear when you exercise? (2) All exercise clothing should be lose enough to permit freedom of movement and should make you feel comfortable and self-assured. (3) As a general rule, you should wear lighter clothes than temperatures might indicate, exercise generates great amounts of body heat. (4) Light-colored clothing who reflects the sun's rays is cooler in summer, and dark clothes are warmer in winter. (5) Sometimes the weather is cold, and when this happens, it's better to wear several layers of light clothing rather than one or two heavy layers. (6) The extra layers help trap heat, and it's easy to shed one of them if you become too warm. (7) In cold weather and in hot, sunny weather it's a good idea to wear something on your head. (8) Ski caps are recommended for winter wear, and some form of tennis or sailor's hat that provides shade and can be soaked in water are good for summer. (9) Never wear rubberized or plastic clothing such garments interfere with the evaporation of perspiration and can cause body temperature to rise to dangerous levels. (10) You can choose many methods of exercise, and you should be comfortable but, at the same time, allow your body to keep itself cool.

10. Sentence 2: **All exercise clothing should be lose enough to permit freedom of movement and should make you feel comfortable and self-assured.**

What correction should be made to this sentence?

(1) replace lose with loose
(2) change the spelling of enough to enuff
(3) change to permit to permitting
(4) insert a comma after movement
(5) change should make to will make

(1) (2) (3) (4) (5)

11. Sentence 3: **As a general rule, you should wear lighter clothes than temperatures might indicate, exercise generates great amounts of body heat.**

Which of the following is the best way to write the underlined portion of this sentence? If you think the original is the best way, choose option (1).

(1) indicate, exercise
(2) indicate exercise
(3) indicate, or exercise
(4) indicate; moreover, exercise
(5) indicate because exercise

(1) (2) (3) (4) (5)

12. Sentence 4: **Light-colored clothing who reflects the sun's rays is cooler in summer, and dark clothes are warmer in winter.**

What correction should be made to this sentence?

(1) replace who with that
(2) change is to are
(3) remove the comma after summer
(4) remove the word and
(5) no correction is necessary

(1) (2) (3) (4) (5)

GO ON TO THE NEXT PAGE.

13. Sentence 5: **Sometimes the weather is cold, and when this happens, it's better to wear several layers of light clothing rather than one or two heavy layers.**

If you rewrote sentence 5 beginning with

When the weather is

the next words should be

(1) cold and wearing
(2) cold. It's better
(3) cold, and this happens
(4) cold, wear
(5) cold. Wear

(1) (2) (3) (4) (5)

14. Sentence 6: **The extra layers help trap heat, and it's easy to shed one of them if you become too warm.**

Which of the following is the best way to write the underlined portion of this sentence? If you think the original is the best way, choose option (1).

(1) heat, and
(2) heat and
(3) heat. And
(4) heat, and in addition
(5) heat since

(1) (2) (3) (4) (5)

15. Sentence 7: **In cold weather and in hot, sunny weather it's a good idea to wear something on your head.**

What correction should be made to this sentence?

(1) remove the comma after hot
(2) insert a comma after sunny weather
(3) replace it's with its
(4) change wear to have worn
(5) replace your with you're

(1) (2) (3) (4) (5)

16. Sentence 8: **Ski caps are recommended for winter wear, and some form of tennis or sailor's hat that provides shade and can be soaked in water are good for summer.**

Which of the following is the best way to write the underlined portion of this sentence? If you think the original is the best way, choose option (1).

(1) are good
(2) is good
(3) be good
(4) must be good
(5) were good

(1) (2) (3) (4) (5)

17. Sentence 9: **Never wear rubberized or plastic clothing such garments interfere with the evaporation of perspiration and can cause body temperature to rise to dangerous levels.**

What correction should be made to this sentence?

(1) insert a comma after clothing
(2) insert because after clothing
(3) change the spelling of interfere to interfear
(4) change can cause to causing
(5) no correction is necessary

(1) (2) (3) (4) (5)

18. Sentence 10: **You can choose many methods of exercise, and you should be comfortable but, at the same time, allow your body to keep itself cool.**

If you rewrote sentence 10 beginning with

Whatever method of exercise you choose, keep comfortable while

the next words should be

(1) you should
(2) at the same time
(3) allowing your body
(4) keeping itself
(5) cooling yourself

(1) (2) (3) (4) (5)

GO ON TO THE NEXT PAGE.

Items 19–28 refer to the following paragraph.

(1) "Moving Day Blues" is a familiar song for many Americans. (2) You will be in a minority, if you maintain your present residence for the rest of your life. (3) About one in five persons move each year. (4) The key to a successful move is preparation, which includes the best information available that suits one's particular moving needs. (5) Although commercial movers have been around for many years, there have always been heads of households who thought they could do the job better. (6) Moving their household goods, today, millions of Americans use their own or borrowed vehicles. (7) This operation can work very well if you have the strenth, facilities, and knowledge to do the job. (8) If you prefer not to move yourself hire a commercial carrier. (9) Select a moving company with a good reputation in the community, and ask for free estimates. (10) Before the move, plan to be flexible by avoiding the Summer season and the hectic days preceding the first of any month. (11) The last step before moving is to make certain that the contract between you and the mover is fully understood by both parties. (12) Protecting yourself is a good idea, and the best way to do that is to get a written estimate from the movers.

19. Sentence 2: **You will be in a minority, if you maintain your present residence for the rest of your life.**

Which of the following is the best way to write the underlined portion of this sentence? If you think the original is the best way, choose option (1).

(1) minority, if
(2) minority if
(3) minority, and if
(4) minority; if
(5) minority. If

① ② ③ ④ ⑤

20. Sentence 3: **About one in five persons move each year.**

Which of the following is the best way to write the underlined portion of this sentence? If you think the original is the best way, choose option (1).

(1) persons move
(2) persons moving
(3) persons are moving
(4) persons moves
(5) persons who move

21. Sentence 4: **The key to a successful move is preparation, which includes the best information available that suits one's particular moving needs.**

What correction should be made to this sentence?

(1) change is to are
(2) remove the comma after preparation
(3) replace which with that
(4) replace one's with your
(5) change the spelling of particular to particlar

① ② ③ ④ ⑤

22. Sentence 5: **Although commercial movers have been around for many years, there have always been heads of households who thought they could do the job better.**

What correction should be made to this sentence?

(1) change the spelling of Although to Allthough
(2) change have been to having been
(3) remove the comma after years
(4) replace who with which
(5) no correction is necessary

① ② ③ ④ ⑤

GO ON TO THE NEXT PAGE.

23. Sentence 6: **Moving their household goods, today, millions of Americans use their own or borrowed vehicles.**

If you rewrote sentence 6 beginning with

Today millions of Americans

the next word(s) should be

(1) moving
(2) moved
(3) move
(4) had moved
(5) having moved

(1) (2) (3) (4) (5)

24. Sentence 7: **This operation can work very well if you have the strenth, facilities, and knowledge to do the job.**

What correction should be made to this sentence?

(1) change can work to should have worked
(2) insert a comma after well
(3) change the spelling of strenth to strength
(4) change the spelling of facilities to facilitys
(5) change the spelling of knowledge to knowlege

(1) (2) (3) (4) (5)

25. Sentence 8: **If you prefer not to move yourself hire a commercial carrier.**

Which of the following is the best way to write the underlined portion of this sentence? If you think the original is the best way, choose option (1).

(1) yourself hire
(2) yourself; hire
(3) yourself, hire
(4) yourself and hire
(5) yourself. Hire

(1) (2) (3) (4) (5)

26. Sentence 9: **Select a moving company with a good reputation in the community, and ask for free estimates.**

What correction should be made to this sentence?

(1) change Select to Selecting
(2) change moving company to Moving Company
(3) replace and with or
(4) change ask to asks
(5) no correction is necessary

(1) (2) (3) (4) (5)

27. Sentence 10: **Before the move, plan to be flexible by avoiding the Summer season and the hectic days preceding the first of any month.**

What correction should be made to this sentence?

(1) remove the comma after move
(2) insert a comma after flexible
(3) change avoiding to having avoided
(4) change Summer to summer
(5) change the spelling of preceding to preceeding

(1) (2) (3) (4) (5)

28. Sentence 12: **Protecting yourself is a good idea, and the best way to do that is to get a written estimate from the movers.**

If you rewrote sentence 12 beginning with

To protect yourself,

the next words should be

(1) a written estimate
(2) a good idea
(3) the best way
(4) get a written
(5) you might try

(1) (2) (3) (4) (5)

GO ON TO THE NEXT PAGE.

Items 29–37 refer to the following passage.

(1) Twenty-six-mile marathons becoming a familiar part of the physical fitness program of many Americans. (2) Bicycle enthusiasts have their own special marathon called a "century ride." (3) A century ride is the distance that a rider can comfortably cover in a day, and a century ride is 100 miles long. (4) The average time for a cyclist who has trained for long-distance cycling to complete the course is nine hours, yet not unheard of are riders taking as little as four hours. (5) Most century rides are held in September, when the whether is cool and the cyclists are in top shape after a summer of riding. (6) Each cyclist used a map of the route marked with places to stop and rest. (7) There are even "sag wagons" along the route to help cyclists who's bikes or bodies have given out. (8) During the ride, it is necessary to eat snacks and drink frequently from the bike's water bottle. (9) Some bikers "ride to eat," yet many other people are attracted by the social aspects of a century ride. (10) Since a century ride is so strenuous, many cyclists lose weight after one, even though they eat frequently during the ride. (11) One East Coast touring club, organized an "Eat-a-thon" ride with the sole purpose of biking from city to city and restaurant to restaurant.

29. Sentence 1: **Twenty-six-mile marathons becoming a familiar part of the physical fitness program of many Americans.**

What correction should be made to this sentence?

(1) insert a comma after marathons
(2) insert is after marathons
(3) insert are after marathons
(4) change becoming to became
(5) change the spelling of familiar to familliar

(1) (2) (3) (4) (5)

30. Sentence 3: **A century ride is the distance that a rider can comfortably cover in a day, and a century ride is 100 miles long.**

If you rewrote sentence 3 beginning with

Covering 100 miles,

the next words should be

(1) the rider
(2) a comfortable distance
(3) a day
(4) a century ride
(5) the length

(1) (2) (3) (4) (5)

31. Sentence 4: **The average time for a cyclist who has trained for long-distance cycling to complete the course is nine hours, yet not unheard of are riders taking as little as four hours.**

What correction should be made to this sentence?

(1) replace who with which
(2) replace course with coarse
(3) change is to are
(4) change are to is
(5) no correction is necessary

(1) (2) (3) (4) (5)

GO ON TO THE NEXT PAGE.

32. Sentence 5: **Most century rides are held in September, when the whether is cool and the cyclists are in top shape after a summer of riding.**

What correction should be made to this sentence?

(1) change are held to is held
(2) change September to september
(3) replace when with whereas
(4) replace whether with weather
(5) change summer to Summer

(1) (2) (3) (4) (5)

33. Sentence 6: **Each cyclist used a map of the route marked with places to stop and rest.**

Which of the following is the best way to write the underlined portion of this sentence? If you think the original is the best way, choose option (1).

(1) cyclist used
(2) cyclist who used
(3) cyclist uses
(4) cyclist had used
(5) cyclist using

(1) (2) (3) (4) (5)

34. Sentence 7: **There are even "sag wagons" along the route to help cyclists who's bikes or bodies have given out.**

What correction should be made to this sentence?

(1) replace There with They're
(2) change are to is
(3) replace who's with whose
(4) change given to gave
(5) no correction is necessary

(1) (2) (3) (4) (5)

35. Sentence 8: **During the ride, it is necessary to eat snacks and drink frequently from the bike's water bottle.**

What correction should be made to this sentence?

(1) remove the comma after ride
(2) change is to had been
(3) insert a comma after snacks
(4) change drink to be drinking
(5) no correction is necessary

(1) (2) (3) (4) (5)

36. Sentence 9: **Some bikers "ride to eat," yet many other people are attracted by the social aspects of a century ride.**

If you rewrote sentence 9 beginning with

Although some bikers "ride to eat," the social aspects of a century ride

the next word(s) should be

(1) attract
(2) attracts
(3) attracted
(4) are attracted
(5) are attracting

(1) (2) (3) (4) (5)

37. Sentence 11: **One East Coast touring club, organized an "Eat-a-thon" ride with the sole purpose of biking from city to city and restaurant to restaurant.**

Which of the following is the best way to write the underlined portion of this sentence? If you think the original is the best way, choose option (1).

(1) club, organized
(2) club organized
(3) club, organizing
(4) club organized,
(5) club. It organized

(1) (2) (3) (4) (5)

GO ON TO THE NEXT PAGE.

Items 38–46 refer to the following paragraph.

(1) A philatelist, according to the dictionary is someone who collects or studies stamps. (2) It's estimated that twenty million people in the United States fit that category. (3) Pursuing what is said to be the world's most popular hobby. (4) You begin your collection by saving the stamps from mail delivered to your home or you can go to your local post office and buy each new issue of stamp. (5) You can trade with people interested in collecting, or you can join a stamp club, or you can buy from stamp dealers. (6) It doesn't matter what your collecting area is because you will probably find that these colorful bits of paper capture the spirit and history of their places of origin. (7) There are many ways to collect; for example topical collecting is popular today. (8) To form such a collection, choose a subject that interests you, this could be sports, music, animals, or ships. (9) If you have chosen one that is broad enough, you will find it quiet easy to create a fascinating and personally meaningful collection. (10) Stamp collecting will provide you with a fun-filled way to use your leisure time.

38. Sentence 1: **A philatelist, according to the dictionary is someone who collects or studies stamps.**

Which of the following is the best way to write the underlined portion of this sentence? If you think the original is the best way, choose option (1).

(1) dictionary is
(2) dictionary, is
(3) dictionary; is
(4) dictionary. Is
(5) dictionary, and is

(1) (2) (3) (4) (5)

39. Sentences 2 and 3: **It's estimated that twenty million people in the United States fit that category. Pursuing what is said to be the world's most popular hobby.**

Which of the following is the best way to write the underlined portion of these sentences? If you think the original is the best way, choose option (1).

(1) category. Pursuing
(2) category pursuing
(3) category, pursuing
(4) category; pursuing
(5) category, as well as pursuing

40. Sentence 4: **You begin your collection by saving the stamps from mail delivered to your home or you can go to your local post office and buy each new issue of stamp.**

What correction should be made to this sentence?

(1) change begin to began
(2) insert a comma after home
(3) replace or with but
(4) change post office to Post Office
(5) change buy to buying

(1) (2) (3) (4) (5)

GO ON TO THE NEXT PAGE.

41. Sentence 5: **You can trade with people interested in collecting, or you can join a stamp club, or you can buy from stamp dealers.**

If you rewrote sentence 5 beginning with

You can trade with people who collect, join a stamp club, or

the next word should be

(1) you
(2) can
(3) with
(4) buy
(5) from

① ② ③ ④ ⑤

42. Sentence 6: **It doesn't matter what your collecting area is because you will probably find that these colorful bits of paper capture the spirit and history of their places of origin.**

If you rewrote sentence 6 beginning with

Whatever your collecting area,

the next word should be

(1) it
(2) is
(3) you
(4) because
(5) these

① ② ③ ④ ⑤

43. Sentence 7: **There are many ways to collect; for example topical collecting is popular today.**

Which of the following is the best way to write the underlined portion of this sentence? If you think the original is the best way, choose option (1).

(1) collect; for example
(2) collect for example
(3) collect, for example
(4) collect for example,
(5) collect; for example,

① ② ③ ④ ⑤

44. Sentence 8: **To form such a collection, choose a subject that interests you, this could be sports, music, animals, or ships.**

What correction should be made to this sentence?

(1) remove the comma after collection
(2) replace choose with chose
(3) replace that with who
(4) replace this could be with such as
(5) remove the comma after sports

① ② ③ ④ ⑤

45. Sentence 9: **If you have chosen one that is broad enough, you will find it quiet easy to create a fascinating and personally meaningful collection.**

What correction should be made to this sentence?

(1) replace If with Since
(2) change chosen to chose
(3) remove the comma after enough
(4) replace quiet with quite
(5) change the spelling of fascinating to fascinateing

① ② ③ ④ ⑤

46. Sentence 10: **Stamp collecting will provide you with a fun-filled way to use your leisure time.**

What correction should be made to this sentence?

(1) change will provide to provided
(2) replace you with one
(3) replace your with you're
(4) change the spelling of leisure to liesure
(5) no correction is necessary

① ② ③ ④ ⑤

GO ON TO THE NEXT PAGE.

Items 47–55 refer to the following paragraph.

(1) Herbs can provide creative, tasty alternatives to salt for flavoring foods. (2) Through the skillful use of herbs and spices, imaginative flavors can be created, and simple foods can be made into gourmet delights. (3) Herbs and spices differing only in that herbs tend to be plants grown in temperate areas, while spices grow in tropical regions. (4) If herbs are being grown for drying, the harvesting should be done in the Morning after the dew has evaporated but before the sun is very bright. (5) The essential oils in herbs will evaporate into the atmosphere during the day it is important to collect them when their flavor is at its peak. (6) The herbs should be dried in bunches or laid on screens in a warm, dark, well-ventilated spot. (7) The length of time, whether it is short or long, required for drying will vary according to the thickness of the plant parts. (8) Most dried herbs kept in glass or plastic containers can be stored for at least one year. (9) That won't destroy their flavor. (10) There are no strict limits to the use of herbs. (11) To become familiar with the specific flavor of an herb, try mixing it with butter or cream cheese let it sit for at least an hour, and spread it on a plain cracker. (12) Don't mix two very strong herbs together, but rather one strong herb with one or more milder flavors to compliment both the strong herb and the food.

47. Sentence 2: **Through the skillful use of herbs and spices, imaginative flavors can be created, and simple foods can be made into gourmet delights.**

Which of the following is the best way to write the underlined portion of this sentence? If you think the original is the best way, choose option (1).

(1) created, and
(2) created; and
(3) created. And
(4) created and
(5) created for

(1) (2) (3) (4) (5)

48. Sentence 3: **Herbs and spices differing only in that herbs tend to be plants grown in temperate areas, while spices grow in tropical regions.**

What correction should be made to this sentence?

(1) change differing to differ
(2) insert a comma after that
(3) change tend to tending
(4) change grow to grown
(5) no correction is necessary

(1) (2) (3) (4) (5)

49. Sentence 4: **If herbs are being grown for drying, the harvesting should be done in the Morning after the dew has evaporated but before the sun is very bright.**

What correction should be made to this sentence?

(1) change are being grown to being grown
(2) remove the comma after drying
(3) remove the words should be
(4) change Morning to morning
(5) no correction is necessary

(1) (2) (3) (4) (5)

GO ON TO THE NEXT PAGE.

50. Sentence 5: **The essential oils in herbs will evaporate into the atmosphere during the day it is important to collect them when their flavor is at its peak.**

Which of the following is the best way to write the underlined portion of this sentence? If you think the original is the best way, choose option (1).

(1) day it
(2) day, it
(3) day, and it
(4) day, so it
(5) day; so it

(1) (2) (3) (4) (5)

51. Sentence 7: **The length of time, whether it is short or long, required for drying will vary according to the thickness of the plant parts.**

If you rewrote sentence 7 beginning with

The time

the next words should be

(1) whether short or long
(2) required for drying
(3) and the length
(4) according to the thickness
(5) and the drying vary

(1) (2) (3) (4) (5)

52. Sentences 8 and 9: **Most dried herbs kept in glass or plastic containers can be stored for at least one year. That won't destroy their flavor.**

The most effective combination of sentences 8 and 9 would include which of the following groups of words?

(1) one year, and that
(2) Most dried herbs won't
(3) one year and will not
(4) one year without destroying
(5) herbs can be kept and stored

(1) (2) (3) (4) (5)

53. Sentence 10: **There are no strict limits to the use of herbs.**

What correction should be made to this sentence?

(1) replace There with Their
(2) replace There with They're
(3) change are to is
(4) replace no with know
(5) no correction is necessary

(1) (2) (3) (4) (5)

54. Sentence 11: **To become familiar with the specific flavor of an herb, try mixing it with butter or cream cheese let it sit for at least an hour, and spread it on a plain cracker.**

What correction should be made to this sentence?

(1) change the spelling of familiar to familar
(2) remove the comma after herb
(3) insert a comma after cheese
(4) change let to to let
(5) change the spelling of plain to plane

(1) (2) (3) (4) (5)

55. Sentence 12: **Don't mix two very strong herbs together, but rather one strong herb with one or more milder flavors to compliment both the strong herb and the food.**

What correction should be made to this sentence?

(1) change mix to be mixing
(2) replace two with too
(3) replace but with and
(4) replace compliment with complement
(5) insert a comma after both

(1) (2) (3) (4) (5)

GO ON TO THE NEXT PAGE.

Part II

Directions: This is a test to find out how well you write. The test has one question that asks you to present an opinion on an issue or to explain something. In preparing your answer for this question, you should take the following steps:

1. Read all of the information accompanying the question.
2. Plan your answer carefully before you write.
3. Use scratch paper to make any notes.
4. Write your answer.
5. Read carefully what you have written and make any changes that will improve your writing.
6. Check your paragraphing, sentence structure, spelling, punctuation, capitalization, and usage, and make any necessary corrections.

You will have 45 minutes to write on the question you are assigned. Write legibly and use a ball-point pen.

Computers have made possible the storage of vast amounts of information about people: their medical histories, bills, credit ratings, vital statistics, political preferences, and so on. Computers have also made it possible to "access," or get, such information about people.

Think about the possible consequences of having access to personal information. Discuss the advantages of this situation, the disadvantages, or both in a composition of about 200 words. Be specific, and give examples.

END OF EXAMINATION

Answers: Posttest B

1. (5) No error.

2. (4) In the original wording, *they* seems to refer to *authorities.* To make the meaning of the sentence clear, option (4) is the best choice.

3. (4) Commas are not used to join two words (*parent* and *child*).

4. (5) *Conscious* means "to be awake or aware." Your *conscience* tells you the difference between right and wrong.

5. (4) Careful pronunciation will help you spell *library* correctly.

6. (5) *Volunteers can perform all types of duties, including assisting parents in completing forms that record vital statistics.* This revision gets rid of repeated information by using the subject *(Volunteers)* only once. The second sentence is made into a dependent part.

7. (3) The original wording is a run-on. Option (2) creates a comma splice. *Yet* and *and* do not correctly express the relationship between the two sentences. Therefore, option (3) is the best revision.

8. (1) The original sentence is a fragment because it lacks a complete verb. Since the passage is about an action taking place in present time, option (1) is the best choice.

9. (2) Again, the passage is about a current action. *Made* and *had made* show past actions. *Communities* and *makes* do not agree.

Corrected passage:

A Child Safety Day (CSD) is an event that attracts attention to the tragedy of missing children and educates the community about the problem. A Child Safety Day provides parents and guardians with preventive information. It also arms them with materials that can be provided to authorities to assist them if the parent or guardian ever has a missing child. Perhaps most important, a CSD can open the lines of communication between parent and child. When children, in the company of their parents, receive safety tips and information, they learn to be safety conscious. Any community, regardless of size, can organize a Child Safety Day with the cooperation of local civic organizations and volunteers. A CSD is held at a public facility such as a town hall, shopping mall, civic center, fire house, school, church, or library. Volunteers can perform all types of duties, including assisting parents in completing forms that record vital statistics. Volunteer dentists prepare a dental chart of each child, while law enforcement agents or trained volunteers fingerprint the children. Child Safety Days bring about greater community awareness of the growing problem and stress, "It can happen to the children of this community." With this new awareness, communities make a commitment that the safety of every child is a responsibility of every adult in the community.

10. (1) *Lose* is a verb that is the opposite of *find. Loose clothing* is the opposite of *tight clothing.*

11. (5) The original wording is a comma splice. *Because* logically joins the two thoughts since it tells *why* you should wear light clothes.

12. (1) *Who* cannot refer to a thing *(clothing),* only *that* or *which* can.

13. (4) *When the weather is cold, wear several layers of light clothing rather than one or two heavy layers.* The revision gets rid of a lot of unnecessary words. A comma is needed after an introductory dependent thought.

14. (1) The two independent thoughts are correctly joined by the comma and the word *and.*

15. (2) *In cold weather and in hot, sunny weather* is an introductory descriptive phrase and needs a comma placed after it.

16. (2) Since *form* is the subject of the second independent thought, it must match with a singular verb *(is).* All the words that come between don't change that fact.

17. (2) The original wording is a run-on. *Because* correctly shows the cause-and-effect relationship between the two thoughts.

18. (3) *Whatever method of exercise you choose, keep comfortable while allowing your body to keep itself cool. While* correctly expresses the time relationship between the two thoughts.

Corrected passage:

What should you wear when you exercise? All exercise clothing should be loose enough to permit freedom of movement and should make you feel comfortable and self-assured. As a general rule, you should wear lighter clothes than temperatures might indicate because exercise generates great amounts of body heat. Light-colored clothing that reflects the sun's rays is cooler in summer, and dark clothes are warmer in winter. When the weather is cold, wear several layers of light clothing rather than one or two heavy layers. The extra layers help trap heat, and it's easy to shed one of them if you become too warm. In cold weather and in hot, sunny weather, it's a good idea to wear something on your head. Ski caps are recommended for winter wear, and some form of tennis or sailor's hat that provides shade and can be soaked in water is good for summer. Never wear rubberized or plastic clothing because such garments interfere with the evaporation of perspiration and can cause body temperature to rise to dangerous levels. Whatever method of exercise you choose, keep comfortable while allowing your body to keep itself cool.

19. (2) When a dependent thought comes at the end of a sentence, you usually don't need a comma before the connecting word *(if)*. Insert a comma only if there is a pause before the connecting word.

20. (4) *One* (not *persons*) is the subject of the sentence. *One* and *moves* agree because they both are singular.

21. (4) The pronouns *you* and *your* are used throughout this passage. *One's* does not follow through with this usage.

22. (5) No error.

23. (3) *Today millions of Americans move their household goods using their own or borrowed vehicles.* Options (1) and (5) create fragments. Options (2) and (4) are incorrect because they express past action.

24. (3) *Strength* is difficult to spell because the *g* is often not pronounced. Careful pronunciation of *strength* will help you spell it correctly.

25. (3) A comma is needed after an introductory dependent part.

26. (5) No error.

27. (4) The names of seasons are not capitalized.

28. (4) *To protect yourself, get a written estimate.* In the revision, *To protect yourself* correctly describes the subject *you* (the *you* in the command *get a written estimate* is understood). *To protect yourself* does not describe *a written estimate, a good idea,* or *the best way.*

Corrected passage:

"Moving Day Blues" is a familiar song for many Americans. You will be in a minority if you maintain your present residence for the rest of your life. About one in five persons moves each year. The key to a successful move is preparation, which includes the best information available that suits your particular moving needs. Although commercial movers have been around for many years, there have always been heads of households who thought they could do the job better. Today millions of Americans move their household goods using their own or borrowed vehicles. This operation can work very well if you have the strength, facilities, and knowledge to do the job. If you prefer not to move yourself, hire a commercial carrier. Select a moving company with a good reputation in the community, and ask for free estimates. Before the move, plan to be flexible by avoiding the summer season and the hectic days preceding the first of any month. The last step before moving is to make certain that the contract between you and the mover is fully understood by both parties. To protect yourself, get a written estimate.

29. (3) The original wording is a fragment. *Marathons are* (not *marathons is*) agrees. *Are becoming* shows that an event is currently happening and will continue to happen.

30. (4) *Covering 100 miles, a century ride is the distance that a rider can comfortably cover in a day. Covering 100 miles* describes a century ride (not *the rider, a comfortable distance, a day,* or *the length*).

31. (5) No error. If you chose option (4), you probably did not realize that *riders* is the subject of the independent thought after *yet. Riders are* agrees.

32. (4) *Weather* refers to outside conditions. *Whether* indicates a choice.

33. (3) *Uses* shows present time and matches the other present verbs in the passage.

34. (3) *Who's* stands for *who is.* It would not be logical to write *who is bikes. Whose* shows ownership. The bikes and bodies belong to the cyclists.

35. (5) No error.

36. (1) *Although some bikers "ride to eat," the social aspects of a century ride attract many other people.* The subject of the revised sentence (*aspects*) agrees with *attract.*

37. (2) A comma is not used to separate a subject (*club*) and its verb (*organized*).

Corrected passage:

Twenty-six-mile marathons are becoming a familiar part of the physical fitness program of many Americans. Bicycle enthusiasts have their own special marathon called a "century ride." Covering 100 miles, a century ride is the distance that a rider can comfortably cover in a day. The average time for a cyclist who has trained for long-distance cycling to complete the course is nine hours, yet not unheard of are riders taking as little as four hours. Most century rides are held in September, when the weather is cool and the cyclists are in top shape after a summer of riding. Each cyclist uses a map of the route marked with places to stop and rest. There are even "sag wagons" along the route to help cyclists whose bikes or bodies have given out. During the ride, it is necessary to eat snacks and drink frequently from the bike's water bottle. Although some bikers "ride to eat," the social aspects of a century ride attract many other people. Since a century ride is so strenuous, many cyclists lose weight after one, even though they eat frequently during the ride. One East Coast touring club organized an "Eat-a-thon" ride with the sole purpose of biking from city to city and restaurant to restaurant.

38. (2) *According to the dictionary* is a descriptive phrase that comes in the middle of the sentence and must be separated by commas.

39. (3) Sentence 3 is actually a fragment because it lacks a subject. *Pursuing what is said to be the world's most popular hobby* is an explanatory phrase that should be separated from the rest of the sentence with a comma.

40. (2) A comma and *or* are used to connect two independent thoughts. *Or* correctly shows that there is a choice of how to begin your stamp collection.

41. (4) *You can trade with people who collect, join a stamp club, or buy from stamp dealers.* In the original wording, three independent thoughts are joined with commas and the connecting word *or.* The revision combines the common subject *you* with the three related verbs (*trade, join,* and *buy*).

42. (3) *Whatever your collecting area, you will probably find that these colorful bits of paper capture the spirit and history of their places of origin.* The subject of this sentence is *you.*

43. (5) The semicolon is correct because it is separating two independent thoughts. A comma is needed to set off the interrupting phrase *for example.*

44. (4) The comma incorrectly joins two independent thoughts. Option (4) changes the second independent thought into an explanatory phrase that lists topics.

45. (4) *Quiet* and *quite* are often confused because they are mispronounced.

46. (5) No error.

Corrected passage:

A philatelist, according to the dictionary, is someone who collects or studies stamps. It's estimated that twenty million people in the United States fit that category, pursuing what is said to be the world's most popular hobby. You begin your collection by saving the stamps from mail delivered to your home, or you can go to your local post office and buy each new issue of stamp. You can trade with people who collect, join a stamp club, or buy from stamp dealers. Whatever your collecting area, you will probably find that these colorful bits of paper capture the spirit and history of their places of origin. There are many ways to collect; for example, topical collecting is popular today. To form such a collection, choose a subject that interests you, such as sports, music, animals, or ships. If you have chosen one that is broad enough, you will find it quite easy to create a fascinating and personally meaningful collection. Stamp collecting will provide you with a fun-filled way to use your leisure time.

47. (1) The comma and the connecting word *and* correctly join the two independent thoughts.

48. (1) The original wording is a fragment. Option (1) correctly adds a verb.

49. (4) Time periods like *morning* and *afternoon* are not capitalized.

50. (4) The original wording is a run-on because two complete thoughts are written together with no punctuation or connecting word. Option (4) combines them correctly, with a comma and a connecting word.

51. (2) *The time required for drying will vary according to the thickness of the plant parts.* The original wording contains too many extra words.

52. (4) *Most dried herbs kept in glass or plastic containers can be stored for at least one year without destroying their flavor.* This combination is correct, clear, and concise.

53. (5) No error.

54. (3) In sentence 11, three complete thoughts are written as items in a series. *Try mixing it with butter or cream cheese* is the first item in the series.

55. (4) If you did not choose option (4), you might want to add *compliment* and *complement* and their definitions to your Target List.

Corrected passage:

Herbs can provide creative, tasty alternatives to salt for flavoring foods. Through the skillful use of herbs and spices, imaginative flavors can be created, and simple foods can be made into gourmet delights. Herbs and spices differ only in that herbs tend to be plants grown in temperate areas, while spices grow in tropical regions. If herbs are being grown for drying, the harvesting should be done in the morning after the dew has evaporated but before the sun is very bright. The essential oils in herbs will evaporate into the atmosphere during the day, so it is important to collect them when their flavor is at its peak. The herbs should be dried in bunches or laid on screens in a warm, dark, well-ventilated spot. The time required for drying will vary according to the thickness of the plant parts. Most dried herbs kept in glass or plastic containers can be stored for at least one year without destroying their flavor. There are no strict limits to the use of herbs. To become familiar with the specific flavor of an herb, try mixing it with butter or cream cheese, let it sit for at least an hour, and spread it on a plain cracker. Don't mix two very strong herbs together, but rather one strong herb with one or more milder flavors to complement both the strong herb and the food.

Sample essay:

Computers have made possible the storage of vast amounts of information—everything from medical histories to credit ratings. This storage, along with its fairly easy accessibility, presents questions that must be resolved before technology progresses even further.

Some people say, "My life is an open book. I don't have anything to hide because I've never done anything to be ashamed of. If people want secrecy, they must have done something wrong." If such people really mean what they say, they would not mind if everything they've ever told their doctor, bought on credit, or checked out of the library was recorded in a computer file available to friends and strangers. If the police had ever questioned them—for good reason or not—if they had ever been issued a speeding ticket or been involved in a fender-bender, that fact could never be forgotten.

The problem is that everyone makes mistakes, and most people have had experiences they would rather forget. Information about our finances or our politics can be used to gain unfair advantage. And mistakes do get into computer records.

For these reasons, computer data on individuals should be more restricted. Our personal data should be given only to people who truly need and have a right to know it. Except where public safety is involved, as in law enforcement, no personal data should be released without permission from the person who is the subject of the file.

In addition, information entered into the file should be double-checked for accuracy. Each person should know what is in his or her file and must be able to get errors corrected.

Computer records are a powerful tool that can help people or be turned against them. We must work to make sure that the latter does not happen.

Answer Key

Use this answer key and the directions on page 249 for scoring your essay to determine your final score on Posttest B.

1. (5)
2. (4)
3. (4)
4. (5)
5. (4)
6. (5)
7. (3)
8. (1)
9. (2)
10. (1)
11. (5)
12. (1)
13. (4)
14. (1)
15. (2)
16. (2)
17. (2)
18. (3)
19. (2)
20. (4)
21. (4)
22. (5)
23. (3)
24. (3)
25. (3)
26. (5)
27. (4)
28. (4)
29. (3)
30. (4)
31. (5)
32. (4)
33. (3)
34. (3)
35. (5)
36. (1)
37. (2)
38. (2)
39. (3)
40. (2)
41. (4)
42. (3)
43. (5)
44. (4)
45. (4)
46. (5)
47. (1)
48. (1)
49. (4)
50. (4)
51. (2)
52. (4)
53. (5)
54. (3)
55. (4)

Style Guide

Capitalization

1. Capitalize names and initials of persons.

   John M. Brown　　Lucille Ball

2. Capitalize names of family members if they stand alone *or* precede a proper name.

   "I'll be home at eight, Mother."
   He takes after his Uncle Paul.

3. However, do not capitalize names of family members if they are used as common nouns *or* with a possessive.

   Everyone's mother is invited.
   My uncle is younger than I am.

4. Capitalize titles of government, military, or religious offices; professions; or nobility if they form part of a personal name. However, most titles are not capitalized when used as common nouns.

Governor Thompson	The governor spoke for an hour.
General Grant	The general rode up on horseback.
Emperor Maximilian	Maximilian was emperor of Mexico.
Professor Stason	The professor published an article.
Bishop Erickson	The bishop plans to retire next year.

5. Capitalize names of peoples, races, and tribes. However, do not capitalize such names when they are based on color.

Negro	Oriental
Afro-American	black
Navaho	white

6. Capitalize names of nationalities and languages.

German	Chinese
Arabic	Turkish

7. Capitalize divisions and features of the earth's surface.

North Pole	South Pacific
Rocky Mountains	Great Lakes
Hudson River	Antarctic

8. Capitalize a general geographic name that precedes two or more proper names.

   Mounts Rainier and Hood
   Lakes Huron and Erie

9. However, do not capitalize the general name if it follows the proper name.

   the Mississippi and Missouri rivers

10. But names of political divisions, such as *state*, are generally capitalized when they follow a proper name, but not when they precede it.

   the state of Washington
   Washington State

11. Capitalize cultural divisions of the world or of a country.

   the Middle East　　Central America
   New England

12. Capitalize points of the compass and descriptive words derived from them when they designate specific regions—but not when they simply indicate direction.

   the Midwest　　the Western nations
   western Utah　　the northern Atlantic
   The sun seems to move from east to west.

13. Capitalize accepted names of localities, even if they are not official.

the Loop (Chicago)	the Bay Area
the Badlands	the Badger State

14. Capitalize the official names of streets, highways, buildings, monuments, and so on.

Golden Gate Bridge	Wrigley Building
Washington Monument	Michigan Avenue

15. Capitalize the names of important historical events and periods.

Industrial Revolution	Reformation
Louisiana Purchase	Middle Ages

16. Capitalize the names of government judicial, legislative, and administrative bodies.

Supreme Court	House of Representatives
Census Bureau	Evanston City Council

17. Do not capitalize the words *federal* and *government* unless they form part of a formal name.

   He works for the Federal Reserve Bank.
   He works for the federal government.

18. Capitalize official names of political parties (though not the word *party*), associations, unions, societies, and companies.

the Democratic party
Northwestern University
The American Federation of Labor; the AFL
Sears, Roebuck and Company

19. Capitalize trademarked names.

Xerox   Coke   ChapStick

20. Capitalize references to one God, revered persons, sacred texts, holy days, religions, and denominations.

Jehovah	the Koran	Good Friday
Saint Paul	Buddhism	Lutheran

Punctuation

Period

1. A period ends any sentence that is not a question or an exclamation.

2. The period is placed inside quotation marks.

He remarked, "I'm not feeling well today."

3. A period is placed inside the closing parenthesis when the idea is a complete sentence; otherwise, the period comes after the parenthesis.

I asked that a window be opened. (The room was very warm.)

I admired the roses (which were an unusual shade of pink).

4. Abbreviations are followed by periods except in scientific usage.

Dr. Madison arrived late.

She measured out 50 cc of blood plasma.

5. Use only one period at the end of a sentence in which an abbreviation is the last word. However, if the sentence is a question or an exclamation, the abbreviation is followed by a period *and* a question mark or exclamation point.

In walked Roberta Fisher, Ph.D.

Has he finished the work for his Ph.D.?

Question Mark

1. A question mark is used at the end of a sentence intended as a question.

Do you understand?

2. A question mark is used inside quotes or parentheses when it is part of the quoted or parenthetical matter. Otherwise, the question mark follows the quotation mark or parenthesis.

"Who's there?" she called.

I believe the date is the twenty-third (is that correct?).

Did you watch "Hill Street Blues"?

Won't we have a holiday on February 22 (Washington's birthday)?

3. When the complete sentence and the quoted sentence are both questions, the final question mark is *inside* the final quotation mark.

Was it Mary who asked, "Who's going to pay?"

4. Polite requests and statements in the form of a question end with a period.

"Will the audience please rise."

Exclamation Point

1. An exclamation point is used to mark an exclamation or an emphatic comment.

We won!

2. The exclamation point is placed inside quotation marks or parentheses when it is part of the quoted or parenthetical material. Otherwise it should follow the final quotation mark or parenthesis.

Then the sergeant shouted, "Ready, aim, fire!"

Let's see you top that (if you can)!

3. A sentence may end with an exclamation point inside quotation marks. However, if the final exclamation point is inside parentheses, a final period should be added.

He shouted, "Watch out!"

Our candidate won the nomination (hurray!).

Comma

1. Use a comma between two independent thoughts that could be separate sentences but are joined into one sentence by a connecting word: *and, but, for, nor, or, so,* or *yet.*

 I went upstairs to look for the magazine, and I found it on the bed.

2. If the independent thoughts are very short, the comma may be omitted. On the other hand, if the sentence is long and has many commas, a semicolon may be used in place of a comma.

 Debbie played the guitar and Jay sang.

 John, who was by this time soaking wet, took off his hat, coat, and shoes; but he refused to remove any other clothing.

3. Use commas to set off dependent thoughts that are not essential to the sentence. If the thought could not be omitted without changing the meaning of the sentence, it should not be set off by commas.

 The bill, which is on the table, is due Friday.
 (Not essential: the bill happens to be on the table.)

 The bill that is on the table is due Friday.
 (Essential: there are several bills, but only the one on the table is due.)

4. When a noun phrase merely gives added information about the noun that precedes it, set off the phrase with commas.

 Wilma Ford, the typist, introduced her boss, Jean Schwartz.

However, if the noun phrase is needed to identify which noun is being discussed, the phrase should not be set off by commas.

 The book *Gone with the Wind* is one of my all-time favorites.

5. Use commas to set off short phrases such as *for example, however, in deed, in fact,* and *nevertheless* if they interrupt the flow of the sentence.

 The Zacks are thoughtless people; they are, for example, always late.

6. Use a comma before *and, or,* or *nor* at the end of a series of three or more words, phrases, or clauses.

 We have a choice of chocolate, vanilla, or yellow for the wedding cake.

7. Do not use a comma where connecting words join all the words in a series.

 We can have chocolate or vanilla or yellow wedding cake.

8. Use a comma between descriptive words in a series only if they all describe the noun in the same way. That is, use a comma if they could be separated by the word *and* or stated in reverse order without changing the meaning of the sentence.

 Although it was a hot, sticky day, Belinda looked cool in her sundress.

 I could not eat the ice-cold scrambled eggs.

9. Commas are used to set off direct quotations.

 She said angrily, "I have no idea what you mean."

 "I meant to ask you to dinner, actually," he replied.

10. Do not use a comma before direct quotes that are built into the sentence structure.

 The answer to your question is "Under no circumstances."

11. Use comma and quotes with thoughts that could be spoken statements.

 The soldier thought, "If I only knew."

12. Use a comma between two repeated words.

 What he does, does not interest me.

13. A comma is always placed inside quotation marks but outside parentheses or brackets.

 He said, "The sky's the limit," but he didn't really mean it.

 If I were she (and I'm glad I'm not), I would probably do the same.

14. Use commas to set off elements in dates, locations, and addresses.

 I was born on July 4, 1968, in Salt Lake City, Utah.

 My address is 324 King Drive, Mobile, Alabama.

Semicolon

1. Use a semicolon between two independent thoughts in a sentence that are *not* separated by a connecting word (*and, but, or, nor, for, so, yet*).

> I'm leaving for San Francisco today; my sister leaves tomorrow.
>
> You're doing a good job; consequently, you're being promoted.

2. A semicolon is used to separate units of a sentence that contain smaller elements that are separated by commas.

> The vote was yes, 4; no, 6; and undecided, 3.

3. The semicolon should be placed outside quotation marks or parentheses.

> He told me, "Forget it"; I did.

Colon

1. A colon is used to introduce a formal statement, a very long passage in quotes, or a speech in dialogue.

> The rule may be stated like this:
> Always . . . .
>
> I quote from the speech: "When the time is ripe . . . ."
>
> KING: Come here at once.
> QUEEN: I will not.

2. A colon is used to introduce a list or a series at the end of a sentence.

> There are four main operations in arithmetic: (1) addition, (2) subtraction, (3) multiplication, and (4) division.
>
> The words are as follows: *look, is, run.*

3. However, do not use a colon if the verb leads naturally into the items that follow:

> The cats were called Fluff, Boots, and Ms. Maggie.

Apostrophe

1. The possessive of a singular noun is formed by adding an apostrophe and *s.*

> My cousin's handwriting
>
> Charles's childhood

2. The possessive of a plural noun ending in *s* is formed by adding an apostrophe.

> the girls' hats
>
> the trees' leaves

3. For a plural noun not ending in *s,* the possessive is formed by adding an apostrophe and *s.*

> the children's storybooks

4. An apostrophe marks the omission of letters or numbers to form a contraction or shorten a year.

> the drought of '86
>
> I'm going now.

5. The possessive pronoun *its* does not have an apostrophe. The contraction *it's* (*it is* or *it has*) always has an apostrophe.

> The kitten raised its head.
>
> It's a cold day.
>
> It's been cold for three weeks.

Other possessives without the apostrophe are *hers, ours, yours, theirs.*

Parentheses

1. Parentheses are used within a sentence to enclose words that could be omitted without changing the main idea of the sentence. The enclosed material does not begin with a capital letter or end with a period, even if it is a complete sentence.

> Murphy's Law (if anything can go wrong, it will) was certainly operating.

2. However, a parenthetical sentence within a sentence may close with an exclamation point or question mark; even so, it does not open with a capital letter.

> He got his start (wasn't it in Chicago?) in the early 1920s.
>
> Phyllis Barker (how exhausted she looked!) was the last to finish the marathon.

3. Use parentheses for a separate sentence that is somewhat outside the flow of the main body of material. Such a sentence does begin with a capital letter and end with a period.

> I had not gone. (She knew that.)

Dash

1. Use a dash to mark an abrupt change of thought or to set off a phrase that adds emphasis or explanation.

> Do they—no, of course they are not going.
>
> His explanation—which satisfied the court but did not satisfy me—was that he had not been given advance notice.

2. The first word of the interrupting expression begins with a small letter. If the expression is in the middle of a sentence, it does not end with a period, but it may end with an exclamation point or a question mark.

> The pitcher—there he goes!—threw a curve.

3. Use a dash to end a deliberately uncompleted sentence.

> He said he was late because he had a flat tire, but—

4. In a quotation, use a comma to separate a dash from words that identify a speaker.

> "But—but—," sputtered Jim.

Quotation Marks

1. Use quotation marks to enclose the exact words of a speaker (except for dialogue in a play).

> "Hurry up!" he shouted.

2. Omit quotation marks with statements introduced by *that.*

> She replied that she would be ready in a minute.

3. Use quotation marks to set off material quoted from another source.

> Benjamin Franklin advised his readers, "A penny saved is a penny earned."

4. Use quotation marks for radio or television programs or episodes in a series, song titles, chapter titles, and poems. Titles of movies, magazines, newspapers, books, plays, long works of music, and works of art should be underlined.

5. When you put a quotation within a quotation, use single quotes within the double quotes.

> "The first few I asked answered, 'No, thank you,' " Mrs. Johnson complained.

6. Do not quote the words *yes* and *no* except in direct quotations.

> Stephen said, "Yes, we should all get to work at once."
>
> Stephen said yes, so we went to work at once.

Glossary of Usage

accept, except These words are frequently confused because of their similar pronunciations. *Accept* means "take or receive; consent to receive; say yes to." It is always a verb. *Except* means on any other condition or with the exclusion of something or someone.

> The policeman wouldn't accept Gary's excuse.
>
> Everyone went skating except Carol.

advice, advise *Advice* is a noun meaning "recommendation; counsel." *Advise* is a verb meaning "to recommend; suggest."

> Please advise me; you know how much I appreciate your advice.

affect, effect *Affect,* which is always a verb, means "influence; pretend to have or feel."

> The loss did not affect the team's standing.
>
> Tom Sawyer affected an interest in whitewashing the fence.

Effect can be a noun meaning "result; influence" or a verb meaning "make happen; bring about."

> The low lighting created an eerie effect. (noun)
>
> The committee could not effect a change. (verb)

all right, all-right *All right* is used as a descriptive term.

> Pete will be all right, once he has had some rest. (Descriptive term about the noun *Pete.*)
>
> Sarah will come all right; she never misses a party. (Descriptive term meaning "certainly.")
>
> All right, you can stay up another hour. (Decriptive term meaning "very well; yes.")

All-right is slang, meaning "very good": He's an all-right guy.

almost, most See **most, almost.**

a lot The overuse of this informal expression, which is often misspelled *alot,* should be avoided.
among, between See **between, among.**
amount, number Use *amount* to refer to things that are measured or weighed; use *number* to refer to things that are counted.

the large amount of junk mail

the number of "occupant" letters

as See **like, as.**
awhile, a while *Awhile* is a descriptive word.

They stayed awhile after the program.

While is a noun.

They stayed with us for a while.

bad, badly Both are generally used as descriptive words. *Bad* describes nouns; *badly* describes verbs.

Don't bring bad news; I take it badly.

In formal English and in informal writing, *bad* is used after a linking verb (*smell, feel, taste, appear, become, look, seem,* and parts of the verb *to be*).

The fish smells bad.

beside, besides *Beside* (without the *s*) is most commonly used to mean "next to" or "by the side of."

Our dog likes to lie beside the fire.

Besides (with the *s*) is used as a descriptive word.

No one besides the immediate family knows their good news. (meaning "except")

Besides being difficult to read, the book is very boring. (meaning "in addition to")

The booklet contains excellent explanations and many colorful drawings besides. (meaning "in addition")

between, among *Among* is used in referring to three or more people, places, or things.

It was difficult to choose among the three movies.

A shouting match started among those attending the meeting.

Between is generally used in referring to only two people, places, things, or groups.

It was difficult to choose between the two movies.

A shouting match started between the two aldermen.

Caution: Be careful to use *and*—not *or*—as a connector.

Illogical: I had to choose between Julian or Jason.

Logical: I had to choose between Julian and Jason.

borrow When *borrow* is used, it should be followed by *from,* not *off* or *off of.*

I can borrow the rest of the money from my brother.

breath, breathe The word *breath* is a noun; *breathe* is a verb.

Let me catch my breath; I can't seem to breathe.

buy *Buy,* like *borrow,* is followed by *from,* not *off* or *off of.*
effect, affect See **affect, effect.**
etc. This abbreviation stands for the Latin words *et cetera,* meaning "and others," and should be spelled *etc.*, not *ect.* It is set off by commas—one if it comes at the end of a sentence, two if it comes within a sentence.

Before immunization shots were introduced, many children suffered from measles, chicken pox, mumps, etc.

Childhood diseases like measles, chicken pox, mumps, etc., have been greatly reduced because of immunization.

Because the *et* of *et cetera* means "and," the word *and* should not be used before *etc.* Also, do not overuse *etc.*

everywheres Incorrectly used for *everywhere.*
except, accept See **accept, except.**
fewer See **less, fewer.**
formerly, formally *Formerly* means "in the past"; *formally* means "in a formal manner."

The team coach was formerly a quarterback.

He shook hands formally.

good, well Usually both are descriptive words.

Incorrect: You pitched good today.

Correct: You pitched well today.

Correct: The work is done well. [*Well* refers to the verb.]

*Correct:*The work is good. [*Good* refers to the noun.]

However, *well* meaning "healthy" describes nouns, and *good* may be a noun meaning "good works."

> You look well; I'm glad you've recovered.
>
> The holy man went about doing good.

had ought, hadn't ought These are nonstandard for *ought* and *ought not.*

> *Incorrect:* You had ought to check the furnace.
>
> *Correct:* You ought to check the furnace.
>
> *Incorrect:* They hadn't ought to go alone.
>
> *Correct:* They ought not to go alone.

To avoid problems with *ought,* use *should* instead.

> They shouldn't go alone.

have got, have gotten *Have got,* expressing emphatic obligation, and *have gotten,* expressing possession, are used in informal speech, but are generally avoided in formal English and careful informal writing.

> *Informal speech:* I have got to study tonight.
>
> *Formal and written:* I have to study tonight.
>
> *Informal speech:* I have gotten three electronic games so far.
>
> *Formal and written:* I have received (*or* bought) three electronic games so far.

hisself Incorrectly used for *himself.*

irregardless Since *less* makes the word negative, the prefix *ir-,* which is also a negative, is unnecessary.

> Regardless of his wife's fears, Caesar went to the Capitol. [*Not:* Irregardless of]

kind, sort The singular descriptive words *this* and *that* are used to modify the singular nouns *kind* and *sort.*

> This kind of music is very popular.
>
> That sort of music is not.

The plural descriptive words *these* and *those* are used to modify the plural nouns *kinds* and *sorts.*

> Do you find these kinds of fishes in freshwater?
>
> No, those sorts are found in salt water.

In both speech and writing, *them kind* is incorrect.

less, fewer Formal English usually makes a distinction between these two words, using *less* to refer to amount or quantity (to things that can be measured or weighed) and *fewer* to refer to number (to things that can be counted).

> Mr. and Mrs. Hodges get less mail than their son does.
>
> I myself get fewer personal letters every year.

lie, lay *To lie* means either "to tell an untruth" or "to rest in a horizontal position." *To lay* is "to set down" an object.

> Soon I will lay down my book and lie down.

like, as In both formal and informal English, *like*—not *as*—is used in comparisons.

> Alice looks like her mother.

In writing and informal speech, *as, as if,* and *as though* are used as connecting words to introduce dependent thoughts.

> Did you check for frozen pipes, as the newscaster suggested?
>
> Renata stared at the window as if she had seen a ghost.
>
> It looks as though we can go after all.

In informal speech, *like* is often used as a connecting word in sentences like the preceding ones.

> It looks like we can go after all.

However, this usage is still not considered appropriate in writing.

lose, loose The verb *lose* should not be confused with the descriptive word *loose.*

> That child is going to lose his shoes; they are so loose.

most, almost The use of *most* for *almost* is not appropriate in writing except for written dialogue. Use *almost, almost always, almost all,* and so on.

> They almost always drop in on a Sunday.
>
> Almost all of the turkey was eaten.
>
> Erik could excel in almost any sport.

nowheres Incorrectly used for *nowhere.*

number *A number of,* meaning "several" or "many," is followed by a plural verb; *the number,* meaning "the quantity," takes a singular verb.

A number of cities have good public transportation.

The number of cities without public transportation is staggering.

off, off of, from The use of *off* and *off of* for *from* is nonstandard.

Incorrect: May I copy off your list?

Correct: May I copy from your list?

Incorrect: Phil got free tickets off of his uncle.

Correct: Phil got free tickets from his uncle.

ourself, ourselfs Incorrectly used for *ourselves.*

reason is because *The reason . . . is because* is often used in informal speech and sometimes in informal writing.

The reason we are late is because the bus broke down.

But in formal English and most informal writing *the reason . . . is that* is used.

The reason we are late is that the bus broke down.

respectively, respectfully *Respectively* means "each one in the order mentioned"; *respectfully* means "in a way that shows respect or honor."

The introduction, the speech, and the closing were presented by Bob, Greg, and Jeff respectively.

David answered the judge's questions respectfully.

sort, kind See **kind, sort.**

supposed to Be careful not to omit the *d* at the end of *supposed.*

Incorrect: I don't know what we are suppose to do.

Correct: I'm supposed to be there at noon.

that *That* is used to refer to people, things, or animals.

Is she the woman that snored during the play?

The book that I like best is falling apart.

theirself, theirselves Incorrectly used for *themselves.*

this here, that there Incorrectly used for *this* and *that.*

Incorrect: This here album is on sale.

Correct: This album is on sale.

used to Be careful not to omit the *d.*

My parents used to play cards every Friday. [Not: *use* to play.]

Exception: When *did . . . use to* is used as a negative or a question, the *d* is dropped.

Did you use to think there was a tooth fairy?

way, ways In informal speech, *ways* is often used instead of *way* to mean "distance." In formal speech or writing, *way* should be used.

It is only a short way to the swimming pool.

well, good See **good, well.**

where . . . at, where . . . to The *at* and *to* are unnecessary and should be omitted in written English.

Where is she performing? [*Not:* Where is she performing *at?*]

Where has the team gone? [*Not:* Where has the team gone *to?*]

which *Which* is used to refer to things, including animals.

The can in which we keep nails is missing again.

The turkeys, which gobble almost constantly, will be sold next week.

who *Who* is used to refer to people and to animals, especially when the animals are thought of as having personalities.

We gave our tickets to Kathy, who was desperate to attend the concert.

Frisky, who is extremely jealous, jumped onto my lap when Bruce came in.

whose The possessive form *whose* is generally used in referring to ownership by a person or group of people.

The neighbor whose lawn I mow not only pays me well but also gives me tickets to Astro games.

Irregular Verbs

Here is a chart listing some of the most commonly used irregular verbs.

PRESENT		PAST		PRESENT OR PAST
Use with *I, you, we, they* and plural nouns	Use with *he, she, it* and singular nouns	Use alone	Use with helping verb *(has, have)*	Use with helping verb *(am, is, are, was, were, has been, have been)*
am, are	is	was, were	been	being
begin	begins	began	begun	beginning
bite	bites	bit	bitten	biting
blow	blows	blew	blown	blowing
break	breaks	broke	broken	breaking
bring	brings	brought	brought	bringing
buy	buys	bought	bought	buying
dig	digs	dug	dug	digging
do	does	did	done	doing
draw	draws	drew	drawn	drawing
drink	drinks	drank	drunk	drinking
eat	eats	ate	eaten	eating
fall	falls	fell	fallen	falling
fight	fights	fought	fought	fighting
fly	flies	flew	flown	flying
forget	forgets	forgot	forgotten	forgetting
freeze	freezes	froze	frozen	freezing
give	gives	gave	given	giving
go	goes	went	gone	going
grow	grows	grew	grown	growing
hang	hangs	hung	hung	hanging
have	has	had	had	having
hear	hears	heard	heard	hearing
hide	hides	hid	hidden	hiding
hold	holds	held	held	holding
know	knows	knew	known	knowing
lay	lays	laid	laid	laying
lie	lies	lay	lain	lying
lose	loses	lost	lost	losing
ring	rings	rang	rung	ringing
run	runs	ran	run	running
say	says	said	said	saying
see	sees	saw	seen	seeing
shake	shakes	shook	shaken	shaking
sing	sings	sang	sung	singing
sit	sits	sat	sat	sitting
sleep	sleeps	slept	slept	sleeping
speak	speaks	spoke	spoken	speaking
stand	stands	stood	stood	standing
steal	steals	stole	stolen	stealing
swear	swears	swore	sworn	swearing
take	takes	took	taken	taking
teach	teaches	taught	taught	teaching
tear	tears	tore	torn	tearing
throw	throws	threw	thrown	throwing
wear	wears	wore	worn	wearing
write	writes	wrote	written	writing

GED Spelling List

The following is the list of frequently misspelled words that the GED Testing Service uses to pick the words it tests. Different forms of these words may also be tested. For example, the word *boundaries* could be tested as well as *boundary, awfully* as well as *awful,* and *easier* and *easiest* as well as *easy.*

Don't try to memorize the spelling of each of these words. Instead, take the time every now and then to work with one group of words at a time (there are 42 groups in all and no more than 26 words in a group). Look at each word quickly and then write it without looking at it.

If you've misspelled any words, use one of the techniques you learned about on page 162 to practice them. (Remember that *saying* the letters of a word—either aloud or to yourself—is one good way to fix the spelling of a word in your mind.) Then add any ending to the word that you can (*-s, -ly, -er,* or *-est*). The rules for adding these endings and other spelling rules are explained in the Spelling Breaks.

A
a lot
ability
absence
absent
across
abundance
accept
acceptable
accident
accommodate
accompanied
accomplish
accumulation
accuse
accustomed
ache
achieve
achievement
acknowledge
acquaintance
acquainted

---

acquire
across
address
addressed
adequate
advantageous
advantage
advertise
advertisement
advice
advisable
advise
advisor
aerial
affect
affectionate
again
against
aggravate
aggressive
agree

---

aisle
all right
almost
already
although
altogether
always
amateur
American
among
amount
analysis
analyze
angel
angle
annual
another
answer
antiseptic
anxious

---

apologize
apparatus
apparent
appear
appearance
appetite
application
apply
appreciate
appreciation
approach
appropriate
approval
approve
approximate
argue
arguing
argument
arouse
arrange
arrangement

---

article
artificial
ascend
assistance
assistant
associate
association
attempt
attendance
attention
audience
August
author
automobile
autumn
auxiliary
available
avenue
awful
awkward

B
bachelor
balance
balloon
bargain
basic
beautiful
because
become
before
beginning
being
believe
benefit
benefited
between
bicycle
board
bored

---

borrow
bottle
bottom
boundary
brake
breadth
breath
breathe
brilliant
building
bulletin
bureau
burial
buried
bury
bushes
business

C
cafeteria
calculator
calendar
campaign
capital
capitol
captain
career

careful
careless
carriage
carrying
category
ceiling
cemetery
cereal
certain
changeable
characteristic
charity
chief

---

choose
chose
cigarette
circumstance
citizen
clothes
clothing
coarse
coffee
collect
college
column
comedy
comfortable
commitment
committed
committee
communicate
company
comparative
compel

---

competent
competition
compliment
conceal
conceit
conceivable
conceive
concentration
conception
condition
conference
confident
congratulate
conquer
conscience
conscientious
conscious
consequence
consequently
considerable
consistency
consistent

---

continual
continuous
controlled
controversy
convenience
convenient
conversation
corporal
corroborate
council
counsel
counselor
courage
courageous
course
courteous
courtesy
criticism
criticize
crystal
curiosity
cylinder

D

daily
daughter
daybreak
death
deceive
December
deception
decide
decision
decisive
deed
definite
delicious
dependent
deposit
derelict
descend
descent

---

describe
description
desert
desirable
despair
desperate
dessert
destruction
determine
develop
development
device
dictator
died
difference
different
dilemma
dinner
direction

---

disappear
disappoint
disappointment
disapproval
disapprove
disastrous
discipline
discover
discriminate
disease
dissatisfied
dissection
dissipate
distance
distinction
division
doctor
dollar
doubt
dozen

E

earnest
easy
ecstasy
ecstatic
education
effect
efficiency
efficient
eight
either
eligibility
eligible
eliminate
embarrass
embarrassment
emergency
emphasis
emphasize

---

enclosure
encouraging
endeavor
engineer
English
enormous
enough
entrance
envelope
environment
equipment
equipped
especially
essential
evening
evident

---

exaggerate
exaggeration
examine
exceed
excellent
except
exceptional
exercise
exhausted
exhaustion
exhilaration
existence
exorbitant
expense
experience
experiment
explanation
extreme

F

facility
factory
familiar
fascinate
fascinating
fatigue
February
financial
financier
flourish
forcibly
forehead
foreign
formal
former
fortunate
fourteen

fourth
frequent
friend
frightening
fundamental
further

G
gallon
garden
gardener
general
genius
government
governor
grammar
grateful
great
grievance
grievous
grocery
guarantee
guess
guidance

H
half
hammer
handkerchief
happiness
healthy
heard
heavy
height
heroes
heroine
hideous
himself
hoarse
holiday
hopeless
hospital
humorous
hurried
hurrying

I
ignorance
imaginary
imbecile
imitation
immediately
immigrant
incidental
increase
independence
independent
indispensable
inevitable
influence
influential
initiate
innocence
inoculate
inquiry
insistent

---

instead
instinct
integrity
intellectual
intelligence
intercede
interest
interfere
interference
interpreted
interrupt
invitation
irrelevant
irresistible
irritable
island
its
it's
itself

J–K
January
jealous
judgment
journal
kindergarten
kitchen
knew
knock
know
knowledge

L
labor
laboratory
laid
language
later
latter
laugh
leisure
length
lesson
library
license
light
lightening
likelihood
likely
literal
literature
livelihood
loaf
loneliness
loose
lose
losing
loyal
loyalty

M
magazine
maintenance
maneuver
marriage
married
marry
match
material
mathematics
measure
medicine
million
miniature
minimum
miracle

---

miscellaneous
mischief
mischievous
misspelled
mistake
momentous
monkey
monotonous
moral
morale
mortgage
mountain
mournful
muscle
mysterious
mystery

N
narrative
natural
necessary
needle
negligence
neighbor
neither
newspaper
newsstand
nickel
niece
noticeable

O
o'clock
obedient
obstacle
occasion
occasional
occur
occurred
occurrence
ocean
offer
often
omission
omit
once
operate
opinion
opportune
opportunity
optimist
optimistic
origin
original
oscillate
ought
ounce
overcoat

P
paid
pamphlet
panicky
parallel
parallelism
particular
partner
pastime
patience
peace
peaceable

pear
peculiar
pencil
people
perceive
perception
perfect
perform
performance

---

perhaps
period
permanence
permanent
perpendicular
perseverance
persevere
persistent
persuade
personality
personal
personnel
persuade
persuasion
pertain
picture
piece
plain
playwright

---

pleasant
please
pleasure
pocket
poison
policeman
political
population
portrayal
positive
possess
possession
possessive
possible
post office
potatoes
practical
prairie
precede
preceding

---

precise
predictable
prefer
preference
preferential
preferred
prejudice
preparation
prepare
prescription
presence
president
prevalent
primitive
principal
principle
privilege
probably
procedure
proceed

---

produce
professional
professor
profitable
prominent
promise
pronounce
pronunciation
propeller
prophecy
prophet
prospect
psychology
pursue
pursuit

Q
quality
quantity
quarreling
quart
quarter
quiet
quite

R
raise
realistic
realize
reason
rebellion
recede
receipt
receive
recipe
recognize
recommend
recuperate
referred
rehearsal
reign
relevant
relieve
remedy

---

renovate
repeat
repetition
representative
requirements
resemblance
resistance
resource
respectability
responsibility
restaurant
rhythm
rhythmical
ridiculous
right
role
roll
roommate

S
sandwich
Saturday
scarcely
scene
schedule
science
scientific
scissors
season
secretary
seige
seize
seminar
sense
separate
service
several
severely
shepherd
sheriff
shining
shoulder
shriek

---

sight
signal
significance
significant
similar
similarity
sincerely
site
soldier
solemn
sophomore
soul
source
souvenir
special
specified
specimen
speech
stationary
stationery
statue
stockings

---

stomach
straight
strength
strenuous
stretch
striking
studying
substantial
succeed
successful
sudden
superintendent
suppress
surely
surprise
suspense
sweat
sweet
syllable
symmetrical
sympathy
synonym

T
technical
telegram
telephone
temperament
temperature
tenant
tendency
tenement
therefore
thorough
through
title
together
tomorrow
tongue
toward
tragedy
transferred
treasury
tremendous
tries
truly
twelfth
twelve
tyranny
____

U–V
undoubtedly
United States
university
unnecessary
unusual
useful
usual
vacuum
valley
valuable
variety
vegetable
vein
vengeance
versatile
vicinity
vicious
view
village
villain
visitor
voice
volume
____

W
waist
weak
wear
weather
Wednesday
week
weigh
weird
whether
which
while
whole
wholly
whose
wretched
____

Index

When a word and page number are in **bold** type, the word is defined in a Coming to Terms on that page.